Azure Arc-Enabled Kubernetes and Servers

Extending Hyperscale Cloud Management to Your Datacenter

Steve Buchanan
John Joyner

Foreword by Thomas Maurer, Sr. Cloud Advocate, Microsoft

Apress®

Azure Arc-Enabled Kubernetes and Servers: Extending Hyperscale Cloud Management to Your Datacenter

Steve Buchanan
Minneapolis, MN, USA

John Joyner
Little Rock, AR, USA

ISBN-13 (pbk): 978-1-4842-7767-6
ISBN-13 (electronic): 978-1-4842-7768-3
https://doi.org/10.1007/978-1-4842-7768-3

Managing Director, Apress Media LLC: Welmoed Spahr
Acquisitions Editor: Joan Murray
Development Editor: Laura Berendson
Coordinating Editor: Jill Balzano

Cover designed by eStudioCalamar

Cover image designed by Freepik (www.freepik.com)

Distributed to the book trade worldwide by Springer Science+Business Media LLC, 1 New York Plaza, Suite 4600, New York, NY 10004. Phone 1-800-SPRINGER, fax (201) 348-4505, e-mail orders-ny@springer-sbm.com, or visit www.springeronline.com. Apress Media, LLC is a California LLC and the sole member (owner) is Springer Science + Business Media Finance Inc (SSBM Finance Inc). SSBM Finance Inc is a **Delaware** corporation.

For information on translations, please e-mail booktranslations@springernature.com; for reprint, paperback, or audio rights, please e-mail bookpermissions@springernature.com.

Apress titles may be purchased in bulk for academic, corporate, or promotional use. eBook versions and licenses are also available for most titles. For more information, reference our Print and eBook Bulk Sales web page at http://www.apress.com/bulk-sales.

Any source code or other supplementary material referenced by the author in this book is available to readers on GitHub via the book's product page, located at www.apress.com/9781484277676. For more detailed information, please visit http://www.apress.com/source-code.

Printed on acid-free paper

I would like to dedicate this book to my Mom and Dad for always supporting me and encouraging me to pursue all my dreams and aspirations.

—Steve Buchanan

Dedicated to the true greatest accomplishment of my life, my daughter Ava.

—John Joyner

Table of Contents

About the Authors

Steve Buchanan is a Director, Azure Platform Lead, and Containers Services Lead on a Cloud Transformation team with a large consulting firm. He is a ten-time Microsoft MVP, a Pluralsight author, and the author of eight technical books. He has presented at tech events, including DevOpsDays, Open Source North, Midwest Management Summit (MMS), Microsoft Ignite, BITCon, Experts Live Europe, OSCON, Inside Azure management, and user groups. He stays active in the technical community and enjoys blogging about his adventures in the world of IT at `www.buchatech.com`.

John Joyner is Senior Director, Technology, at AccountabilIT, a managed services provider of 24x7 Network Operations and Security Operations Center (NOC and SOC) services. As an Azure Solutions Architect Expert, he designs and builds modern management and security solutions based on Azure Lighthouse, Azure Arc, Azure Monitor Logs, Microsoft Sentinel, and Microsoft Defender for Cloud. John is also an authority on System Center products in private cloud and hybrid cloud environments and has been awarded Microsoft MVP 14 times. John is a retired US Navy Lt. Cmdr., where he was a computer scientist, worked for NATO in Europe, and served aboard an aircraft carrier in the Pacific. He is a veteran of the Persian Gulf War.

About the Contributor

Fred Limmer is the Cloud Architecture Group Manager with a large Microsoft-focused consulting firm. He is a regular contributor to local and regional events focusing on the organizational journey to the cloud and a frequent speaker and SME at Microsoft-sponsored events and other engagements.

Fred's primary focus is fueling enterprise growth through cloud adoption and transformation via a well-architected Microsoft Azure cloud platform implementation.

About the Technical Reviewer

Adnan Hendricks, Creative Director Cloud Solutions at Microspecialist Consulting, is a leading Azure infrastructure consultant, a Microsoft MVP, and trainer and is actively involved in Microsoft TAP programs.

His day-to-day job is implementing and architecting solutions with a focus on cloud, public/hybrid infrastructure, and the modern workspace.

As an international speaker and trainer, he often spends his time flying around the globe, consulting, teaching, and speaking at IT community events.

Acknowledgments

First and foremost, thanks to God for continued blessings and opportunities like this in my life and career. Thank you to my wife, Ayasha, for being patient with me and supporting me as I pursue opportunities like this. Thank you to my sons (Malcolm, Jalen, Sean, and Isaac) for being one of the reasons I stay motivated and want all of you to succeed in life.

A huge shout-out and thank you to my coauthor John Joyner. I know you did not plan on writing another book. Thanks for taking up this opportunity. As someone whom I respect and have looked up to in the Microsoft and MVP community, it means a lot to collaborate with you on a project like this.

A big thanks to Fred Limmer for jumping in and contributing to this book.

I would also like to thank the team at Apress, Joan Murray and Jill Balzano, for being great and easy to work with.

Finally, thanks to Chris Sanders, Lior Kamrat, Thomas Maurer, and the rest of the Arc team at Microsoft for bringing this exciting technology to the market.

—Steve Buchanan

Thank you, Steve Buchanan, for inviting me to coauthor the book; it has been a pleasure and an honor to collaborate with you to bring this content to our shared community.

Probably, Steve and I might not be in a position to author this book without the resources and opportunities afforded to recipients of the Microsoft MVP award. I know we are both grateful and appreciative for the MVP program's existence and our continued participation.

Much appreciation also to my employer AccountabilIT LLC, which graciously provides me the space to keep learning and writing and also supports a private cloud lab environment that is key for my research and development.

—John Joyner

Foreword

Today, hybrid and multicloud scenarios are critical for many organizations. There is a lot of momentum for building and implementing a hybrid and multicloud strategy. Based on studies, 90% of enterprises depend on hybrid and 93% have a multicloud strategy.

Microsoft Azure is an open, flexible, enterprise-grade cloud computing platform that provides all the services and features required to help you build and operate your technology solutions in the cloud. However, we understand that there are several reasons and motivations that drive the necessity of using multiple private and/or public clouds. Avoiding single cloud provider lock-in, addressing regulatory and data sovereignty requirements, improving business continuity, and maximizing performance by running applications close to user locations to avoid latency are all common business drivers to architect and build hybrid and multicloud environments. That is why Microsoft Azure is built from the ground up to support hybrid environments.

To quote our Azure Engineering lead and Executive Vice President Jason Zander at Microsoft: "Hybrid is not just an in-between state until everything is moved to the cloud, it will be an end state for many of our customers."

Running in hybrid, multicloud, and edge environments not only adds more complexity, but also often leads to an increase in operating costs and challenges when it comes to governance and compliance. With the Azure Resource Manager and additional Azure management services, Microsoft offers a strong management solution for resources and services deployed in Microsoft Azure. With Azure Arc, we are extending the management capabilities, and a number of the services to environments outside of the Azure cloud, to address these challenges. Now you can use Azure as a single control plane for your hybrid and multicloud environments.

With Azure Arc we offer two high level pillars: Azure Arc enabled infrastructure and Azure Arc enabled services. Azure Arc enabled infrastructure allows you to connect existing infrastructure, such as Windows and Linux servers, as well as Kubernetes clusters running outside of Azure to the Azure control plane to get visibility, and to organize and manage these resources. Azure Arc enabled services allow you to deploy

Azure services such as Azure data or Azure application services anywhere. This allows you to build consistent hybrid and multicloud architectures, as well as using the cloud-native tooling for your IT operations, DevOps, and developer processes.

This book, by two industry leading Azure experts, introduces you to the fundamentals of hybrid, multicloud, and edge computing. I have known Steve Buchanan and John Joyner for more than a decade now as valued members in the Microsoft MVP program and personally as friends. Their book provides you insights into Azure Native Management tooling for managing servers and Kubernetes clusters, running both on-premises and other cloud providers. They teach you how to leverage the Azure control plane to get visibility and management capabilities with Azure Arc, which are extremely useful to strengthen your security and governance posture. They also show how to leverage Azure Arc to seamlessly deliver Azure Monitor and/or Azure Sentinel, and achieve regulatory compliance with industry standards using Azure Arc, delivering Azure Policy from Microsoft Defender for Cloud.

An added bonus—their book also provides context on how to set up GitOps using Azure Arc in a hybrid and multicloud environment to empower your DevOps teams to perform tasks that typically fall under IT operations, and much more. In short, if you and your organization are running workloads in a hybrid or multicloud environment, this is the book for you.

–Thomas Maurer
Senior Cloud Advocate
Microsoft
October 2021

Introduction

This book is a practical guide to Microsoft's Azure Arc service. The goal of this book is to take you from 0 to 100 using Microsoft's new multicloud management tool, bringing Azure Management features to your servers and Kubernetes clusters, no matter where they are.

This practical guide on Azure Arc scales back on theory content, giving just enough to grasp important concepts while focusing on practical straight to the point knowledge that can be used to go spin up and start utilizing Azure Arc in no time.

In this book, you will learn about Azure Resource Manager, Git, GitHub, GitOps, Azure Management, and using Azure Arc to extend the Microsoft control plane for management of Kubernetes clusters and Servers in other environments and multiple clouds.

CHAPTER 1

Azure Arc As an Extension of the Azure Control Plane

Welcome to the first chapter in this *Azure Arc-Enabled Kubernetes and Servers* book. This book overall is going to take you on a journey into the world of both Azure Arc-enabled Kubernetes and Azure Arc-enabled servers. Azure Arc has many offerings, and we wanted to focus in this book on Azure Arc's Kubernetes and Server offerings to give you the most value we can on two focused topics.

Before we dive into Azure Arc offerings themselves, it is important to understand how Azure Arc fits as an Extension of the Azure Control Plane. This is what we are going to explore in this chapter. This will help to build foundational knowledge for the remaining chapters in this book.

Hybrid, Multicloud, and Edge

Hybrid cloud, Multicloud, and Edge cloud computing are areas that are all growing at a fast rate. Let's briefly define what each of these are:

Hybrid Cloud

Hybrid cloud combines on-premises data center (private cloud) with a public cloud to create a single cloud environment for an organization. Hybrid cloud gives you workload portability between public cloud and on-premises, a.k.a. private cloud. Hybrid cloud allows an enterprise to choose the optimal computing location for each workload as needed.

S. Buchanan and J. Joyner, *Azure Arc-Enabled Kubernetes and Servers*,
https://doi.org/10.1007/978-1-4842-7768-3_1

Multicloud

Multicloud is when an enterprise combines the use of two or more public clouds from different cloud providers. Multicloud is not something that is provided by a single cloud provider. Multicloud is often a mix of a couple or more of these major cloud providers: Amazon Web Services (AWS), Google Cloud Platform (GCP), Microsoft (Azure), Alibaba, and IBM.

Edge Cloud Computing

Edge cloud computing is extending cloud services, computing, and data storage to or near the source of data. Edge cloud computing saves bandwidth and is ideal for workloads with latency concerns. IoT and data-intensive workloads are common use cases for edge cloud computing.

It is important to look at some stats for these areas to understand the growth. A great resource that is published yearly is the Flexera State of the Cloud Report. This report breaks down all things cloud and gives some hard stats on what is happening in the cloud space with enterprises. Let's take a look at some stats from the Flexera 2021 State of the Cloud Report.

1. **Enterprises are embracing hybrid-cloud**

   87% of enterprises that responded to the Flexera 2021 State of the Cloud Report reported adopting a hybrid cloud strategy.

2. **Enterprises are embracing multicloud**

   93% of enterprises that responded to the Flexera 2021 State of the Cloud Report reported having a multicloud strategy. They also reported combining public and private clouds in their strategy.

3. **Enterprises are embracing edge cloud computing**

   49% of enterprises that responded to the Flexera 2021 State of the Cloud Report are experimenting with or plan to use edge services.

To sum this up, most enterprises have adopted Hybrid as their cloud model, which includes multicloud. The following image from the Flexera 2021 State of the Cloud Report shows this.

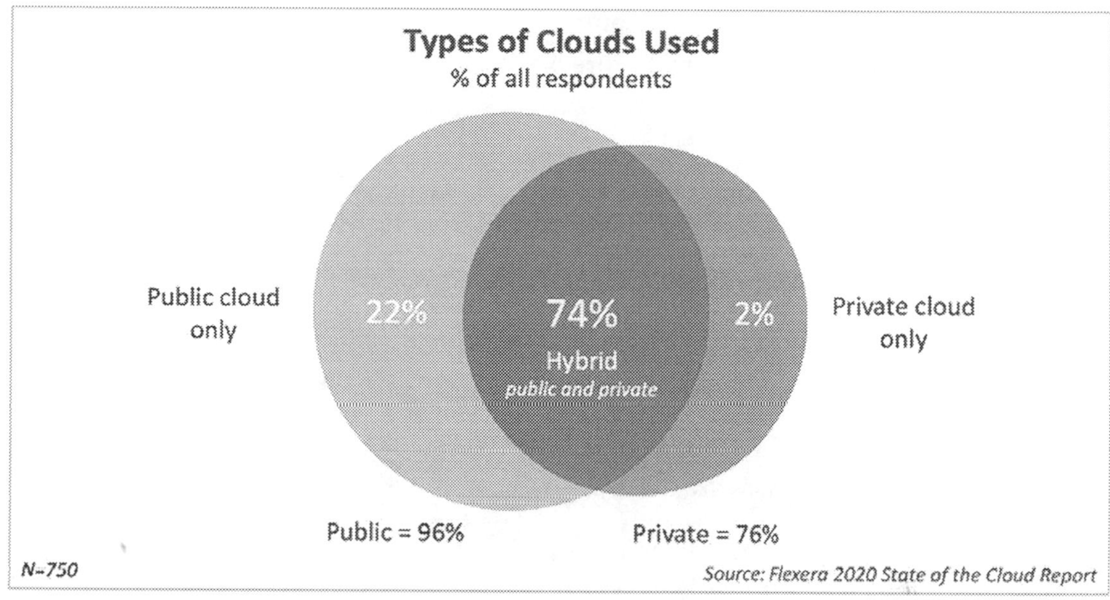

Figure 1-1. *Types of clouds used chart from the Flexera 2021 State of the Cloud Report*

This demonstrates that the growth in cloud is in hybrid, multicloud, and edge cloud computing.

Overview of Azure Arc

As we saw from the previous section, there is a growing demand for hybrid cloud, multicloud, and edge cloud computing in the world of tech today. With running workloads across hybrid cloud, multicloud, and edge cloud computing environments, the complexity to manage them is also increasing.

In 2019, at Microsoft's large technical conference, Microsoft Ignite announced Azure Arc. Azure Arc extends Azure capabilities to environments outside of Azure such as on-premises data centers and other private and public clouds. Azure Arc sets out to simplify complex and distributed environments by bringing the Azure Resource Manager (ARM) and its management tools to environments regardless of what cloud they are on. Azure Arc gives technical teams the power to deploy workloads and manage resources, regardless of where they exist.

Arc is a response to the increasing complexities that on-premises and multicloud management needs enterprises have. Azure Arc enables you to create and manage resources as well as workloads on

- On-premises
- Non-Azure clouds (i.e., GCP, AWS, Alibaba, etc.)
- Private clouds
- Microsoft Hybrid (Azure Stack Hub, Azure Stack HCI, Azure Stack Edge)

Arc all up consists of multiple offerings to help meet an organization's various multienvironment needs. Here are three key areas where Azure Arc provides value:

Consistency

Arc gives you consistent governance, inventory, and management of resources and workloads.

Zero-touch compliance and configuration

With Arc, you can gain zero-touch compliance and configuration across resources and workloads such as servers, Kubernetes, and more.

Unified experience

Azure Arc gives you a unified experience for a single pane and single control plane across environments and resources/workloads running on them. The same tooling is used regardless of where the workloads and resources are running through management with the Azure portal, Azure CLI, Azure PowerShell, or Azure REST API.

Now, Azure Arc extends Azure services to resources and workloads running outside of Azure. The services that are extended will differ based on the Azure Arc offering. Here is a list of many of the Azure services that can be extended via Azure Arc:

- Management Groups
- Subscriptions
- Resource Groups
- Role-Based Access Control
- Tagging

- Security Center/Azure Defender
- Azure Sentinel
- Azure Key Vault
- Azure Policy/Azure Policy Guest Configuration
- Azure Backup
- Update Management, Change Tracking, and Inventory
- Azure Monitor
- Azure Automation
- Viewing and Access in the Azure portal
- Azure SDK
- ARM Templates
- And more

Currently, Azure Arc is offered at no additional cost when managing Azure Arc-enabled servers and Azure Arc-enabled Kubernetes. Azure Arc control plane functionality is offered for free. The services that are considered as a part of the Azure Arc Control plane are

- Attaching servers and Kubernetes clusters to Azure
- Resource organization through Azure management groups and Tagging
- Searching and indexing through Resource Graph
- Access and security through Azure RBAC and Azure subscriptions
- Patch management through Update Management
- Environments and automation through ARM templates and Azure extensions

Azure Arc Offerings

When Azure Arc was launched, it had a few offerings available, the first being Azure Arc-enabled servers. Since its launch, Microsoft has been quickly adding additional offerings to Arc and extending the functionality of the current offerings. Azure Arc offerings break down into two categories. Infrastructure is your infrastructure to run workloads. Services are Azure services being extended out of Azure through Arc. The first category is infrastructure, and the second category is services. Azure Arc offerings and the resource types it is able to manage include the following:

Infrastructure

- **Servers:** Supports Linux and Windows, supports bare-metal servers, on-premises servers, AWS EC2 virtual machines, GCP computer engine virtual machines, VMWare virtual machines, and Hyper-V virtual machines
- **Azure Arc-enabled SQL Server:** Manages instances of SQL Server from Azure, extending Azure services to SQL Server instances hosted outside of Azure
- **Kubernetes:** On-premises Kubernetes clusters, Rancher K3s, AWS EKS clusters, GCP GKE clusters
- **Azure Arc IoT:** Via Azure Arc-enabled Kubernetes, centrally manages and deploys IoT workloads at the edge

Services

- **Data services:** Run Azure data services outside of Azure including SQL Managed Instance and PostgreSQL.
- **Azure Arc with Lighthouse:** The combination of Azure Arc and Azure Lighthouse for expanded Lighthouse management capabilities to non-Azure environments.
- **Azure application services with Azure Arc:** Azure Application PaaS services (App service, Functions, Logic Apps, Event Grid, API Management) and other PaaS services can run on any Kubernetes cluster via Arc.

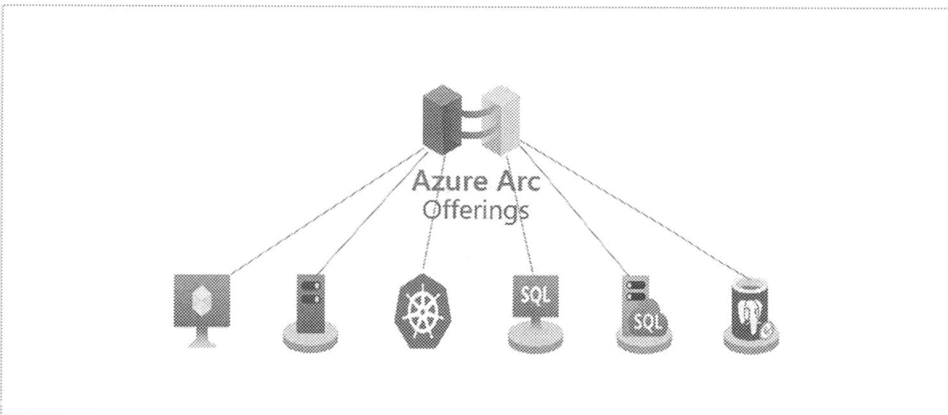

Figure 1-2. *Azure Arc offerings*

Why Would I Want to Use Azure Arc for My Organization?

Multicloud architectures are often more complex and more of a challenge to manage. From the Flexera 2021 State of the Cloud Report, 68% of enterprises that responded to the report are not utilizing multicloud management tools currently. Only 32% are utilizing multicloud management tools. The report goes on to cover multicloud governance, security, and cost management tool stats. The percentages in these other areas have low adoption as well. This means there is a tremendous opportunity of growth in multicloud management tooling. Microsoft set out to fill this gap with Azure Arc.

Use Cases

Here are some use cases that make sense for using Azure Arc:

Legal Jurisdiction

Some workloads are legally required to process and retain data within a specific region, country, etc., requiring infrastructure across multiple data centers and cloud providers.

Latency

Some workloads have latency requirements that have to be met by locating the workload in a specific geography.

Legacy Infrastructure

Some legacy infrastructure is old and is challenging and sometimes can't be moved to the cloud. Arc can extend the cloud to that on-premises legacy infrastructure.

Availability

The ability to run the same services across multiple cloud providers and even on-premises for greater availability in the event of cloud provider or on-premises outages.

Developer Options

The ability to provide a choice to developers to run workloads on any environment that best fits their needs.

Edge Compute Needs (local)

As organizations continue to expand their edge and local footprint for running workloads, i.e., stores, warehouses, factories, in the field, etc., extending cloud and centralizing management can reduce complexity in managing across edge locations.

Hybrid Cloud Scenario

There are many scenarios for organizations when it comes to utilizing Azure Arc. Let's walk through one of these scenarios. In this example, the organization is running a container-based web application that has components spread across Azure cloud and their on-premises data center.

In this specific scenario, the organization needs to have low latency for users that will utilize the web app from on-premises, and they want public traffic to come into the web app; running on Azure as cloud can better handle the external traffic load.

This organization is utilizing Azure Arc to manage both the on-premises Kubernetes cluster and the cloud-based Azure Kubernetes Service (AKS) cluster. They are also utilizing GitOps to ensure the on-premises Kubernetes cluster and the cloud-based AKS cluster configuration and application deployment match at all times. Also, they are utilizing Azure Container Instance (ACI) for very fast burstable capacity as needed on the AKS cluster. The following image visualizes the architecture for this hybrid-based application.

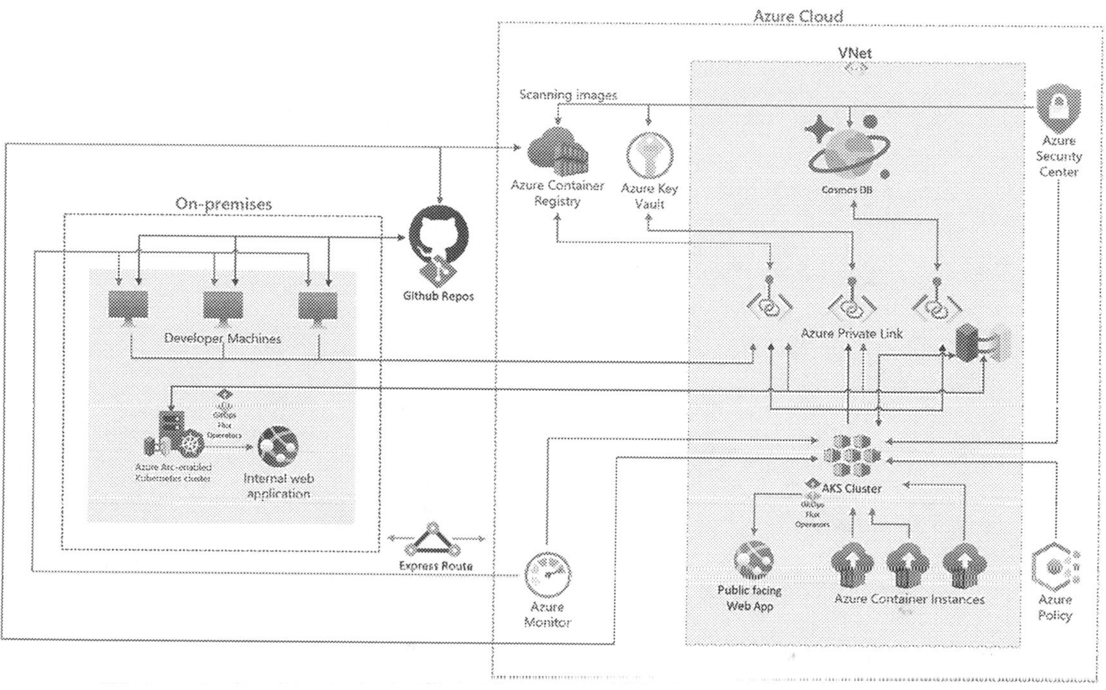

***Figure 1-3.** Container based web app running in hybrid cloud model*

Summary

This brings us to a close of the first chapter. In this chapter, we took time to understand hybrid, multicloud, and edge areas and the challenges that come with managing them. We worked through an overview of Azure Arc. We dove into Azure Arc's offerings to give an understanding of what Azure Arc is made up of. We finally explored why your organization might adopt Azure Arc. This all is to set you up with a solid foundation of knowledge of Azure Arc to help as you further embark on the remaining chapters in this book, moving deeper into the world of hybrid, multicloud, and edge and Azure Arc.

CHAPTER 2

Azure Resource Manager Insights

Introduction

In this section, we'll be examining the Azure Resource Manager or "ARM" platform management layer in Microsoft Azure. We'll talk about what it is, how it works, what you can do with it, and tips and tricks for how to use it effectively in your Azure ARC deployment and other implementation projects in Azure.

What Is Azure Resource Manager?

ARM, at its core, is the deployment and management service for Azure. It allows for the creation, configuration, and management of resources, such as virtual machines or virtual networks, and Platform as a Service, or "PaaS," offerings such as Azure App Service, ARC, and Azure SQL.

In Azure's infancy, a system of management and structure referred to as the Azure Service Manager, or "ASM," was implemented to manage the platform. This immature system quickly exposed its limitations regarding governance, security controls, resource organization, structure, and environment management.

ASM was eventually supplanted with a more flexible and capable management layer called Azure Resource Manager or "ARM." ASM, however, still exists in the Azure environment, and ASM-based resources are labeled as "Classic."

S. Buchanan and J. Joyner, *Azure Arc-Enabled Kubernetes and Servers*,
https://doi.org/10.1007/978-1-4842-7768-3_2

The ARM management layer essentially executes tasks like creating resources and managing them with identity and access controls (IAM), organizing and grouping with tags, or adding locks to prevent unauthorized changes.

Think of ARM as the interpreter between you and Azure. You tell it WHAT you want to do, and it figures out HOW to do it.

ARM enables you to perform a host of tasks inside of the Azure platform. It allows for the management of infrastructure through declarative means rather than static scripts or other actions. This means that you can deploy, manage, configure, and monitor resources as a group rather than attempting to manage them separately. For example, you can apply a defined Access Control design to a group of resources rather than having to configure each one individually, saving time and reducing potential for human error.

This approach not only allows for a simpler management approach to a scope of resources, but it allows you to easily redeploy that same group of resources as part of another separate deployment. This comes in quite handy when you need to deploy resources for a solution using a life cycle approach where you might start initially with a Development environment and then move to a Testing or QA environment before eventually reaching Production.

When determining your Azure deployment strategy, there are a number of different considerations that you need to take into account.

Firstly, once you start down a path, it can sometimes be very difficult to change course. For example, if you decide that you want to deploy resources with PowerShell scripts but later decide that you want to switch to using another deployment method like Terraform, that change can be very difficult and might require a significant amount of effort. Take the time to review the options and decide on the best path for you.

Consider the technological investment. What will you need to buy to take this path? Do you need to build and host servers? Will you need to purchase software licensing? Will you require a third-party service? Will you need to train your team? What are the costs and what is the value?

Additionally, what are the future cloud adoption plans for the organization? What is the plan for Azure? Do you have a road map to follow? What external situations exist that might drive additional Azure adoption or consumption? Does the company need to plan a data center exit in the near future or close a key location?

Your people will also be key to the success of your program. Who on your team has the knowledge necessary to make use of the tools, services, or applications? Is there a skill gap? How will you close it? How will you manage the knowledge documentation and transfer to new or junior resources in the future?

Keep in mind that your choice here will not only affect the team(s) using ARM to deploy infrastructure resources but will potentially affect how your application development or data and analytics teams will function when they are deploying solutions to the Azure environment as well. Be sure to get everyone engaged as early as possible so every perspective is considered, and the best choice made.

These are all key areas that will require organization-wide thought, discussion, and group decisions before charting your course.

Secondly, planning what you actually want to do with Azure up front is key to success. You shouldn't build anything in Azure until you have at least defined basic requirements, a list of resources, and a road map.

Will you only be using Azure for a web application, or will you be using it solely for data analytics? Will you extend your data center into the environment and use Azure to operate and manage your core infrastructure across the organization?

Each of these varying scenarios will drive you down a diverging path and will require vastly different resources to accomplish.

Understanding ARM

ARM is structured in a standard hierarchy with five levels of scope with each level inheriting the settings from the level above.

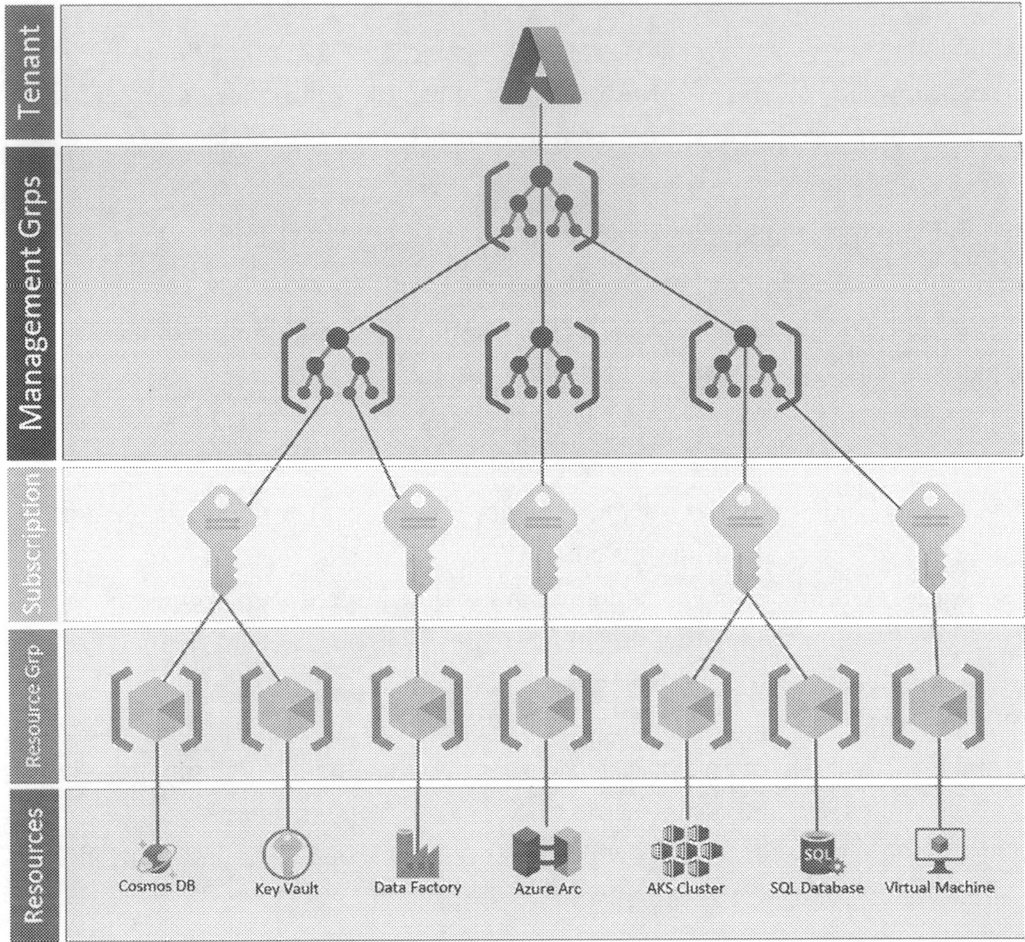

Figure 2-1. *Azure management scopes*

At the top of the hierarchy is the Azure Tenant. This is also often referred to as the "Enrollment" or the "Directory." From the perspective of our organization discussion, the name doesn't really matter. It's simply the highest level of the hierarchy.

The first scope level commonly utilized for structure, administration, policy, or other broader administration is the Management Group. This level of the hierarchy generally contains Subscriptions but can also have multiple tiers of Management Groups in scenarios where you may have different policies for different geopolitical regions such as North America vs. Europe, or Asia Pacific.

Settings can be applied at any level in the hierarchy, but access controls, permissions, and policies for governance and/or security will often be created in a Management Group so that they are inherited by the Subscriptions and everything below them in the structure.

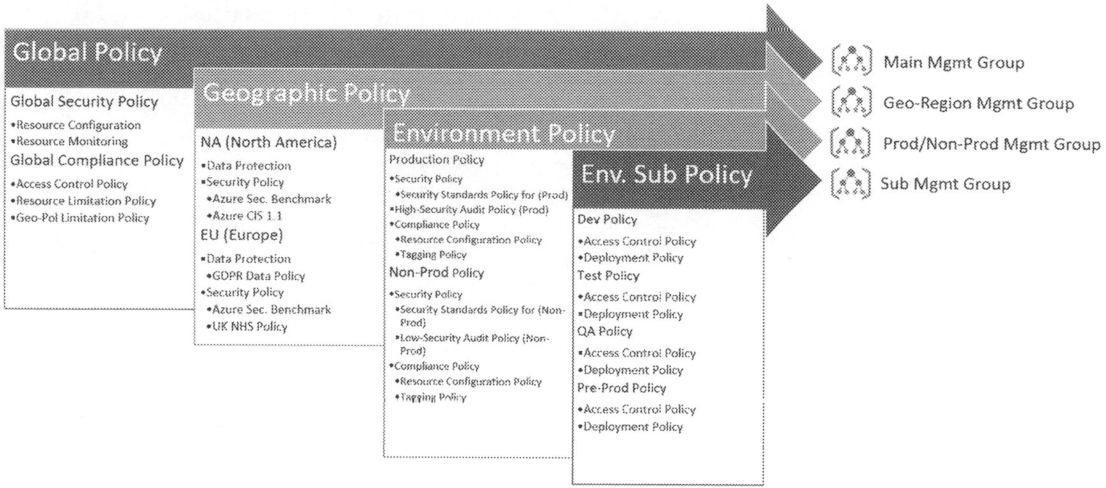

Figure 2-2. *Azure hierarchy*

This hierarchical approach with inheritance enables the configuration and management of the Azure environment at multiple levels with continually restrictive policies moving down the hierarchy from a global or corporate-wide configuration down to a highly specific set of policies applied to a very specific set of resources.

Key Definitions

Tenant/Directory/Enrollment: This is the top layer of organization for Azure. It represents the organization as a whole, and all other constructs such as Management Groups and Subscriptions fall under the Tenant.

Management Group: An organization object at the top of the structure which contains Subscriptions and everything below them in the hierarchy.

Subscription: A logical construct in Azure that contains Resource Groups and represents a boundary for many different aspects or management and organization.

Policy: A construct in Azure that allows for the creation of requirements specifications that can audit for proper configuration, prevent misconfiguration, or change the configuration of a resource.

Geography: Represents a disparate geographic region that may have varying sovereignty requirements/policies such as Europe.

There are some limitations to consider with Management Groups that should be taken into account when designing the organizational structure.

Table 2-1. *Management Group Limitations*

Resource	Limit
Management Groups per Tenant	10,000
Subscriptions per MG	Unlimited
Levels of Hierarchy	Root plus 6 levels
Direct parent Management Groups	One
MG-level Deployments per Location	800
Locations of MG-level deployments	10

Regarding Management Group Limitations, the important items to consider are the hierarchy level limitation and the maximum deployment locations.

If you are embarking on a large-scale Azure Cloud Transformation journey for an international organization that operates in multiple countries, these limitations should be considered and incorporated into your Management Group design:

1. You would need resources in more than ten Azure Regions.
2. You need to segregate different Subscriptions based on factors such as geopolitical regions, business unit, and responsibility separation.
3. You have a need for regional deployments with reduced latency to meet business requirements.

Below the Management Group level, you will find the Azure Subscription.

The Subscription level contains Resource Groups and will often be the scope where responsibilities begin to separate and constrict.

While it is typical to implement broad RBAC controls to the Management Group, it's frequently necessary to allow different levels of access to one Subscription vs. another. One example of this would be if your organization utilized a Production and a Nonproduction Subscription model. It's likely that permissions in Production would need to be more restrictive than those for Nonproduction.

Key Definitions

Subscription: A logical construct in Azure that contains Resource Groups and represents a boundary for many different aspects or management and organization.

Resource Group: A container object that holds Resources. Typically, these resources are related to one another as part of an application, or solution, or are similar resources such as Route Tables or Virtual Networks that might be grouped together for management through role-based access control, or RBAC.

RBAC: Refers to role-based access control which is a feature of ARM that allows for the assignment of predefined or custom roles to a user or group of users.

Location: Azure Locations represent the overall area within the Azure geography that Resources are deployed to such as "EastUS2," "SouthCentralUS," and "WestUS."

Tag: Tags are used to organize Azure resources into a logical taxonomy. Tags consist of a Key/Value pair, meaning that there is a "Key" and a "Value." For example, you may have a tag with a Key name of "Environment" and a Value name of "Prod."

Subscriptions are frequently used as an administrative boundary where users can be granted access to every resource in the subscription. To a lesser degree, it is used as a logical unit of scale by which the number of specific types of Azure Resources can be limited on a per-Azure Region basis.

The following are two examples of using Subscription-level admin boundaries:

1. Granting owner-level permissions on a Subscription to a high-level administrator so that person can manage access controls.

2. Granting "Network Contributor" role to a network administrator in your organization so that they can access various networking resources and tools to test performance and troubleshoot problems.

As with Management Groups and Subscriptions, there are some limitations related within the ARM framework to consider when designing your Subscription strategy.

Table 2-2. *Subscription Limitations*

Resource	Limit
Subscriptions per Tenant	Unlimited
Co-administrators per Subscription	Unlimited
Resource Groups per Subscription	980
ARM API request size	4,194,304 bytes
Tags per Subscription	50
Unique tag calculations per Subscription	80,000
Subscription-level Deployments per Location	800
Locations of Subscription-level Deployments	10

The most important items to consider here are the number of Resource Groups per Subscription and the locations per Subscription. If your Resource Group strategy will require an extensive number of RGs, consider spanning them across multiple subscriptions, and if you're planning a multiregional deployment, plan around the ten-location limit per Subscription. In some instances, the Locations limit can be exceeded by using nested templates for deployment across multiple locations.

The Resource Group or "RG" level is used to further refine permissions and begin separation of duties within the organization. For example, if you placed all of your networking resources in a "network" Resource Group, you might grant Reader access to the Subscription to your Networking Team, but Contributor access to that network RG.

When designing and implementing a Resource Group structure, there are a number of things to keep in mind. The task may seem simple at first, but as the complexity of the environment escalates, it will increasingly get more daunting.

Resources in a Resource Group should share life cycles and should be deployed, updated, and ultimately deleted together. An example of this would be creating a "Network Resource Group" that contained Virtual Networks, Virtual Network Gateways, VPN Connections, and Route Tables. These resources are all logically grouped together, would likely have the same RBAC structure, and should maintain the same life cycle within the organization.

Resources can only exist in a single Resource Group and can't be part of multiple groups, so RBAC structure should consider the contents of the Resource Group and the configuration designed accordingly.

Most resources can be moved to a different RG, at any time. This is often helpful when it is necessary to reorganize the hierarchy as the complexity in the environment increases.

There are different limitations per Resource when changing Resource Groups. Ensure that you review the documentation regarding changing Resource Groups on your resources before attempting the move.

Resources can be located in a Resource Group in a different Azure Region, but it is recommended to keep Resources in the same region as the RG as any control plane issues in one Region could affect the Resources in another if your RG is in the failing Region. This limits potential impact from a failure in a single Region.

Additionally, the Resource Group provides necessary metadata to the resources contained within it. If that metadata becomes unavailable, the Resource may fail.

Resource Groups are a logical construct to enable organization and access controls for users, not limit access to/from other resources.

Resource Groups do not act as a barrier between resources! Resources in one Resource Group can freely interact with Resources in another.

Tags can be applied to a Resource Group, but Resources don't inherit the Tags automatically; however, Azure Policy or PowerShell can help with this.

An Out-of-Box or "OOB" Policy can be applied that can copy down missing tags from a Resource Group to the Resources in that Group. This greatly simplifies the process of ensuring required Tags are present on Resources.

Deleting a Resource Group will delete all Resources in that Group. Be careful when deleting an RG! Triple-check that every Resource can be deleted without impact.

There are some additional limitations to keep in mind regarding Resource Groups as with the other levels in the hierarchy.

Table 2-3. *Resource Group Limitations*

Item	Limit
Resources per RG	Resources are limited by resource type within a resource group
Resources per Type	800 instances of a resource type per RG
Deployments per RG in History	800
Resources per Deployment	800
Management Locks per Scope	20
Number of Tags per Resource or RG	50
Tag Key length	512
Tag Value length	256

For Resource Group Limitations, the main issues to consider in your design are the number of like Resources per Resource Group and Deployments per RG in History. If you are deploying multiple iterations of a resource like Storage Accounts in a Subscription, or it's a particularly dynamic environment where you expect to exceed the 800 deployment history limitation, you need to consider ways to mitigate those limitations.

Resource Groups can be created through multiple means including the Azure portal, Azure CLI, PowerShell, and ARM or other deployment templates.

In addition to limitations on the hierarchy in ARM, there are some limitations on deployment templates that should be considered in an overall implementation strategy for your environment.

Table 2-4. *ARM Template Limitations*

Value	Limit
Parameters	256
Variables	256
Resources (including copy count)	800
Outputs	64
Template expression	24,576 characters
Resources in exported templates	200
Template size	4 MB
Parameter file size	4 MB

Key Definitions

Azure Resource Manager (ARM) Template: Commonly referred to as an "ARM Template," this is a JavaScript Object Notation, or JSON-formatted file that is used to deploy Resources through ARM. This file is written in a Declarative Syntax structure, meaning that you are declaring what you intend to create rather than having to write extensive code sequences to create the objects.

When Resources are deployed through ARM, or by any other means, there are always two pieces of information that are required before ARM will execute the request. You must provide a Resource Group for the Resource and an Azure Location where the Resource will be deployed.

We've already reviewed Resource Groups in depth, so let's talk about the organization of ARM from a geographic perspective.

Resources in Azure are delivered in one of two ways geographically speaking. They are either a "Nonregional Service," meaning that they are not homed in a particular data center and the services source from essentially everywhere, or they are delivered from a specific Azure Region and to use that service, you must use a Region where it is available.

An Azure Region is a group of Azure data centers that are located in close proximity to one other. Resources within an Azure Region will typically have a 1-2 ms latency across the region. Each Region is connected to the Azure edge network which will have at least 5 ms of latency between Regions, but it depends on the source and destination. If you're moving data between East US and Sydney, it will be significantly higher.

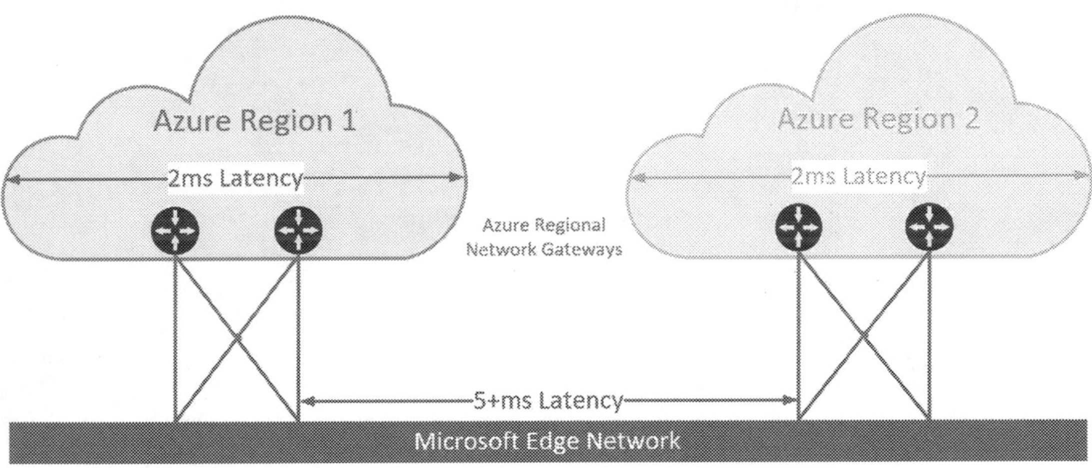

Figure 2-3. *Azure Region resources*

Key Definitions

Azure Region: A collection of data centers deployed within a latency-defined geographical area and connected with high-bandwidth, low-latency network connections.

In each Azure Region, there are two or more data centers or "Availability Zones."

These Availability Zones represent a completely separate Azure data center within a Region that has its own power, cooling, and Internet connectivity.

If any data center in a Region goes down, the workloads in that data center will roll over to the other two data centers assuming that this has been accommodated for in your Regional strategy design.

There are multiple categories of services provided by the Azure platform.

Foundation Service: A core Azure service that is available across all Azure Regions. This would be basic services like Virtual Networks, Virtual Machines, and Storage Accounts.

Mainstream Service: An Azure service that is available in recommended Regions but may not have support in other Regions.

Specialized Service: A very specific service that is demand driven and typically requires specialized hardware to deliver. SAP HANA Large Instance on Azure is a good example of a Specialized Service as it requires dedicated servers in the Azure data center that can support the special operating system required as well as the HANA database.

When considering your Regional strategy, it's very important to validate that all of the services that you want to use in Azure are available in your selected Region.

While a particular type of Resource may be available in one particular Region, it doesn't mean it's available in all Regions. Plan your Regions based on the Resources that you expect to use!

You can check the Azure Product Availability by Region website at

`https://azure.microsoft.com/en-us/global-infrastructure/services/`

In addition to choosing a Primary Region, you should determine a Secondary Region for Disaster Recovery and cross-Regional Operations. Microsoft pairs specific Azure Regions with similar services that are generally over 300 miles apart and continuously replicates between them.

This protects workloads from the potential impact of natural disasters, power outages, or connectivity issues that could potentially cause a Region to go offline.

Utilizing paired Regions enables you to more quickly overcome either a disaster within your primary Region or a disaster within your environment.

While you must duplicate Compute workloads from Region to Region, Geo-Redundant Storage or "GRS" and Azure SQL with Geo-replication are automatically replicated between paired Regions as well as Management Services like ARM Resource Metadata, IAM, and Activity Logs.

Additionally, platform updates are scheduled sequentially across paired Regions to prevent both pairs from being affected by an update window or problems with an update.

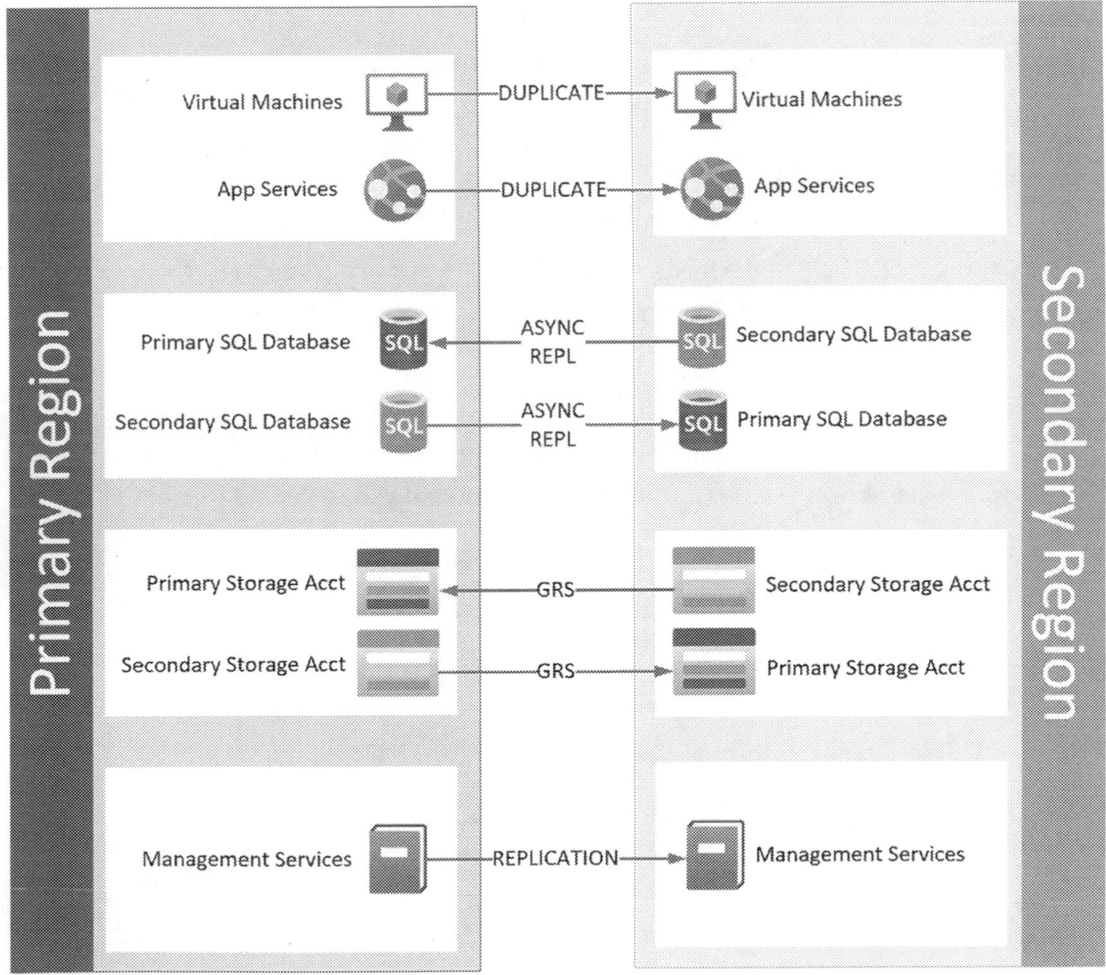

Figure 2-4. *Azure paired regions*

Microsoft uses a "Blast Radius" approach to inform design recommendations for Application Resiliency.

This essentially means that you need to design your application for Resiliency based on the blast radius and potential impact on operations.

Key Definitions

Blast Radius: This represents the impact of an event on your environment across your landscape. This can be represented at many levels:

1. **Loss of Resource:** Server that has gone offline due to hardware failure.

2. **Loss of Resource Collection:** This might represent a rack in a data center that has gone offline due to a power distribution failure.

3. **Loss of Data Center Zone:** This would represent a loss of a zone in an Azure data center that resulted in a major failure for services like Storage, Networking, or Compute instances.

4. **Loss of Region:** This represents a catastrophic failure in a geographical region that has forced all of the data centers in an Azure Region to go offline. This would likely be either a natural disaster like a hurricane or earthquake, a catastrophic failure in the power grid, or some other major event.

Azure Region: A collection of Azure data centers in close proximity with low-latency connections and separate power, cooling, and Internet connectivity.

Availability Zone: Identifies a specific subset of an Azure Region that allows for distribution of Resources and enables protection from the loss of a single Azure data center.

Resiliency: The ability of an application to adapt or adjust to failure and continue operating and continue delivering the service based on the Service Level Agreement or "SLA."

When considering how and where you will deploy your Resources with ARM, you will need to consider how to plan Resiliency for your deployments.

The first question that you should ask for any workload is, "Do I need Resilience for this deployment?" Often, nonproduction workloads will not require high availability or disaster recovery, but there will be varying requirements for production systems.

If you do need Resiliency for the workload, then your next question is, "How much?" This is often answered by the Service Level Agreement for your application. If you have a Business Critical application, it may have very high SLAs tied to it, such as 99.99% uptime, with downtime at no more than 2 hours per incident, and data loss of 1 hour or less.

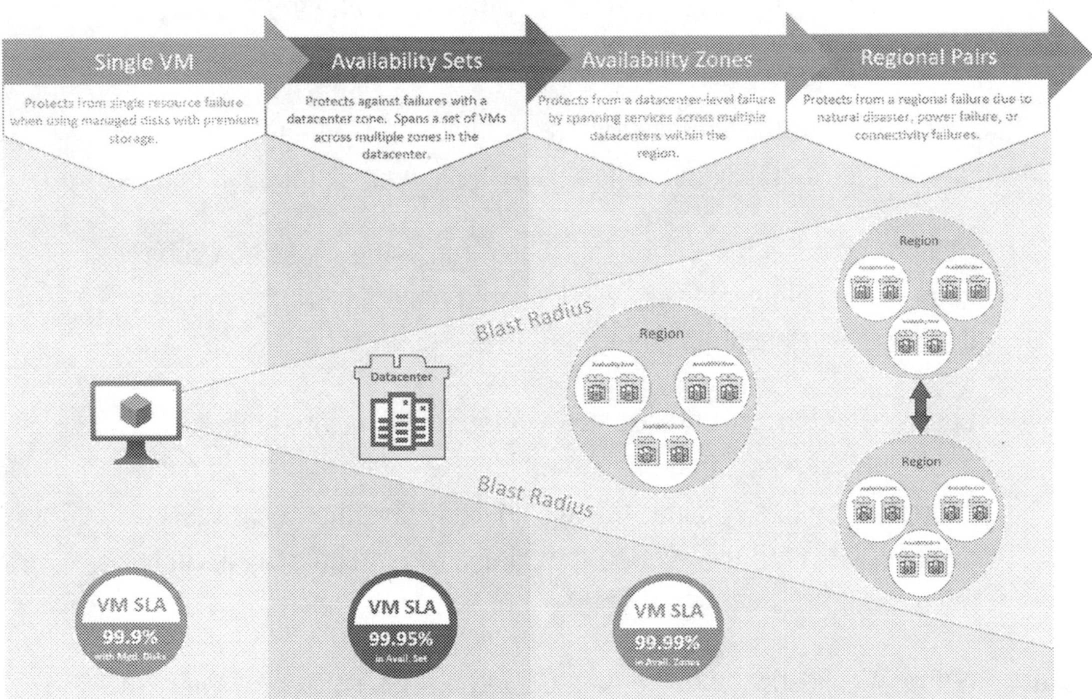

Figure 2-5. *Azure blast radius*

Once you've identified your requirements, you can build your application based on the blast radius approach. Once you've identified your approach, then you're ready to deploy your workloads to Azure using ARM.

ARM Development and Management

Before we dive into using ARM, let's quickly discuss how Azure is continually maintained and updated by Microsoft.

Azure is a platform that is continuously undergoing transformation (sometimes on a weekly basis), and as a result, it can often be quite confusing as individual Azure resource features or behaviors can be different or function differently from one day to the next due to Azure infrastructure updates across the region or platform.

This seemingly chaotic service model may appear so at first glance, but behind the scenes, service changes, updates, and feature expansions are heavily vetted and tested by multiple customers willing to invest the time to test and vet the changes/updates and work with Microsoft to refine them to achieve General Availability (GA).

Azure services and features are released in a cycle that incorporates feedback and refinement from Microsoft teams, clients, and partners before becoming GA.

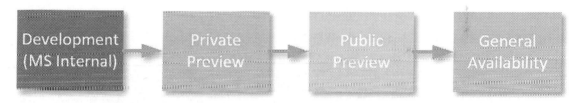

***Figure 2-6.** Azure development life cycle phases*

In the Development phase, only Microsoft resources are engaged and developing the features and functionality of the specific service. Once Microsoft has determined that they are ready for the next phase, they will invite customers that have expressed interest or have requested access to the service to develop solutions around the offering. This is referred to as "Private Preview."

Once the service has been tested and updated and has achieved a state where it's ready to start operating under normal usage, the stage is changed to "Public Preview." In this stage, the service is available to any customer that chooses to implement it, but there are limitations on the service such as reduced or eliminated Service Level Agreement and "Best Effort" support, and some features may either be unavailable or unconfigurable.

Once the product management team feels that the service is fully vetted and ready for operation, it will be deemed "Generally Available" or simply "GA."

It is highly recommended that you do not deploy production workloads using services that are not GA. Functions, features, capabilities, and deployment models can all change between the Preview and GA releases. Always wait for a service to become Generally Available in your Region(s) before deploying production workloads that utilize them.

Once the product is Generally Available, all Azure SLAs and Support guarantees apply, and the service can be implemented in production.

You can view the status and availability of any Azure service, in any region, by visiting the Azure Products by Region website:

```
https://status.azure.com/en-us/status
```

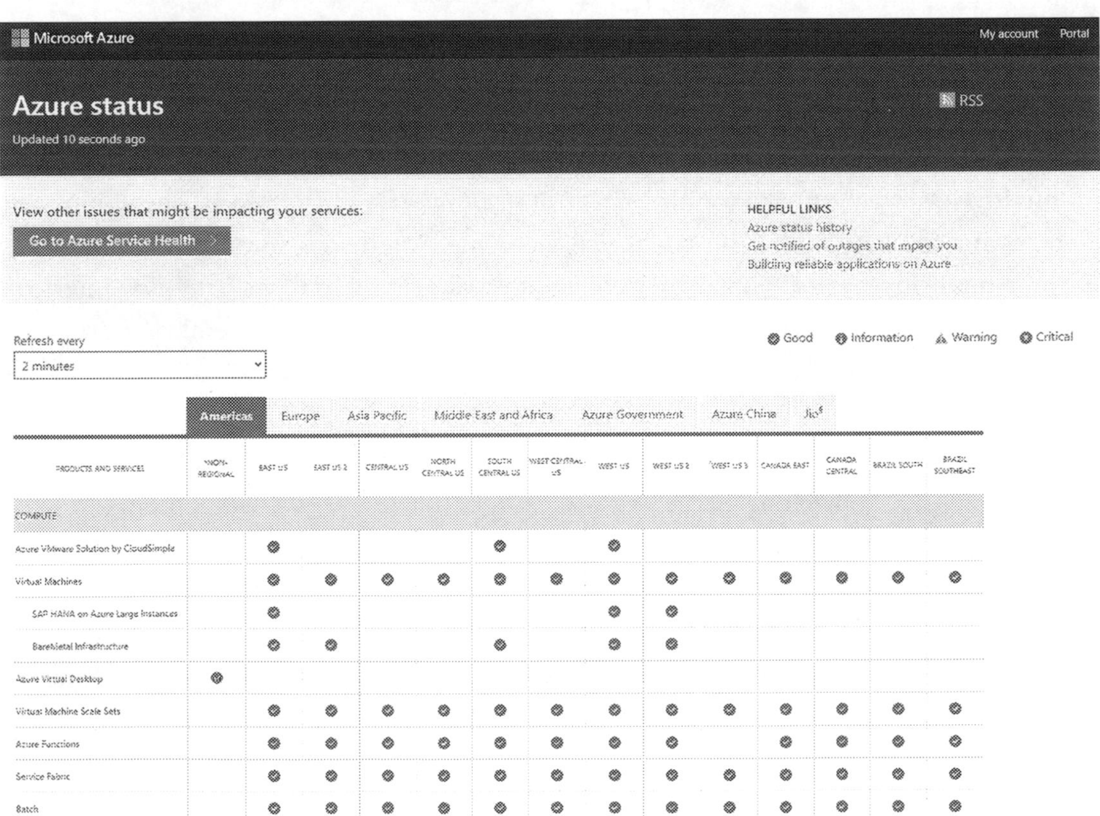

Figure 2-7. *Azure status website*

Using Azure Resource Manager

Let's take a look at some of the mechanisms available for you to interface with ARM, how they work, and what recommendations and best practices should be followed when deploying workloads through ARM.

ARM is significantly more flexible than the previous ASM system, and there are a number of ways to interface with it. You can simply log in to the Azure web portal and use the web-based graphical interface, you can use command-line tools like PowerShell or Azure CLI, or you can even connect directly via the Azure API through REST or third-party systems like HashiCorp's Terraform or other deployment tools like Chef or Octopus.

The Azure portal and the Azure API interface directly with ARM, while PowerShell and Azure CLI interact with the Azure SDK, which manages translation and hand-off to ARM for request processing.

Once requests are submitted to ARM, either directly or through the SDK, ARM will validate the identity of the user or Service Principal making the request and will validate permissions through RBAC and execute if the process is authorized.

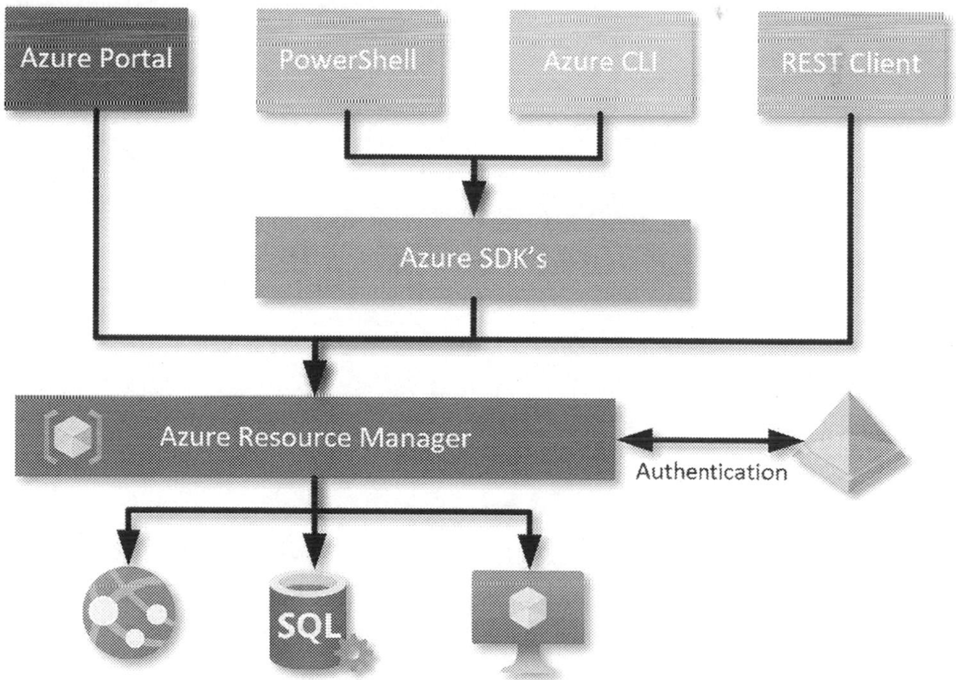

Figure 2-8. *Azure resource manager operation*

This process turns something simple like "Create VM" into all of the complex commands and subcommands required to build the pieces across the Azure data center(s) like allocating storage, creating network interfaces, locking processor/RAM resources, connecting them together, and configuring them to return a functional Virtual Machine based on your request.

ARM via Azure Portal

The most common and least organizationally mature interaction with ARM is via the Azure portal. Using the Azure portal allows for substantial potential for human error as well as architectural failures for the application or solution due to human error and limited or no validation of configuration options.

The Azure portal consists of four main areas that will be consistently used to interact with the ARM platform to create, modify, or manage resources.

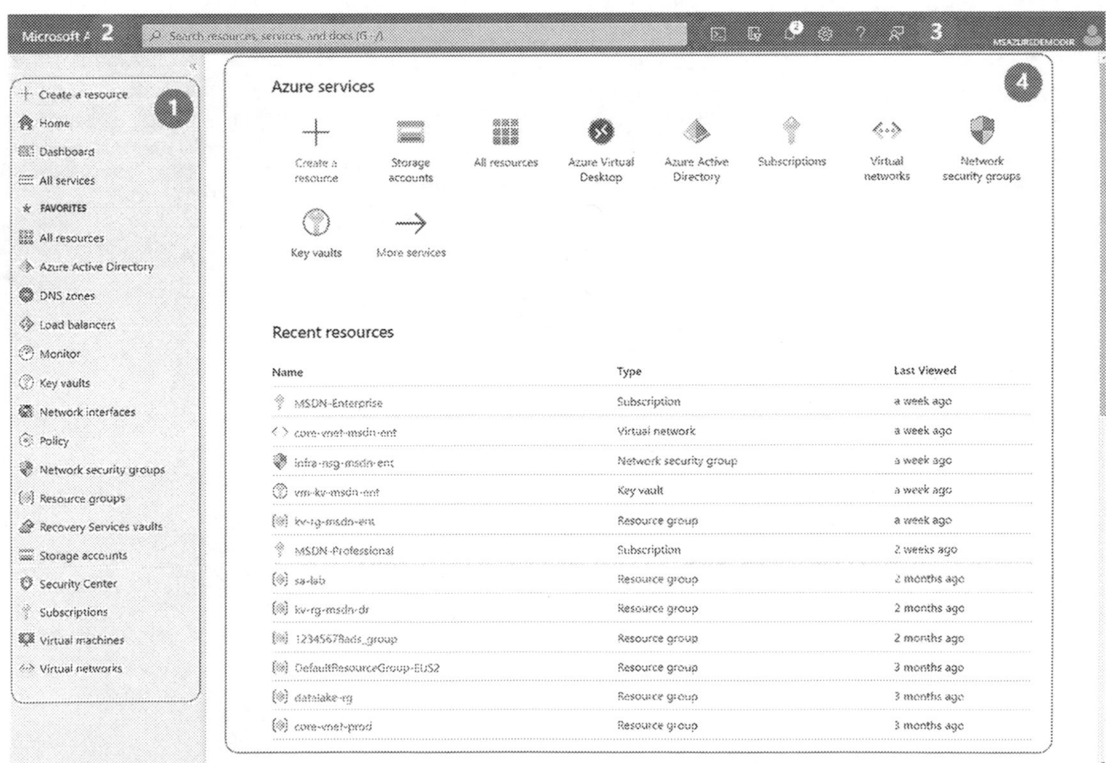

Figure 2-9. The Azure portal

1. **Main navigation:** This area contains quick links to the most commonly used Azure Resources and objects. The menu is customizable, and items can be added, removed, or reorganized to suit the user's needs.

2. **Search box:** The search box is a highly useful tool for quickly finding specific Resource types or resources.

3. **Utility menu:** The utility menu contains shortcuts to frequently used portal utilities such as the Azure Cloud Shell that is used to execute Azure CLI commands, through the portal, and the Settings options for changing the portal's theme or layout.

4. **Interaction pane:** This is the main interactional area of the portal. This is where Resources can be viewed or modified within the portal.

The majority of interaction with Resources in the Azure portal will occur in the interaction pane. Once a Resource Type has been selected, all resources, based on any filters in place, will be displayed in the pane.

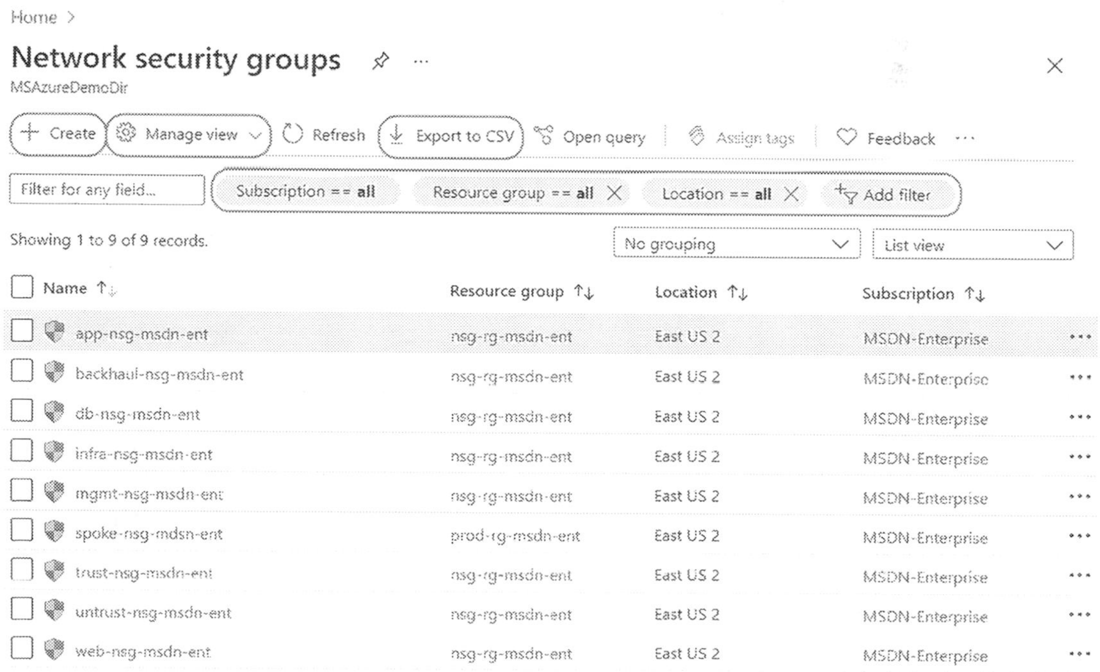

Home >

Network security groups

MSAzureDemoDir

Create | Manage view | Refresh | Export to CSV | Open query | Assign tags | Feedback

Filter for any field... | Subscription == all | Resource group == all | Location == all | Add filter

Showing 1 to 9 of 9 records. | No grouping | List view

Name	Resource group	Location	Subscription
app-nsg-msdn-ent	nsg-rg-msdn-ent	East US 2	MSDN-Enterprise
backhaul-nsg-msdn-ent	nsg-rg-msdn-ent	East US 2	MSDN-Enterprise
db-nsg-msdn-ent	nsg-rg-msdn-ent	East US 2	MSDN-Enterprise
infra-nsg-msdn-ent	nsg-rg-msdn-ent	East US 2	MSDN-Enterprise
mgmt-nsg-msdn-ent	nsg-rg-msdn-ent	East US 2	MSDN-Enterprise
spoke-nsg-mdsn-ent	prod-rg-msdn-ent	East US 2	MSDN-Enterprise
trust-nsg-msdn-ent	nsg-rg-msdn-ent	East US 2	MSDN-Enterprise
untrust-nsg-msdn-ent	nsg-rg-msdn-ent	East US 2	MSDN-Enterprise
web-nsg-msdn-ent	nsg-rg-msdn-ent	East US 2	MSDN-Enterprise

***Figure 2-10.** Portal interaction pane 1*

From this view, you can create a new resource of the current type; you can modify the view by adding, removing, or reordering the columns. You can also apply a number of different types of filters to the view, and you can export the view to a comma-separated value file for viewing and manipulating in an application such as Microsoft Excel.

Additionally, you can create a Microsoft Graph query to get additional information based on the Graph query structure, and tags can be created and assigned to resources.

If you select an individual Resource, the view will change to display the specific details for that resource. Here, you can manage the resources and perform most configuration tasks.

You can assign RBAC roles to the resource, view the activity or diagnostic logs, or modify the Resource's configuration options.

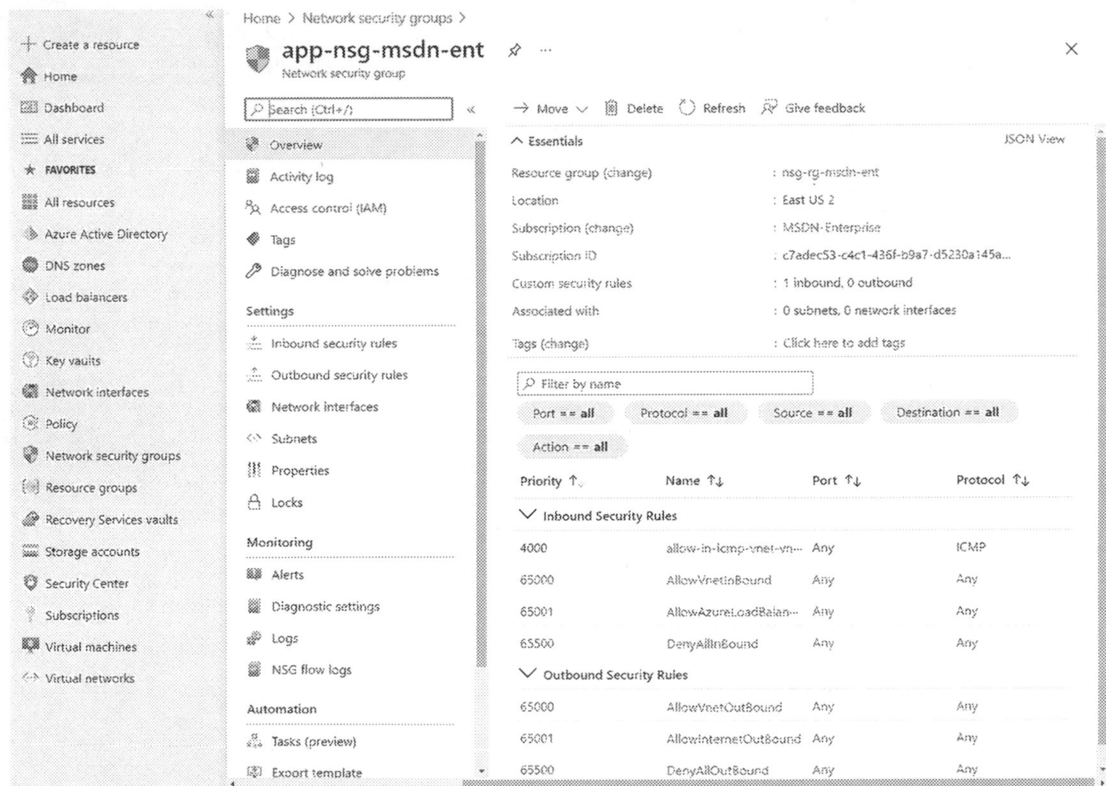

***Figure 2-11.** Portal interaction pane 2*

ARM via Command Line

Azure Cloud Shell is an interactive browser-based command-line utility for managing Resources. Cloud Shell can present with a PowerShell-style CLI, or it can use BASH to process commands.

The Cloud Shell can be accessed in two ways:

1. Direct link: Open a browser and navigate to `https://shell.azure.com`
2. Azure portal: Select the Cloud Shell icon in the Azure portal Utility Menu.

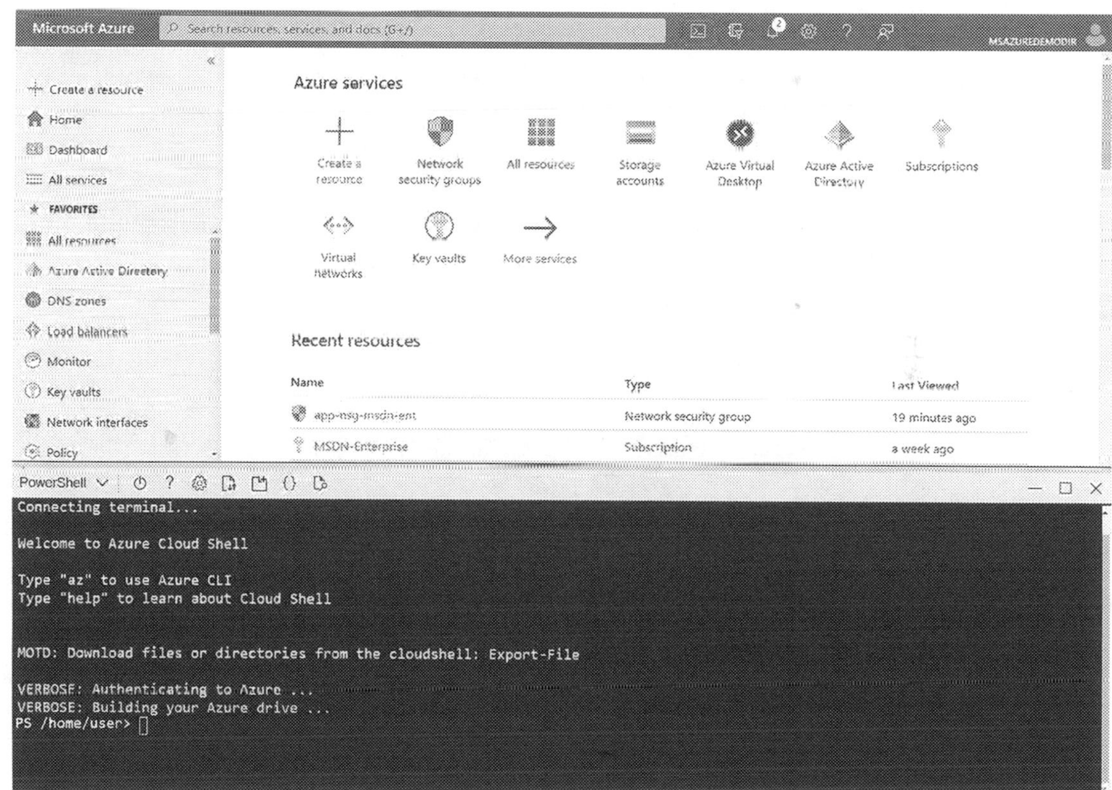

Figure 2-12. *Azure Cloud Shell*

The Azure Cloud Shell can process multiple languages to execute commands.

PowerShell is often used in the Cloud Shell to execute specific commands or scripts. In Listing 2-1, a PowerShell command has been executed to show all Network Security Groups that are in the specific Resource Group.

Code Snippet 1. Get-AzResource

```
Get-AzResource -ResourceType "Microsoft.Network/NetworkSecurityGroups"
-ResourceGroupName "nsg-rg-msdn-ent"
```

This will return the following information.

Listing 2-1. PowerShell Command in Cloud Shell

```
Name              : app-nsg-msdn-ent
ResourceGroupName : nsg-rg-msdn-ent
ResourceType      : Microsoft.Network/networkSecurityGroups
Location          : eastus2
ResourceId        : /subscriptions/c7abfg3-c4c1-436f-b9a7-d5230a145a6b/
                    resourceGroups/nsg-rg-msdn-ent/providers/Microsoft.
                    Network/networkSecurityGroups/app-nsg-msdn-ent
Tags              :
```

In addition to PowerShell, Azure CLI can also be used in the Cloud Shell. In the example in Listing 2-2, an Azure CLI command has been executed to show all Network Security Groups that are in the specific Resource Group.

Code Snippet 2. Az Resource List

```
az resource list -g nsg-rg-msdn-ent --resource-type "Microsoft.Network/
NetworkSecurityGroups"
```

Running what is essentially the same command in AzCLI returns different information in a different format.

Listing 2-2. Azure CLI Command in Cloud Shell

```
{
  "changedTime": "2021-08-01T22:37:30.018120+00:00",
  "createdTime": "2021-08-01T22:27:12.392913+00:00",
  "extendedLocation": null,
  "id": "/subscriptions/c7adec53-c4c1-436f-b9a7-d5230a145a6b/
  resourceGroups/nsg-rg-msdn-ent/providers/Microsoft.Network/
  networkSecurityGroups/app-nsg-msdn-ent",
  "identity": null,
```

```
    "kind": null,
    "location": "eastus2",
    "managedBy": null,
    "name": "app-nsg-msdn-ent",
    "plan": null,
    "properties": null,
    "provisioningState": "Succeeded",
    "resourceGroup": "nsg-rg-msdn-ent",
    "sku": null,
    "tags": {},
    "type": "Microsoft.Network/networkSecurityGroups"
  }
```

Azure PowerShell and AzCLI can also be used from a Windows command prompt, PowerShell prompt, or PowerShell ISE instance.

When running commands or scripts, it's generally a good idea to use PoweShell ISE so that you can more easily review your code, execute snippets, and troubleshoot issues.

Commonly, you may deploy resources using ARM templates. ARM templates use JSON-based declarative structure to identify resources, properties, and configurations for a group of resources to be deployed to Azure.

ARM templates use three components to make up the definition of a deployment.

Parameters: Provides values used during the deployment process. Parameter files can be reused as they are typically used to identify standard data and would be consistent across Subscriptions, Resource Groups, and Azure Environments.

Variables: Parameters that are specific to your template and wouldn't normally be reusable.

Resources: Identifies the Resources to be created during the deployment. Configuration information for Resources is generally obtained from the Parameters or Variables and applied during Resource creation.

When you deploy an ARM template, ARM translates the declarative code in your template to REST API operations and executes them sequentially.

Let's take a look at the components of the structure in a basic ARM template.

States that this section is for Resource creation	`"resources": [`
	`{`
Identifies the type of resource that is being deployed by Resource Provider	`"type": "Microsoft.Storage/storageAccounts",`
Declares the Azure API version to use	`"apiVersion": "2019-04-01",`
Identifies the Resource Name	`"name": "storageaccount1",`
Sets the location where the Resource will be deployed	`"location": "centralus",`
Selects the SKU for the Resource	`"sku": {`
Identifies a sub-SKU if one is required	`"name": "Standard_LRS"`
	`},`
Specifies any specific properties for the Resource	`"kind": "StorageV2",`
	`"properties": {}`
	`}`
	`]`

Once you deploy your ARM template, it is converted into a PUT API operation and executed against the Azure API, and your Resources are created based on your request.

```
PUT
https://management.azure.com/subscriptions/{subscriptionId}/resourceGroups/
{resourceGroupName}/providers/Microsoft.Storage/storageAccounts/
mystorageaccount?api-version=2019-04-01
REQUEST BODY
{
  "location": " centralus ",
  "sku": {
    "name": "Standard_LRS"
  },
  "kind": "StorageV2",
  "properties": {}
}
```

ARM via DevOps

The typical code creation>storage>execution process for deploying in Azure via ARM is relatively simple.

Code is usually developed using a tool like VS Code that supports ARM, Terraform, Chef, and a vast array of coding languages and plug-ins.

The two most common code formats are ARM templates and Terraform templates. Either can be developed in VS Code and deployed to Azure. The benefit of Terraform is that it maintains a state file in Azure and will refer to it when the code pipeline is executed and only modifies what is required.

ARM templates don't keep track of the current Azure landscape and have somewhat less flexibility in deploying and maintaining your Azure IaC landscape.

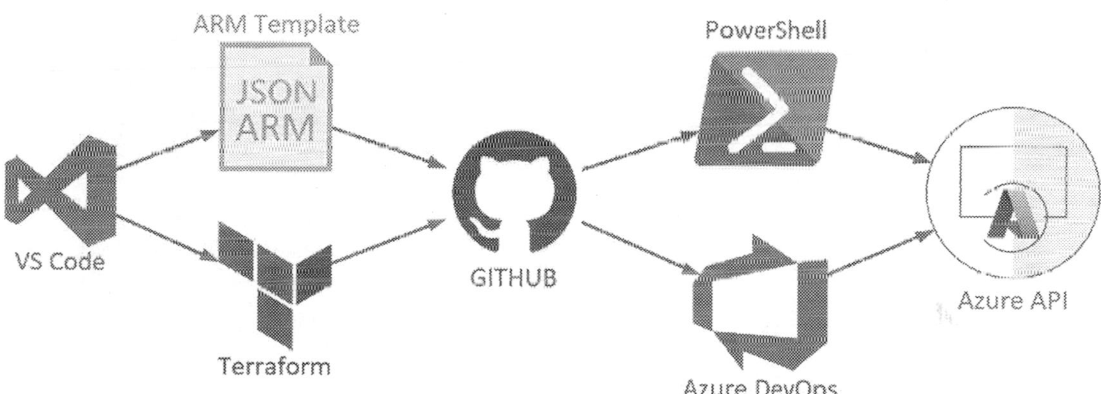

Figure 2-13. *Azure development cycle (simple)*

Once the templates are created, they are stored in a Code Repository (Repo) of some kind. The most common Repo in use today is GIT, but code can also be stored in an Azure Repo or a number of other third-party Repos as well.

Once you have your code created and ready to deploy, you can either deploy through a PowerShell command or better yet an Azure DevOps pipeline. Once you execute your command, or run the pipeline, ARM will receive your request, translate it, and pass it off to the Azure API for servicing.

Summary

In this chapter, we have discussed Azure Resource Manager, what it is, how to use it, and things to consider when planning your ARM deployments.

While the Azure Resource Manager may seem a little overwhelming at first, if you take it in parts and focus on one thing at a time, it's not difficult to wrap your head around.

From this chapter, you should have gained a basic understanding of ARM and insights around planning deployments using it and found things to think about regarding how you can incorporate it into your cloud journey.

CHAPTER 3

Azure Management Insights

In the IT world, management is defined as the process of overseeing all matters related to operations and resources. The raison d'être of Azure Arc is performing management by extending monitoring and control services that exist in the Azure cloud to computers and services that exist outside Azure, such as in on-premises networks or in other clouds. Azure Arc by itself doesn't provide much management value. Rather, it is the rich hybrid set of Azure-based management capabilities, extended to Azure Arc-connected computers and services, where the business value arises.

While many chapters in this book focus on the planning and deployment aspects of Azure Arc, the objective of this chapter is to equip you with the knowledge to imagine what is possible. You will discover what you can do with Azure Arc by learning the monitoring and control features that Azure Arc offers. You will use these valuable building blocks, sometimes called *microservices*, to deliver the solutions that we'll cover in Chapter 6, "Hybrid Server Monitoring Solution," and in Chapter 7, "Regulatory and Security Compliance for Azure Arc Servers."

Azure Policy

Azure Policy underpins all functionality of Azure Arc. Put another way, you need to assign one or more policies to Azure Arc objects to get work done. It is not inaccurate to view Azure Arc as an Azure Policy distribution and enforcement framework.

Figure 3-1 illustrates how Azure Arc servers and Azure Arc Kubernetes instances (at the bottom) are assigned Azure policies (lower left and lower right) to enforce Microsoft Defender for Cloud and Azure Monitor configurations. Those settings in turn enable Microsoft Sentinel, Azure Log Analytics, and Azure Automation solutions.

S. Buchanan and J. Joyner, *Azure Arc-Enabled Kubernetes and Servers*,
https://doi.org/10.1007/978-1-4842-7768-3_3

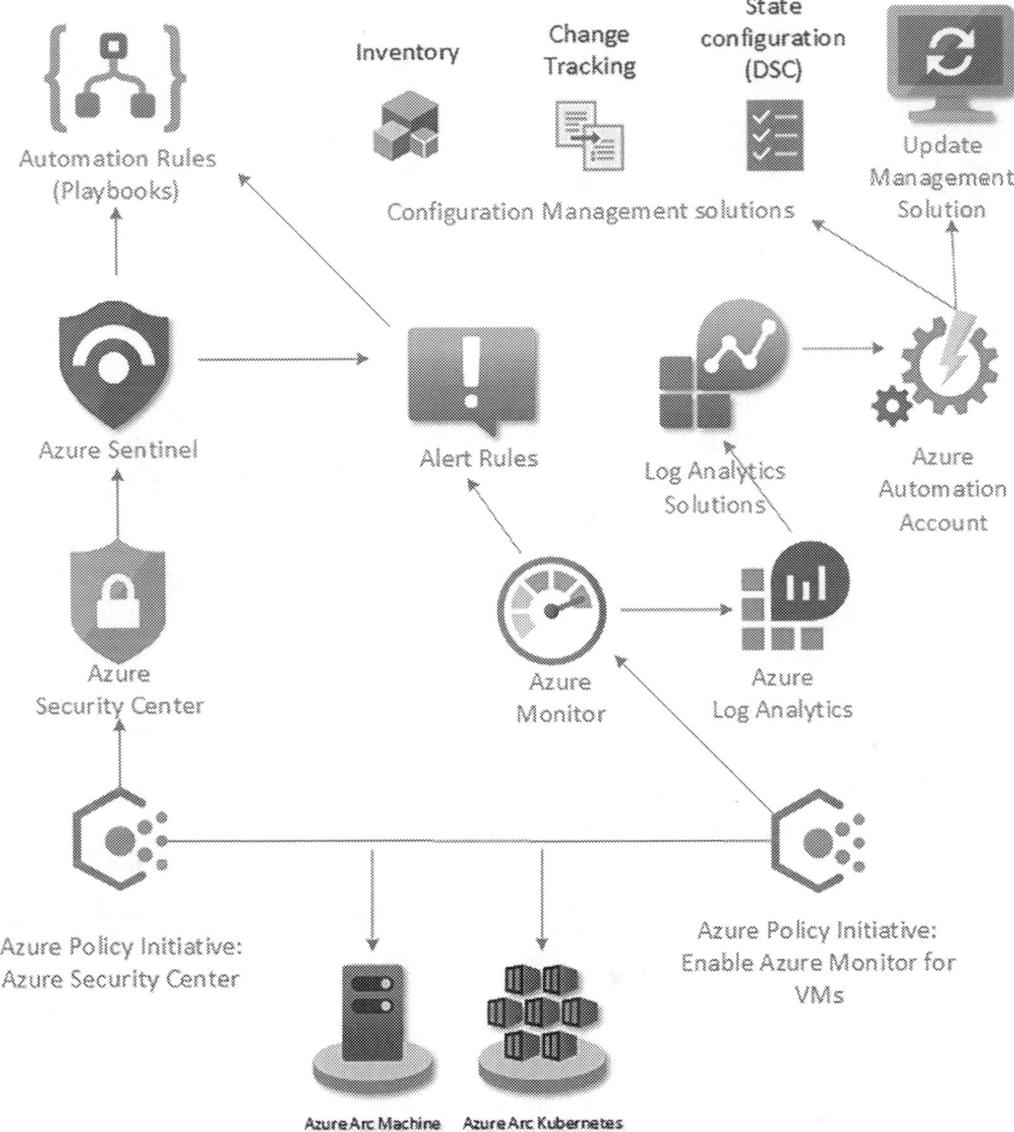

Figure 3-1. *Azure Policy assignments to Azure Arc objects enable access to Azure management services*

Single Source of Truth

Azure Policy enforces organizational standards and assesses compliance at scale. Using a compliance-based model for security-sensitive governance, resource consistency, and regulatory compliance is a best practice for organizations of all sizes. Essentially, you manage by exception to policy. If you achieve 100% policy compliance and you monitor that compliance continuously, you have done your best job. What better way to achieve that level of confidence than by enforcing the same policies with the same tool everywhere?

Having a "single source of truth" for security compliance is critical to assuring integrity of your security posture. Figure 3-2 illustrates the power of Azure Policy and Azure Arc working together. In the upper right, see that Azure Policy is pushing out initiatives for Azure Monitor and Microsoft Defender for Cloud consistently to Windows and Linux computers located both in Azure and on-premises or in any cloud. Other clouds certainly include AWS and private cloud service providers.

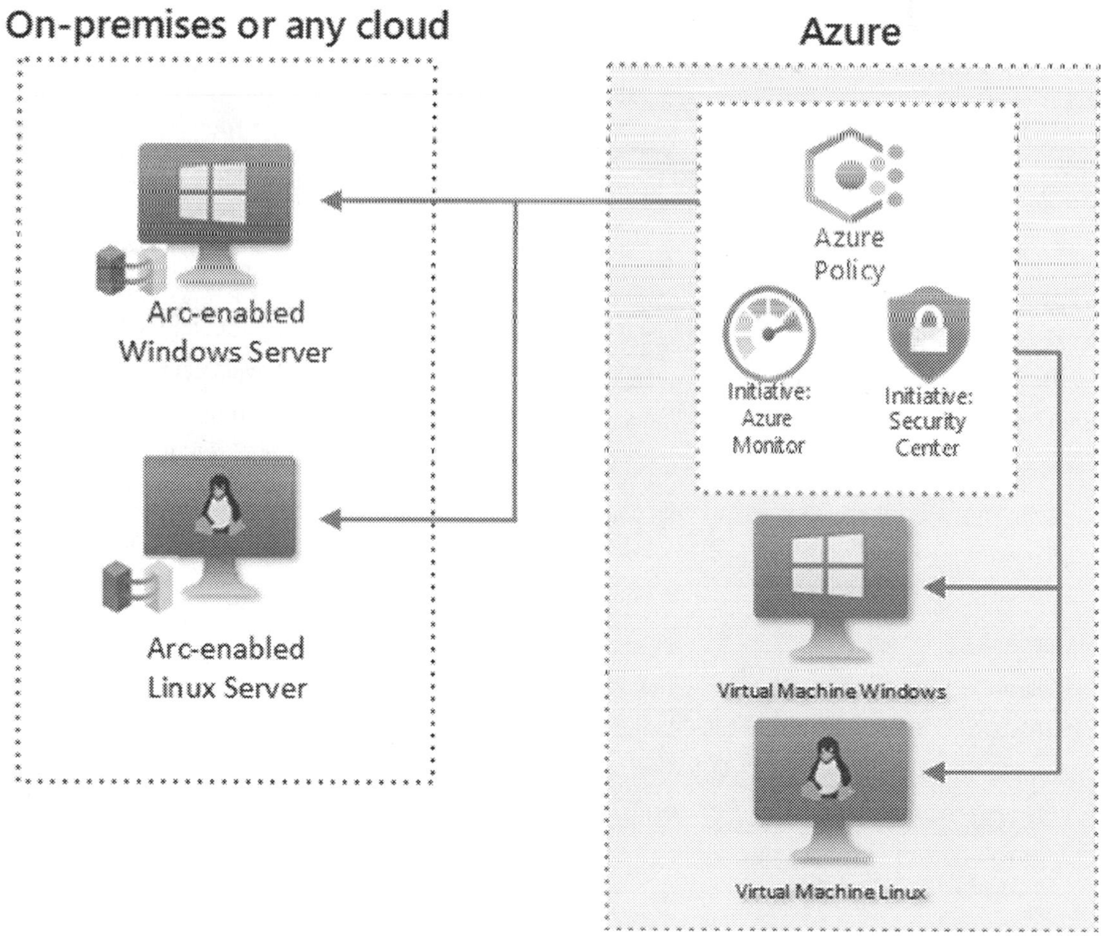

***Figure 3-2.** Azure Policy assigning Azure Monitor and Azure Defender for Cloud initiatives*

Comparison to Active Directory

Those of you familiar with Microsoft Windows Active Directory (AD) can equate Azure Policy to Active Directory Group Policy. If you are not familiar with AD, think about a directory service for user and computer names that assigns and enforces uniform policies for everything happening on the network.

Just as Group Policy Objects (GPOs) in AD are applied to a specified scope such as an OU (organizational unit) or a security group, Azure Policy is assigned to scopes such as to an Azure Subscription or Resource Group. In both cases, a large number of computers in many locations share a single instance of a policy, resulting in efficiency and uniformity. Table 3-1 helps understand Azure Policy concepts by comparing them to familiar Active Directory Group Policy components.

Table 3-1. *Comparing Azure Policy to Active Directory Group Policy*

Azure Policy	Active Directory Group Policy
Azure policies enforce settings on computers in the scope of an assignment. Multiple policies can be bundled in an Initiative. Computers can have multiple initiatives applied.	GPOs can contain settings for many and different settings. Computers can have multiple GPOs applied.
The scope of policy assignment is at the Azure subscription and resource group levels. Exceptions can be applied to specific computers in the scope(s).	GPOs are generally applied to the Domain and OU levels. They can also be applied to security groups and specific exemptions are supported.
The following are the times or events that cause a policy to be evaluated: • A resource is created, updated, or deleted in a scope with a policy assignment. • A policy or initiative is newly assigned to a scope. • A policy or initiative already assigned to a scope is updated. • During the standard compliance evaluation cycle, which occurs once every 24 hours.	GPOs are applied and processed at boot time and every 90 minutes while the computer is running.

(*continued*)

Table 3-1. *(continued)*

Azure Policy	Active Directory Group Policy
Example Azure Policy: "Audit Windows machines that do not have a minimum password age of 1 day"	Example GPO setting: Default Domain Policy ➤ Computer Configuration ➤ Policies ➤ Windows Settings ➤ Security Settings ➤ Account Policies ➤ Password Policy ➤ "Minimum password age" Policy Setting "1 days"

> **Tip** Azure Policy can also be assigned to Azure Management Groups, logical containers that allow Azure Administrators to manage access, policy, and compliance across multiple Azure Subscriptions at once.

Figure 3-3 is the Overview pane of the Policy blade in the Azure portal. The names of five initiatives that have been assigned to resources are seen in the left column. The fourth and fifth columns show the number of noncompliant resources and the number of noncompliant policies inside the assigned initiatives. Noncompliant resources can be reduced in number by remediating relevant noncompliant policies one by one.

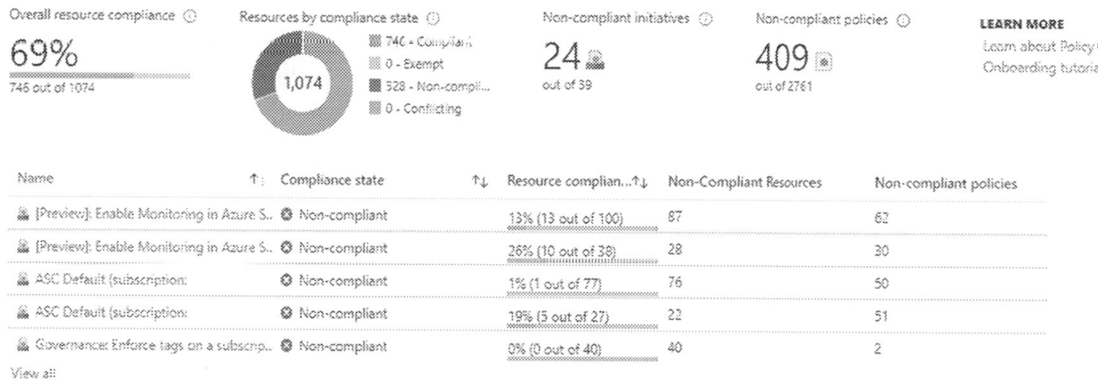

Figure 3-3. *Azure Policy definitions enforce rules uniformly for in-Azure and on-prem assets*

In summary, Azure Policy is used in Azure Arc to deliver policy assignments to Azure Arc servers. Common uses of Azure Policy in this model are to enable monitoring for Azure Monitor and Microsoft Sentinel and to enforce security policies that are contained in relevant compliance initiatives.

Microsoft Defender for Cloud

Microsoft Defender for Cloud is an optional service to enable within your Azure subscription. As a best practice, turn on Microsoft Defender for Cloud to strengthen your cloud security posture. Unique features of Microsoft Defender for Cloud include *Secure Score*, a measure of the security posture of your subscription, and *Regulatory Compliance*, a robust governance and benchmark solution.

Use Microsoft Defender for Cloud to protect your hybrid cloud workloads. When Microsoft Defender for Cloud (formerly Azure Security Center) was originally released, the only computers supported were Azure virtual machines (VMs). Now with Azure Arc, Microsoft Defender for Cloud support extends to on-premises computers or VMs in any cloud. Key benefits of Microsoft Defender for Cloud for the Azure Arc scenario include the following:

(1) Establishing a data-driven metric that assesses the security state of your resources in Azure, on-premises, and in other clouds with **Azure Secure Score**.

(2) Simplifying enterprise compliance and view your compliance against **regulatory requirements**.

(3) Microsoft Defender for Server provides deep security inspection over vulnerability-prone workloads like servers, SQL databases, and Kubernetes.

These key benefits map to the top-level dashboard tiles in Microsoft Defender for Cloud seen in Figure 3-4. Through Azure Arc, Windows and Linux servers and Kubernetes outside Azure fully participate in Microsoft Defender for Cloud coverage just like their in-Azure counterparts.

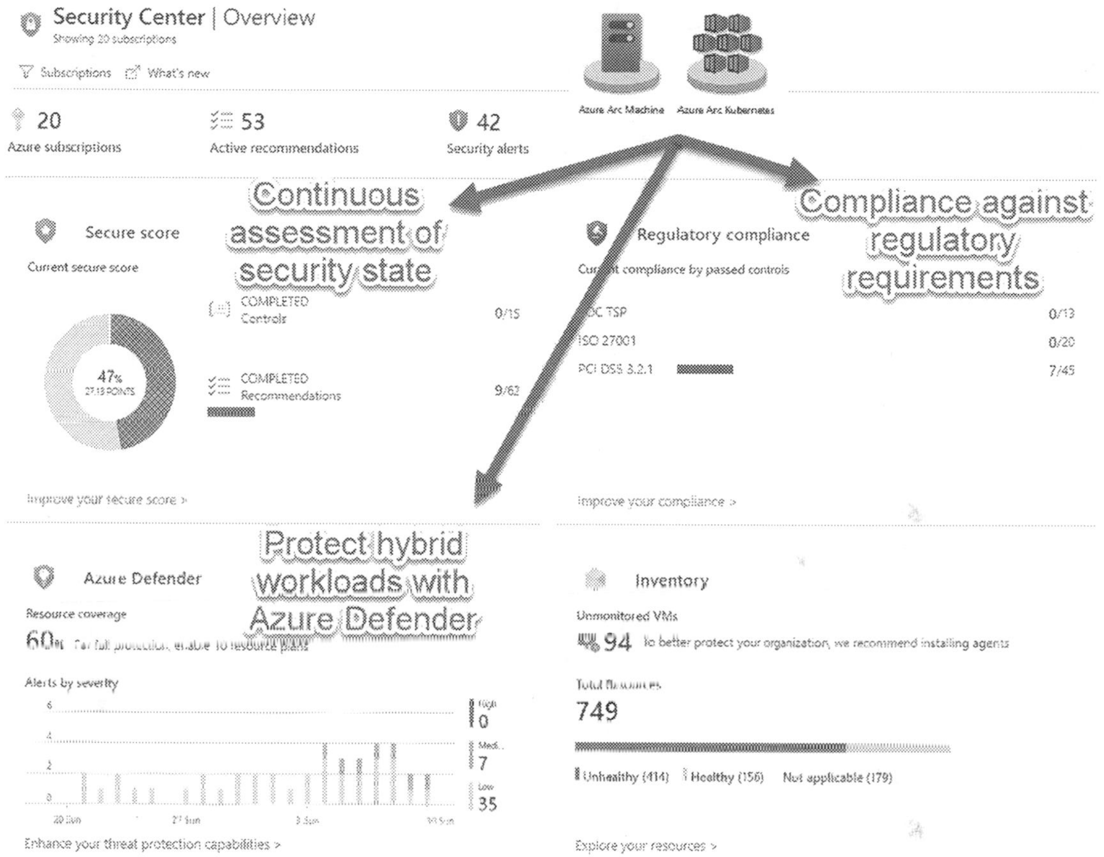

***Figure 3-4.** Microsoft Defender for Cloud (formerly Azure Defender) is key to security for Azure Arc machines and Kubernetes*

Microsoft Defender for Cloud has a monthly cost of $15 per Azure Arc server, with an additional $15 for SQL server on machines. Azure Arc Kubernetes costs are $2/VM core/month, and Container registries are $0.29 per image. Exact pricing varies by region; get updated pricing at this link:

`https://azure.microsoft.com/en-us/pricing/details/azure-defender`

Security-Focused Dashboard

There are many consoles and portals one would need to watch in order to monitor all security-sensitive aspects of your enterprise within each technology silo. Can you really say you'd rather watch your antimalware application portal at the expense of watching your firewall health portal? Of course, you need to watch both portals and likely many others. And while security settings exist almost everywhere in Azure, Microsoft Defender for Cloud, through its Secure Score methodology, achieves a strategic high ground from which you can assess your enterprise security posture.

Customers running Microsoft Sentinel rightfully can consider Microsoft Sentinel their top-level security operations console. However, distinct from the real-time incident processing and investigation that goes on in Microsoft Sentinel, Microsoft Defender for Cloud provides relevant dashboard views as well as insights into the "Most prevalent recommendations (by resources)" and "Controls with the highest potential increase."

Without Microsoft Sentinel integration, Microsoft Defender for Cloud has built-in alerting and notification workflow features that can signal you when configured to do so. Like Microsoft Sentinel, workflow automations take the form of Azure Logic Apps. For example, you could author a Logic App that takes the output of Microsoft Defender for Cloud alerts and sends an O365 email with the details.

Tip You can enable granular suppression rules for security alerts arising from Microsoft Defender for Cloud. Find the settings at Microsoft Defender for Cloud ➤ General ➤ Security Alerts ➤ Suppression rules. Create overrides based on IP, DNS, Host, and Azure Resource entities

---

Microsoft Defender for Cloud for servers

For many customers, this might be the top reason to activate Microsoft Defender for Cloud. Microsoft Defender for Cloud for servers includes Microsoft Defender for Endpoint at no extra cost. Together, they provide comprehensive endpoint detection and response (EDR) capabilities. The Microsoft Defender for Endpoint sensor is automatically enabled on Windows servers that use Microsoft Defender for Cloud.

Among the many feature parities there are between Azure VMs and Azure Arc servers is how the Security blade is populated with data from Microsoft Defender for Cloud. Figure 3-5 is almost identical to what you would see for an Azure VM with Microsoft Defender for Cloud coverage enabled, but this Azure Arc server is a VM running in an on-premises private cloud. A prioritized list of security recommendations and a historical list of security incidents and alerts for the computer are provided.

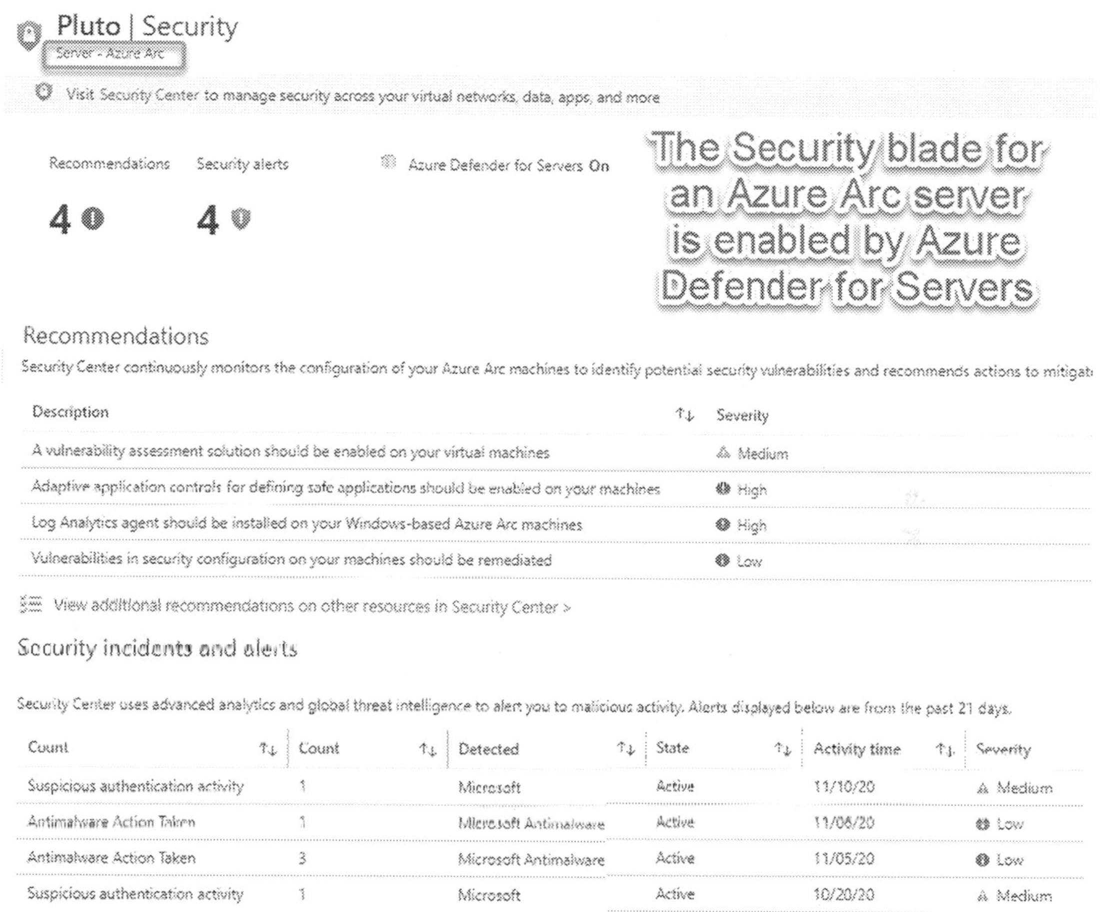

Figure 3-5. *Microsoft Defender for Cloud coverage is extended to on-prem servers by Azure Arc*

Compliance Against Regulatory Requirements

For some organizations, such as financial institutions that must comply with PCI DSS, or healthcare organizations that must comply with HIPAA, compliance is a key reason to deploy Azure Arc with Microsoft Defender for Cloud. The Secure Score of a compliance assignment is based on how well the resources in the scope conform to the desired security policies. Having a well-defined and industry-accepted security model to adhere to gives your team a meaningful goal to work toward.

A variety of industry and regional regulatory standards are available to assign to scopes via policy. These regulatory standards are predeployed (out of the box) to each Microsoft Defender for Cloud instance:

- PCI DSS 3.2.1 (Payment Card Industry Data Security Standard for organizations that handle branded credit cards from the major card schemes)
- ISO 27001 (An international standard on how to manage information security)
- SOC TSP (Internal control reports on the services provided by a service organization)

Additional regulatory compliance standards easily added in the Microsoft Defender for Cloud portal:

- NIST SP 800-53 R4 (Security and Privacy Controls for Federal Information Systems and Organizations)
- NIST SP 800 171 R2 (Protecting Controlled Unclassified Information in Nonfederal Systems and Organizations)
- UK OFFICIAL and UK NHS
- Canada Federal PBMM
- Azure CIS 1.1.0 (New) (Microsoft Azure Foundations Benchmark Regulatory Compliance)
- Azure Security Benchmark
- HIPAA HITRUST (Health Insurance Portability and Accountability Act for healthcare organizations)
- SWIFT CSP CSCF v2020 (Customer Security Controls Framework consists of mandatory and advisory security controls for SWIFT users)

Recommended Security Life Cycle Approach

Consider these high-level steps to use the regulatory compliance feature of Microsoft Defender for Cloud with Azure Arc resources:

1. Place Azure Arc servers and Azure Arc Kubernetes in Azure resource groups suitable as policy scopes.
2. Assign one or more Azure Policy Initiatives to resource groups containing Azure Arc servers and/or Kubernetes.

3. Observe the compliance status of all policies in the initiative after initial assignment.

4. Create an Exemption for those policies that are judged as mitigated or waived in your environment.

5. Working from the short list of outstanding noncompliant resources, perform necessary remediation to achieve 100% compliance.

6. Monitor for sustained full compliance, alerting when an exception occurs.

7. Alerts result in manual or automated repair and remediation tasks that restore full compliance.

Figure 3-6 shows what full compliance with an initiative looks like. You will have a 100% Secure Score, and each listed control in the initiative will be marked Completed.

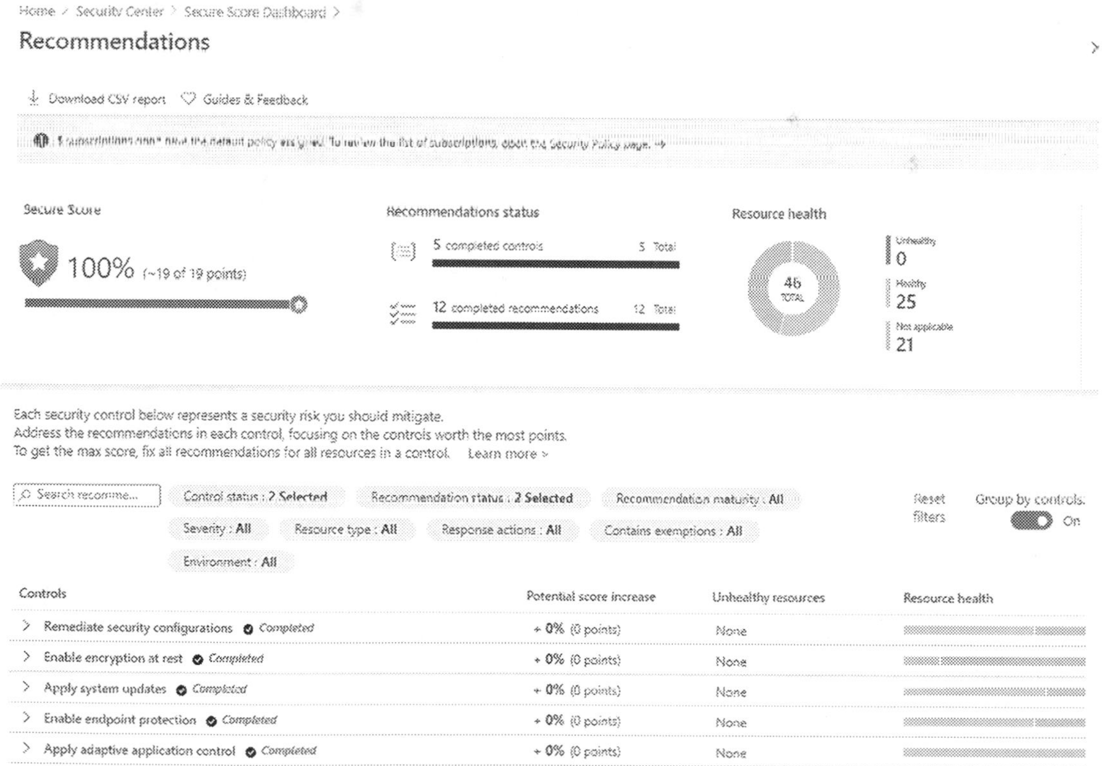

***Figure 3-6.** What success looks like when you achieve a 100% Secure Score*

Azure Monitor

Azure Monitor is an Azure service that collects, analyzes, and acts on telemetry data from your Azure and on-premises environments. Think of "Azure Monitor" as a brand that encompasses a variety of solutions, much like "Microsoft Office," which includes Word, Excel, Outlook, and a slew of common underpinnings that help the individual applications and components work together.

There's a lot to Azure Monitor; consult Figure 3-7 to understand what tools and microservices are in play. If you have any resources in Azure or you are using Azure Arc, you are already using Azure Monitor. Every Azure and Azure Arc resource produces logs, and many resources also supply metrics on utilization and performance.

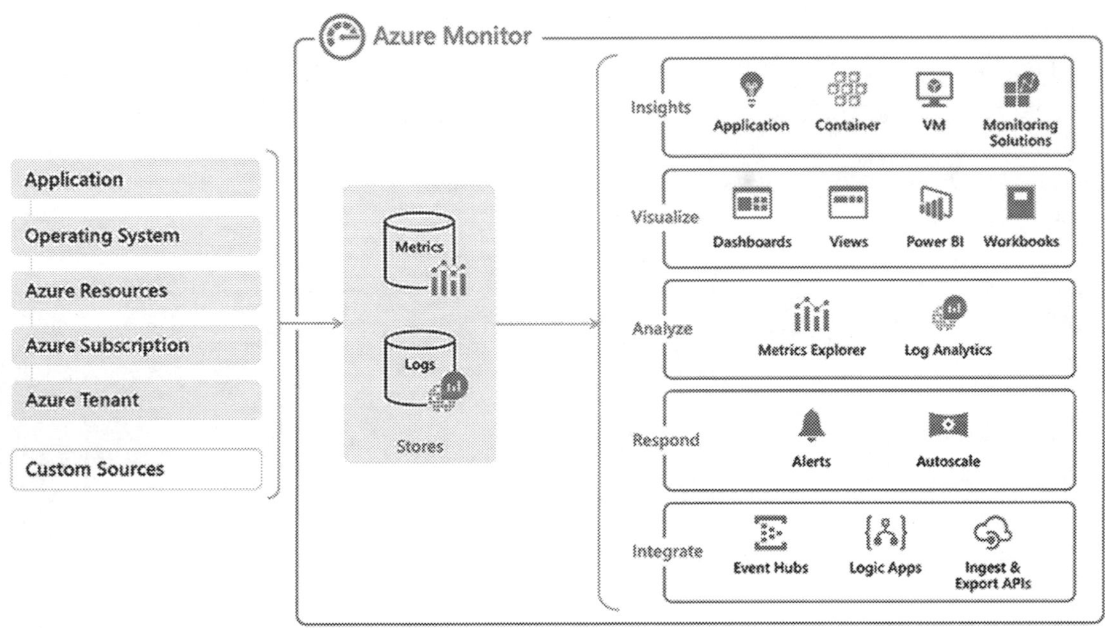

Figure 3-7. *Azure Monitor collects, analyzes, and acts on telemetry data*

Tip *Understanding Azure Monitor product names*

Azure Monitor, Log Analytics, and Application Insights are a single service that provides monitoring. Some features in Log Analytics and Application Insights have been rebranded to Azure Monitor, but their function has not changed. The log data engine and query language of Log Analytics is referred to as **Azure Monitor Logs**.

Azure Monitor Data Sources and Solutions

On the left in Figure 3-7 are data sources that input to Azure Monitor, such as a Windows computer OS, Azure services like Key Vault, or activity from an Azure subscription. The database icons for Metrics and Logs in the center represent your data repository where telemetry data flows and is stored. Consumers and users of the data ("solutions") are on the right and include Azure dashboards and workbooks for visualization and Log Analytics for running scheduled queries that raise alerts when availability, performance, configuration, or security issues occur.

Azure Monitor stores data from multiple sources together so that the data can be correlated and analyzed using a common set of tools. You are fully abstracted from the data repository (you can think of it as an infinite capacity data lake). Data in the repository is read-only and subject to the retention polices of your workspace. Microsoft handles the security access via normal Azure role-based access control and automatically purges data at the end of its retention period, which is 30 days by default but can be extended up to 2 years.

Different sources of data for Azure Monitor will write to either a Log Analytics workspace (Logs) or the Azure Monitor metrics database (Metrics) or both. Data is stored in tables, and each workspace or database will have different tables depending on what data sources have been written to them.

Azure Monitor Scope Targeting

Azure Monitor is enabled the moment that you create a new Azure subscription, and Activity log and platform metrics are automatically collected. Resources that produce logs are seen as "scopes" when it comes to log queries.

Figure 3-8 demonstrates the concept that Azure Monitor Logs require a scope to execute queries against. By scoping Azure Monitor Logs to any particular Azure resource that produces logs, you can run focused queries against the log data of that resource. Alternatively, by setting the scope to a Log Analytics workspace, you can search across database tables from all data sources reporting logs to that workspace.

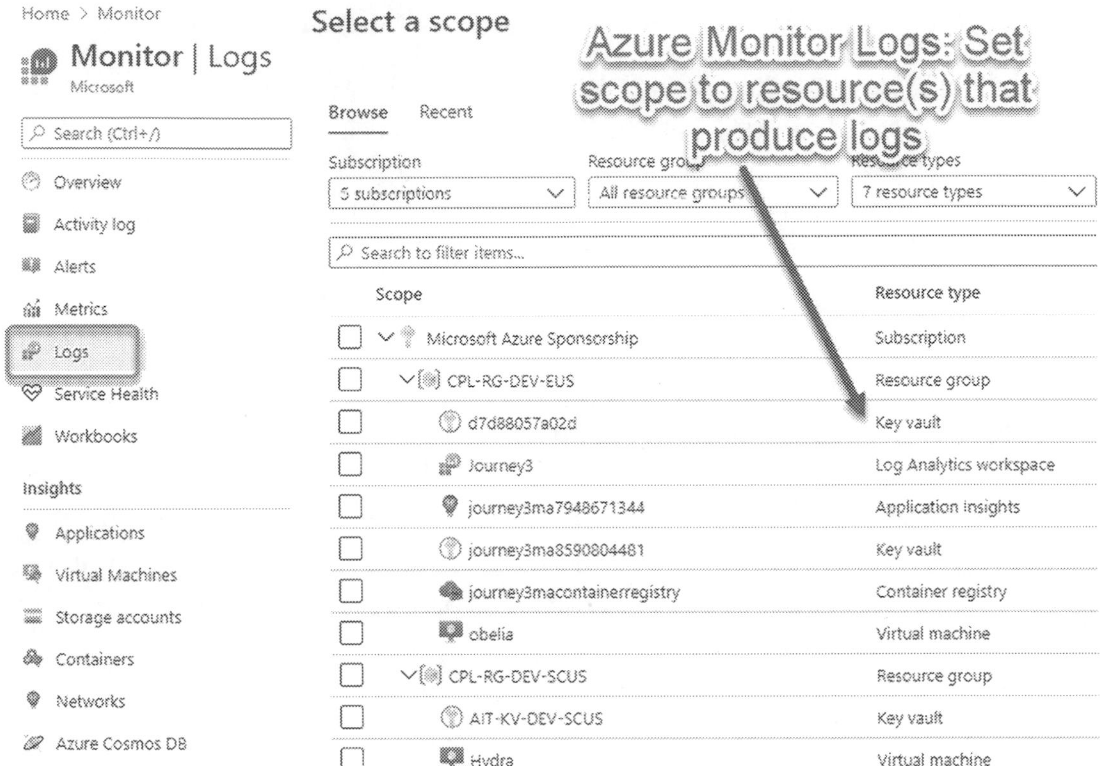

Figure 3-8. *Azure Monitor Logs require selection of a scope in order to target queries*

For example, Figure 3-9 shows the logs blade of an Azure Arc server. Since this server is running Windows Defender for antimalware defense and the *Security and Audit* or *SecurityCenterFree* solutions are deployed, the *ProtectionStatus* table is present in the logs view, and you can query that table directly.

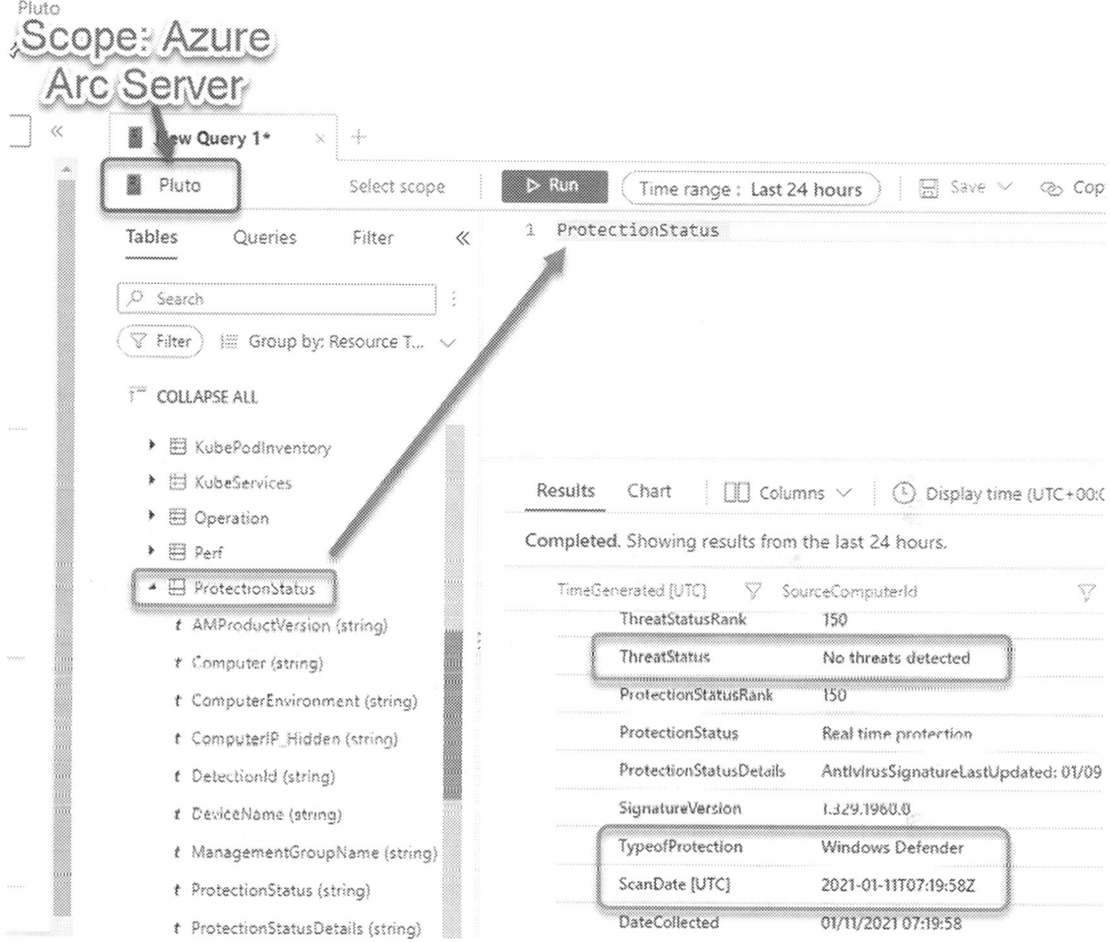

***Figure 3-9.** Using Azure Monitor Logs to check the status and last scan date of Windows Defender on an Azure Arc server*

Needless to say, an identical *ProtectionStatus* table is also present in the logs view of an Azure VM running Windows Defender. Consider that you can run the same query against the *ProtectionStatus* tables of all computers, in-Azure and non-Azure, to learn if any computers have detected threats or have outdated scans. This is a powerful example of how Azure Arc elevates on-premises computers to the same management paradigm as in-Azure VMs, making your life easier when it comes to hybrid administration tasks.

Tip The *Query Explorer*, *Save*, and *New alert rule* buttons are not available in Azure Monitor Log view when the query scope is set to a specific resource. To create alerts, save, or load a query, Log Analytics must be scoped to a workspace.

Log Analytics and Microsoft Sentinel

Deploying one or both of these Azure services to support infrastructure monitoring (Log Analytics) and/or security monitoring (Microsoft Sentinel) is an excellent and common scenario for Azure Arc. By doing so, you will achieve the "single pane of glass" that colocates your in-Azure and your non-Azure resources in the same alerting infrastructure and portal views. Both solutions use the same agent and have an identical rollout plan.

If your enterprise has any number of servers running outside Azure and you plan to monitor them from Azure, you want to

(1) Use Azure Arc to ...

(2) Assign Azure Policy that ...

(3) Install the Microsoft Monitoring Agent (MMA) and dependencies

For both Azure Log Analytics and Microsoft Sentinel scenarios, that's all there is to it. All the other monitoring solutions described in this chapter require only the MMA (and dependencies) to be installed.

Log Analytics Workspaces

Monitoring solutions like *VM Insights* (which include Azure Arc servers) and *Container Insights* for AKS deployments install into a Log Analytics workspace. *Microsoft Sentinel* installs as a superset solution (*Security Insights*) into an existing Log Analytics workspace. (There is a 1:1 relationship between Azure Log Analytics workspaces and Microsoft Sentinel instances.) Whether your end goal is to monitor servers with Log Analytics or manage their security with Microsoft Sentinel (or both), you need the MMA installed on your Windows and Linux servers.

Here are three common things you will do with your Log Analytics workspace:

1. Deploy solutions that monitor and manage specific services.
2. Run scheduled query rules to raise alerts.
3. Create visualizations such as Workbooks and Dashboards.

We will take a look at each of these next.

Tip Avoid workspace sprawl. Consider creating a Log Analytics workspace in a new production Azure subscription as almost the first resource you create. Doing so enables other log-generating resources you create such as Virtual Machines and Key Vaults to have a common destination.

- When enabling Application Insights, Container Insights, and VM Insights and installing Azure Sentinel, select the preexisting workspace.
- Configure automatic assignment of your central Log Analytics workspace in Azure Security Center at Pricing and Settings ➤ Subscription ➤ Settings ➤ Auto provisioning.

Log Analytics Solutions

Monitoring solutions in Log Analytics provide analysis of the operation of a particular Azure application or service. After you deploy a Log Analytics workspace, monitoring solutions appropriate for your environment are automatically added to provide specific features. For example, when you enable Microsoft Defender for Cloud, the *Security* solution is installed in your selected Log Analytics workspace.

Installing solutions is not necessary to use the basic functionality of Azure Monitor logs; however, most all production Log Analytics workspaces will have several solutions installed along the way.

Solutions that are particularly useful for Azure Arc servers include *Change Tracking* and *Updates*, which are installed by Azure Automation, and *SecurityInsights*, which is the solution name for Microsoft Sentinel. Figure 3-10 shows these solutions installed in a Log Analytics workspace. If you ever need to delete a solution from a workspace, you can do it from here.

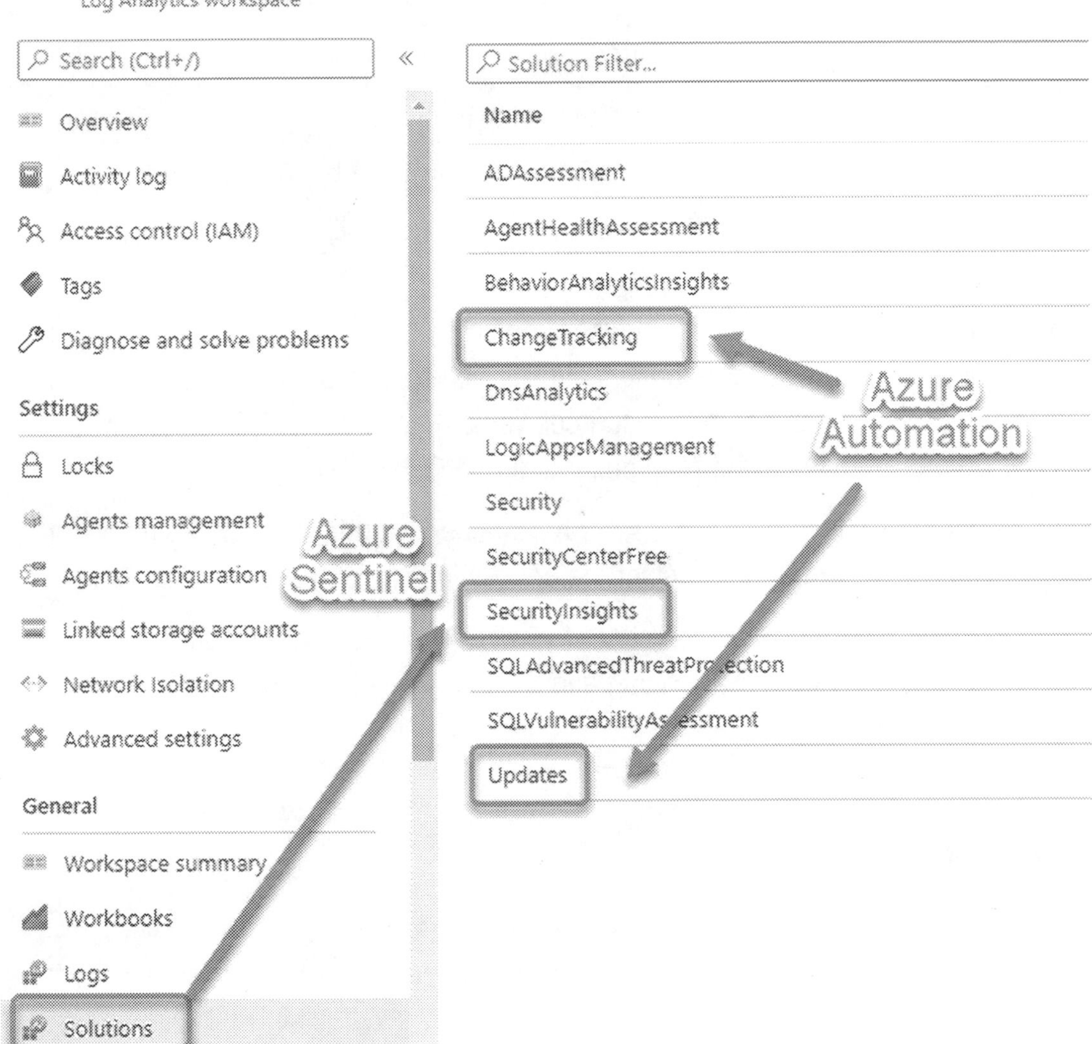

Figure 3-10. *The Solutions blade of a Log Analytics workspace lists the solutions installed into the workspace*

Log Analytics Costs

Azure Monitor has a log ingestion cost that is measured in gigabytes per day (GB/day). This is the main cost of using log analytics. Monitoring servers contributes from 1 to 3 GB per month in log and metric data; domain controllers running DNS server will be up to

10 GB per month. As a rule of thumb, budget $5 per month per Azure Arc server for Log Analytics processing. (Microsoft Sentinel ingestion costs, not estimated here, are also measured in GB/day and are additive to Log Analytics charges.)

There are smaller costs you will incur for running scheduled query rules and microcosts for such things as Azure Logic App and Azure Functions executions. The most expensive monitor runs every 5 minutes and costs about $1.50 per month. Monitors that run every hour or once a day cost much less, as low as $0.05 per day. The average organization spends much less than $50 a month on these combined small charges.

To obtain a precise estimate of Azure Monitor charges for metric queries and alerts, enter your sizing data in the Azure Pricing Calculator at this link:

`https://azure.microsoft.com/en-us/pricing/calculator/?service=monitor`

Contributors to microcharges include metric queries ($0.01 per 1,000 API calls, first 1,000,000 are free), ITSM connections ($5.00 per 1,000 tickets created, first 1,000 are free), and email notifications (2.00 per 100,000 emails, first 1,000 are free).

Log Alert Rules

Log alerts allow you to use a Log Analytics query to evaluate logs on a recurring schedule and fire an alert based on the results. Rules can trigger one or more actions using Action Groups. Action Groups can include notification tasks like sending an email or creating an ITSM ticket, as well as automation tasks like launching an Azure Automation Runbook or a Logic App.

Traditional State-Based vs. Analytics-Based Monitoring

This is where the real monitoring work happens. Traditional network monitoring tools, like Microsoft System Center Operations Manager (SCOM) or *Orion* from SolarWinds, Inc., consist of a database that represents the health state of monitored servers. Agents or probes use proprietary workflow to check a particular attribute or metric and write that to the database. For example, a monitor might "ping" a server and record ping reply status to the database. When you want to know if the server is online, you examine the state value in the database to learn when the last successful ping was.

A more modern and scalable approach is to use log-based analytics. Popular implementations of this approach include products from *Splunk, Sumo Logic,* and *ELK (Elasticsearch, Logstash, and Kibana).* Enterprises often select Splunk for functionality and feature set, cloud-native Sumo Logic for simplicity, or ELK for its open source design.

In this model, a lightweight agent process streams the log data from the server to a repository. The thinking is that if we log everything the server is doing, we can learn anything we want by searching the copy of the logs. Questions about the status of a server are answered in a two-step process: (1) first by running a query that searches the repository and then (2) looking for a match (or the absence of a match) of the search query criteria.

How a Query-Based Alert Rule Works

For example, consider a common scenario you want to alert on; this is the loss of contact with a monitored server. A query that will alert on a loss of contact consists of searching for "heartbeat" log entries from the computer in the recent past. Finding no recent heartbeat log entry when you run the query constitutes a loss of contact. Running that query every 5 minutes (a *scheduled alert rule*) can produce an alert in near real time when contact with a server is lost.

See the Rules blade of an Azure Log Analytics workspace in Figure 3-11. The first column shows the names of the alert-generating rules, and the second column shows the actual query language checking for the conditions of interest.

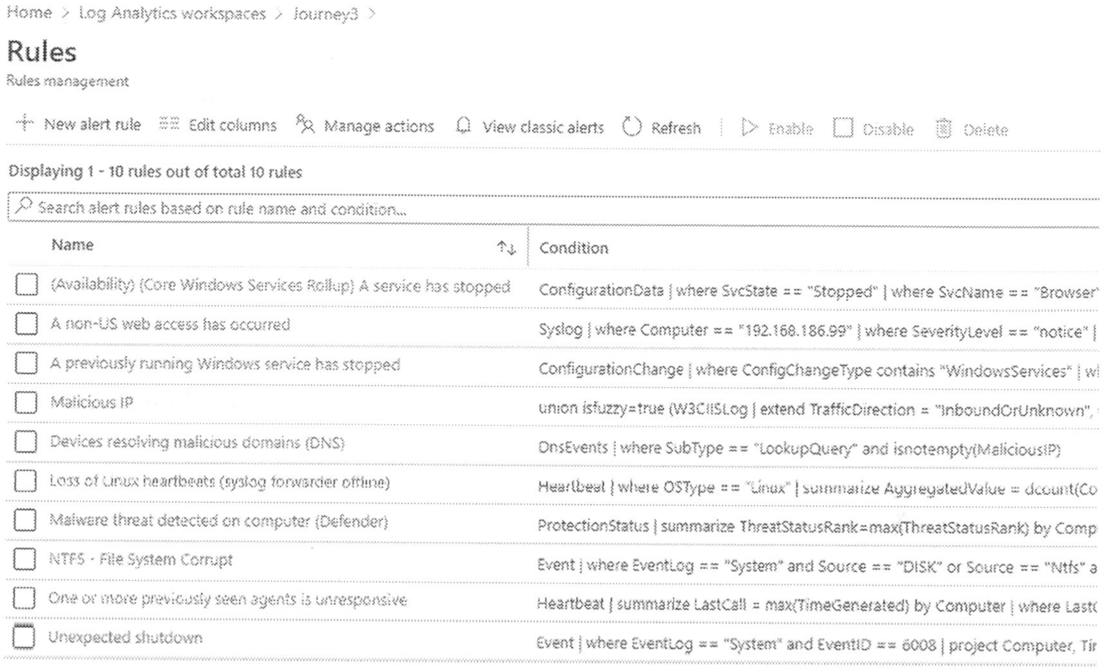

Home > Log Analytics workspaces > Journey3 >

Rules

Rules management

+ New alert rule | Edit columns | Manage actions | View classic alerts | Refresh | Enable | Disable | Delete

Displaying 1 - 10 rules out of total 10 rules

Search alert rules based on rule name and condition...

Name	Condition
(Availability) (Core Windows Services Rollup) A service has stopped	ConfigurationData | where SvcState == "Stopped" | where SvcName == "Browser"
A non-US web access has occurred	Syslog | where Computer == "192.168.186.99" | where SeverityLevel == "notice" |
A previously running Windows service has stopped	ConfigurationChange | where ConfigChangeType contains "WindowsServices" | wl
Malicious IP	union isfuzzy=true (W3CIISLog | extend TrafficDirection = "InboundOrUnknown",
Devices resolving malicious domains (DNS)	DnsEvents | where SubType == "LookupQuery" and isnotempty(MaliciousIP)
Loss of Linux heartbeats (syslog forwarder offline)	Heartbeat | where OSType == "Linux" | summarize AggregatedValue = dcount(Co
Malware threat detected on computer (Defender)	ProtectionStatus | summarize ThreatStatusRank=max(ThreatStatusRank) by Comp
NTFS - File System Corrupt	Event | where EventLog == "System" and Source == "DISK" or Source == "Ntfs" a
One or more previously seen agents is unresponsive	Heartbeat | summarize LastCall = max(TimeGenerated) by Computer | where Last(
Unexpected shutdown	Event | where EventLog == "System" and EventID == 6008 | project Computer, Tir

Figure 3-11. *Scheduled rules check for conditions you want to alert on*

Many queries that work for Azure VMs work for Azure Arc servers as well. As an example, consider this simple query that returns a list of monitored computers with their most recent heartbeat:

```
Heartbeat
| summarize arg_max(TimeGenerated, *) by Computer
```

Since both Azure VMs and Azure Arc servers produce heartbeat messages every minute and both kinds of servers are of the “Computers” class of Azure objects, a homogeneous list is achieved.

Investments you make in building a library of useful monitoring rules for Azure Arc servers will keep working with little or no modification if you migrate to Azure VMs in the future. Scheduled query-based rules work identically in Microsoft Sentinel, where they are called *Analytics Active Rules*.

Workbooks and Dashboards

Once you have alerts arriving when adverse or unusual events occur, consider the flip side of effective monitoring is visualization. In particular, to assess the state of a computer's performance metrics, a list of alerts (or even the absence of alerts) does not do the job. You need a chart or graph-based visual display of some sort in many situations to perform management.

Azure Monitor (and likewise both Azure Log Analytics and Microsoft Sentinel) solves the visualization requirement with the same core function as alert-generating rules: Queries. A feature of the query language used in Azure Monitor, Kusto Query Language, or KQL, is that queries can return data in graphical as well as list format. Think of it this way: while a scheduled alerting rule contains a query to run and actions to perform depending on the query results, Azure Monitor *visualizations* like workbooks and dashboards contain multiple queries. Each query executes and renders graphical output immediately and in real time for you to view when you open the workbook or dashboard.

Azure Workbooks

The workbook seen in Figure 3-12 is a demonstration of the power of cross-platform query analysis in a hybrid environment. The sorted chart with bar graphs and color shading assesses server performance. This view is of CPU utilization of Windows and Linux servers that are both in-Azure VMs and on-premises physical and virtual computers. With Azure Arc and the Microsoft Monitoring Agent (MMA), you achieve a "single pane of glass" for server performance using Azure management tools that extends to your entire estate.

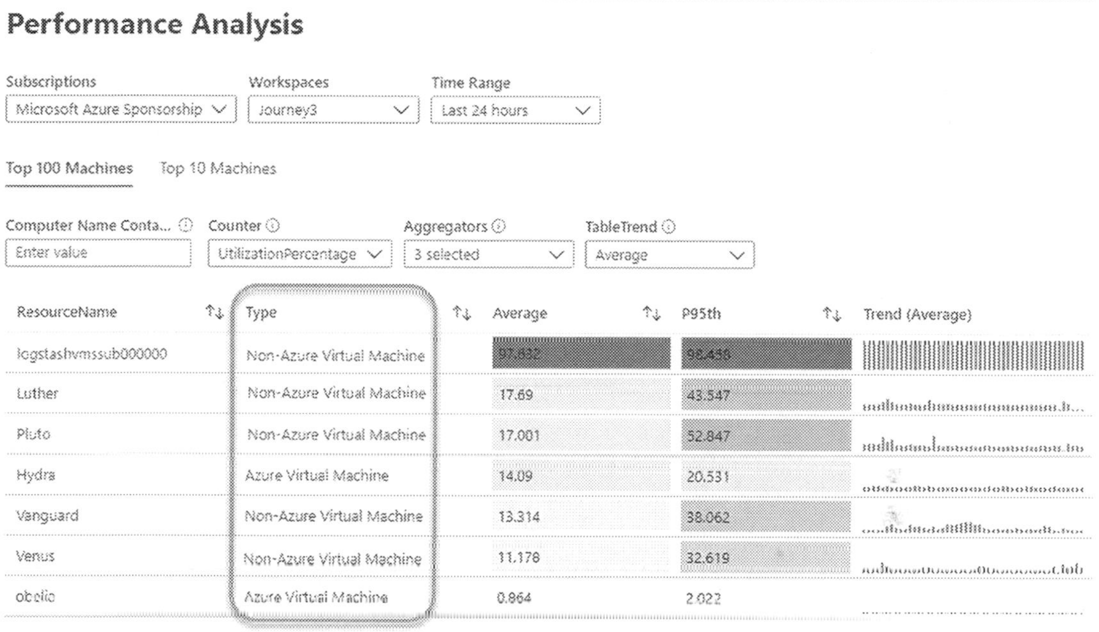

Figure 3-12. *Queries return data as charts and diagrams in an Azure Workbook*

Workbooks are saved in your Azure subscription and are sharable with team members in various ways. Microsoft Sentinel environments have only shared workbooks, while Azure Monitor and Log Analytics environments have only private workbooks. In all environments, private workbooks are sharable by sending recipients a unique URL.

Workbooks support parameter-enabled interactive reports—that is, selecting an element in a table will dynamically update associated charts and visualizations (see the drop-down selection boxes in Figure 3-12 like *Counter* and *TableTrend*). This lets you pivot and focus the visualizations to "fly around" in your data.

Azure Dashboards

Another visualization product in Azure Monitor is the Dashboard. Just like Azure workbooks, Azure dashboards are assemblages of KQL queries configured to return data in chart and graph format. Dashboards can be private to your user account or shared with teammates.

Figure 3-13 is a dashboard, *Infrastructure insights* that is displaying network traffic metrics for all monitored servers, both in-Azure VMs and on-premises Azure Arc servers. This visualization helps you quickly identify the "top talkers" in your estate–wherever they are and whatever OS they are running.

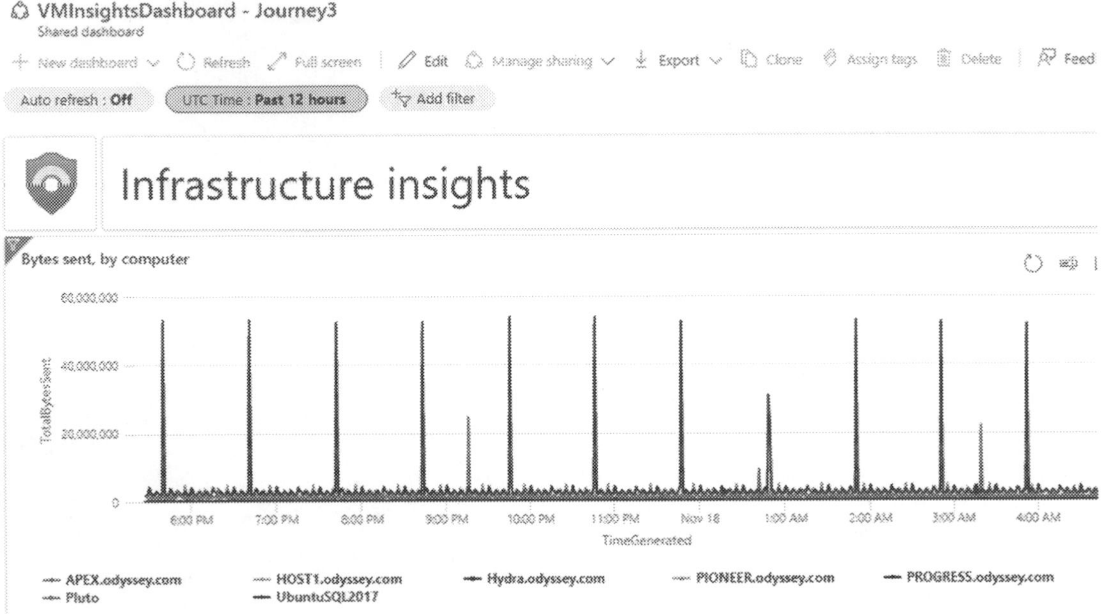

***Figure 3-13.** Azure dashboards feature auto-refresh and full-screen modes*

Key reasons to use dashboards include that, like workbooks, dashboards have an auto-refresh setting that is customizable from every 5 minutes to once a day. Dashboards also have a useful "Full screen" mode. By combining these features, you can create an infinite number of live kiosk-style dashboards that run on any computer with a web browser.

Azure Automation Solutions

An Azure Automation account is linked to a given Azure Log Analytics workspace to enable a variety of solutions. In Azure Automation, you can enable the Update Management, Change Tracking, and Inventory features for your Azure Arc servers and in-Azure VMs. These features have a dependency on a Log Analytics workspace and therefore require linking the workspace with an automation account.

It's a best practice to create an automation account immediately after creating an Azure Log Analytics workspace and proceed to perform the procedure to link them. However, only certain regions are supported to link them together. Table 3-2 lists the supported mappings to successfully enable and use these features. Be sure and select the region(s) for your Azure Log Analytics workspace(s) in awareness of this table.

Table 3-2. *Supported Mappings Azure Log Analytics ↔ Azure Automation*

Log Analytics Workspace Region	Azure Automation Region
AustraliaSoutheast	AustraliaSoutheast
CanadaCentral	CanadaCentral
CentralIndia	CentralIndia
ChinaEast2	ChinaEast2
EastUS	EastUS2
EastUS2	EastUS
FranceCentral	FranceCentral
JapanEast	JapanEast
NorthEurope	NorthEurope
SouthCentralUS	SouthCentralUS
SoutheastAsia	SoutheastAsia
SwitzerlandNorth	SwitzerlandNorth
UKSouth	UKSouth
USGovArizona	USGovArizona
USGovVirginia	USGovVirginia
WestCentralUS	WestCentralUS
WestEurope	WestEurope
WestUS2	WestUS2

You will be glad you created an automation account not only for the update and configuration management features we will describe next in this chapter but for the general-purpose **process automation** you will gain:

- **Runbooks**: PowerShell or Python scripts that can be launched automatically
- **Hybrid worker groups**: Automation instrumentality to execute runbooks on-premises that are launched from cloud-based Azure processes
- **Watcher tasks**: Launch pairs of runbooks that watch for events and then perform selected automations when they occur

With an automation framework in place, you can specify runbooks as automated responses to Azure Monitor alerts. Further, you can stage PowerShell and Python script-based runbooks to launch in response to webhooks activated by Microsoft Sentinel playbooks (Azure Logic Apps).

Tip To link an Azure Automation account with an Azure Log Analytics workspace, navigate to one of the Configuration Management solutions or to the Update management solution in the automation account. In the right-hand details pane, you will be able to select your paired Log Analytics workspace and push the **Enable** button.

Azure Automation Costs

Azure Automation has two excellent features in the Azure Arc scenario: *Update Management* and *Configuration Management*. One is free everywhere; the other has a cost outside of Azure:

- **Update Management:** Free (all Azure VMs and Azure Arc servers)
- **Configuration Management:** Free for Azure VMs, $6.00 per month "Configuration Management for Non-Azure Nodes" for Azure Arc servers

In addition to these features, Azure Automation also has a process automation capability with microcharges like *job run time* ($0.002/minute, 500 included per month) and *watcher* nodes ($002/hour, 744 per month included).

To obtain an estimate of Azure Automation charges for process automation and configuration management, select your region and currency at the Azure Automation Pricing page:

`https://azure.microsoft.com/en-us/pricing/details/automation/`

Update Management

The Update Management feature of Azure automation is a tremendous value because there is no license cost to use this solution for Azure VMs or Azure Arc servers. Other than microcharges for log analytics data processing, this is a fully free solution to monitor and manage Windows and Linux operating system (OS) updates. There is really nothing like it in the industry.

If you are paying for a third-party server updating solution or using Microsoft Endpoint Manager (formerly System Center Configuration Manager) for OS updates, or WSUS (Windows Server Updating Server), consider migrating to this free and full-featured solution to handle your server OS updating. It is simple and elegant and fully integrated with Azure Arc and Microsoft Defender for Cloud.

After you enable the Update Management solution, each of your Azure Arc servers will have a live updates dashboard inside their Azure Arc server blade in the Azure portal as seen in Figure 3-14. Not only do you have an accurate live view into the update status of the selected computer, but you can also create and launch a cloud-based updating task against the on-premises server effortlessly.

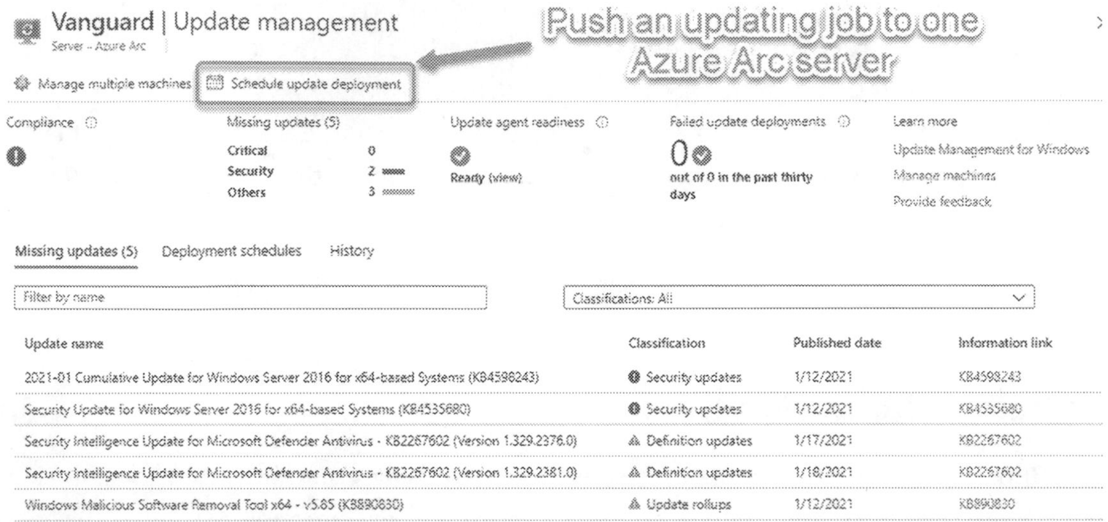

***Figure 3-14.** The Update management blade of an Azure Arc server*

In addition to the update management view added to each Azure Arc server, there is a view to manage updates on *multiple machines* in the Azure Automation account blade as seen in Figure 3-15. From this page, you can launch an immediate or scheduled updating job against multiple Windows and Linux computers in both Azure VM and Azure Arc server settings.

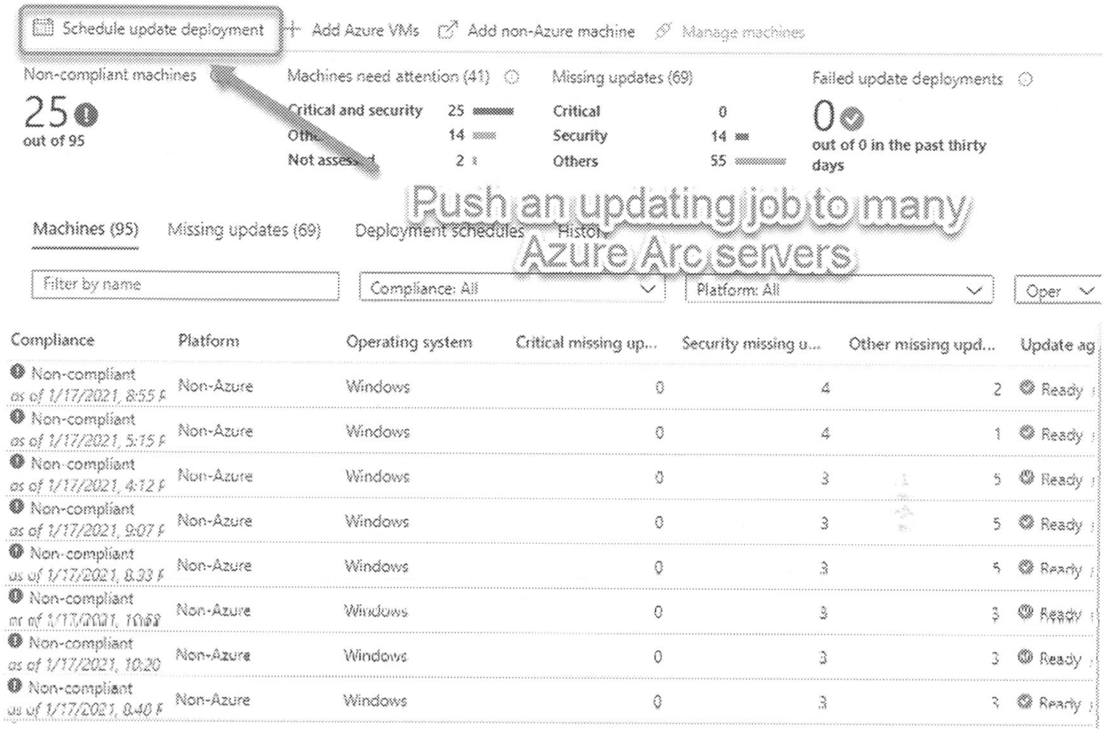

Figure 3-15. *The Update management blade of an Azure Automation account*

Configuration Management

The Configuration Management features of Azure automation are free for Azure VMs, and there is an Azure consumption cost of $6 per month for Azure Arc servers (billed as "Configuration Management for Non-Azure Nodes"). There are three microservices bundled in this feature: State Configuration (DSC), Inventory, and Change Tracking.

State Configuration (DSC)

Azure Automation State Configuration is an Azure configuration management service that allows you to write, manage, and compile PowerShell Desired State Configuration (DSC) configurations for nodes in any cloud or on-premises data center.

If you are not ready to manage machine configuration from the cloud, you can use Azure Automation State Configuration as a report-only endpoint. This feature allows you to set (push) configurations through DSC and view reporting details in Azure Automation.

If your environment is already using DSC outside of Azure, consider that Azure Automation State Configuration provides several advantages. This service enables scalability across thousands of machines quickly and easily from a central, secure location.

The Azure Automation State Configuration service is to DSC what Azure Automation runbooks are to PowerShell scripting. In other words, in the same way that Azure Automation helps you manage PowerShell scripts, it also helps you manage DSC configurations.

Inventory

The Azure Automation Inventory feature discovers what software is installed in your environment. You can collect and view inventory for software, files, Linux daemons, Windows services, and Windows Registry keys on your computers. Tracking the configurations of your machines can help you pinpoint operational issues across your environment and better understand the state of your machines.

Providing functionality like a traditional CMDB (configuration management database), the inventory solution tracks what software is installed and what services are running on all your monitored Windows and Linux servers—both Azure VMs and on-premises Azure Arc servers. Real time and historical inventory status are equally tracked.

See Figure 3-16 for the inventory view into 39 servers (mainly Azure Arc Windows servers with some Linux). Over the previous 24-hour period, over 12,000 software changes, almost 800 Windows services, and 200 Linux daemon status changes were tracked by Azure Automation.

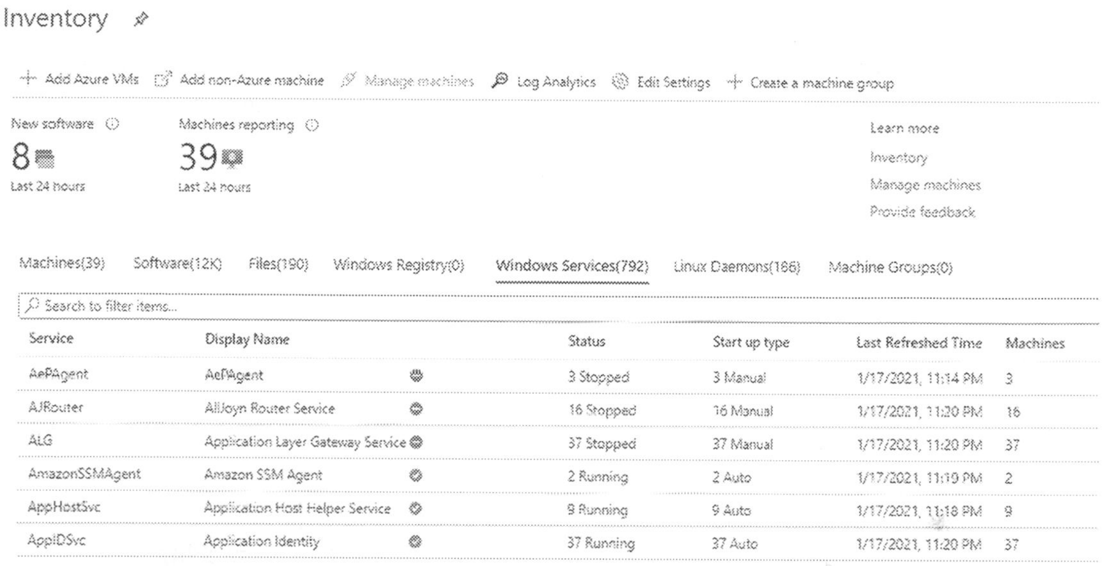

Inventory

+ Add Azure VMs | Add non-Azure machine | Manage machines | Log Analytics | Edit Settings | + Create a machine group

New software 8 Last 24 hours | Machines reporting 39 Last 24 hours

Learn more
Inventory
Manage machines
Provide feedback

Machines(39) | Software(12K) | Files(190) | Windows Registry(0) | Windows Services(792) | Linux Daemons(166) | Machine Groups(0)

Search to filter items...

Service	Display Name	Status	Start up type	Last Refreshed Time	Machines
AePAgent	AePAgent	3 Stopped	3 Manual	1/17/2021, 11:14 PM	3
AJRouter	AllJoyn Router Service	16 Stopped	16 Manual	1/17/2021, 11:20 PM	16
ALG	Application Layer Gateway Service	37 Stopped	37 Manual	1/17/2021, 11:20 PM	37
AmazonSSMAgent	Amazon SSM Agent	2 Running	2 Auto	1/17/2021, 11:19 PM	2
AppHostSvc	Application Host Helper Service	9 Running	9 Auto	1/17/2021, 11:18 PM	9
AppIDSvc	Application Identity	37 Running	37 Auto	1/17/2021, 11:20 PM	37

Figure 3-16. *Azure Automation Inventory: A live configuration management database of software installed in your environment*

Change Tracking

Change Tracking in Azure Automation monitors for changes in virtual machines hosted in Azure, on-premises, and other cloud environments to help you pinpoint operational and environmental issues. For example, if an Azure Arc server starts having a problem, you can consult the Server - Azure Arc Change Tracking blade of the computer and see if any unexpected software or registry changes occurred in the last few hours or days. Items that are tracked by Change Tracking include

- Windows software
- Linux software (packages)
- Windows and Linux files
- Windows registry keys
- Microsoft services
- Linux daemons

Change Tracking builds on the inventory features of Azure Automation. Changes occurring to monitored inventory are captured, both to permit replay of the changes during an investigation and to provide metrics on the nominal change rates in an environment. Figure 3-17 is the Change Tracking blade of an Azure Automation account set to a 30-day view.

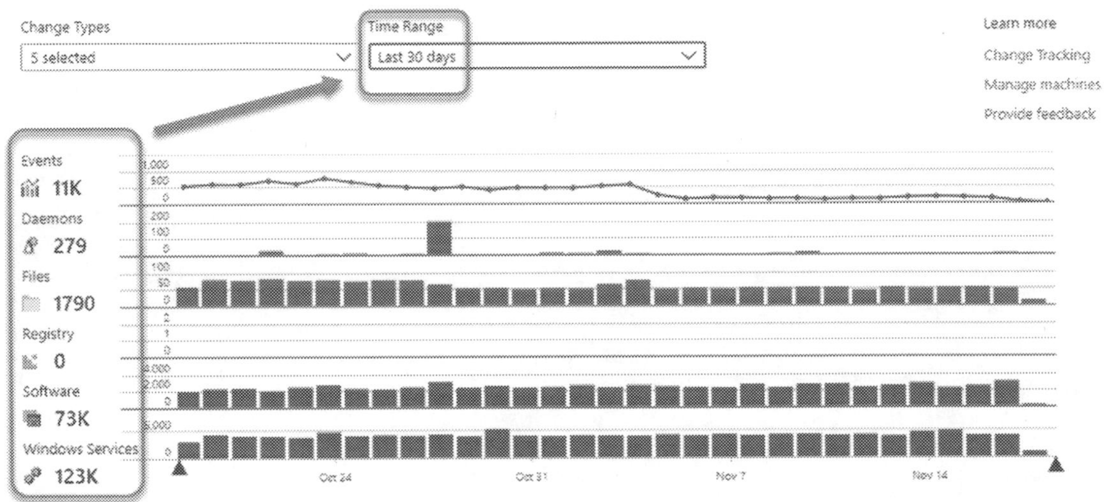

***Figure 3-17.** Azure Automation Change Tracking: Detecting changes across platforms and applications*

It is simple to focus and filter the Change Tracking summary to drill down into individual changes reflected in the graph. Change Tracking is in some ways the "crown jewel" of the Azure Automation configuration management solution because of its value in the forensic and security roles.

When unexplained issues occur in your environment, an early and valid question is, *What changed?* With Azure Automation Change Tracking, you have a valuable tool to answer that question. When checking the change details of a change event, the "before and after" values of the change are preserved and presented as seen in Figure 3-18.

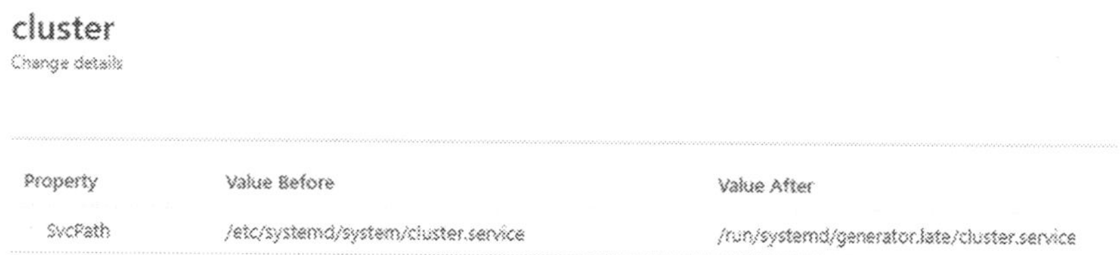

***Figure 3-18.** Detail view of a software version change detected on a Linux computer*

While Change Tracking is useful to reconstruct changes that occurred on an individual computer, another role is monitoring and assessing the overall rate and scope of change during normal conditions across your estate. Then when anomalous volumes of changes occur, they can be detected by the aggregate monitoring features of Azure Automation.

Detected changes in individual computers are written to the *ConfigurationChange* table in Azure Log Analytics. Queries to detect comparatively large differences from normal change volume indicate something happened in the environment that merits investigation.

In fact, anomalous change detection is a very valuable security monitoring technique. Figure 3-19 is a snippet from the Microsoft Sentinel overview page that might appear in this situation. If you saw this, you would know unusually large volumes of changes were experienced twice in the last 24 hours. Investigating unexpected changes can be the first tip-off that unwanted processes are taking place and require remediation.

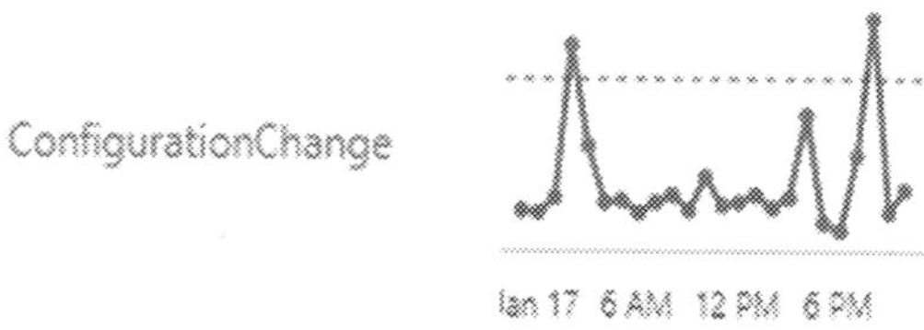

***Figure 3-19.** Data source anomalies detection from the Azure Sentinel overview blade*

Summary

In this chapter, you learned all about what you can do with Azure Arc. You became familiar with the monitoring and control features in Azure Arc and have a basic understanding of what they make possible. Now that you are inspired, let's move on to the next chapter where we'll dive into how to plan for, deploy, and support Azure Arc servers.

CHAPTER 4

Azure Arc Servers: Getting Started

Azure Arc represents a wholly new concept that emerged organically from the cloud. That secret ingredient signals Azure Arc's natural disposition toward cloud essential characteristics like *broad network access* and *rapid elasticity*. "Cloudy" systems will naturally prevail over legacy and traditional ones that do not continuously adapt. Consider that Azure Arc brings to your organization hyperscale *resource pooling* benefits—projecting your non-Azure resources into the Azure Resource Manager (ARM) control plane where they join billions of well-managed objects.

Creating that projected object, an *Azure Arc server*, and getting value from doing so is what this chapter is about. This chapter introduces and dives deep into what an Azure Arc server object looks like in Azure and all about its agent footprint on your Windows and Linux computers. We focus in this chapter on installing Azure Arc agents one at a time for testing and evaluation, and in Chapter 5, "Azure Arc Servers: Using at Scale," there will be details on deploying Azure Arc agents in production.

Management Platform as a Service

Azure Arc is a destination architecture for server management functions because it moves management tasks into a proven hyperscale cloud. What those tasks are—server availability, configuration, performance, and security—has not changed since the early days of networking. What's changed is where management tasks are best delivered from.

Before there was *cloud*, there was *on-premises*, which most people called the LAN and/or WAN (Local Area Network/Wide Area Network). There was also a VPN (Virtual Private Network), and these network-centric constructs defined the canvas where

S. Buchanan and J. Joyner, *Azure Arc-Enabled Kubernetes and Servers*,
https://doi.org/10.1007/978-1-4842-7768-3_4

management and monitoring occurred. Every object to be monitored was inside the LAN/WAN/VPN boundaries, so the tools for management were located there as well.

Fast forward to the modern hybrid era where physical location is often irrelevant to service delivery or consumption. It is natural and expected that server management tasks will emerge that can be "peeled away" and delivered from a cloud service more efficiently than remaining on-premises. Think of Disaster Recovery as a Service (DRaaS) offerings for on-premises servers protected to public clouds off-site. DR traditionally required a lot of expensive infrastructure to build a hot site, so spinning off DR to the cloud was an early industry trend driven by economics.

Figure 4-1 pictures server management functions as an iceberg, with most of the server management burden moved to Azure. The vast global Azure Resource Manager is your back-end service provider with Azure Arc. Azure Arc represents a new paradigm produced by cloud economics: no cost Management as a Service (MaaS). Put another way, Azure Arc is an infinitely scalable management tool framework provided by Microsoft as a free platform service.

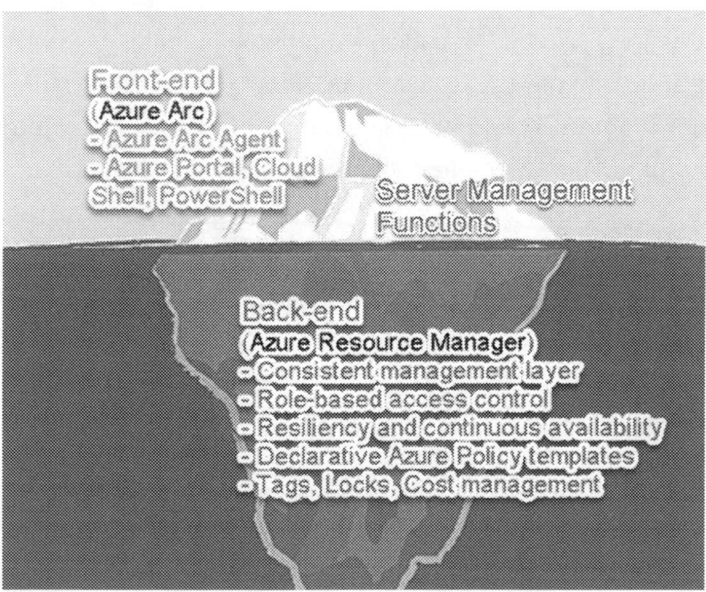

Figure 4-1. *Azure Arc moves many server management functions to Azure Resource Manager*

Cloud service management can be described from the perspective of business support, provisioning, and configuration and from the perspective of portability and interoperability. Azure Arc allows your servers to experience these economies of scale, normally reserved to cloud services, even though they do not exist in the cloud! Ask yourself: Why not "snap into" a set of proven management, monitoring, and security best practices for your servers? Why should you pay for and maintain any legacy management tools when you can unload the cost and the maintenance burden?

Here is a final "gut check" on the wisdom of investing in Azure Arc for your server management: as a cloud-based management technology, Azure Arc passes the "mutual alignment" test for managed services. The most fundamental underpinnings of the offering are a "win-win" for the consumer and the service provider. Microsoft wins because by using Azure Arc, you are more likely to consume Microsoft services that there *is* a charge for, and you win because Azure Arc lowers your servers' total cost of ownership (TCO).

What Is an Azure Arc Server?

At the front end, an Azure Arc server is a computer managed by Azure but running outside Azure. In the back end, an Azure Arc server is a *machine* instance of the Azure Resource Manager (ARM) resource "type" *Microsoft.HybridCompute/machines*.

Azure Resource Manager (ARM) Resource Types

True to its hybrid nature, an Azure Arc server consists of separate physical and logical entities:

- **Physical location:** A computer, physical or virtual, running anywhere in the world except in the Azure cloud
- **Virtual location:** An Azure resource of the "type" *Microsoft.HybridCompute/machines* that exists in a specific Azure subscription, resource group, and location

For comparison, an Azure VM that exists completely in Azure has this taxonomy:

- **Azure VM:** An Azure resource of the "type" *Microsoft.Compute/virtualMachines* that exists in a specific Azure subscription, resource group, and location

Like every other object in Azure, both Azure VMs and Azure Arc servers are Azure resources defined by their resource types, subscriptions, resource groups, and locations. Tags assigned to Azure VMs and Azure Arc computers work identically for purposes of governance and billing.

Figure 4-2 is a side-by-side JSON view of the Azure Resource Manager (ARM) definitions of a running Azure Arc server (on the left) and an Azure VM (right). These common underpinning software structures explain why managing on-premises servers with Azure-based tools is logical and efficient.

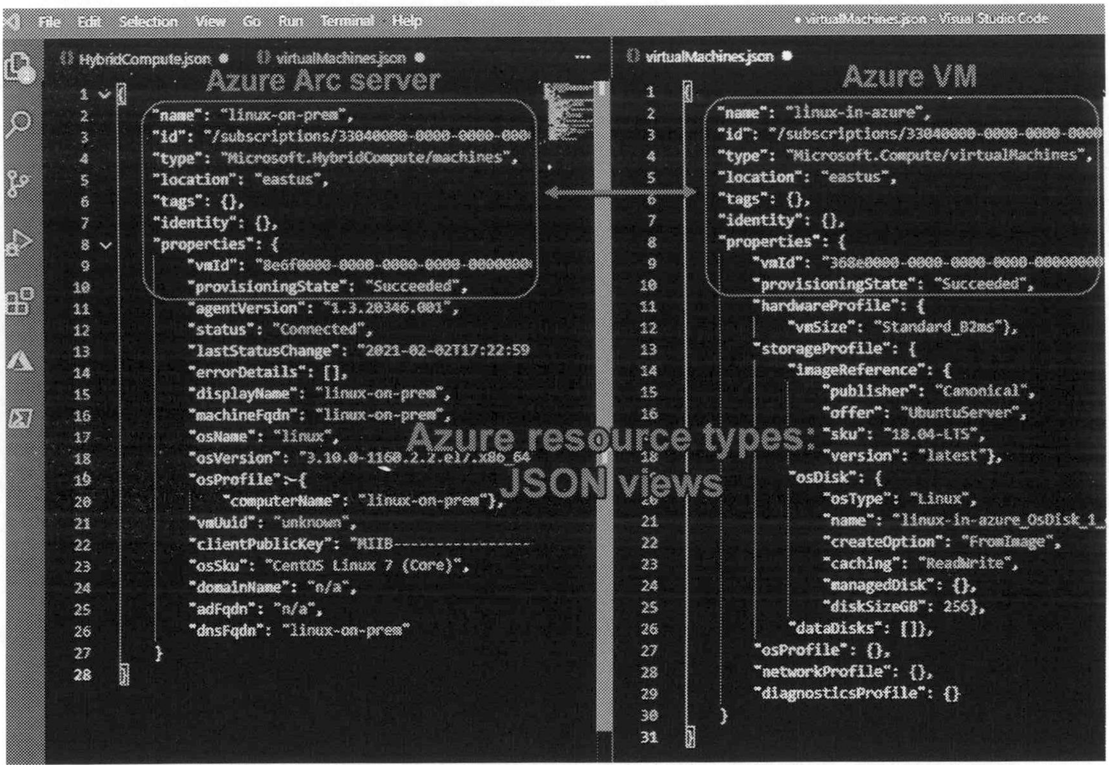

***Figure 4-2.** Side-by-side JSON views in Visual Studio Code highlight ARM commonality of Azure Arc servers and Azure VMs*

Tip Use Azure PowerShell to query lists of Azure Arc servers or Azure VMs using their ARM resource type names:

```
get-AzResource -ResourceType Microsoft.HybridCompute/machines

get-AzResource -ResourceType Microsoft.Compute/
virtualMachines
```

Azure Arc Servers in the Azure Portal

The Azure portal (`https://portal.azure.com`) is a graphical view of the JSON template elements that define the resource groups in your Azure subscription. As seen in Figure 4-3, you can inspect the contents of your resource groups in the Azure portal at the *Export template* blade in your Azure resource group. Your Azure Arc servers will be included alongside all the other Azure resource types in your resource group.

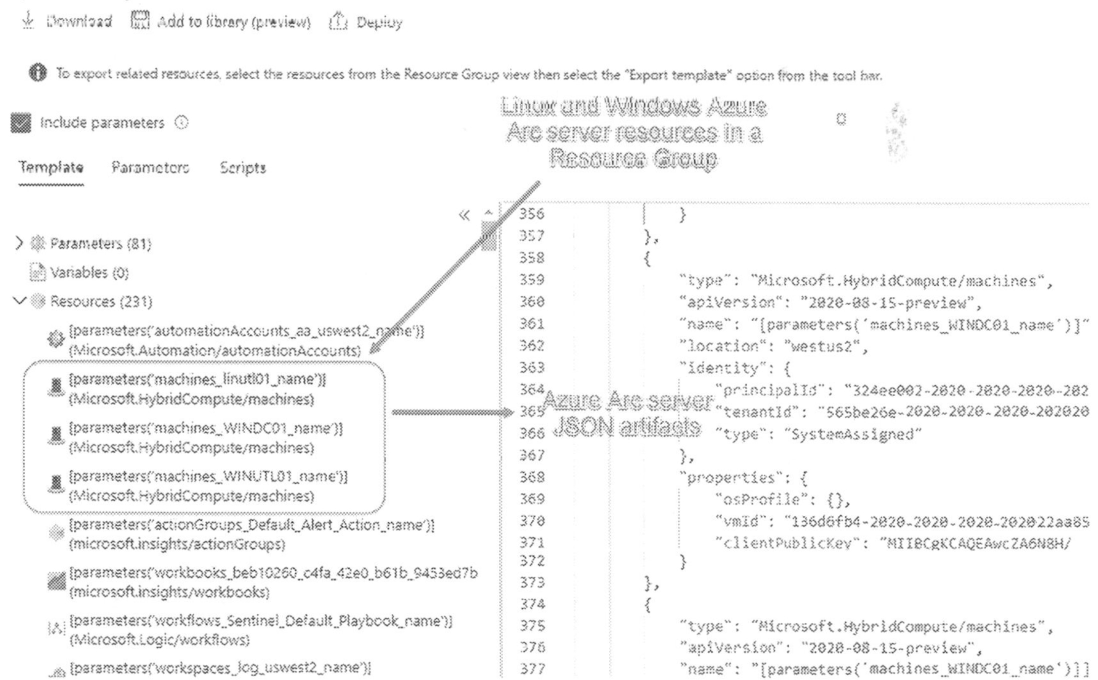

***Figure 4-3.** Exporting an entire resource group to a JSON document*

Of course, the Azure portal has a whole set of dedicated Azure Arc views that surface Azure Arc infrastructure resources like servers, Kubernetes clusters, SQL servers, and Azure Stack HCI deployments. Figure 4-4 shows the Azure Arc servers page where all the Azure Arc servers in all subscriptions you have access to can be found.

Servers - Azure Arc

+ Add | Manage view | Refresh | Export to CSV | Open query | Assign tags | Feedback

Filter for any field... | Subscription == all | Resource group == all | Location == all | Add filter

Showing 1 to 100 of 150 records.

Name	Status	Location	Tags	Operating system
mgmp03	Connected	East US	environment: product...	Linux
mgmt06	Connected	East US		Linux
mgmt07	Connected	East US		Linux
cgip01	Connected	East US		Linux
linutl01	Connected	West US 2		Linux
CDC2	Connected	East US 2		Windows
Luther	Offline	West US 2		Windows
Pluto	Connected	West US 2	CountryOrRegion: US...	Windows
Vanguard	Connected	West US 2		Windows
Venus	Connected	East US		Windows

Figure 4-4. *Azure Arc servers as they present in the Azure portal*

As the columns of the view in Figure 4-4 show, you can sort and filter on parameters such as Status (Connected or Offline), Location (the Azure region where the Azure Arc server resource was created), Operating system (Linux or Windows), and Tags you may have optionally assigned at creation or later.

What you should understand at this point is that an Azure Arc server is a logical construct in the Azure control plane. The actual technical process of onboarding an Azure Arc server is the creation of an Azure resource record of the "type" *Microsoft.HybridCompute/machines*. To onboard an Azure Arc server with the interactive method, you need these things:

(i) A login credential to an Azure subscription that has permission to create Azure Arc resources

(ii) A resource group in an Azure subscription suitable for your organization to contain Azure Arc server resources

(iii) An Azure region (location) to host the Azure Arc server object, which does not need to be the same region as the resource group

Azure Arc Server Location Selection

In most cases, the location you select when you onboard an Azure Arc server should be the Azure region geographically closest to your machine's location. Here are some considerations in selecting the region(s) to use:

- Data at rest is stored within the Azure geography containing the region you specify, which may also affect your choice of region if you have data residency requirements.
- If the Azure region your machine connects to is affected by an outage, the connected machine is not affected, but management operations using Azure may be unable to complete.

In the event of a regional outage, if you have multiple locations that support a geographically redundant service, it is best to connect the Azure Arc servers in each location to a different Azure region.

Tip Azure Arc-enabled servers support up to 5,000 machine instances in a resource group. For very large deployments, plan for multiple resource groups.

Register Azure Resource Providers

Azure Arc-enabled servers depend on the following Azure resource providers in your subscription to use the service:

- Microsoft.HybridCompute
- Microsoft.GuestConfiguration

If they are not registered, you can register them using the following commands:

Azure PowerShell

```
Login-AzAccount
Set-AzContext -SubscriptionId [subscription you want to onboard]
Register-AzResourceProvider -ProviderNamespace Microsoft.HybridCompute
Register-AzResourceProvider -ProviderNamespace Microsoft.GuestConfiguration
```

Azure CLI

```
az account set --subscription "{Your Subscription Name}"
az provider register --namespace 'Microsoft.HybridCompute'
az provider register --namespace 'Microsoft.GuestConfiguration'
```

You can also register the resource providers in the Azure portal by following the steps under the **Register resource provider Azure portal** section at this link on Azure resource providers and types:

https://docs.microsoft.com/en-us/azure/azure-resource-manager/management/resource-providers-and-types#azure-portal

After you have registered the two specified providers, the *Resource providers* blade of your Azure subscription should look like Figure 4-5.

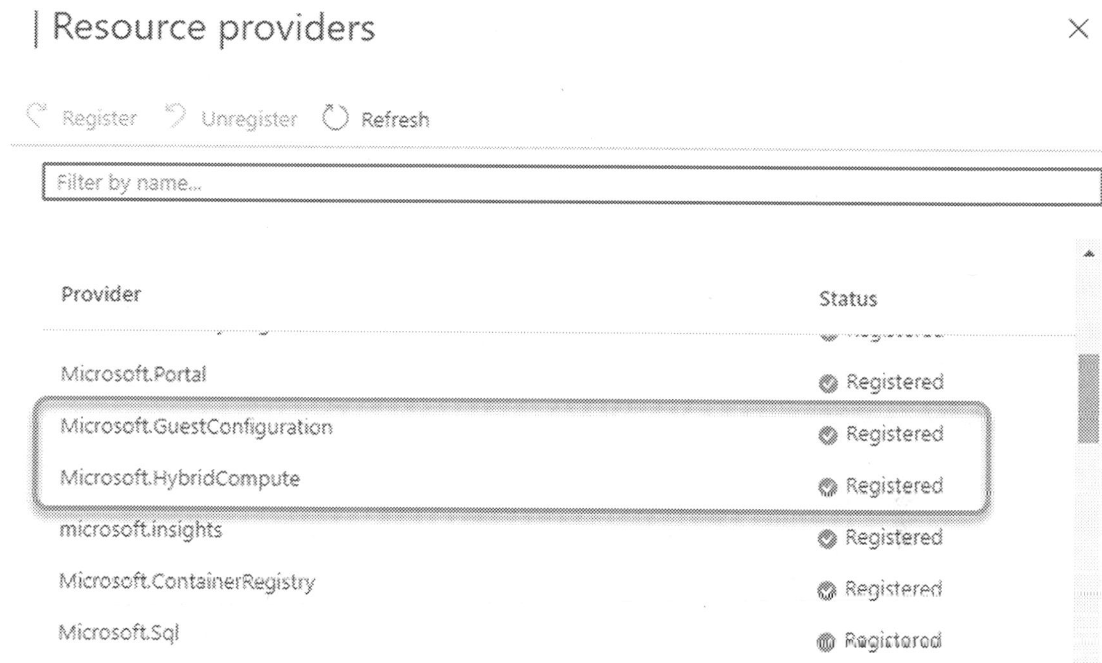

Figure 4-5. *Resource providers to be registered in your Azure subscription to create Azure Arc-enabled servers*

Connect Azure Arc to Windows and Linux Servers

Installing the Azure Arc agent might be the last agent you ever need to install because through Azure Policy and Azure Arc, you can manage all the current and future management and security agents your hybrid computer might need. The "Azure Arc agent" is called the **Azure Connected Machine Agent**.

At installation time, the Azure Connected Machine Agent needs to authenticate with Azure AD to validate the new Azure Arc server is authorized to be associated with your Azure subscription. There are two ways to do this:

- **Add servers manually with an interactive script**. This is suitable for small deployments and testing. You log into Azure with your individual user credential for each install. *This chapter steps through this method.*

- **Add servers at scale**. This method uses the identity and client secret (application password) of an Azure App Registration that you create in your Azure AD. Run the agent install with switches via any scripting or management tool you like. *Covered in Chapter 5, "Azure Arc Servers: Using at Scale."*

Prerequisites: Add Azure Arc Servers Using Interactive Script (Windows and Linux Computers)

Before attempting to onboard an Azure Arc server, be aware of these parameters:

- Local administrator or root permission on the server is required.
- The minimum built-in Azure subscription security role needed to onboard Azure Arc servers is **Azure Connected Machine Onboarding**.
- Make sure you have performed the procedure covered previously in the "Register Azure Resource Providers" section of this chapter on all involved Azure subscriptions.
- Confirm the server to be onboarded has access to the Internet on port TCP 443 to the following URLs:
    - management.azure.com
    - login.windows.net
    - login.microsoftonline.com
    - dc.services.visualstudio.com
    - agentserviceapi.azure-automation.net
    - *-agentservice-prod-1.azure-automation.net
    - *.guestconfiguration.azure.com
    - *.his.arc.azure.com
    - *.blob.core.windows.net
    - azgn*.servicebus.windows.net
    - pas.windows.net

Step by Step: Add Azure Arc Windows Servers Using Interactive Script

1. In your Azure portal, click **New** and select **Azure Arc for servers**, and then click **Create**.
2. At the Select a method blade seen in Figure 4-6, click ***Generate script***.

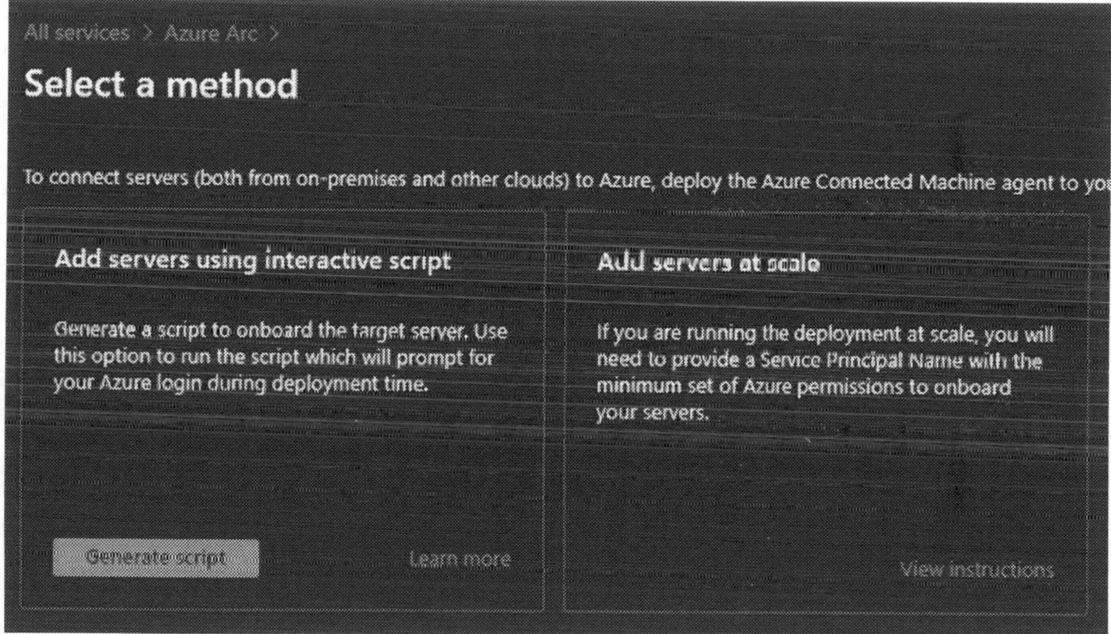

Figure 4-6. *There are two primary ways to connect servers on-premises and in other clouds to Azure*

3. Enter the Resource details and Tags appropriate for your environment, and then click ***Download and run script*** to arrive at the blade seen in Figure 4-7.

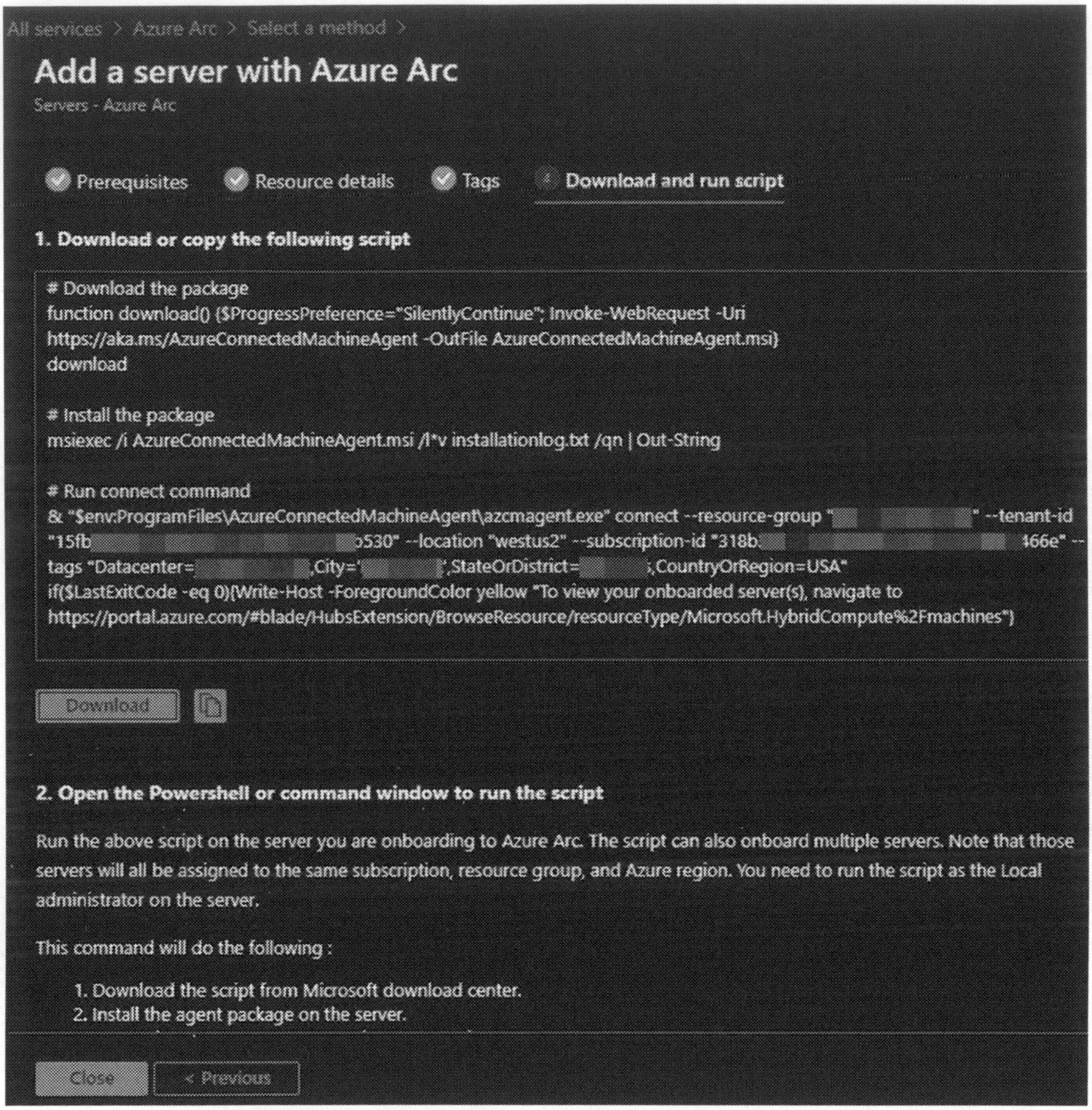

All services > Azure Arc > Select a method >

Add a server with Azure Arc

Servers - Azure Arc

Prerequisites Resource details Tags Download and run script

1. Download or copy the following script

```
# Download the package
function download() {$ProgressPreference="SilentlyContinue"; Invoke-WebRequest -Uri
https://aka.ms/AzureConnectedMachineAgent -OutFile AzureConnectedMachineAgent.msi}
download

# Install the package
msiexec /i AzureConnectedMachineAgent.msi /l*v installationlog.txt /qn | Out-String

# Run connect command
& "$env:ProgramFiles\AzureConnectedMachineAgent\azcmagent.exe" connect --resource-group "          " --tenant-id
"15fb          b530" --location "westus2" --subscription-id "318b          466e" --
tags "Datacenter=          ,City='          ',StateOrDistrict=          ,CountryOrRegion=USA"
if($LastExitCode -eq 0){Write-Host -ForegroundColor yellow "To view your onboarded server(s), navigate to
https://portal.azure.com/#blade/HubsExtension/BrowseResource/resourceType/Microsoft.HybridCompute%2Fmachines"}
```

Download

2. Open the Powershell or command window to run the script

Run the above script on the server you are onboarding to Azure Arc. The script can also onboard multiple servers. Note that those servers will all be assigned to the same subscription, resource group, and Azure region. You need to run the script as the Local administrator on the server.

This command will do the following :

1. Download the script from Microsoft download center.
2. Install the agent package on the server.

Close < Previous

Figure 4-7. *The Azure portal will automatically generate a custom script that onboards a computer to Azure Arc*

4. Download the script (OnboardingScript.ps1) and copy it to the server you are adding to Azure Arc.

   a. Run the script in an elevated PowerShell session. Note the code the script prints out.

b. Open a web browser to `https://microsoft.com/devicelogin`.

c. Log in with an Azure AD credential in your tenant and enter the code as shown in Figure 4-8.

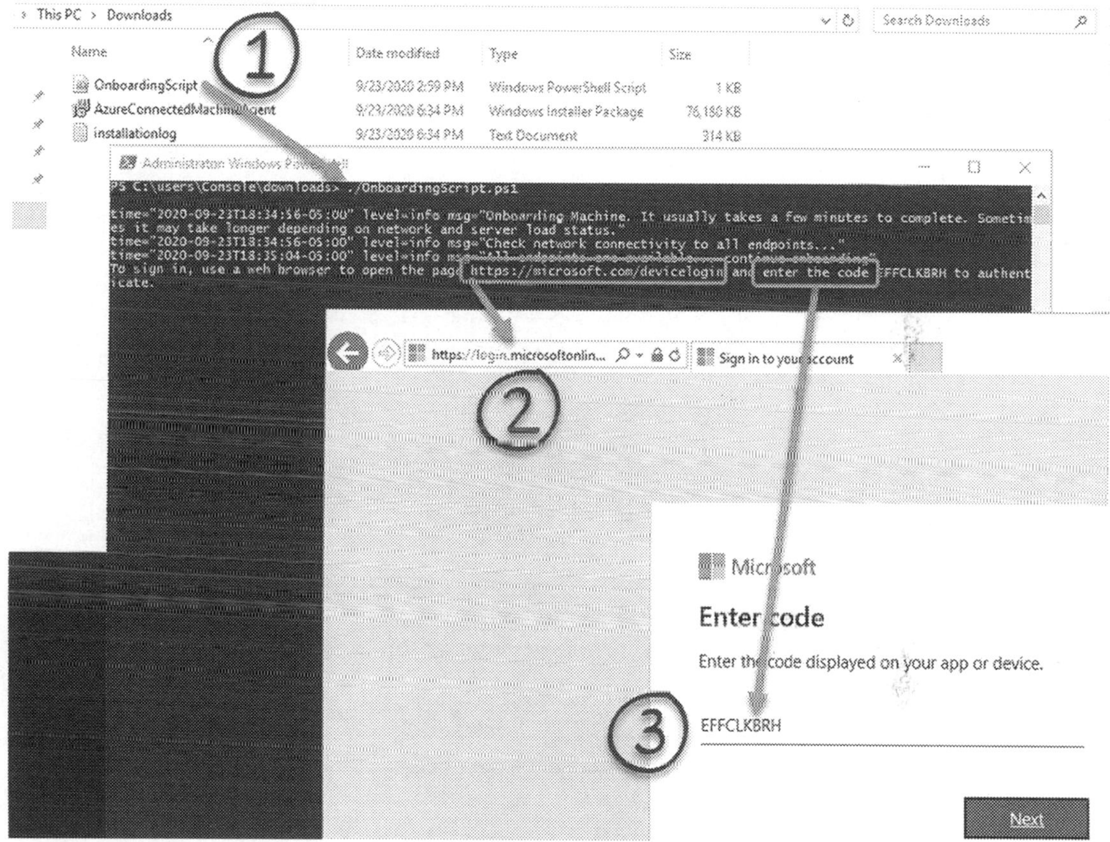

***Figure 4-8.** Three steps to install the Azure Arc agent manually with onboarding script*

Notice in Figure 4-8 that the script will download the **AzureConnectedMachineAgent** Windows Installer Package to the folder where you executed the script. A log file **installationlog** is also created at the same location. (You have a limited time to complete login with a given code before it expires.)

5. After you have installed the agent, you will find **Azure Connected Machine Agent** listed in Add/Remove Programs as shown in Figure 4-9.

a. Agent files are located at C:\Program Files\AzureConnectedMachineAgent.

b. Two Windows services are created:

   i. **Guest Configuration Arc Service** (GCArcService): This service monitors desired state of the machine.

   ii. **Guest Configuration Extension Service** (ExtensionService): The service installs the requested extensions.

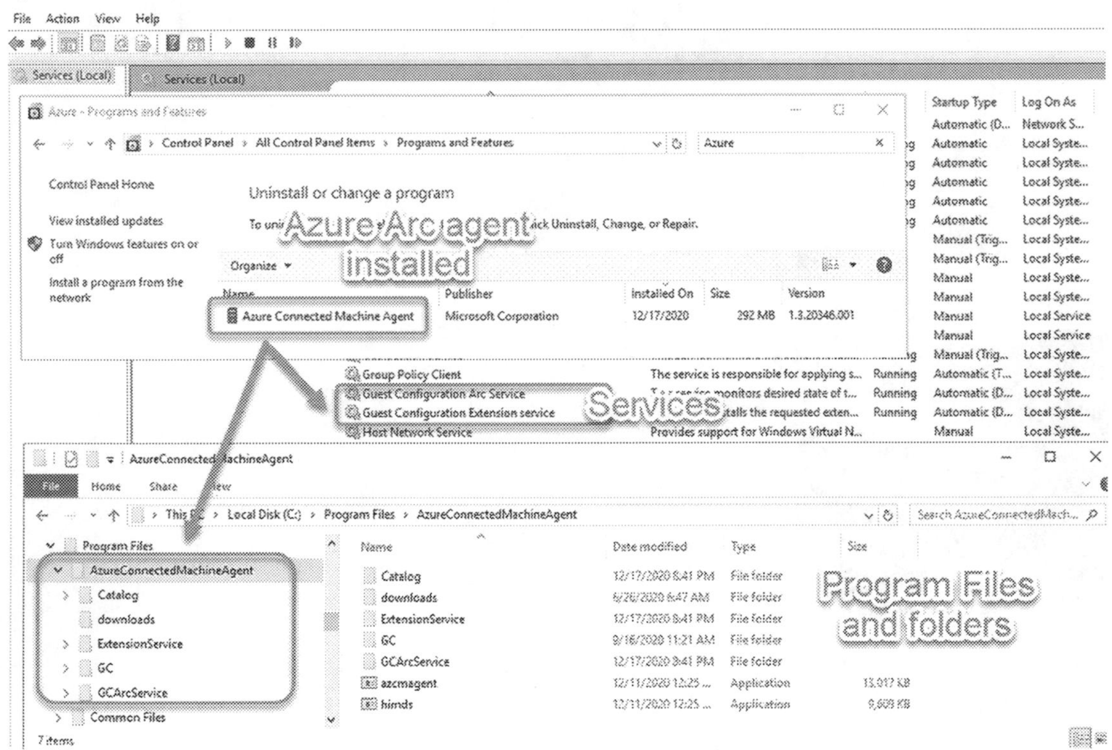

***Figure 4-9.** Tear-down of the Azure Connected Machine Agent folders and services*

c. After the Azure Arc agent is installed, you can open your Azure portal to view the new hybrid computer object:

```
https://portal.azure.com/#blade/HubsExtension/BrowseResource/resourceType/
Microsoft.HybridCompute%2Fmachines
```

Figure 4-10 shows what you might see soon after adding an Azure Arc server. If you specified Tags for your Azure Arc server at creation time, you would see them on the Overview blade. You can also add tags manually by clicking the **change** link, or programmatically at any time during your Azure Arc server life cycle. We will cover advanced use of tags in Chapter 6, "Hybrid Server Monitoring Solution."

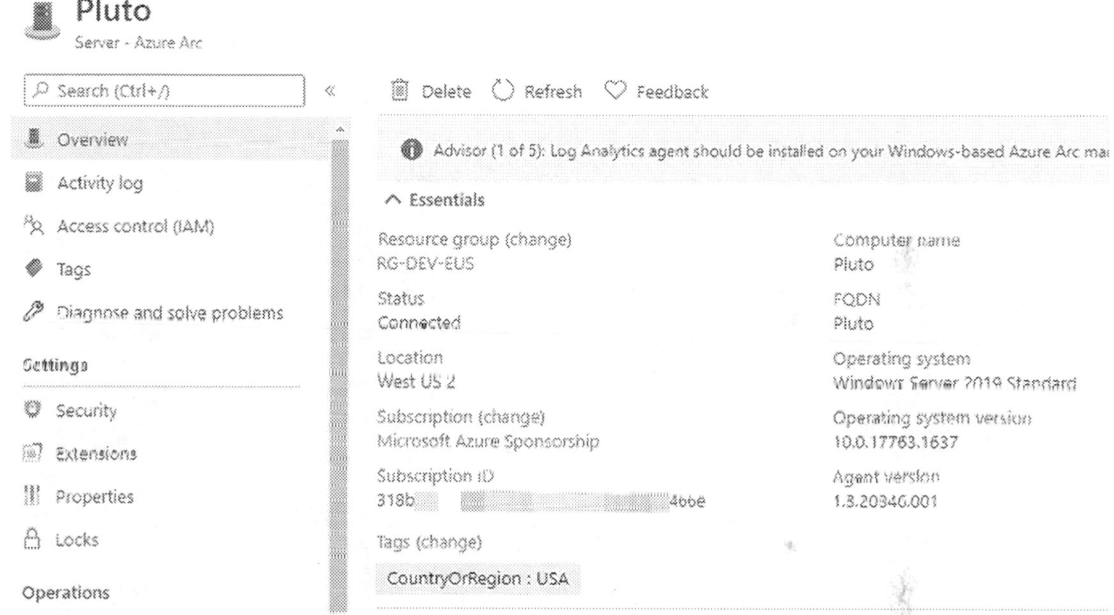

Figure 4-10. *The Overview blade of a Windows Azure Arc server immediately after onboarding*

Step by Step: Add Azure Arc Linux Servers Using Interactive Script

The procedure to connect Linux servers using the manual method is very similar to that for Windows servers. You must comply with the "Prerequisites: Add Azure Arc Servers Using Interactive Script (Windows and Linux Computers)" section earlier in this chapter.

1. In your Azure portal, click **New** and select **Azure Arc for servers**,and then click **Create**.

2. At the Select a method blade (previously seen in Figure 4-6), click **Generate script**.

3. Enter the Resource details and Tags appropriate for your environment, and then click **Download and run script** to arrive at the blade seen in Figure 4-11.

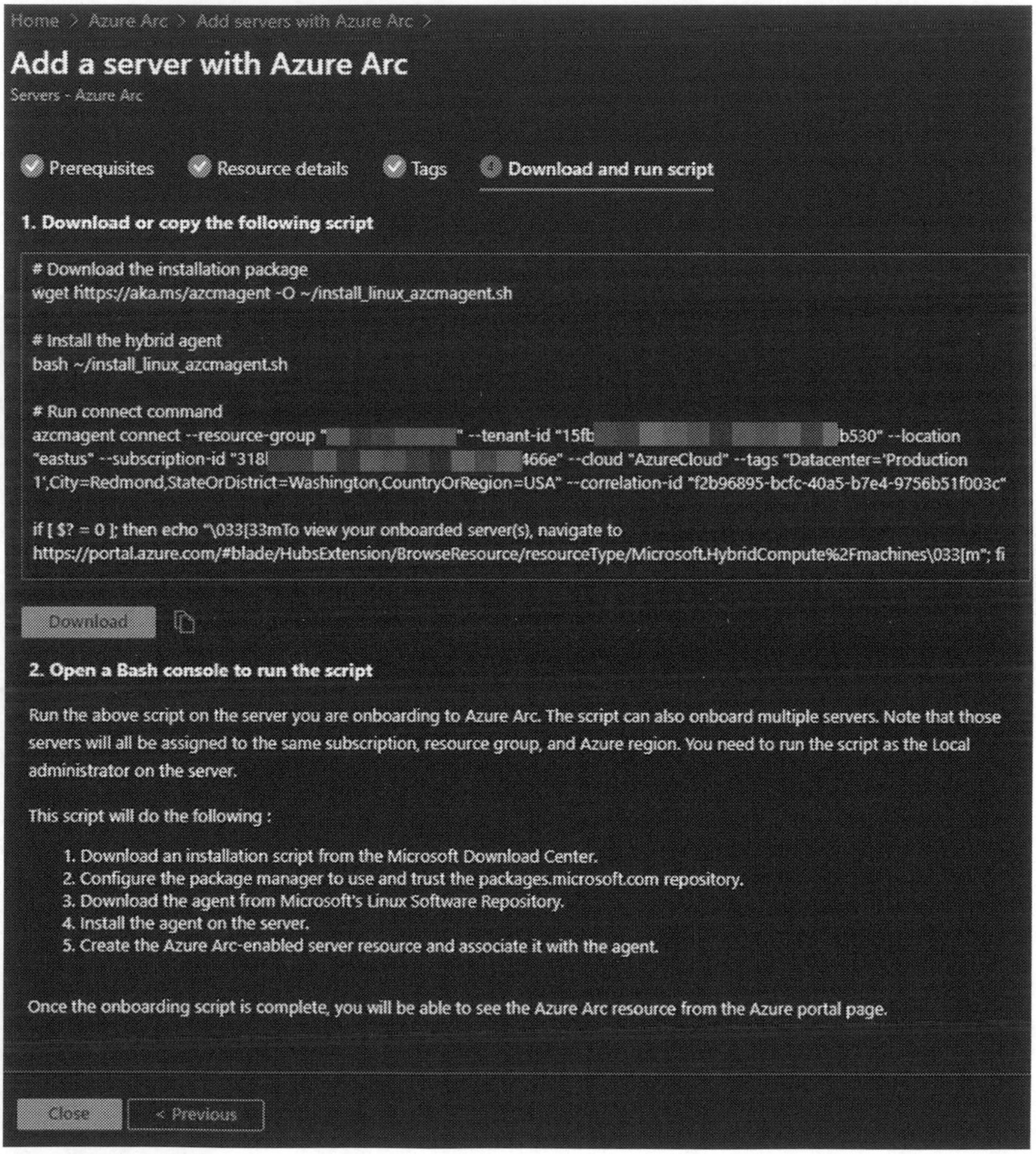

Home > Azure Arc > Add servers with Azure Arc >

Add a server with Azure Arc

Servers - Azure Arc

Prerequisites Resource details Tags **Download and run script**

1. Download or copy the following script

```
# Download the installation package
wget https://aka.ms/azcmagent -O ~/install_linux_azcmagent.sh

# Install the hybrid agent
bash ~/install_linux_azcmagent.sh

# Run connect command
azcmagent connect --resource-group "" --tenant-id "15fb b530" --location "eastus" --subscription-id "318l 466e" --cloud "AzureCloud" --tags "Datacenter='Production 1',City=Redmond,StateOrDistrict=Washington,CountryOrRegion=USA" --correlation-id "f2b96895-bcfc-40a5-b7e4-9756b51f003c"

if [ $? = 0 ]; then echo "\033[33mTo view your onboarded server(s), navigate to https://portal.azure.com/#blade/HubsExtension/BrowseResource/resourceType/Microsoft.HybridCompute%2Fmachines\033[m"; fi
```

Download

2. Open a Bash console to run the script

Run the above script on the server you are onboarding to Azure Arc. The script can also onboard multiple servers. Note that those servers will all be assigned to the same subscription, resource group, and Azure region. You need to run the script as the Local administrator on the server.

This script will do the following :

1. Download an installation script from the Microsoft Download Center.
2. Configure the package manager to use and trust the packages.microsoft.com repository.
3. Download the agent from Microsoft's Linux Software Repository.
4. Install the agent on the server.
5. Create the Azure Arc-enabled server resource and associate it with the agent.

Once the onboarding script is complete, you will be able to see the Azure Arc resource from the Azure portal page.

Close < Previous

Figure 4-11. *Automatically generated custom Bash script that onboards a Linux computer to Azure Arc*

4. Download the script (OnboardingScript.sh) and copy it to the Linux computer you are adding to Azure Arc. (Use any convenient tool such as WinSCP; download at `https://winscp.net`.)

   a. Enable the script to be executed by running this command:

   ```
   sudo chmod 700 OnboardingScript.sh
   ```

   b. Run the script with elevated permissions like this:

   ```
   sudo ./OnboardingScript.sh
   ```

   c. Near the completion of the script run, watch for the script to print out a **device login code** as seen in Figure 4-12.

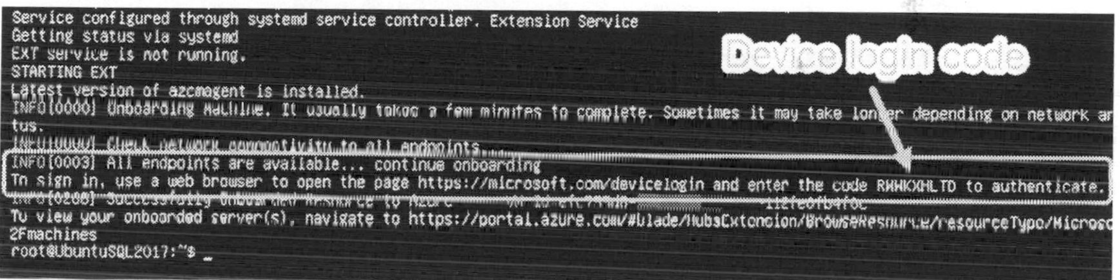

Figure 4-12. *Manually onboarding a Linux computer to Azure Arc*

5. Open a web browser to `https://microsoft.com/devicelogin`. The web browser session can occur on any computer; it does not need to be run from the Linux computer being onboarded.

6. Log in with an Azure AD credential in your tenant as seen in the upper portion of Figure 4-13.

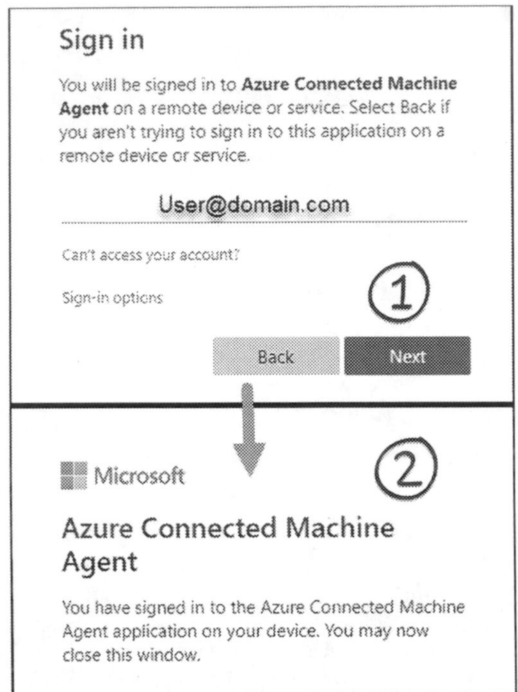

Figure 4-13. *Device login for the Azure Connected Machine Agent*

An Enter Code page like that seen during Windows agent onboarding in Figure 4-8 will appear. After entering the code, you will receive a confirmation message as seen in the lower portion of Figure 4-13. When you see this, the script will finish with a prompt to view your onboarded server(s); navigate to

```
https://portal.azure.com/#blade/HubsExtension/BrowseResource/resourceType/
Microsoft.HybridCompute%2Fmachines
```

1. After you have installed the agent, the following configuration changes are applied:

    a. Agent files are located at

        i. /var/opt/azcmagent (support files)

        ii. /var/lib/GuestConfig.(applied policies from Azure)

        iii. /opt/azcmagent (himdsd.service files)

iv. /opt/GC_Ext, (Guest Configuration agent files and downloaded extension files)

v. /opt/DSC (common DSC artifacts)

b. Three Linux daemons are created:

i. **Azure Connected Machine Agent Service** (himdsd.service): This service implements the Azure Instance Metadata service (IMDS) to manage the connection to Azure and the connected machine's Azure Arc identity.

ii. **GC Arc Service** (gcad.service): Monitors the desired state configuration of the machine.

iii. **Extension Service** (extd.service): Installs the required extensions targeting the machine.

2. You can check that the service daemons are running with this command as demonstrated in Figure 4-14:

```
systemctl -list-units | grep <service name>
```

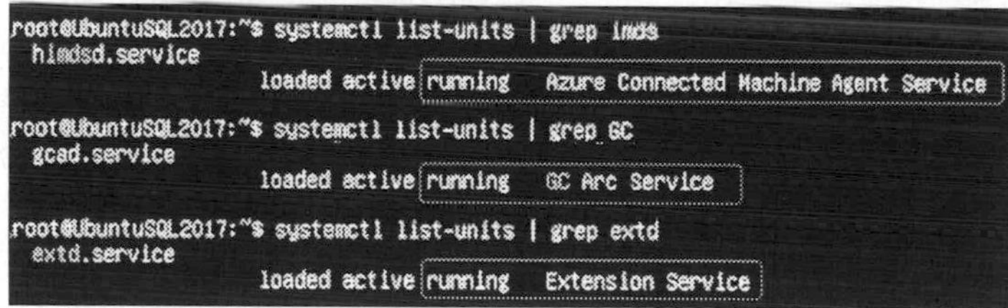

Figure 4-14. *Confirming that all Azure Arc daemons are running*

3. After the Azure Arc agent is installed, you can view the new hybrid computer object in the Azure portal as seen in Figure 4-15.

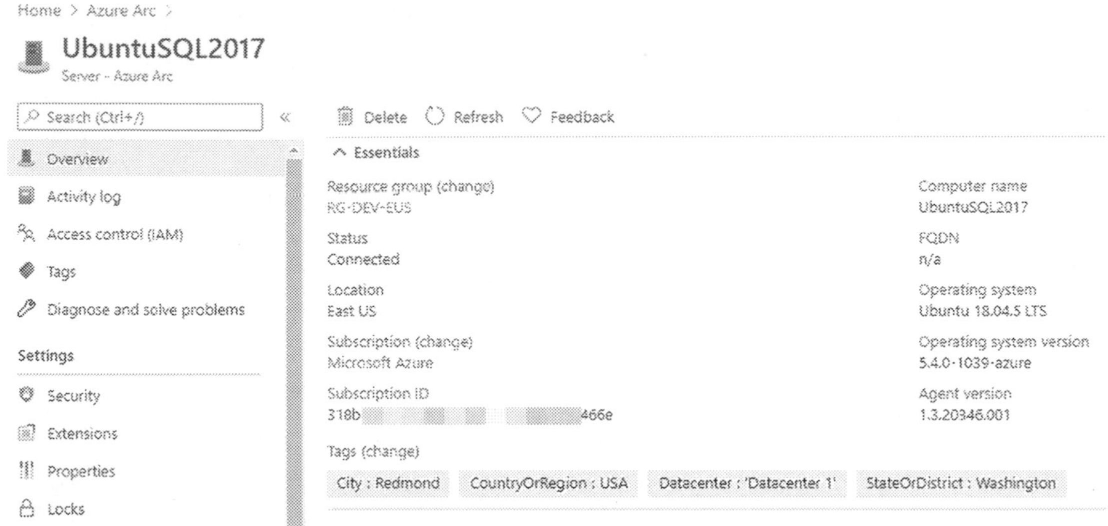

Figure 4-15. *The Overview blade of a Linux Azure Arc server immediately after onboarding*

Manage and Use Azure VM Extensions

Azure virtual machine (VM) extensions are small applications that provide postdeployment configuration and automation tasks on Azure VMs. For example, if a virtual machine requires software installation or to run a script in it, a VM extension can be used in lieu of traditional configuration management tools.

Extensions are essentially an "Out of Band" (OOB) management communications channel created using desired state configuration (DSC) technologies that work equally with Azure VMs and Azure Arc servers. A communications channel that was born in the hyperscale Azure cloud and now via Azure Arc is extended to your servers outside Azure.

Using extensions whenever possible in your computer management tasks is a force multiplier. Traditionally, deploying and auditing software across Linux and Windows servers in both cloud and on-premises environments required multiple management tools. Now, with Azure Arc-enabled servers alongside your Azure VMs, management of your hybrid machines' life cycles is simplified.

Whenever an extension is installed in an Azure VM or Azure Arc server, a hidden resource type–which is a child of the computer object–is created in your Azure resource group as follows:

- Azure Arc server extension resource type:

  Microsoft.HybridCompute/machines/extensions

- Azure VM extension resource type:

  Microsoft.Compute/virtualMachines/extensions

An extension object represents the desired state configuration of that extension on that computer. Viewing all resources in a resource group with the *Show hidden types* option selected will expose the extensions you have deployed. Extensions supplement and extend the Azure Resource Manager framework upon which your infrastructure runs, really a textbook migration of service management functions to platform services.

You can see how, in Figure 4-16, that Microsoft's novel approach—that is, cross-platform configuration extensions–achieves homogenous management across your estate.

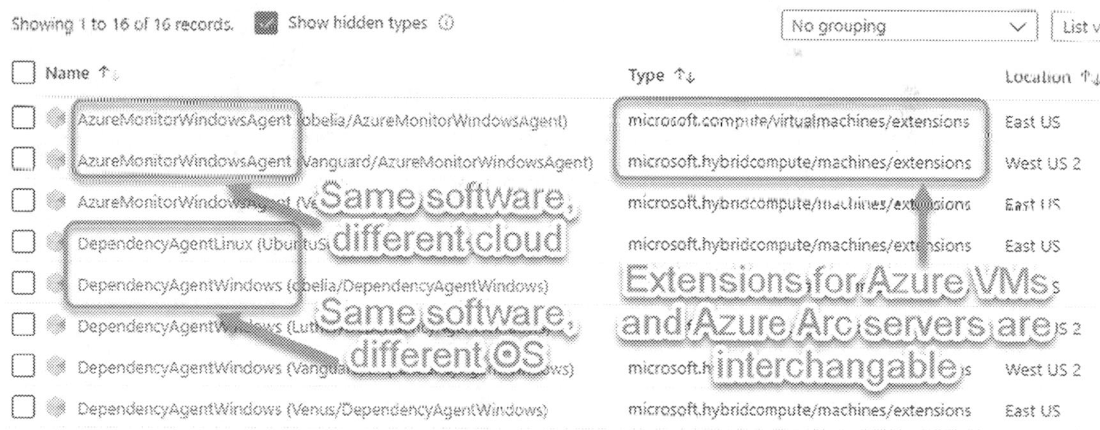

Figure 4-16. *Extensions are hidden resource types in the resource group*

Put in terms of business value, this model means you can accelerate the add/remove/change processes inherent in computer management by having a consistent control point and repeatable processes. There are several ways to leverage extensions at scale and in an automated fashion; we will cover these next.

Use Cases for Azure VM Extensions

Here are some specific use cases for available Azure VM extensions that provide key benefits to Azure Arc-enabled servers:

- **DSC VM extension:** Use Azure Automation State Configuration to centrally store configurations and maintain the desired state of Azure Arc servers. For example, to enforce standard feature deployments like IIS or DNS services on computers.
- **Log Analytics agent VM extension:** Collect log data for analysis with Logs in Azure Monitor and Microsoft Sentinel. This is useful for doing complex analysis across data from different kinds of sources.
- **Azure Monitor for VMs:** Analyzes the performance of your Windows and Linux VMs and monitors their processes and dependencies on other resources and external processes. This is achieved through enabling both the Log Analytics agent and Dependency agent VM extensions.
- **Custom Script Extension:** Download and execute scripts on hybrid connected machines. This extension is useful for postdeployment configuration, software installation, or any other configuration or management tasks. Think of installing antimalware or other security agents on all servers as soon as they are created.

You can learn details about each of these extensions as well as find a current full list of extensions available to use at these links:

- **Discovering VM Extensions for Windows**

  `https://docs.microsoft.com/en-us/azure/virtual-machines/extensions/features-windows`

- **Discovering VM Extensions for Linux**

  `https://docs.microsoft.com/en-us/azure/virtual-machines/extensions/features-linux`

Methods to Manage Azure VM Extensions

Even though they influence machines in many locations, extensions exist only in the Azure control plane, so they are easy to work with and can be executed from any location with access to Azure. There are five methods available to deploy and manage Azure VM extensions, and all methods work with all Azure VM and Azure Arc servers, both Windows and Linux. The methods are Azure portal, Azure PowerShell, Azure CLI, ARM templates, and Azure Policy.

Method 1: Extensions in the Azure Portal

A simple quick way to work with extensions on an individual Azure Arc server is on the Extensions blade of the Azure Arc server's page in the Azure portal. Figure 4-17 shows a typical Azure Arc server that is connected to Azure Log Analytics using VM extensions.

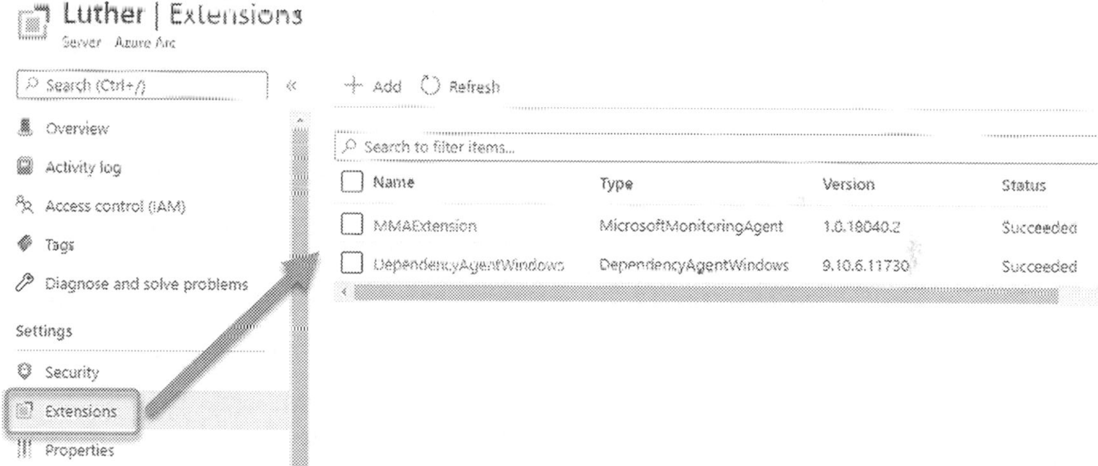

Figure 4-17. *Azure VM extensions added to an Azure Arc server*

To help you understand the net effect of Azure Arc and Azure VM extensions on an Azure Arc server, look at Figure 4-18, the Control Panel ➤ Programs and Features applet inside the Azure Arc server "Luther" from Figure 4-17.

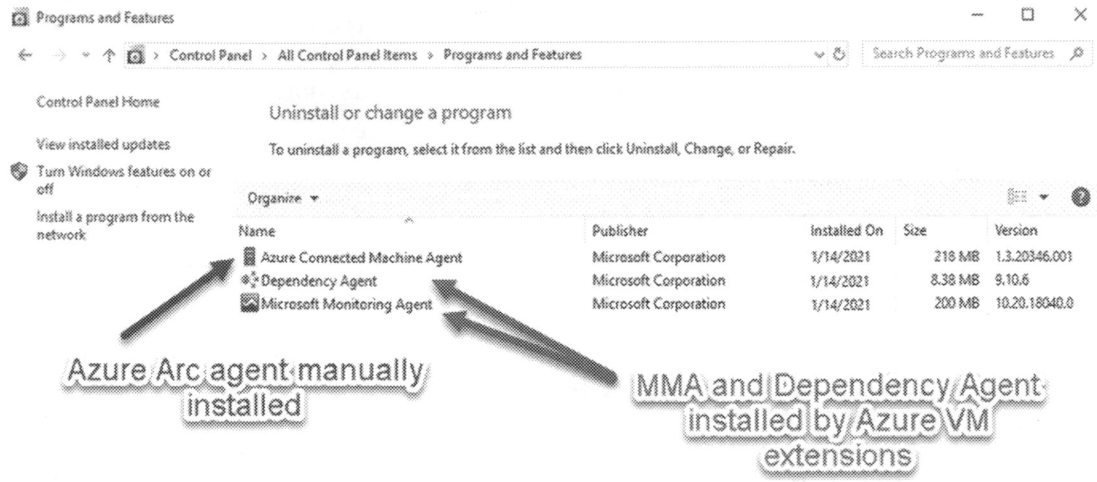

***Figure 4-18.** Extensions are hidden resource types in the resource group*

Figure 4-18 demonstrates how Azure VM extensions (added in the Azure Resource Manager control plane) influence Azure Arc servers that exist outside Azure. The only software the owner of this server needed to install was the Azure Arc agent (the *Azure Connected Machine Agent*). Subsequently, the extensions for Microsoft Management Agent (MMA) and its dependency agent caused those pieces of software to be installed as well—with the installation work accomplished automatically by Azure Arc, powered by Azure Resource Manager.

Reasons to navigate to the extensions page of an Azure Arc server include double-checking that a particular extension is installed as expected, or to manually install or uninstall an extension. If you click the **Add** button on a computer's extensions page (seen in Figure 4-17), a list of extensions available to install manually will be provided as seen in Figure 4-19.

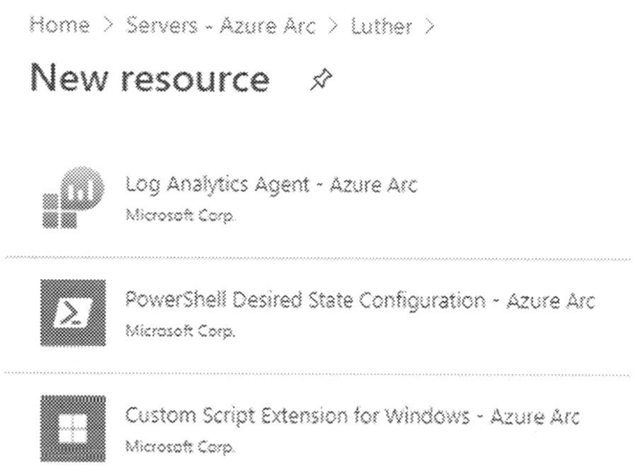

Figure 4-19. *Manually installing new Azure VM extensions on an Azure Arc server from the Azure portal*

Tip The Azure portal only exposes a subset of available Azure VM extensions that also work with Azure Arc servers. Others include *Azure Key Vault VM extension*, *Extension-based User Hybrid Runbook Worker*, and *Azure Defender integrated scanner* that can be installed by ARM template.

Alternately, clicking on the name of an installed extension (again in Figure 4-17) will open a details blade for that extension with an **Uninstall** button as seen in Figure 4-20. If you are having a problem with a particular extension installing properly, you can uninstall the failed extension from here and let Azure Arc try to add the extension again.

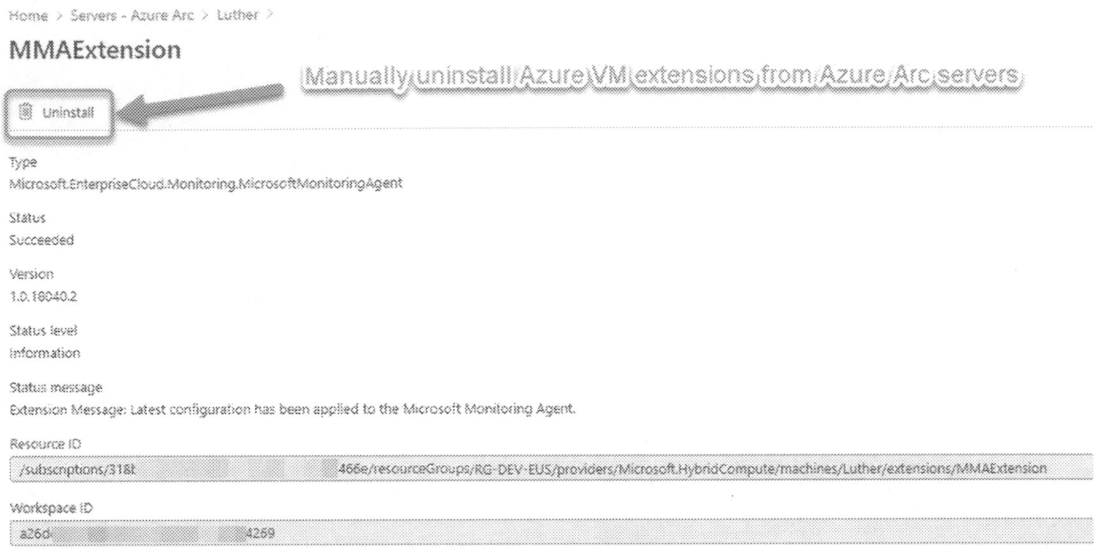

Figure 4-20. *Each installed Azure VM extension has an Uninstall button on its details page*

Method 2: Extensions Using Azure PowerShell

Azure PowerShell commands can be run from any computer with Azure PowerShell installed, or from Azure Cloud Shell in the Azure portal. In either case, you need to add the *Az.ConnectedMachine* module to your PowerShell instance with this cmdlet:

```
Install-Module -Name Az.ConnectedMachine
```

After a one-time install of that module to your PowerShell or Cloud Shell instance, you can run these PowerShell commands to list, add, and remove extensions:

```
Get-AzConnectedMachineExtension -ResourceGroupName <rgname> -MachineName
<machineName>
```

```
New-AzConnectedMachineExtension -Name <extensionName> -ResourceGroupName
<rgname> -MachineName <machineName> -Location <location> -Publisher
<publisher> -ExtensionType <extensionType> -Settings <settings>
```

```
Remove-AzConnectedMachineExtension -MachineName <machineName>
-ResourceGroupName <rgname> -Name <extensionName>
```

Figure 4-21 demonstrates using PowerShell in Azure Cloud Shell to list installed Azure VM extensions on an Azure Arc server. Notice this is the same data as seen in the Azure portal in Figure 4-17.

```
PS /home > Get-AzConnectedMachineExtension -ResourceGroupName RG-DEV-EUS -MachineName Luther

Name                     Location Provisioningstate
----                     -------- -----------------
MMAExtension             westus2  Succeeded
DependencyAgentWindows   westus2  Succeeded
```

***Figure 4-21.** Listing Azure VM extensions installed in a Windows Azure Arc server with Azure PowerShell*

Method 3: Extensions Using the Azure CLI

The Azure CLI is available to install in Windows, macOS, and Linux environments. It can also be run in a Docker container and Azure Cloud Shell. In all scenarios, and as was the case with PowerShell, there is a module to install before using Azure CLI with Azure Arc servers. The command is

```
az extension add --name connectedmachine
```

After a one-time install of that module to your Azure CLI or Cloud Shell instance, you can run commands like these to list, add, and remove extensions:

```
az connectedmachine extension list --machine-name "myMachineName"
--resource-group "myResourceGroup"

az connectedmachine extension create --machine-name "myMachineName"
--name "OmsAgentForLinux or MicrosoftMonitoringAgent" --location
"eastus" --settings '{\"workspaceId\":\"myWorkspaceId\"}' --protected-
settings '{\"workspaceKey\":\"myWorkspaceKey\"}' --resource-group
"myResourceGroup" --type-handler-version "1.13" --type "OmsAgentForLinux
or MicrosoftMonitoringAgent" --publisher "Microsoft.EnterpriseCloud.
Monitoring"

az connectedmachine extension delete --machine-name "myMachineName" --name
"OmsAgentForLinux" --resource-group "myResourceGroup"
```

If you do not have a local installation of Azure CLI, a quick way to run these commands is in an Azure Cloud Shell Bash environment as demonstrated in Figure 4-22.

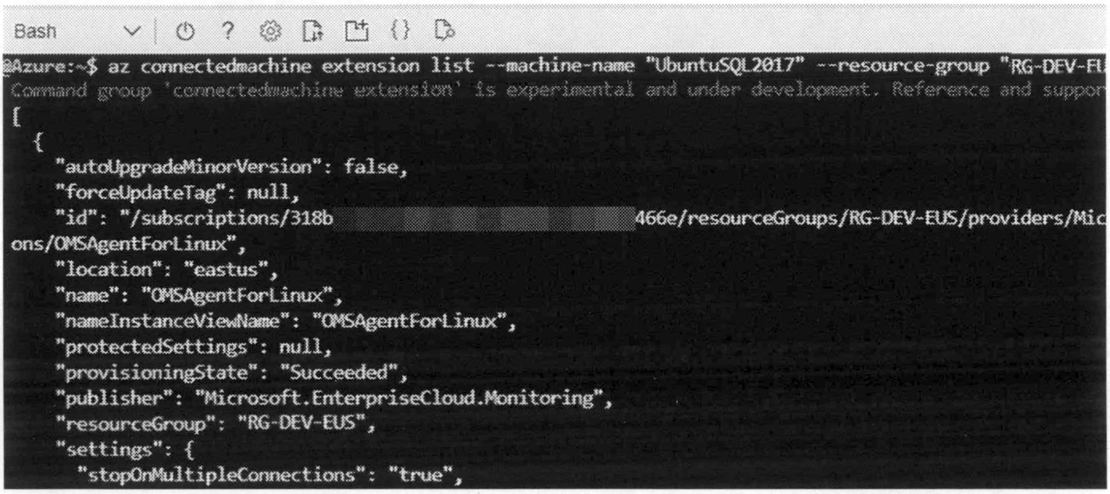

```
Bash
@Azure:~$ az connectedmachine extension list --machine-name "UbuntuSQL2017" --resource-group "RG-DEV-EU
Command group 'connectedmachine extension' is experimental and under development. Reference and suppor
[
  {
    "autoUpgradeMinorVersion": false,
    "forceUpdateTag": null,
    "id": "/subscriptions/318b                    466e/resourceGroups/RG-DEV-EUS/providers/Mic
ons/OMSAgentForLinux",
    "location": "eastus",
    "name": "OMSAgentForLinux",
    "nameInstanceViewName": "OMSAgentForLinux",
    "protectedSettings": null,
    "provisioningState": "Succeeded",
    "publisher": "Microsoft.EnterpriseCloud.Monitoring",
    "resourceGroup": "RG-DEV-EUS",
    "settings": {
      "stopOnMultipleConnections": "true",
```

Figure 4-22. *Listing Azure VM extensions installed in a Linux Azure Arc server with Azure CLI*

Method 4: Extensions as ARM Templates

This is a good approach to consider when you are using template-based deployment and provisioning tools for new Azure Arc servers. Microsoft has published at this link template files and parameters files with sample values for the extensions, listed as follows:

`https://docs.microsoft.com/en-us/azure/azure-arc/servers/manage-vm-extensions`

ARM templates for Windows and Linux Azure Arc computers are available for these extensions:

- Log Analytics VM extension
- Custom Script extension
- PowerShell DSC extension
- Dependency agent extension
- Azure Key Vault VM extension
- Microsoft Defender for Cloud integrated vulnerability scanner
- Azure Automation Hybrid Runbook Worker extension

Method 5: Extensions Deployed with Azure Policy

While listed last, this is the best approach to managing extensions, since using Azure Policy achieves deployment, compliance, and cloud scale in one management action. Azure Policy works with new and existing computers. While any of the previous methods of working with extensions have their use cases, Azure Policy is the most likely way you will deploy Azure VM extensions to your Azure Arc servers.

Azure policies, and *initiatives* that bundle sets of policies, can be applied to vast global scopes of heterogenous computers, thanks to Azure Arc. The built-in compliance and remediation features of Azure Policy are a road map and a toolset to achieve the technical goals of any given extension.

For example, using this approach, you could assign the built-in Azure Policy *Deploy Log Analytics agent to Linux* or *Windows Azure Arc machines* (seen in Figure 4-23) to audit if the Arc-enabled server has the Log Analytics agent installed. If the agent is not installed, the policy can create a predefined remediation task to automatically install the agent via an Azure resource deployment job.

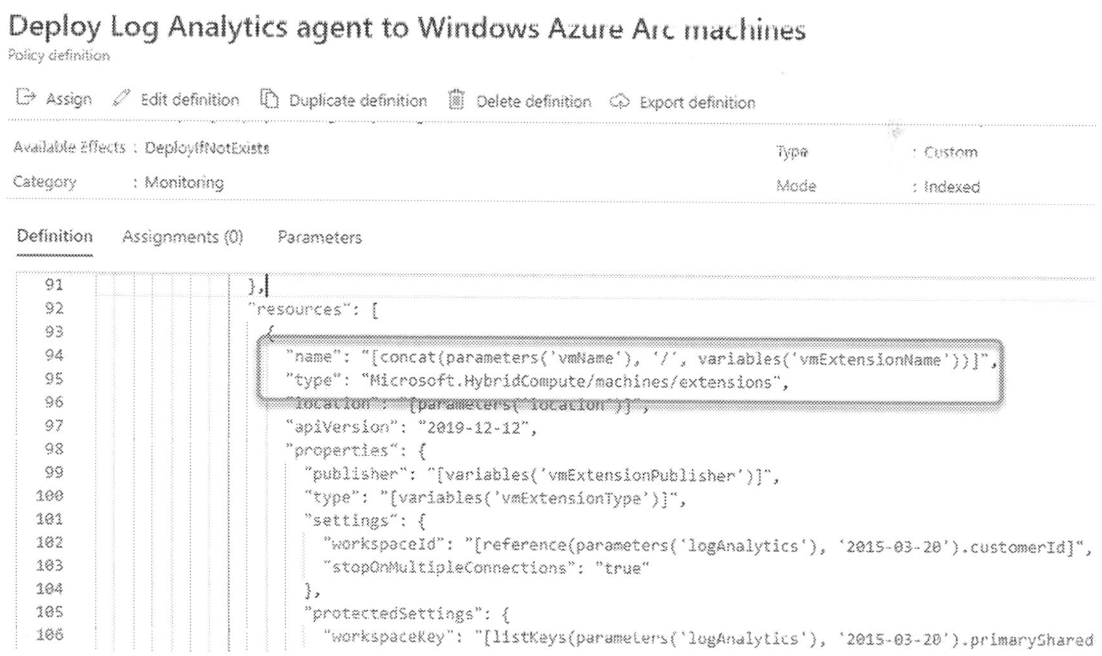

***Figure 4-23.** Built-in Azure Policy to deploy the Log Analytics agent to Windows Azure Arc machines*

Notably, Azure Policy does this check indirectly by looking to see if the appropriate Azure VM extension is successfully installed on the Azure Arc server object, not by interacting with the computer itself. Consider in the architecture of Azure Arc that attestation of the successful state of a desired configuration is delegated to a low and highly distributed level—the DSC agent on the hybrid computer itself. This efficiently leaves Azure Resource Manager only the lightweight task of checking that state value when assessing policy compliance.

Microsoft recommends installing the Log Analytics agent for Windows or Linux using Azure Policy. We cover this method in detail in Chapter 6, "Hybrid Server Monitoring Solution."

Summary

In this chapter, you learned at a deep level what an Azure Arc server is, and you were introduced to manual deployment and extension management concepts. You also gained insight into how Azure Arc servers interact with the Azure control plane through Azure Resource Manager. Now that you understand the fundamentals of working with Azure Arc servers, in the next chapter, you will learn how to deploy and manage Azure Arc servers at scale. We'll also cover more advanced Azure Arc features like tags and dashboarding, as well as troubleshooting Azure Arc servers in all scenarios.

CHAPTER 5

Azure Arc Servers: Using at Scale

When you use Azure Arc for management of your on-premises servers that may not exist in a cloud, you are effectively extending *cloud service management* essential characteristics to noncloud resources. That means all your servers can share the economy of scale benefits enjoyed by cloud consumers from perspectives of *business support, provisioning/configuration*, and *portability/interoperability*. This chapter will help you realize the maximum benefits from these perspectives using Azure Arc in production.

Chapter 4, "Azure Arc Servers: Getting Started," covered installing Azure Arc agents one at a time for testing and evaluation with the interactive method, while this chapter progresses to deploy Azure Arc servers at scale using a *service principal*. Chapter 4, "Azure Arc Servers: Getting Started," also included details on how Azure VM Extensions work with Azure Arc servers to perform postdeployment configuration and automation tasks, all of which apply equally to using extensions with Azure Arc servers at scale.

This chapter adds to your Azure Arc skillset by covering how to use *tags* with Azure Arc servers and how to author Azure Monitor *workbooks* that can serve as dashboards for all servers in your hybrid estate. We conclude with general troubleshooting tips for onboarding and using Azure Arc with Windows and Linux servers.

Create a Service Principal for Onboarding

To connect non-Azure computers to Azure as Azure Arc-enabled servers, you can use an Azure Active Directory service principal instead of using a privileged user identity to interactively connect the machine as we did in Chapter 4, "Azure Arc Servers: Getting Started." Using that method, an admin or user with elevated permissions needs to log into (or use PowerShell remoting to) every computer to be managed and onboard the server interactively.

S. Buchanan and J. Joyner, *Azure Arc-Enabled Kubernetes and Servers*,
https://doi.org/10.1007/978-1-4842-7768-3_5

Recall that installing the Azure Arc agent requires the installer have write access to the Azure subscription in order to create the Azure Resource Manager (ARM) resource of the "type" *Microsoft.HybridCompute/machines* that exists in a specific Azure subscription, resource group, and location. The installer can be a person, or it can be a security principal rather than a person. At scale, you need a process that doesn't require a person—you need a process that can be easily and infinitely repeated by automation or scripting.

A **service principal** is a special limited management identity (an "Azure service account") that is granted only the minimum permission necessary to connect machines to Azure using the **azcmagent** command. This is safer than using a higher privileged account like a *Global Admin* and follows Microsoft access control security best practices. The service principal is used during onboarding and offboarding; it is not used for any other purpose. *Azure Connected Machine Onboarding* is a predefined Azure access role that is sufficient to onboard Azure Arc servers.

The installation methods to install and configure the Connected Machine (Azure Arc) agent do require that the automated method you use, such as by scripting, has elevated permissions on the target machines to be enrolled. On Linux, by using the root account and on Windows, as a member of the Local Administrators group.

Create the Service Principal Using PowerShell

It is quite simple to create your service principal using Azure PowerShell; here are the commands to enter:

```
$sp = New-AzADServicePrincipal -DisplayName "Arc-for-servers" -Role "Azure
Connected Machine Onboarding"
$sp
$credential = New-Object pscredential -ArgumentList "temp", $sp.Secret
$credential.GetNetworkCredential().password
```

Figure 5-1 shows what this looks like running in Azure Cloud Shell. You are performing three actions with these commands:

1. Creating an Enterprise app named *Arc-for-servers*
2. Assigning the app the Azure Connecting Machine Onboarding role in your Azure subscription
3. Creating a secret password that is only visible once

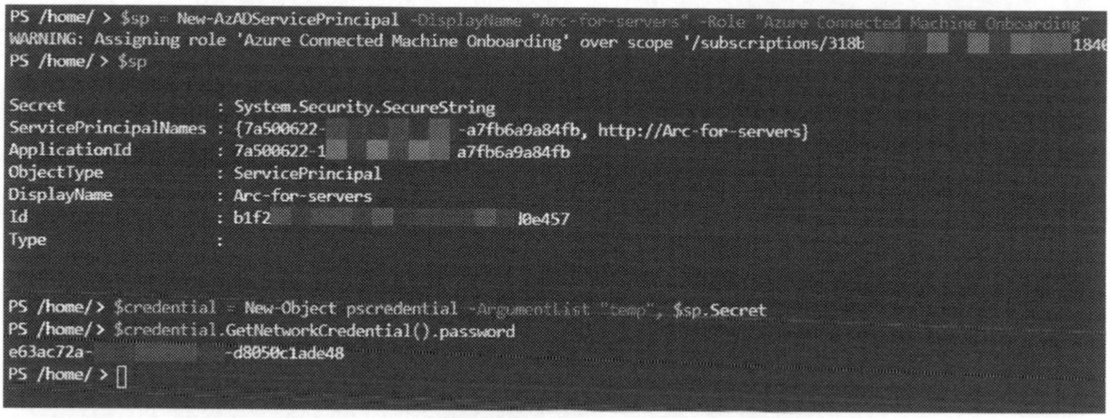

```
PS /home/ > $sp = New-AzADServicePrincipal -DisplayName "Arc-for-servers" -Role "Azure Connected Machine Onboarding"
WARNING: Assigning role 'Azure Connected Machine Onboarding' over scope '/subscriptions/318b                184
PS /home/ > $sp

Secret                : System.Security.SecureString
ServicePrincipalNames : {7a500622-          -a7fb6a9a84fb, http://Arc-for-servers}
ApplicationId         : 7a500622-1          a7fb6a9a84fb
ObjectType            : ServicePrincipal
DisplayName           : Arc-for-servers
Id                    : b1f2                0e457
Type                  :

PS /home/> $credential = New-Object pscredential -ArgumentList "temp", $sp.Secret
PS /home/> $credential.GetNetworkCredential().password
e63ac72a-          -d8050c1ade48
PS /home/ > []
```

***Figure 5-1.** Creating the Azure Arc onboarding service principal using PowerShell*

It is very important that after running these commands, you copy and paste the results into a file that you will save. You will need the *ApplicationId* and the *password* later to edit the script used for onboarding at scale.

Create the Service Principal Using the Azure Portal

If you prefer, you can create your service principal using the Azure portal; the step-by-step procedures are in the **Register an application with Azure AD and create a service principal** and **Assign a role to the application** sections at this link:

`https://docs.microsoft.com/en-us/azure/active-directory/develop/howto-create-service-principal-portal`

Using the same settings as demonstrated using PowerShell, name the application "Arc-for-servers," create a new client secret (password), and assign the application the role *Azure Connected Machine Onboarding* in your Azure subscription. Take note of the Application (client) ID as shown in Figure 5-2 and preserve the password that was created for the onboarding script that we will create next.

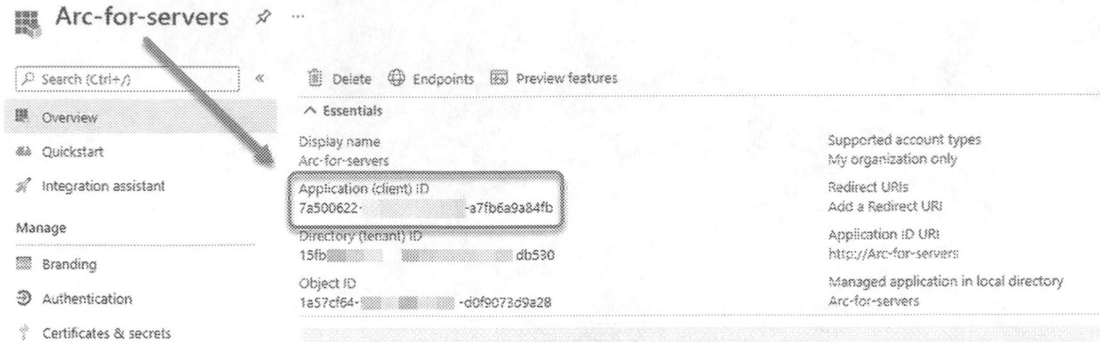

Figure 5-2. *Creating the Azure Arc onboarding service principal using the Azure portal*

Connect Azure Arc to Windows Servers at Scale

With your Azure AD service principal created, Azure subscription permissions assigned, and service principal password in hand, you are ready to add multiple servers to Azure with a script. Of course, all of the content from Chapter 4, "Azure Arc Servers: Getting Started," regarding prerequisites to interactive onboarding also applies to onboarding at scale. In particular, make sure the *Microsoft.HybridCompute* and *Microsoft.GuestConfiguration* Azure resource providers are registered in your Azure subscription.

Step by Step: Add Azure Arc Windows Servers at Scale

1. In your Azure portal, click **New** and select **Azure Arc for servers**, and then click **Create**.

2. At the Select a method blade seen in Figure 5-3, under ***Add multiple servers***, click ***Generate script***.

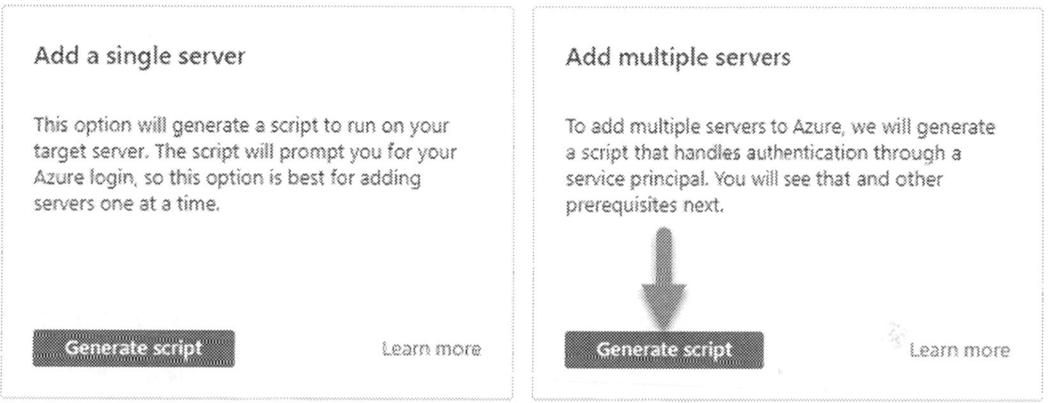

Figure 5-3. *Starting your guided experience to onboard servers at scale*

3. Read the Prerequisites page and click **Next: Resource details.**
4. Enter the Resource details appropriate for your environment, and then click **Next: Authentication**.
5. As seen in Figure 5-4, the service principal you created previously is available to select; then click ***Next: Tags***.

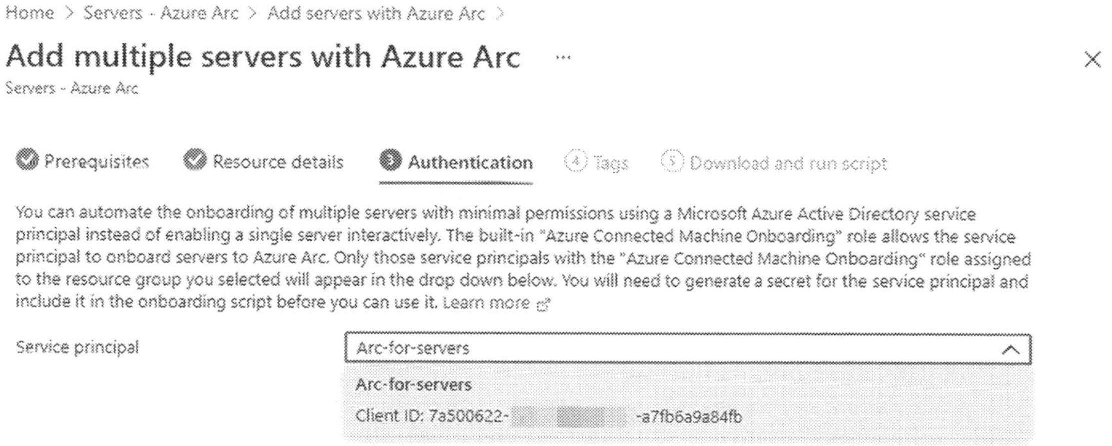

Home > Servers - Azure Arc > Add servers with Azure Arc >

Add multiple servers with Azure Arc ...

Servers - Azure Arc

Prerequisites | Resource details | 3 Authentication | 4 Tags | 5 Download and run script

You can automate the onboarding of multiple servers with minimal permissions using a Microsoft Azure Active Directory service principal instead of enabling a single server interactively. The built-in "Azure Connected Machine Onboarding" role allows the service principal to onboard servers to Azure Arc. Only those service principals with the "Azure Connected Machine Onboarding" role assigned to the resource group you selected will appear in the drop down below. You will need to generate a secret for the service principal and include it in the onboarding script before you can use it. Learn more

Service principal: Arc-for-servers

Arc-for-servers

Client ID: 7a500622- -a7fb6a9a84fb

Figure 5-4. *App registrations with the Azure Connected Machine Onboarding role are listed to select for authentication*

Resource *tags* can optionally be associated with Azure Arc servers onboarded with this script as seen in Figure 5-5.

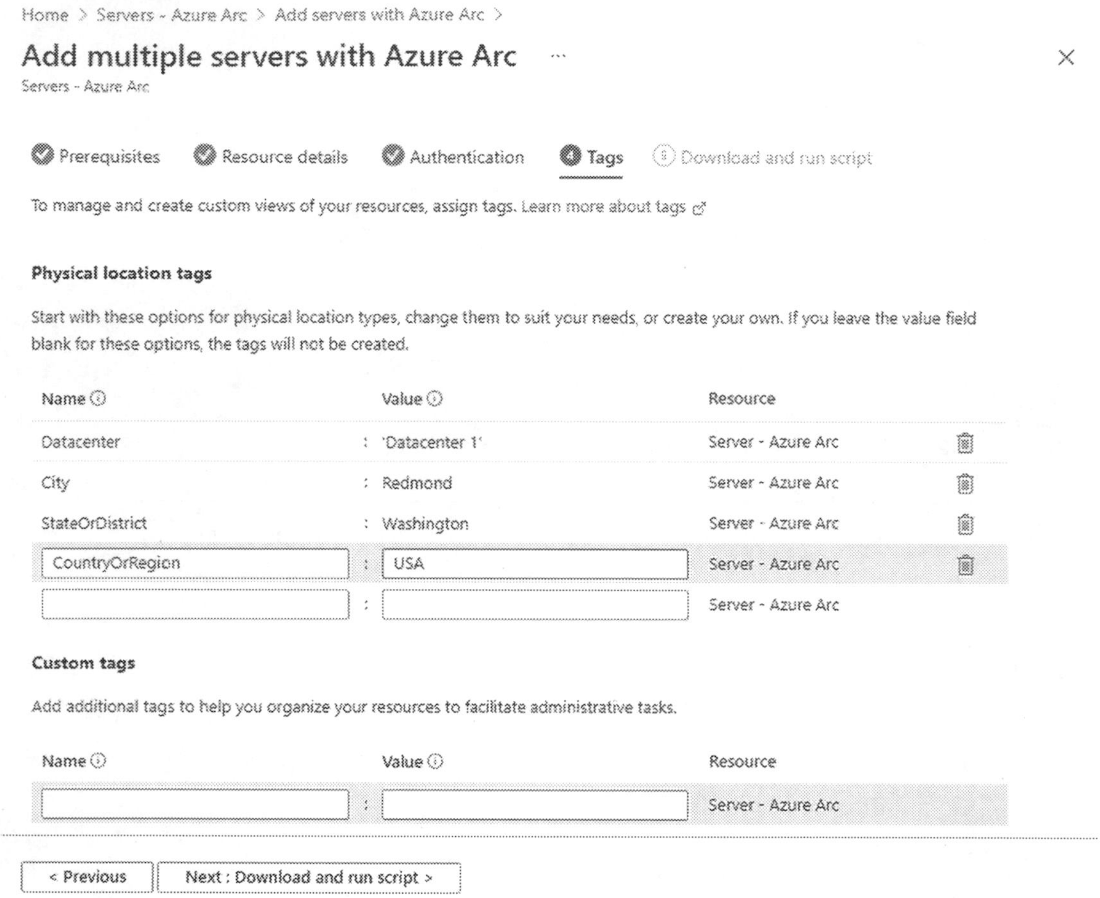

Home > Servers - Azure Arc > Add servers with Azure Arc >

Add multiple servers with Azure Arc

Servers - Azure Arc

Prerequisites   Resource details   Authentication   4 Tags   5 Download and run script

To manage and create custom views of your resources, assign tags. Learn more about tags

Physical location tags

Start with these options for physical location types, change them to suit your needs, or create your own. If you leave the value field blank for these options, the tags will not be created.

Name		Value	Resource
Datacenter	:	'Datacenter 1'	Server - Azure Arc
City	:	Redmond	Server - Azure Arc
StateOrDistrict	:	Washington	Server - Azure Arc
CountryOrRegion	:	USA	Server - Azure Arc
	:		Server - Azure Arc

Custom tags

Add additional tags to help you organize your resources to facilitate administrative tasks.

Name		Value	Resource
	:		Server - Azure Arc

< Previous   Next : Download and run script >

Figure 5-5. *Optionally assign tags for Azure Arc servers. Tags can be added or changed afterward at any time*

6. After entering desired tags, click ***Next: Download and run script*** to arrive at the Download script page shown in Figure 5-6.

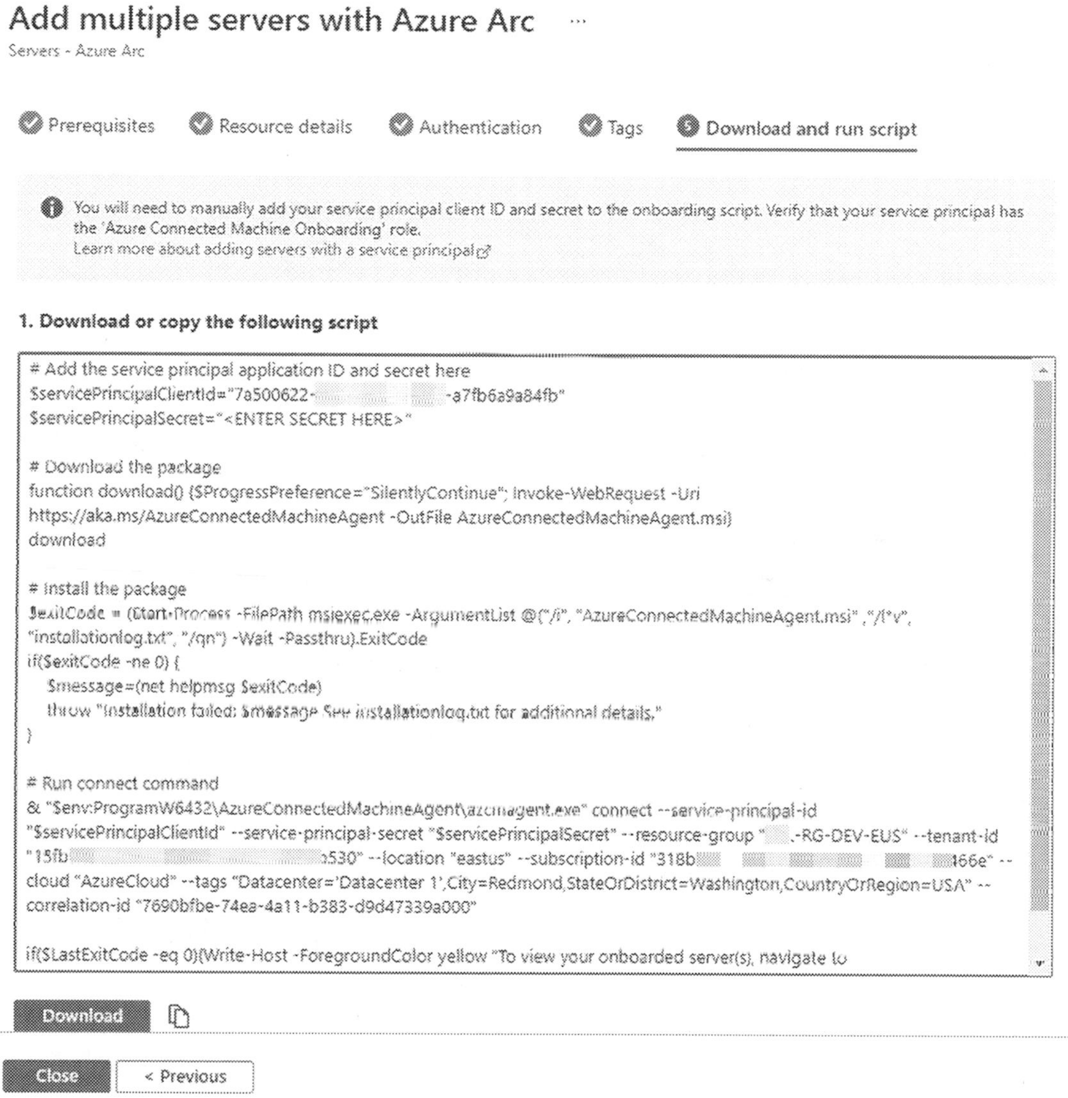

Add multiple servers with Azure Arc ...

Servers - Azure Arc

Prerequisites | Resource details | Authentication | Tags | 5 Download and run script

You will need to manually add your service principal client ID and secret to the onboarding script. Verify that your service principal has the 'Azure Connected Machine Onboarding' role.
Learn more about adding servers with a service principal

1. Download or copy the following script

```
# Add the service principal application ID and secret here
$servicePrincipalClientId="7a500622-                -a7fb6a9a84fb"
$servicePrincipalSecret="<ENTER SECRET HERE>"

# Download the package
function download() {$ProgressPreference="SilentlyContinue"; Invoke-WebRequest -Uri
https://aka.ms/AzureConnectedMachineAgent -OutFile AzureConnectedMachineAgent.msi}
download

# Install the package
$exitCode = (Start-Process -FilePath msiexec.exe -ArgumentList @("/i", "AzureConnectedMachineAgent.msi" ,"/l*v",
"installationlog.txt", "/qn") -Wait -Passthru).ExitCode
if($exitCode -ne 0) {
    $message=(net helpmsg $exitCode)
    throw "Installation failed: $message See installationlog.txt for additional details."
}

# Run connect command
& "$env:ProgramW6432\AzureConnectedMachineAgent\azcmagent.exe" connect --service-principal-id
"$servicePrincipalClientId" --service-principal-secret "$servicePrincipalSecret" --resource-group "   .-RG-DEV-EUS" --tenant-id
"15fb                    530" --location "eastus" --subscription-id "318b                    466e" --
cloud "AzureCloud" --tags "Datacenter='Datacenter 1',City=Redmond,StateOrDistrict=Washington,CountryOrRegion=USA" --
correlation-id "7690bfbe-74ea-4a11-b383-d9d47339a000"

if($LastExitCode -eq 0){Write-Host -ForegroundColor yellow "To view your onboarded server(s), navigate to
```

Download

Close | < Previous

Figure 5-6. *At-scale onboarding script ready to download, edit to add the secret (password), and run on a test server*

You can also elect to author an onboarding script manually using the following script format:

```
# OnboardingScript.ps1
# --------------------

# Download the package
function download() {$ProgressPreference="SilentlyContinue"; Invoke-
WebRequest -Uri https://aka.ms/AzureConnectedMachineAgent -OutFile
AzureConnectedMachineAgent.msi}
download

# Install the package
msiexec /i AzureConnectedMachineAgent.msi /l*v installationlog.txt /qn |
Out-String

# Run connect command
& "$env:ProgramFiles\AzureConnectedMachineAgent\azcmagent.exe" connect `
  --service-principal-id "{serviceprincipalAppID}" `
  --service-principal-secret "{serviceprincipalPassword}" `
  --resource-group "{ResourceGroupName}" `
  --tenant-id "{tenantID}" `
  --location "{resourceLocation}" `
  --subscription-id "{subscriptionID}"
```

Tips on running OnboardingScript.ps1: (applies to Windows and Linux)

(1) The script can onboard multiple servers. Azure Arc servers will all be assigned to the same subscription, resource group, and Azure region.

(2) The script downloaded from the portal will not contain the `$servicePrincipalSecret` value; you need to manually add the service principal password to the downloaded script before running it.

(3) The script must be run with local administrator (or root) privileges.

(4) You can modify the tags to make multiple versions of the script using the pattern `--tags "tag1name=tagvalue,'tag 2 name'='tag value'"`

---

7. While the script might be run on hundreds of servers, it is prudent to validate the script manually on at least one computer. Copy the script (OnboardingScript.ps1) to a prospective Azure Arc server and run the script in an elevated PowerShell session. Figure 5-7 shows the output of the at-scale onboarding script when run manually.

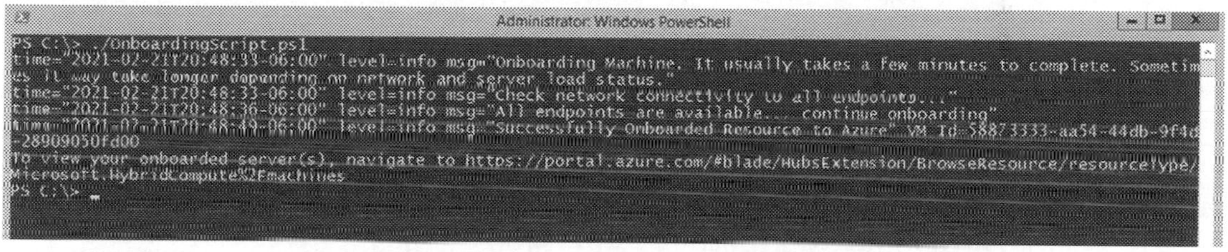

Figure 5-7. *At-scale onboarding script run manually on a server for validation*

After the Azure Arc agent is installed, you can open your Azure Portal to view the new hybrid computer object:

```
https://portal.azure.com/#blade/HubsExtension/BrowseResource/resourceType/
Microsoft.HybridCompute%2Fmachines
```

Run Azure Arc Windows Onboarding Script at Scale

Of course, the main reason for crafting the at-scale onboarding script is to permit running the script automatically and remotely on a large number of computers without further human intervention. Any method in the network administrator's toolkit to run PowerShell scripts with elevated permissions will work. Consider these options:

- PowerShell Remoting using the `Invoke-Command` cmdlet for one-to-many remoting.

- Deploy the PowerShell script as an Application or Program using Microsoft Endpoint Manager (MEM), formerly System Center Configuration Manager (SCCM).
- Run the PowerShell script as an Immediate Scheduled Task with an Active Dircctory Group Policy Object (GPO).

The third option is recommended since the GPO scheduled task method lets you run the script immediately and with admin rights, and the script only runs once because each time group policy refreshes, it will remove the task. Follow these steps to deploy the Azure Arc Windows onboarding script to many or all servers in your Active Directory (AD) domain.

1. Copy the OnboardingScipt.ps1 file to a network shared location; in our example, we will use the domain "sysvol" scripts folder: `%LOGONSERVER%\sysvol\%USERDNSDOMAIN%\scripts\OnboardingScript.ps1`
2. Open the Group Policy Management Console (GPMC) and navigate to the location in your AD forest that contains the systems to be onboarded to Azure Arc server. Right-click and select "Create a GPO in this domain, and Link it here." When prompted, assign the name *Install Azure Arc Agent*.
3. Right-click the new GPO and select **Edit**. Navigate to Computer Configuration ➤ Preferences ➤ Control Panel Settings ➤ Scheduled Tasks, and then right-click and select New ➤ Immediate Task (at least Windows 7) as shown in Figure 5-8.

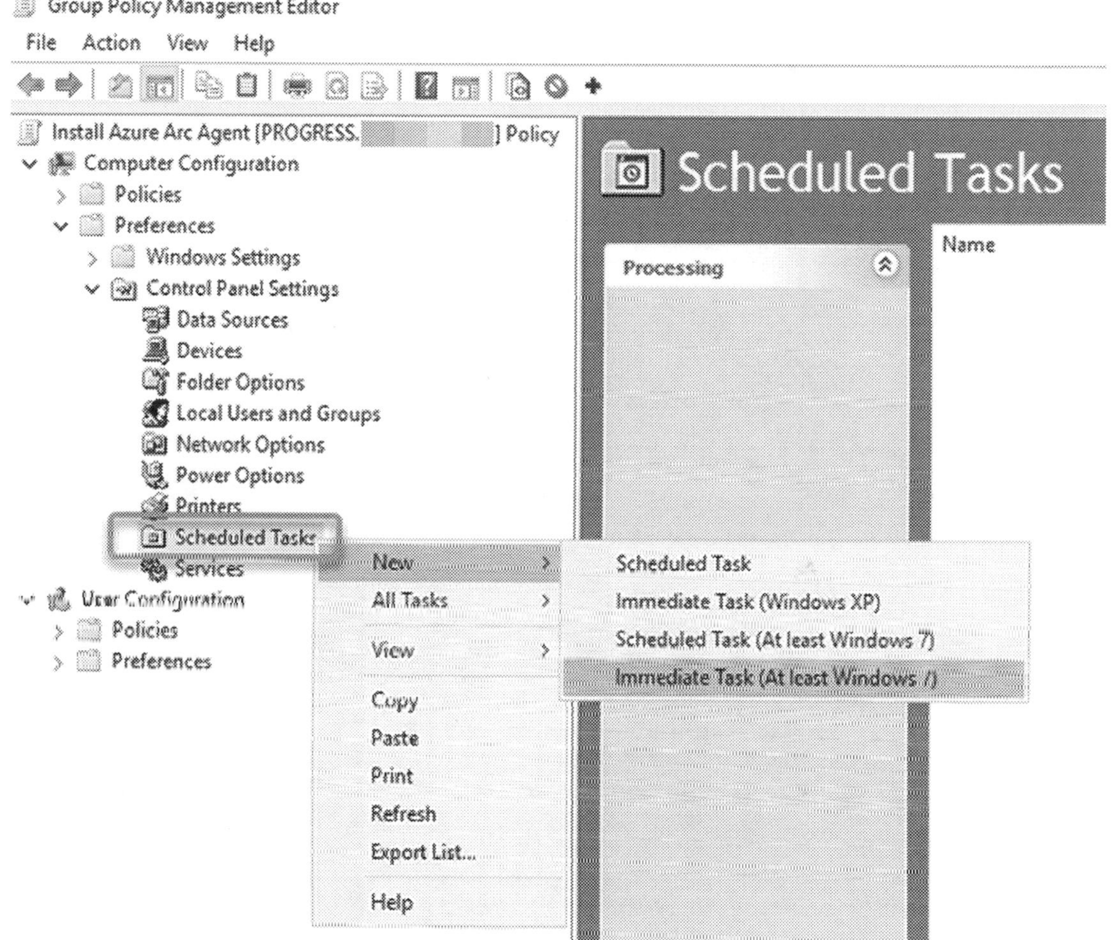

Figure 5-8. *Creating an immediate scheduled task using Group Policy*

4. On the General tab of the new task, set the Action to Create, enter the name Immediate Task to Install Azure Arc Agent, change the user account to SYSTEM, select to Run whether user is logged on or not, to Run with highest privileges, and Configure for Windows 7, Windows Server 2008 R2 as shown in Figure 5-9.

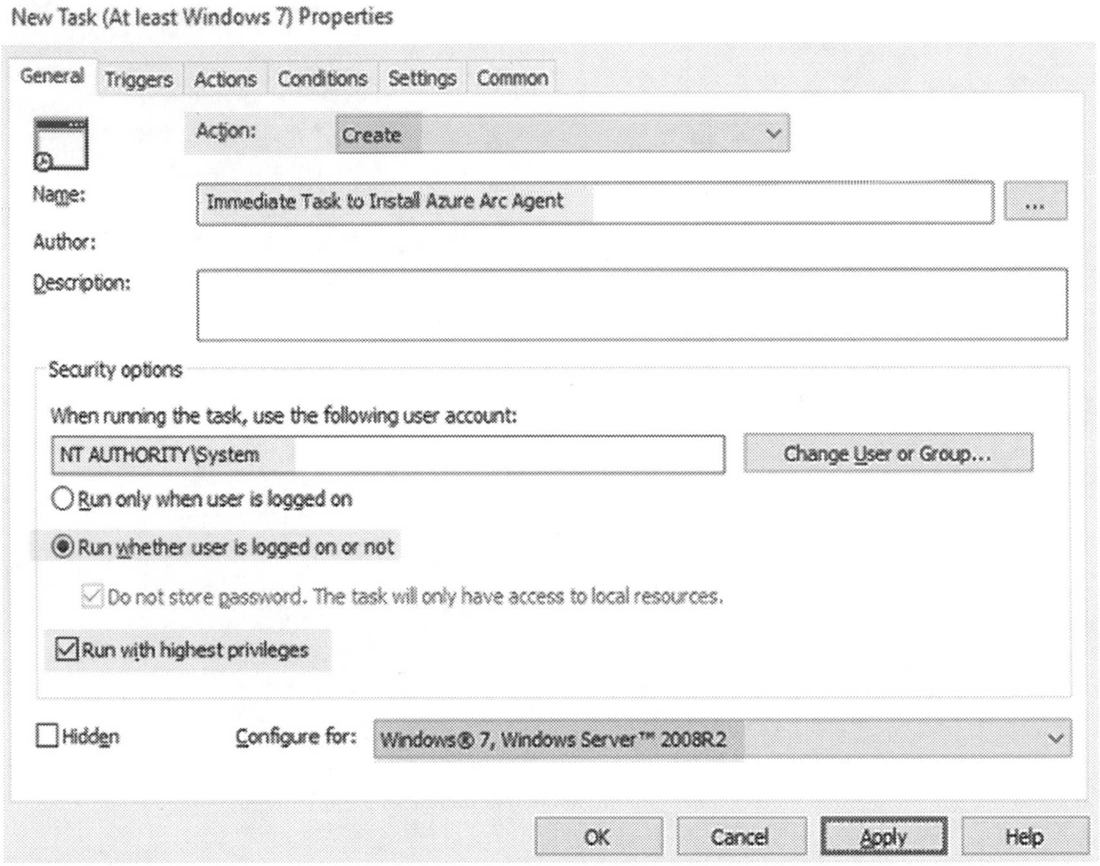

Figure 5-9. *Configure the General tab of the new task*

5. Move to the Actions tab of the new task and enter this information:

   - Action = "Start a program"
   - Program/Script =

     `C:\WINDOWS\system32\WindowsPowerShell\v1.0\powershell.exe`

   - Add Arguments (optional) =

     `-ExecutionPolicy Bypass -command "& \\SERVER\SHARE\OnboardingScript.ps1"`

     (replace SERVER and SHARE with the names you used in your environment)

6. Finally, move to the Common tab and select the **Apply once and do not reapply** option.

7. Save the new task, and the Azure Arc agent will be installed on computers the GPO applies to at the next group policy refresh interval, which is every 90 minutes with a randomized offset of up to 30 minutes.

Connect Azure Arc to Linux Servers at Scale

To onboard Linux servers at scale, you will use the same Azure AD service principal and secret password developed for at-scale onboarding of Windows servers. The procedure to connect Linux servers at scale is very similar to that for Windows servers at scale.

Step by Step: Add Azure Arc Linux Servers at Scale

You must comply with the "Prerequisites: Add Azure Arc Servers Using Interactive Script (Windows and Linux Computers)" section in Chapter 4, "Azure Arc Servers: Getting Started."

1. In your Azure portal, click **New** and select **Azure Arc for servers**, and then click **Create**.

2. At the Select a method blade previously seen in Figure 5-3, under **Add multiple servers**, click **Generate script**.

3. Read the Prerequisites page and click **Next: Resource details**.

4. Enter the Resource details appropriate for your environment, set the Operating system to **Linux**, and then click **Next: Authentication**.

5. As previously seen in Figure 5-4, the service principal you created previously is available to select; then click **Next: Tags**.

6. After entering desired tags, click **Next: Download and run script** to arrive at the Download script page shown in Figure 5-10.

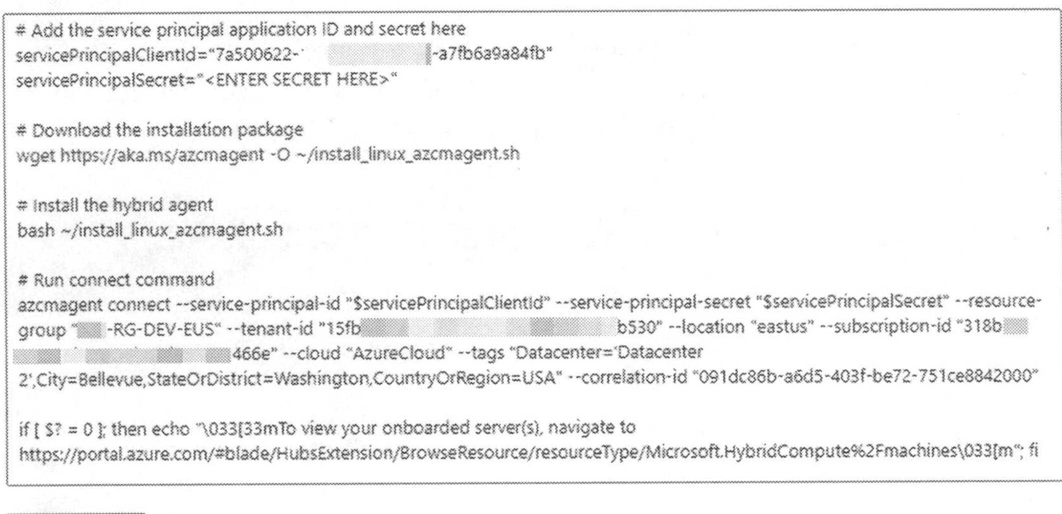

***Figure 5-10.** Automatically generated custom bash script that onboards a Linux computer to Azure Arc using a service principal*

Here is the format for authoring your Linux at-scale onboarding script manually:

```
# OnboardingScript.sh
# --------------------

# Download the installation package
wget https://aka.ms/azcmagent -O ~/install_linux_azcmagent.sh

# Install the hybrid agent
bash ~/install_linux_azcmagent.sh
```

```
# Run connect command
azcmagent connect \
  --service-principal-id "{serviceprincipalAppID}" \
  --service-principal-secret "{serviceprincipalPassword}" \
  --resource-group "{ResourceGroupName}" \
  --tenant-id "{tenantID}" \
  --location "{resourceLocation}" \
  --subscription-id "{subscriptionID}"
```

7. At this point, your bash script is ready to test on a pilot computer and then deploy at scale using any variety of Linux software management techniques.

Run Azure Arc Linux Onboarding Script at Scale

Popular open source configuration management software may be in use in your Linux environment such as *Chef* or *Puppet,* and these tools are perfectly suited to deploying your Azure Arc at-scale onboarding script. As a simplified walk-through of deploying the onboarding script remotely, consider these steps using Linux built-in **ssh** commands:

1. Copy the onboarding script to your Linux admin computer and enable the script to be executed by running this command:

   ```
   sudo chmod 700 OnboardingScript.sh
   ```

2. Generate a public-private key pair using the **ssh-keygen** utility (see Figure 5-11 as an example). Just hit the Enter key every time you are prompted.

   ```
   ssh-keygen -t rsa
   ```

```
lumaroot@UbuntuSQL2017:~$ ssh-keygen -t rsa
Generating public/private rsa key pair.
Enter file in which to save the key (/home/lumaroot/.ssh/id_rsa):
Enter passphrase (empty for no passphrase):
Enter same passphrase again:
Your identification has been saved in /home/lumaroot/.ssh/id_rsa.
Your public key has been saved in /home/lumaroot/.ssh/id_rsa.pub.
```

Figure 5-11. *Generating an ssh keypair to use for remotely running scripts*

3. Next add the public key to the `~/.ssh/authorized_keys` file on the remote host you want to enroll in Azure Arc:

   ```
   ssh-copy-id -i ~/.ssh/id_rsa.pub <username>@<host>
   ```

4. Now you can execute SSH commands on the remote host from your admin computer without entering a password. The following single command line will (1) copy the script from the admin computer to the target computer, (2) run the onboarding script, and (3) delete the remote copy of the script.

   ```
   scp OnboardingScript.sh <host>:/tmp/ && ssh -t
   <user>@<host> "sudo -s bash /tmp/OnboardingScript.sh" &&
   ssh -t <user>@<host> "rm /tmp/OnboardingScript.sh"
   ```

   At the completion of the script run, watch for the script to print out an INFO notice that onboarding is complete as demonstrated in Figure 5-12.

```
STARTING Arc GC
Getting status via systemd
EXT service is not running.
Configuring EXT service ...
Found systemd service controller...for Extension Service
Created symlink /etc/systemd/system/multi-user.target.wants/extd.service → /lib/
Service configured through systemd service controller. Extension Service
Getting status via systemd
EXT service is not running.
STARTING EXT
Latest version of azcmagent is installed.
INFO[0000] Onboarding Machine. It usually takes a few minutes to complete. Somet
INFO[0000] Check network connectivity to all endpoints...
INFO[0002] All endpoints are available... continue onboarding
INFO[0010] Successfully Onboarded Resource to Azure      VM Id=227af307 9cb1-400
\033[33mTo view your onboarded server(s), navigate to https://portal.azure.com/#
hines\033[m
```

Figure 5-12. *Remotely onboarding a Linux computer to Azure Arc*

Connect Machines to Azure Arc from Windows Admin Center

Microsoft provides a means to onboard Azure Arc servers using **Windows Admin Center**. Windows Admin Center is a locally deployed, browser-based app for managing Windows servers, clusters, hyperconverged infrastructure, as well as Windows 10 PCs. It is a free product in general availability (GA) since 2019 and is already used in production by many organizations. You install the product on a computer in your environment, and then log into a web portal on that computer to interact with Windows Admin Center. The portal surfaces controls for virtually every aspect of server management. It is a viable, even smart alternative to using PowerShell and/or individual GUI-based admin tools for server administration. Table 5-1 lists 27 specific management tools consolidated in Windows Admin Center.

Table 5-1. *Server Management Functions Included in Windows Admin Center*

Azure hybrid services	Firewall	Roles & features
Azure Backup	Installed apps	Scheduled tasks
Azure File Sync	Local users & groups	Services
Azure Monitor	Networks	Storage
Azure Security Center	Performance Monitor	Storage Migration Service
Certificates	PowerShell	Storage Replica
Devices	Processes	System Insights
Events	Registry	Settings: Environment variables
Files & file sharing	Remote Desktop	Settings: Power Configuration

Microsoft continues to invest in Windows Admin Center and directs customers in Windows Server 2022 to consider Windows Admin Center a primary method of server administration. If you are using Windows Admin Center already or were waiting for a use case to deploy it in your environment, consider that you can use it for Azure Arc server onboarding. In some respects, Windows Admin Center is a simplified method for at-scale onboarding to Azure Arc server. Here's a short list of "pro and con" considerations for this method:

Azure Arc Pros: Windows Admin Center

- It does not require or use a service principal.
- It does not require use of scripts for onboarding.
- Windows Admin Center itself is easy to install and use.

Azure Arc Cons: Windows Admin Center

- Servers are onboarded one at a time.
- A user authorized to onboard servers to your Azure subscription must be logged in.
- You can't assign tags to the Azure Arc server at the time of server creation.

This solution uses the Azure credentials of the logged-on user in the same manner as the interactive script method detailed in Chapter 4, "Azure Arc Servers: Getting Started." The difference is there is no need for the user to copy device code(s) and log in separately to validate their Azure user identity (as occurs during the interactive script method).

Additional considerations for using Windows Admin Center to onboard servers to Azure Arc include the following:

- The minimum built-in Azure subscription security role needed to onboard Azure Arc servers is **Azure Connected Machine Onboarding**. The user logged into the Windows Admin Center console must have this right in your Azure subscription. (To delete a machine, the user needs the **Azure Connected Machine Resource Administrator** role.)
- Although connecting your Windows Admin Center instance to your Azure subscription does create an Azure AD App registration (service principal), usually named *WindowsAdminCenter-https://<servername>*, that service principal is not used for the Azure Arc onboarding action.

- You cannot select to onboard the server using a precreated Azure Arc service principal, as described in the "Create a Service Principal for Onboarding" section of this chapter.
- Make sure the *Microsoft.HybridCompute* and *Microsoft.GuestConfiguration* Azure resource providers are registered in your Azure subscription before attempting to onboard an Azure Arc server using Windows Admin Center.

Step by Step: Add Azure Arc Servers Using Windows Admin Center

This procedure assumes you have installed Windows Admin Center on a server in your environment and connected at least one server that you desire to onboard to Azure Arc.

1. Sign into Windows Admin Center.
2. From the *All connections* list on the **Overview** page, in the list of connected Windows servers, select a server from the list to connect to it.
3. From the left-hand pane, select **Settings**.
4. In the Settings page, select **Azure Arc for servers**; click **Get started**.
5. In the Get started with Azure in Windows Admin Center blade, click the **Copy** button as seen in Figure 5-13.

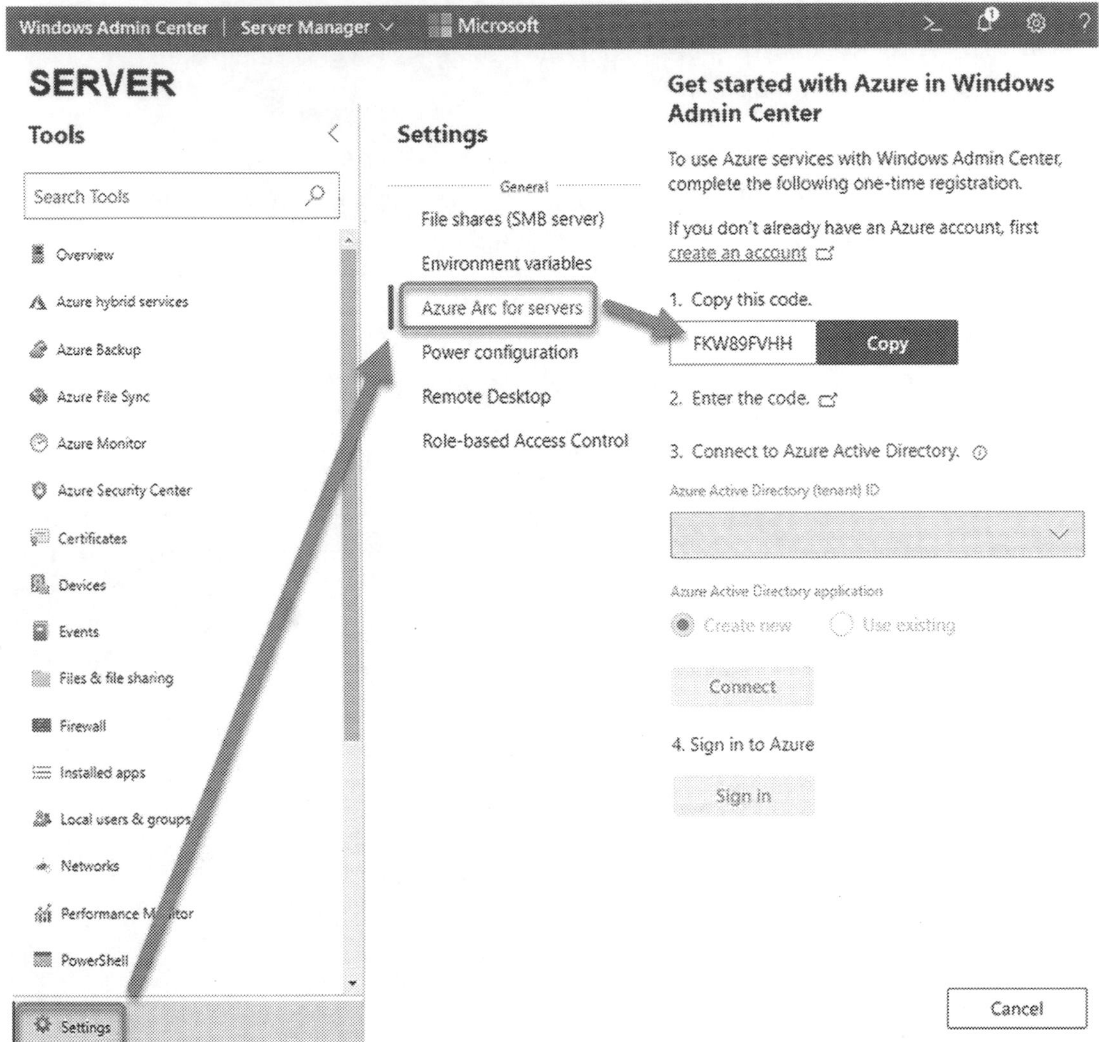

Figure 5-13. *The Settings page of a Windows Admin Center connected server*

6. Click the **Enter the code** link, and in the web page that opens, paste the code.

7. When prompted, pick an Azure login identity with permission to add Azure Arc servers to your subscription.

8. Close the login to Azure page and you will find the Connect to Azure Active Directory step populated with one or more Azure Active Directory tenant IDs. Select your tenant from the drop-down list, and with the **Create new** radio button selected, click **Connect**.

9. Click the **Sign in** button. When a Permissions requested dialog appears, click the **Accept** button.

10. Returning to the **Azure Arc for servers** blade, click the **Get started** button again.

11. At the ***Connect server to Azure*** blade, select the Azure subscription, resource group, and Azure region where you want the Azure Arc server created and click the ***Set up*** button as seen in Figure 5-14.

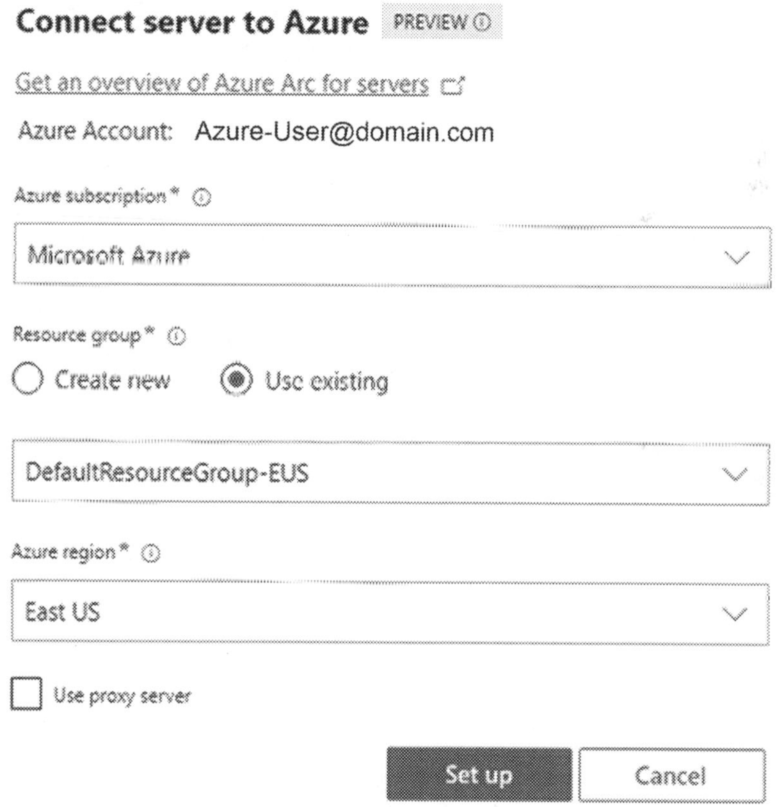

Figure 5-14. *The last step before onboarding an Azure Arc server in the Windows Admin Center console*

12. You will see a Windows Admin Center task "Setting up Azure Arc for servers" that will run for a few minutes.

13. When Azure Arc for server is set up for a connected server in Windows Admin Center, you will see a view like Figure 5-14 with shortcuts to these items:

- *View this server in Azure* opens the Azure Arc server page in the Azure portal for the connected server.
- *This server is connected to* link opens the Resource group page in the Azure portal that the Azure Arc server is a member of.
- A **Disconnect** server button that deletes the Azure Arc server object from the Azure subscription.
- Links to *Azure Policy* and Azure Monitor *Search logs*.

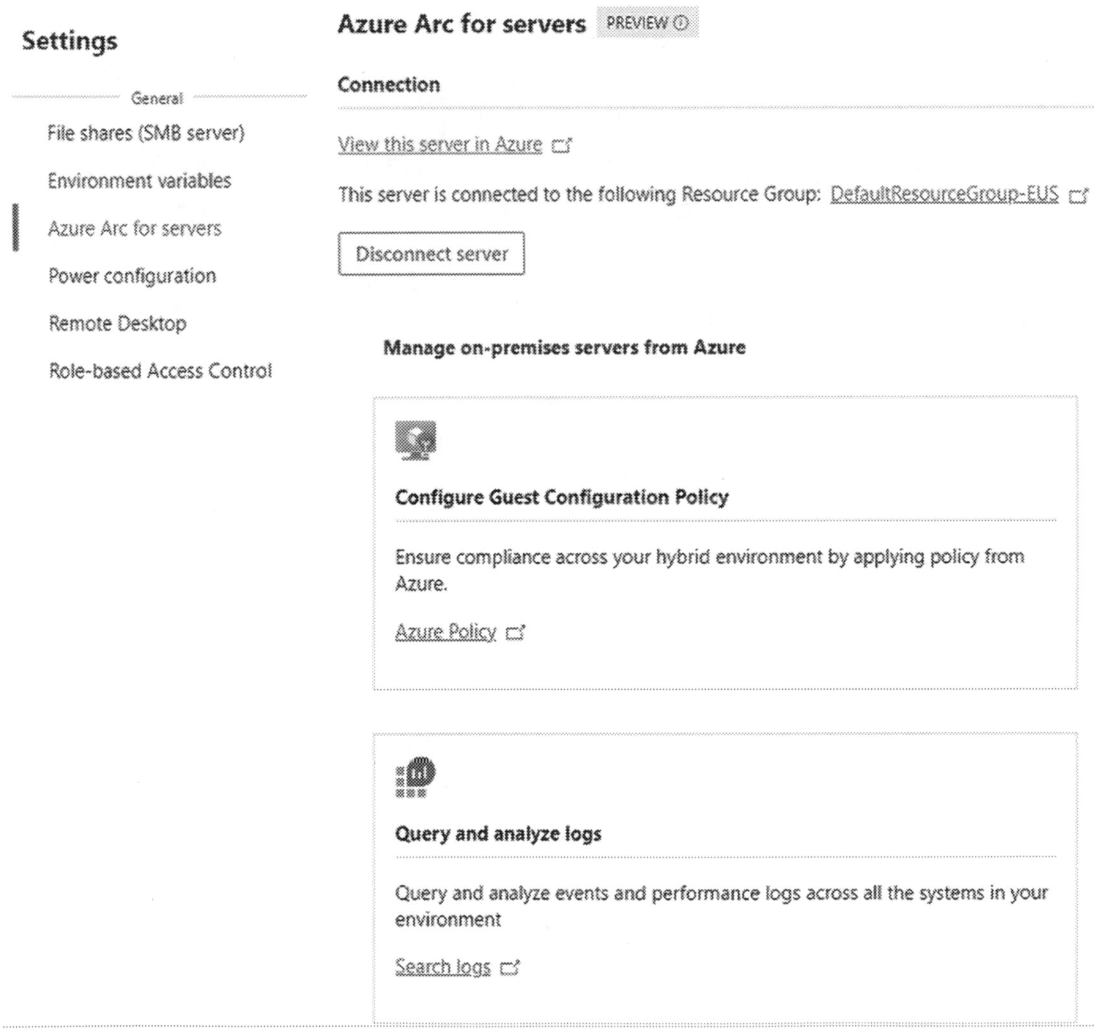

Figure 5-15. *Azure Arc for servers integrated with Windows Admin Center*

To onboard subsequent servers, you don't need to repeat steps 1 to 9; in fact, you can start with step 10: From a connected server's **Setup** blade, open the **Azure Arc for servers** item, and click the **Get started** button. Repeat steps 10 and 11 for all the servers you want to onboard to Azure Arc.

Using Tags with Azure Arc Servers

When a hybrid machine is connected to Azure, it becomes a connected machine and benefits from standard Azure constructs such as Azure Policy and applying tags. The ability to easily organize and manage server inventory using Azure as a management engine greatly reduces administrative complexity and provides a consistent strategy for hybrid and multi-cloud environments. Applying and using tags with Azure Arc servers is a force multiplier for your organization. Figure 5-16 is a reminder of how tags present themselves in the Azure portal Overview page of any given Azure Arc server.

Edit tags

Tags are name/value pairs that enable you to categorize resources and view consolidated billing by applying the same tag to multiple resources and resource groups. Tag names are case insensitive, but tag values are case sensitive. Learn more about tags

Tags

Name		Value
City	:	Bellevue
CountryOrRegion	:	USA
Datacenter	:	'Datacenter 2'
State	:	Washington

Resource

Luther (Server - Azure Arc)

Datacenter : 'Datacenter 2' City : Bellevue State : Washington CountryOrRegion : USA

No changes

Figure 5-16. *Azure resource tags applied to an Azure Arc server*

Add Business Value with Tags

The best tagging schemes include a business-aligned focus, such as accounting, business ownership, and business criticality that reflect business interests and maintain those standards over time. Investing in a tagging system provides improved accounting for costs and value of IT assets to the overall business. This association of an asset's business value to its operational cost is a key activity in changing the cost center perception of IT within your wider organization.

Organizing cloud-based resources is a crucial task for IT, unless you only have simple deployments. Here are some tagging standards to consider for organizing your resources, with example tag `name/value` pairs as they might apply in the management of Azure Arc servers:

- Resource management: `City/Bellevue, Datacenter/West-Campus`
- Cost management and optimization: `Department/Marketing, Promotion/Spring2020`
- Operations management: `Vendor/Dell, Network/HQ-LAN-A`
- Security: `Owner/Jill.Smith@company.com, JIT enabled/Yes`
- Governance and regulatory compliance: `HIPAA HITRUST/Yes, ISO 27001/Yes`
- Automation: `Backup Policy/DailyFull-LRS-Retain365days, Patching Group/Wave2-West`
- Workload optimization: `Shutdown allowed/Weekend-Holiday, Shutdown allowed/Weeknight-Weekend-Holiday`

Figure 5-17 provides a suggestion on getting started with tags, which is the **Tags** page available in your Azure portal. Notice in the left column are listed all the tag name/value pairs found on resources in your Azure subscription. Clicking on any tag pair in the left calls up a detail view on the right of all Azure resources with that same tag name/value pair.

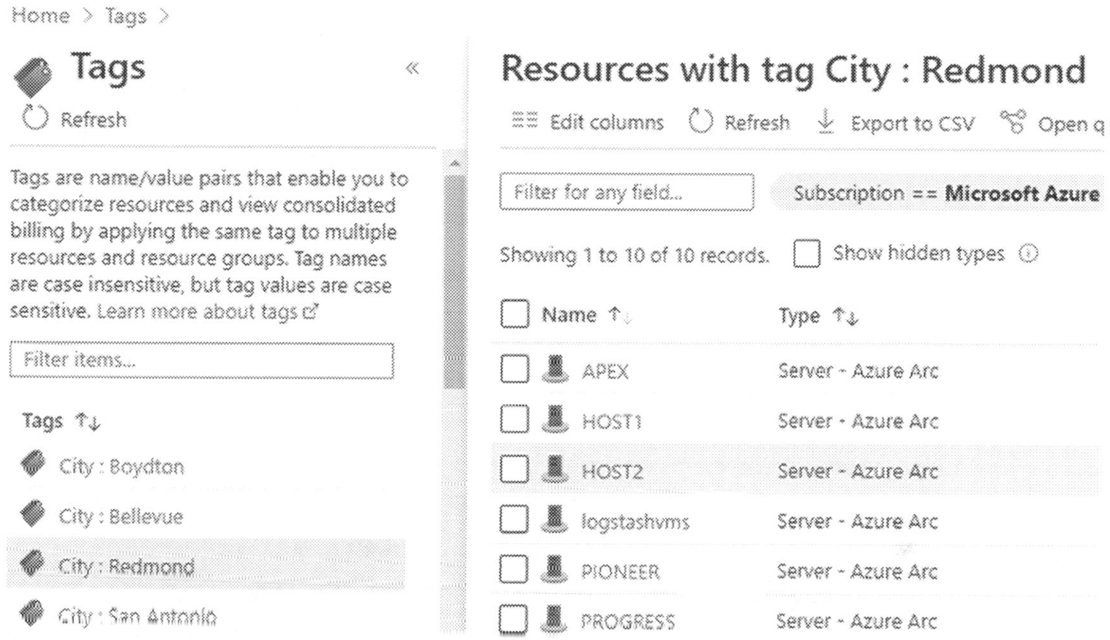

Figure 5-17. *Using the Tags pane in the Azure portal to explore tag associations*

All About Azure Resource Tags

- *Tags* are a semirandom piece of management metadata used by humans and processes to signal and interact with one another. You or a process leaves a tag to be read by another human or process to help make a future decision or select an automated action. Think of them as *flags* or *markers*.
- Azure resource tags have two elements: a tag name and a tag value, like `City/Bellevue`.
- Each Azure Arc server can have one tag of each name (like "City"), so you can only associate one value of the tag type (like "Bellevue") with each server. In other words, you can't have two City tags on one server, and you can only have one value field (like a city name) for each tag.

- The universe of tag names and tag values is remembered by Azure. You can precreate tag names and values to make them available to users to select when creating new resources. Azure also remembers all tags and values already present in the subscription. To avoid tag sprawl, have a tag name and value pair plan in mind and help users stick to it.
- You build management products and solutions like alerting, queries, policies, reports, and dashboards that sort and key on tags. First, you assign tags and values to resources; then you craft management artifacts that look for the tags you have deployed. Think of this simple example: your server admin or a provisioning process adds a tag about a specific backup policy to a server. Backup automation scans for computers with that tag and automatically applies the correct backup policy–backups just start happening. All from adding a single tag.
- Using Azure policies, you can cause Azure resources to automatically inherit tags from their resource groups. Also using Azure policies, you can enforce the presence of specific tags to perform operations tasks. Large Azure estates are well managed with policies and tags.... Azure Arc is your opportunity to leverage this advanced management paradigm across *your* entire estate, both in-Azure and not in-Azure.

Apply Inventory Tagging to Azure Arc-Enabled Servers

The following steps will create a helpful server inventory management capability that demonstrates using tags with Azure Arc servers. Notice we are creating meaningful tag values that match our environment and that we intend to use for our management purposes. (Only create tag values that will be used, not just "nice to have.") Replace the vendor names and virtualization types with values that exist in your environment.

1. Open the Azure CLI in your Azure portal and run the following commands to create a basic taxonomy that lets you query and report on what kind of hardware or virtualization platform your Azure Arc servers are associated with:

```
az tag create --name "Server Platform"
az tag add-value --name "Server Platform" --value "HP Host"
az tag add-value --name "Server Platform" --value "Dell Host"
az tag add-value --name "Server Platform" --value "HV Guest"
az tag add-value --name "Server Platform" --value "ESX Guest"
```

2. Now you need to add the tag name/value pairs to the Azure Arc servers in your subscription. This Azure PowerShell adds the "Server Platform/Dell Host" value to an on-premises physical computer:

   ```
   $tag = @{"Server Platform"="Dell Host"}
   $VM = Get-AzResource -ResourceGroupName RG-DEV-EUS -Name Venus
   Set-AzResource -ResourceId $vm.Id -Tag $tag -Force
   ```

   Rerun this set of PowerShell for each Azure Arc server, changing the Server Platform tag as appropriate.

3. After you have applied *Server Platform* tags to all your Azure Arc servers, use **Resource Graph Explorer** to query them and get insight into your multi-cloud landscape. In the query window, enter the following query:

   ```
   Resources
   | where type =~ 'Microsoft.HybridCompute/machines'
   | where isnotempty(tags['Server Platform'])
   | project name, location, resourceGroup, tags
   ```

   Azure Resource Graph Explorer, part of Azure portal, enables running Resource Graph queries directly in the Azure portal.

4. Click **Run Query** and then select the **Formatted Results** toggle. As seen in Figure 5-18, all Azure Arc-enabled servers and their assigned Server Platform tag values are listed. You can easily query and report on how your server resources are hosted. For example, you could pin the results as a chart that provides real-time dynamic information on Azure Arc servers to your portal workflow.

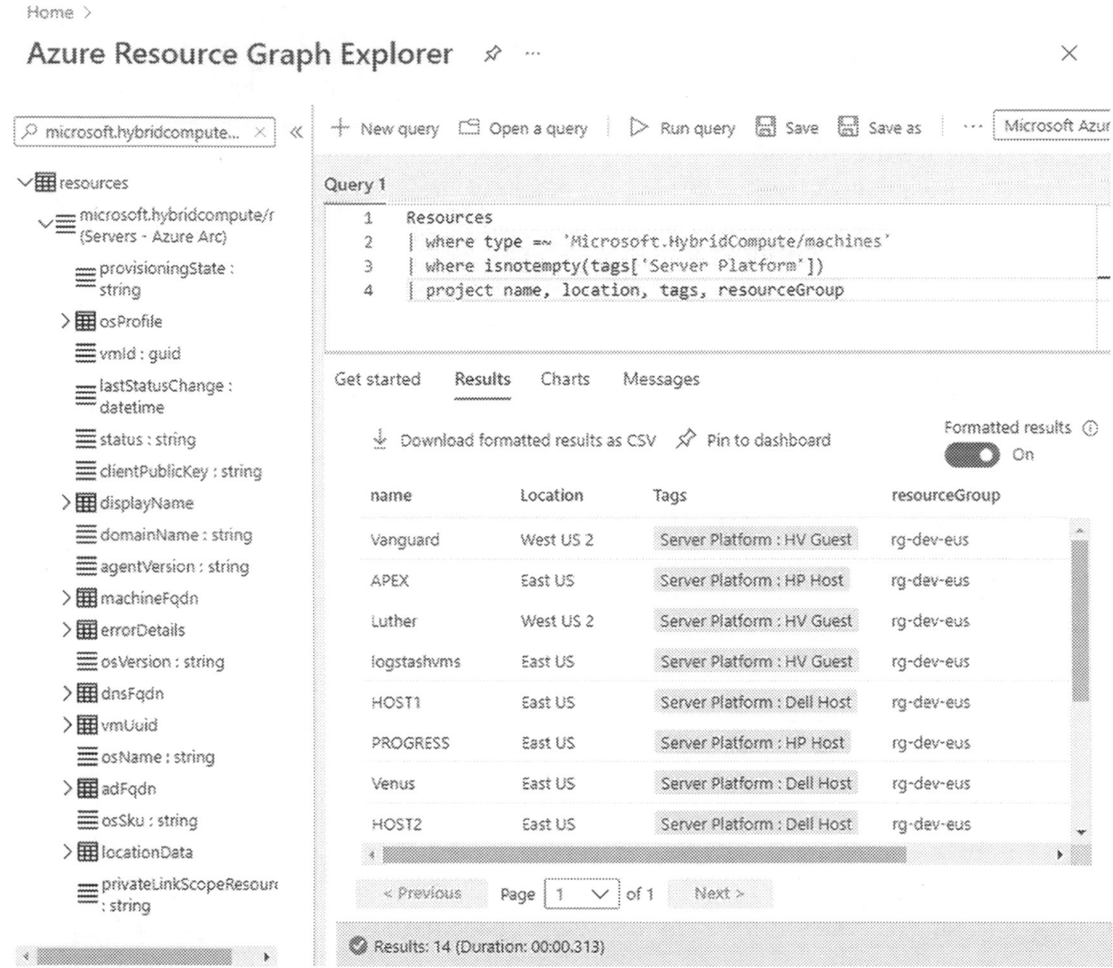

Figure 5-18. *Azure Resource Graph Explorer displaying formatted results*

Dashboard Hybrid Server Data with Azure Monitor Workbooks

Visualizations such as charts and graphs can help you analyze your monitoring data to drill down on issues and identify patterns. Azure Monitor workbooks and dashboards allow you to tap into multiple data sources from across Azure and combine them into single-pane-of-glass experiences.

In the case of Azure Arc servers, we can exploit this capability to create a fused display of all servers in all clouds. Follow these steps to create an Azure Monitor workbook that features a true "All Servers" view:

1. From the **Workbooks** blade of your **Azure Log Analytics** workspace, click the **New** button.

2. Click **Edit** under the New workbook text item and optionally change the title and text, for example, to "Azure Arc workbook," and then click **Done Editing**.

3. In the **Editing query item: query -2** section, change the Query Data source to **Azure Resource Graph**, change the **Visualization** and **Size** to "Grid" and "Full," and paste this query as seen in Figure 5-19. Click Run Query and observe both Azure VMs and Azure Arc servers are listed in the grid.

```
resources
| where type == "microsoft.hybridcompute/machines" or type == "microsoft.
compute/virtualmachines"
| mvexpand prop=properties.provisioningState
| project ComputerName = id,  Status = properties.status, State=prop,
location, resourceGroup, type, tags
```

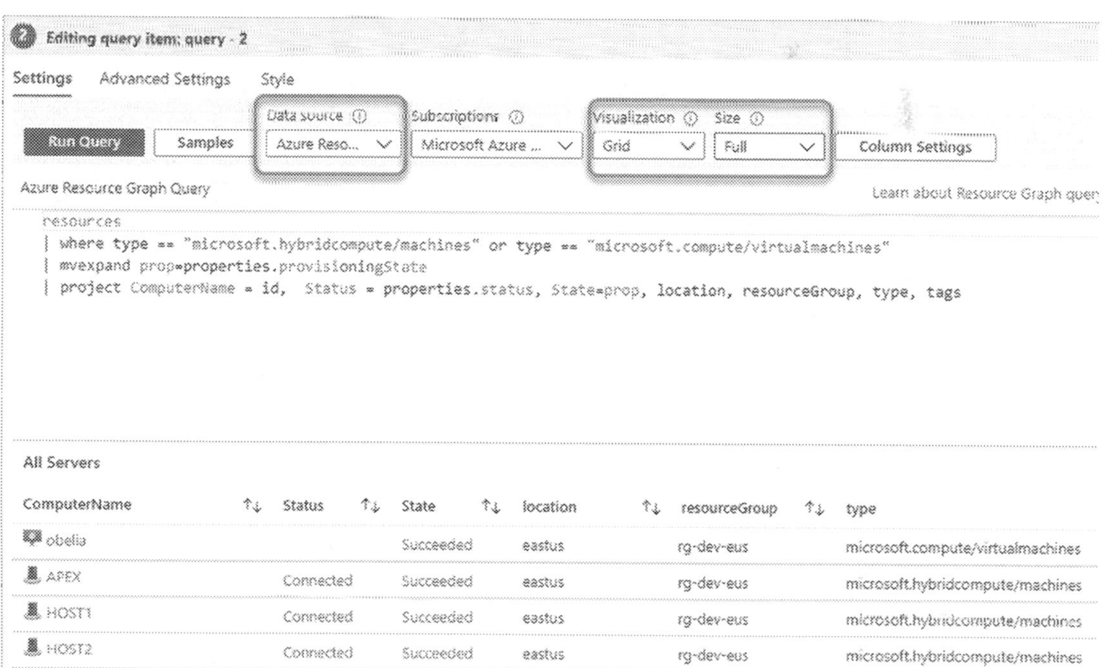

Figure 5-19. *Embedding an Azure Resource Graph grid in an Azure Monitor workbook*

4. Click the Advanced Settings tab and enter "All Servers" for the Chart title, and then click Done Editing.

5. Click Done Editing at the top of the workbook, and then click the Save icon. Give the workbook a name such as "Azure Arc" and click the Save button.

6. Figure 5-20 displays the workbook so far, cleanly listing all Windows and Linux servers in Azure and in other clouds including their tags. Clicking the "pin" icon will save this workbook to your selected dashboard where accurate live data about all your server assets will always be available.

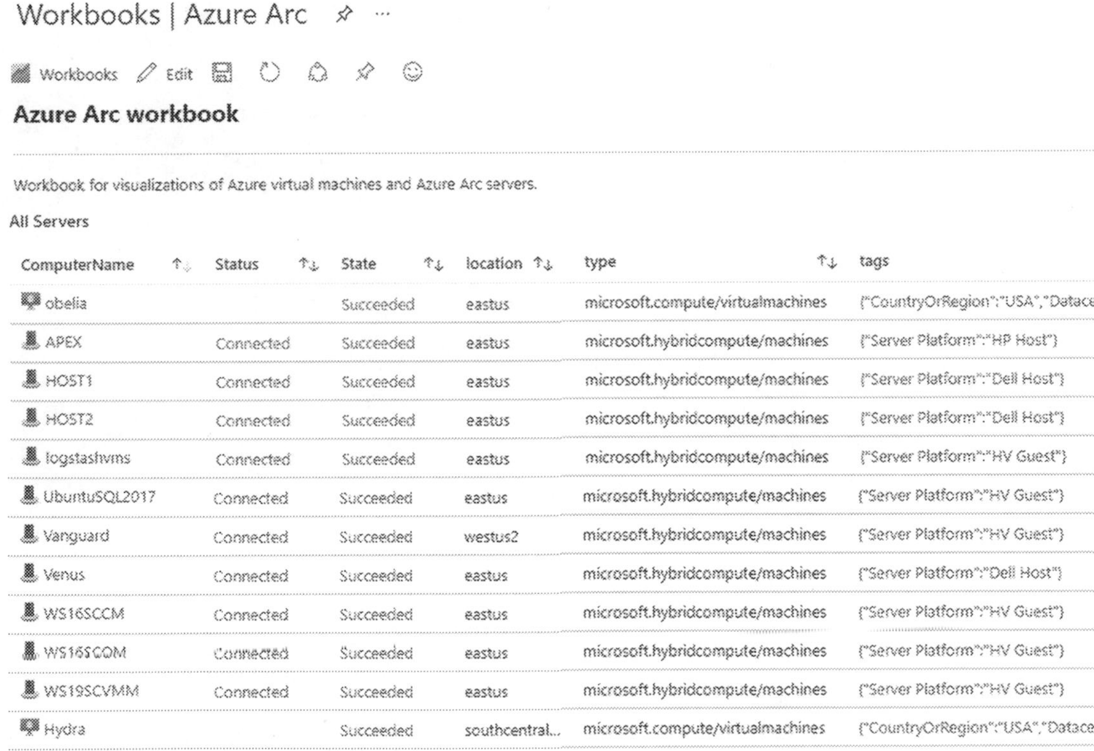

ComputerName	Status	State	location	type	tags
obelia		Succeeded	eastus	microsoft.compute/virtualmachines	{"CountryOrRegion":"USA","Datace
APEX	Connected	Succeeded	eastus	microsoft.hybridcompute/machines	{"Server Platform":"HP Host"}
HOST1	Connected	Succeeded	eastus	microsoft.hybridcompute/machines	{"Server Platform":"Dell Host"}
HOST2	Connected	Succeeded	eastus	microsoft.hybridcompute/machines	{"Server Platform":"Dell Host"}
logstashvms	Connected	Succeeded	eastus	microsoft.hybridcompute/machines	{"Server Platform":"HV Guest"}
UbuntuSQL2017	Connected	Succeeded	eastus	microsoft.hybridcompute/machines	{"Server Platform":"HV Guest"}
Vanguard	Connected	Succeeded	westus2	microsoft.hybridcompute/machines	{"Server Platform":"HV Guest"}
Venus	Connected	Succeeded	eastus	microsoft.hybridcompute/machines	{"Server Platform":"Dell Host"}
WS16SCCM	Connected	Succeeded	eastus	microsoft.hybridcompute/machines	{"Server Platform":"HV Guest"}
WS16SCOM	Connected	Succeeded	eastus	microsoft.hybridcompute/machines	{"Server Platform":"HV Guest"}
WS19SCVMM	Connected	Succeeded	eastus	microsoft.hybridcompute/machines	{"Server Platform":"HV Guest"}
Hydra		Succeeded	southcentral...	microsoft.compute/virtualmachines	{"CountryOrRegion":"USA","Datace

***Figure 5-20.** The hybrid estate visualized: Azure VMs and Azure Arc servers in a single list*

7. Let us add one more visualization that demonstrates the mapping capability of Azure Resource Graph and Azure Monitor workbooks. Click the Add query button at the very bottom of the workbook

8. In the Editing query item section, change the Query Data source to Azure Resource Graph, change the Visualization and Size to "Map" and "Medium," and paste this query.

```
resources
| where type == "microsoft.hybridcompute/machines" or
type == "microsoft.compute/virtualmachines"
| extend location
| summarize VMCount=count() by location
| order by VMCount desc
```

9. Click **Run Query** and observe the world map showing the count of Azure VMs and Azure Arc servers located in each Azure region (Figure 5-21). Using default "heat map" topology, sites with a higher count have larger circles and warmer colors.

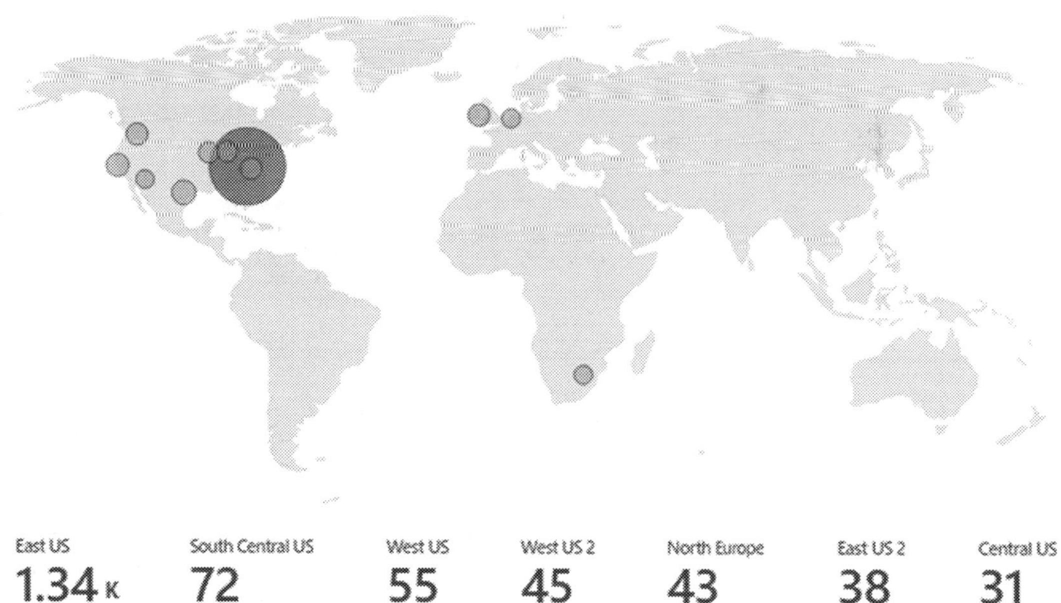

***Figure 5-21.** The hybrid estate mapped: Combined locations of Azure VMs and Azure Arc servers*

10. Click the **Advanced Settings** tab and enter “Server counts by region” for the Chart title, then click **Done Editing** twice, and then click the **Save** icon.

Troubleshooting Azure Arc Server Status

Azure Arc Agent Installation Issues

The Azure Arc agent is very low maintenance and is quick and easy to install and uninstall. Agent installation issues can involve either the Azure subscription side and/or the Azure Arc server side. If your Azure Arc installation script running the **azcmagent** tool can get to Microsoft but fails during installation, look to the *Activity log* in your Azure subscription for clues on cloud-side failure.

For example, Figure 5-22 shows the reason for an Azure Arc machine onboarding failure was that the *Microsoft.HybridCompute* resource provider wasn’t registered with the Azure subscription. Type “Azure Arc machines” in the search filter to show just Azure activity log entries involving Azure Arc servers.

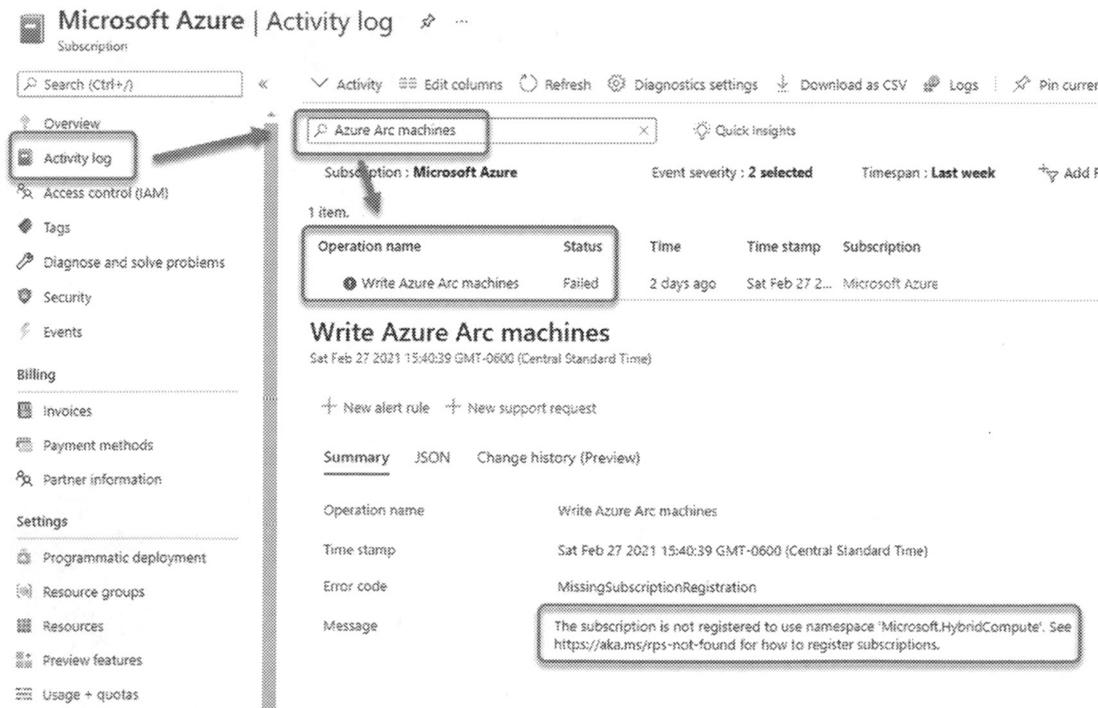

Figure 5-22. *Azure Activity log is key for troubleshooting agent onboarding failure*

If your installation process is blocked by Azure communications or local access issues, the logs of the **azcmagent** tool when set to "verbose" operation will be most relevant. To collect the verbose logs, attempt installation of the Azure Connected Machine Agent using the azcmagent.exe tool and the switch "`--verbose`," and then review the logs at these locations for clues on agent-side failure:

Agent Log locations

- Windows Azure Arc agent installation log location

  `%ProgramData%\AzureConnectedMachineAgent\Log\azcmagent.log`

- Linux Azure Arc agent installation log location

  `/var/opt/azcmagent/log/azcmagent.log`

Agent Installation Command Lines

The following are examples of the commands to enable verbose logging with the Connected Machine agent for Windows and Linux when performing an at-scale installation using a service principal:

- Windows Azure Arc agent installation

```
& "$env:ProgramFiles\AzureConnectedMachineAgent\azcmagent.
exe" connect --resource-group "resourceGroupName" --tenant-
id "tenantID" --location "regionName" --subscription-id
"subscriptionID" -verbose
```

- Linux Azure Arc agent installation

```
azcmagent connect --resource-group "resourceGroupName"
--tenant-id "tenantID" --location "regionName"
--subscription-id "subscriptionID" --verbose
```

Agent Uninstall Procedures

- **Uninstall the Windows agent** from Control Panel ➤ Programs and Features ➤ Azure Connected Machine Agent ➤ Uninstall <u>or</u> run the agent setup wizard by double-clicking the *AzureConnectedMachineAgent.msi* installer package.

- **Uninstall the Linux agent** using one of the following commands depending on your Linux OS:
  - Ubuntu:

    ```
    sudo apt purge azcmagent
    ```

  - RHEL, CentOS, Amazon Linux:

    ```
    sudo yum remove azcmagent
    ```

  - SLES:

    ```
    sudo zypper remove azcmagent
    ```

Azure Arc Agent Operations Issues

In operation, agent communication is simple: about every 5 minutes there is an outbound heartbeat communication to an HTTPS endpoint in the Microsoft cloud in the region where the Azure Arc server exists. Figure 5-23 shows the normal status of the Windows and Linux agents sending heartbeat messages. (An HTTP status code of 204 means "success, no additional content to send.")

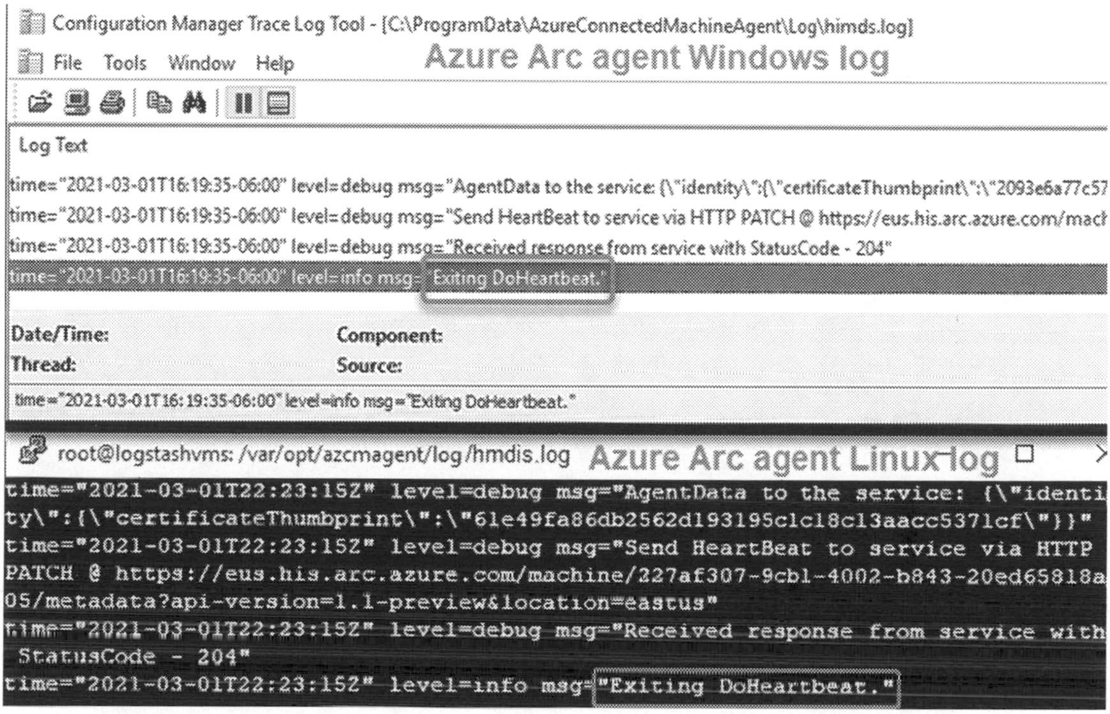

Figure 5-23. *Windows and Linux Azure Arc agents sending heartbeat messages*

If that outbound communication is interrupted, on the client side, you will see error messages in the **himds.log** file of the Azure Arc server. That is, following the "Send Heartbeat to service via HTTP" messages, there will not be an HTTP Status code of 204; there will be something else that might help you understand what's wrong.

Identifying Disconnected Azure Arc Servers

On the Azure cloud side, a loss of the agent heartbeat will cause the Azure Arc server status to change from Connected to Disconnected within 15 minutes. The following Azure Resource Graph query will only return data when one or more Azure Arc servers are not in a connected status:

```
resources
| where type == "microsoft.hybridcompute/machines"
| project ComputerName = id,  Status = properties.status, location,
resourceGroup, type, tags
| where Status != "Connected"
```

Consider saving the preceding Azure Resource Graph query to the Azure Arc workbook we authored previously in this chapter (name it "Azure Arc agents not Connected"). If any Azure Arc server names appear in the grid, you need to investigate the Azure Connected Machine Agent status of the involved servers. Figure 5-24 shows a couple of Azure Arc servers in a disconnected status.

Azure Arc agents not Connected

ComputerName ↑↓	Status ↑↓	location ↑↓
Luther	Disconnected	westus2
Vanguard	Disconnected	westus2

Figure 5-24. *Azure Resource Graph query produces a list of disconnected Azure Arc servers*

Azure Arc Services on Windows and Linux Computers

A common cause of Azure Arc servers having a disconnected status is that one or more Azure Arc services (or daemons) are stopped on the computer. Here are some tips on identifying and restarting the services and daemons used by Azure Arc.

Windows services

- Azure Hybrid Instance Metadata Service (himds)
- Guest Configuration Arc Service (GCArcService)
- Guest Configuration Extension service (ExtensionService)

Commands to restart all Azure Arc services on a Windows computer (which requires running in an elevated PowerShell session):

```
Restart-Service -Name himds
Restart-Service -Name GCArcService
Restart-Service -Name ExtensionService
```

Linux daemons

- Azure Connected Machine Agent Service (himdsd.service)
- GC Arc Service (gcad.service)
- Extension Service (extd.service)

Commands to restart all Azure Arc daemons on a Linux computer:

```
sudo systemctl restart himdsd.service
sudo systemctl restart gcad.service
sudo systemctl restart extd.service
```

Tip If you have deployed the Azure Automation Change tracking solution to your Azure Arc servers, you can run the following scheduled query alert rule to find out when Azure Arc-dependent services are stopped on Windows and Linux computers:

```
ConfigurationChange | where ConfigChangeType contains
"WindowsServices" or ConfigChangeType contains "Daemons"
| where SvcState contains "Stopped" | where SvcPreviousState
contains "Running"
| where SvcName in ("himds", "GCArcService",
"ExtensionService", "himdsd.service", "gcad.service",
"extd.service")
```

Summary

In this chapter, you learned how to deploy and manage Azure Arc servers at scale, which included creating and using an Azure AD service principal. We also covered more advanced Azure Arc features like tags and dashboarding, as well as troubleshooting Azure Arc servers in all scenarios. You have all the knowledge now to expertly deploy and support Azure Arc-connected machines. In the following two chapters, we will build out two enterprise solutions using Azure Arc. Chapter 6, “Hybrid Server Monitoring Solution,” deploys a monitoring and alerting solution, and Chapter 7, “Regulatory and Security Compliance for Azure Arc Servers,” deploys a security solution.

CHAPTER 6

Hybrid Server Monitoring Solution

This chapter describes a stand-alone end-to-end server monitoring solution based on Azure Monitor platform services. Previous chapters helped you build out your Azure-based management framework; now we do something valuable and cost-effective with it. The solution delivers server infrastructure monitoring to Azure VMs and Azure Arc servers in an Azure subscription. The solution will notify your team when monitored servers go down or have a serious issue.

This solution encompasses an assembly of Azure microservices that probe and assess the availability, configuration, and performance of a server's OS. It achieves parity with existing industry-standard tools for monitoring of core server functions (availability, configuration, and performance). Being a cloud-native solution, with the novel Azure Connected Machine Agent (Azure Arc) that extends the cloud framework to noncloud endpoints, there's nothing like it.

This solution represents a new industry paradigm: suitable, low-cost server monitoring delivered via a no-cost cloud service management platform. The solution offers infinite scale and global availability. Organizations that successfully migrate their server monitoring tools from more costly legacy applications will achieve a competitive advantage.

Solution High-Level Features

Consider the solution architecture as having three primary features: management control plane, rule set, and notification workflow. These are described in the following, along with the Azure services in the solution that constitute the feature.

S. Buchanan and J. Joyner, *Azure Arc-Enabled Kubernetes and Servers*,
https://doi.org/10.1007/978-1-4842-7768-3_6

1. A management control plane that delivers monitoring, security, access, and governance
    - Azure Lighthouse and Azure Commercial Marketplace
    - Azure Arc and Azure Resource Manager (ARM)
    - Azure Policy
    - Azure VM Extensions
    - Microsoft Management Agent (MMA)/Azure Management Agent (AMA)
2. A set of monitors and rules that collect and analyze data from managed computers
    - Azure Log Analytics
    - Azure VM Insights Guest Health
    - Azure Automation (Updating and Configuration Management)
    - Azure Scheduled Query Alert Rules
3. Methods of responding to alerts such as performing automated workflow and alert notification to ticketing systems
    - Azure Alert Action Groups
    - Azure Alert Action Rules
    - Azure Logic Apps

What gets monitored: The curated set of monitors and rules that are deployed in this solution–which achieve effective server OS monitoring from Azure Monitor–includes detection of the most common alerts from rules and alert-generating monitors contained in the System Center Operations Center (SCOM) management packs for Windows Server OS.

What it costs: The Azure consumption cost to deliver the specific monitoring services can be estimated at **$5.00 per month per server**. This estimate is in line with the Azure pricing calculator recommendation that most servers produce from 1 GB to 3 GB of log ingestion per month ($1.30 = 1 GB in less expensive region, to $5.10 = 3 GB in more expensive region). Depending on your market and currency, $5 per server is a conservative and validated round number.

Solution Diagram

Figure 6-1 diagrams the Azure services that deliver the solution features. Here is a visual guide to the diagram:

1. Starting in the lower right, either **Azure AD users** or **Azure Lighthouse service provider security groups** are the identities that will access the Azure subscription.
2. **Azure RBAC** (role-based access control) is used to associate Azure AD users with security roles in the Azure subscription. In the **Azure Lighthouse** scenario, an offer is accepted by the customer that associates service provider staff with delegated security rights in the customer Azure subscription.
3. Authorized users or service principals use their RBAC or delegated access to assign **Azure Policy** to **Azure VMs** and **Azure Arc servers**.
4. The policy causes the computers to become monitored by **Azure Monitor** (center) using the MMA and connecting them to a Log Analytics workspace (center right).
5. **Azure VM Extensions** install the AMA and connect the VMs to the VM Guest Health monitor (center left).
6. Continuing left, **VM Guest Health** *Warning* and *Critical* state changes trigger launch of a **Logic App**, which conditionally creates an alert notification (red triangle).
7. **Alert rules** (upper left) are run on a scheduled basis looking for log or metric data indicating problems.
8. Alerts arising from scheduled alert rules (top left) are optionally suppressed **by Azure Monitor alert action rules**; this is how you account for computer-specific overrides on scheduled alert rules.
9. Moving up the right side from the center, **Log Analytics solutions** installed in **the Log Analytics workspace** include linkage with an **Azure Automation account**.
10. Solutions in the automation account include **Update Management** (top right) and **Configuration Management** solutions (top center).

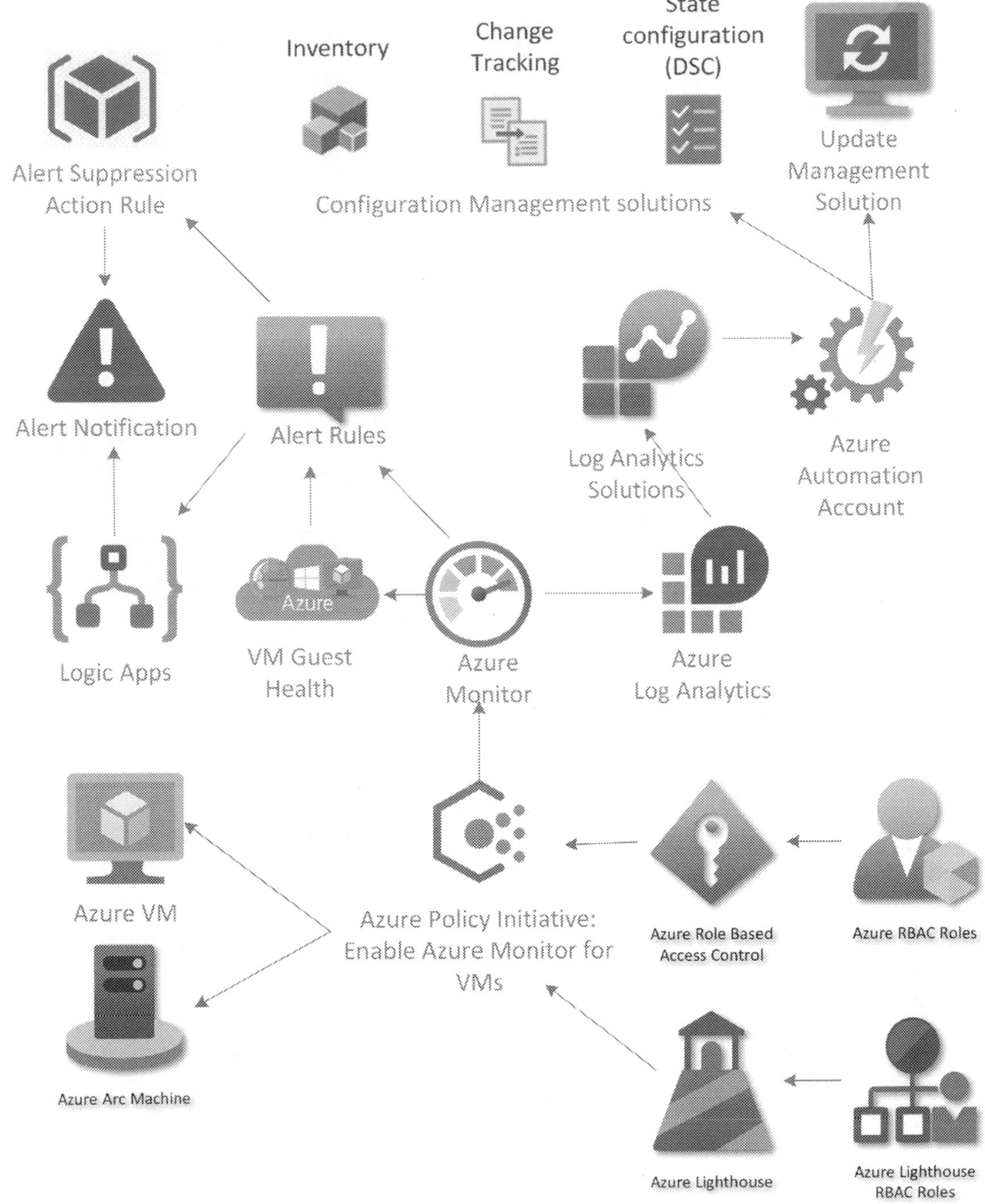

Figure 6-1. *Azure Monitoring solution powered by Azure Arc and Azure Policy*

Specific Monitoring Features

To answer the question *What does the solution monitor?*, the following specific list is provided. The monitor and alert selection, as well as alerting thresholds, are derived from the default monitoring profile of the SCOM management pack for Windows Server.

Rule and Monitor List

1. Azure Monitor heartbeat failure (two or fewer heartbeats in last 5 minutes).
2. Logical disk transfer (reads and writes) latency is too high.
3. Memory Pages Per Second is too High.
4. Logical Disk Free Space is low.
5. Available Megabytes of Memory is too low.
6. Total CPU Utilization Percentage is too high.
7. Logical disk current queue length is too high.
8. Service entered unpredictable state.
9. Duplicate IP Address has been Detected.
10. NTFS–File System Corrupt.
11. Malware threat detected on computer.
12. Unexpected shutdown detected.
13. A core Windows service has stopped (12 specific services are monitored).
14. A previously running Windows service has stopped.

In addition to alerting products from the rule and monitor list, the solution deploys these high-value products:

- **Azure Automation Updating solution** provides server-specific and whole-organization views of installed and missing/needed updates on all Windows and Linux servers in all locations.

- **Azure Automation Configuration Management solutions** perform checks on software, file systems, Windows registry, Windows servers, and Linux daemons. Changes are logged and before-and-after change detection readouts are automatic.
- **Azure Monitor Workbooks** are installed for diagram-based visual assistance in current, trending, and historical availability and performance data. Workbooks can be deployed as Azure Dashboards for management displays.

Azure Lighthouse

Azure Lighthouse was created expressly for service providers, but it also has use in larger organizations that have multiple Azure AD tenants. In enterprise and academic scenarios, the tenant where "shared services" or the "instructor" are located can use "Service Provider" Lighthouse delegations to seamlessly manage Azure subscriptions owned by other Azure AD tenants, such as "Customer" subordinate, "student", or partner companies.

Azure Lighthouse allows a one-to-many approach with service provider staff and Azure artifacts like monitoring rules and ARM templates shared across many customer tenants. That is, one Azure AD tenant (the service provider) gets delegated permissions to an Azure subscription that belongs to a different tenant (the customer). It happens when the service provider makes an "offer" available to the customer. Then the customer accepts the offer and delegates their subscription(s) and/or resource groups to the specific Azure AD security groups that exist in the service provider tenant and that were specified in the offer.

The Azure Lighthouse offer is a revocable, one-way, verifiable, and granular trust that eliminates the need for duplicate accounts to exist in customer domains for each service provider employee (or worse, shared accounts). Customer audit logs show the actual name of the service provider staff member that had activity in the customer subscription. If the service provider enforces multifactor authentication (MFA) for all employee logins, the solution allows the service provider to guarantee that only MFA access occurs on customer resources.

In the solution described in this chapter, any Azure Lighthouse involvement is optional. However, if Azure Lighthouse is employed, the solution is fully functional for all multitenant monitoring scenarios.

Azure Arc

After initial Microsoft Azure successes with the "classic" or original Azure data center fabric controller, there were scaling and other limitations discovered. Microsoft had to invent a way to administer and orchestrate the global Azure cloud at hyperscale. The resulting "V2" technology was called Azure Resource Manager (ARM), sometimes called the Azure *control plane*, and it powers all of Azure today. Think of ARM as Azure's own OS, the "master controller." We communicate fundamentally with ARM using documents written in the JSON format, also called *ARM templates*.

ARM is proven hyperscalable and hyperreliable at managing IT objects and services. **Azure Arc** is a name for a new concept that extends the economies of scale and benefits of ARM to objects that are not in Azure. In this solution, Azure Arc server objects are created in the Azure subscription that, to ARM, resemble Azure VMs. To ARM, both objects are computers, and computer management paradigms can be applied across environments. Azure policies to monitor the computers can be applied to both Azure VMs and non-Azure servers by ARM because of Azure Arc.

Azure Arc makes noncloudy servers cloudy from a management perspective. The economic implications are that using Azure Arc for management of noncloud servers will yield cost benefits. The benefits arise from using Azure management features like policy, tags, and resource groups for free–and from consuming (or delivering) other cloud services like monitoring, security, and backup with almost zero incidental or intermediate "management tool" cost.

Azure Arc Server

As we covered in Chapter 4, "Azure Arc Servers: Getting Started," Azure Arc installs an application on a non-Azure computer–the **Azure Connected Machine Agent** for non-Azure computers–that performs the same functions as the in-Azure **Windows Azure Guest Agent** that runs in every Azure VM by default. The Windows Azure Guest Agent is essentially an out-of-band administration channel for managing the Azure VM. The main thing the Windows Azure Guest Agent does for Azure VMs is install and maintain Azure VM Extensions, which are applets and services that actually do monitoring work. Azure Arc's Azure Connected Machine Agent does the same thing for non-Azure computers. The Azure Arc agent connects the non-Azure server to the Azure control plane as a hybrid machine object.

In this solution, you don't install a monitoring agent on servers. Rather, you install the Azure Arc agent on non-Azure servers. Then configure Azure Policy to install monitoring agents on the computers via Azure Arc. Azure Policy remediation tasks actually install the monitoring agents using a service principal in Azure AD that is created when the policy is assigned. In Figure 6-2, all the listed management applications on this Windows server were installed or verified by the first listed agent, the Azure Arc agent (Azure Connected Machine Agent).

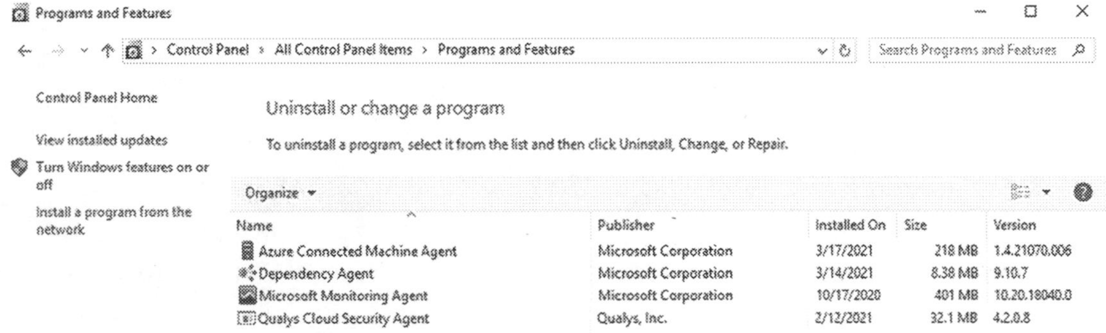

Figure 6-2. *The Azure Connected Machine Agent on this Azure Arc server installed the other programs using Azure VM Extensions*

Azure Arc servers are enrolled using scripts that run on the servers being onboarded. The scripts log into the Azure AD tenant of the person or service principal running the onboarding script. Then if the person or service has the appropriate security access, an ARM resource record (an ARM object) for the Azure Arc server is created in the specified Azure subscription, resource group, and Azure region. The Azure Arc server is silently issued a digital certificate that acts as the computer's unique identity provider to Azure.

Azure Policy

Azure Policy consistently applies monitoring and management settings across Azure VMs and Azure Arc servers. Specifically, in this solution, all Windows and Linux servers–in all locations and clouds–have their compliance with the core monitoring objective assessed with the same, single policy initiative. When servers are ready to start being monitored, deploy an Azure Policy initiative that connects servers to an Azure Monitor instance in the subscription (Figure 6-3).

The core monitoring objective is to connect each computer to a selected Azure Log Analytics workspace by installing two pieces of software on each computer: (1) the Microsoft Monitoring Agent (MMA) and (2) a Dependency agent. The Dependency agent supplements the MMA and provides the network-level information for the Service Map integration in VM Insights.

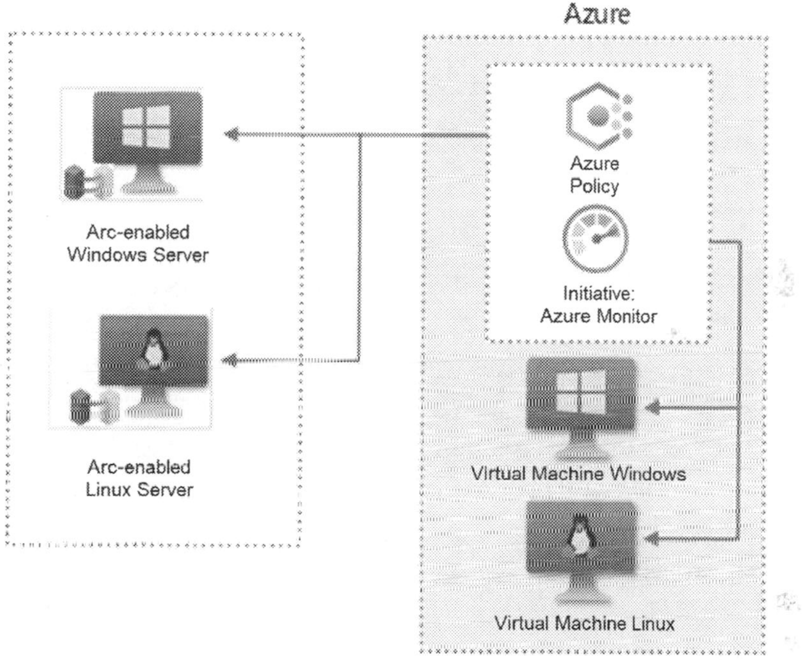

Figure 6-3. *Azure Policy pushes out the Enable Azure Monitor for VMs policy initiative to all servers in all locations*

There is a built-in Azure Policy initiative **Enable Azure Monitor for VMs** (Policy ➤ Authoring ➤ Definitions) that bundles ten policies. Eight policies are capable of *DeployifNotExist* remediation tasks:

1. Deploy Log Analytics agent to Windows Azure Arc machines.
2. Deploy–Configure Log Analytics agent to be enabled on Windows virtual machines.
3. Deploy Log Analytics agent to Linux Azure Arc machines.
4. Deploy Log Analytics agent for Linux VMs.
5. Deploy Dependency agent to Windows Azure Arc machines.

6. Deploy-configure Dependency agent to be enabled on Windows virtual machines.
7. Deploy Dependency agent to hybrid Linux Azure Arc machines.
8. Deploy Dependency agent for Linux virtual machines.
9. Two policies are of the of *AuditifNotExist* type that function to flag when nonstandard Azure VM image types are discovered that would otherwise prevent automatic remediation.
10. Log Analytics Agent should be enabled for listed virtual machine images.
11. Dependency agent should be enabled for listed virtual machine images.

Azure Policy Assignment

The **Enable Azure Monitor for VMs** initiative is assigned to subscription(s) and/or resource group(s) and is the primary vehicle for push-installing and centrally configurating the MMA and Dependency agent on all computers. Doing so will also detect configuration drift if computers fall out of compliance with the core monitoring objective.

At the time the initiative is assigned, a Managed Identity is created, which is an Azure AD Enterprise Application registration (service principal). The service principal is automatically granted the **Log Analytics Contributor** role in the Azure subscription or resource group. The service principal will have a random DisplayName like "27c1377f005d47578cecc397".

You can locate the service principal name by returning to edit the initiative assignment; on the **Remediation** tab is the Principal ID box with a GUID like "75943696-0879-432d-98e6-ae0aa439ed05". That GUID matches the Object ID of the Enterprise Application (service principal). You can cross-reference that Object ID back to the Name of the Azure AD service principal with the Azure PowerShell command Get-AzADServicePrincipal (demonstrated with output):

```
PS /home> Get-AzADServicePrincipal -ObjectId 75943696-0879-432d-98e6-
ae0aa439ed05

ServicePrincipalNames : {57aa357a-8f37-44c5-8fb5-ade220354465,
https://identity.azure.net/TzdI8YgzhpY339TyesufBsnmeXGgqUM56HhUnrT8S2k=}
ApplicationId         : e0ba357a-8f37-44c5-8fb5-ade220354564
ObjectType            : ServicePrincipal
DisplayName           : 27c1377f005d47578cecc397
Id                    : 75943696-0879-432d-98e6-ae0aa439ed05
```

For remediation tasks to work, the DisplayName of the service principal should be found in the subscription or resource group ➤ Access control (IAM) ➤ Role assignments under **Log Analytics Contributor**.

Azure Policy Enforcement Interval

The following are the times or events that will cause a policy resource to be evaluated:

- A resource is created, updated, or deleted in a scope with a policy assignment.
- A policy or initiative is newly assigned to a scope.
- A policy or initiative already assigned to a scope is updated.
- During the standard compliance evaluation cycle, which occurs once every 24 hours.

Tip You can trigger an on-demand Azure Policy enforcement in a resource group with this Azure PowerShell command:

```
Start-AzPolicyComplianceScan -ResourceGroupName '<rgname>'
-AsJob
```

Azure Policy Compliance

The goal of Azure Policy assignment is to achieve a 100% compliance state through a combination of remediation tasks and optional exemptions (Figure 6-4). When below a 100% compliance state, a list of specific computers and the policies that are not compliant is found at Policy ➤ Compliance ➤ Initiative ➤ Non-compliant resources.

The list of noncompliant resources is the worklist during solution deployment to identify computers needing remediation. After solution deployment, monitor that compliance remains at 100%, and when computers and policies fall out of compliance, do what is needed to restore 100% compliance.

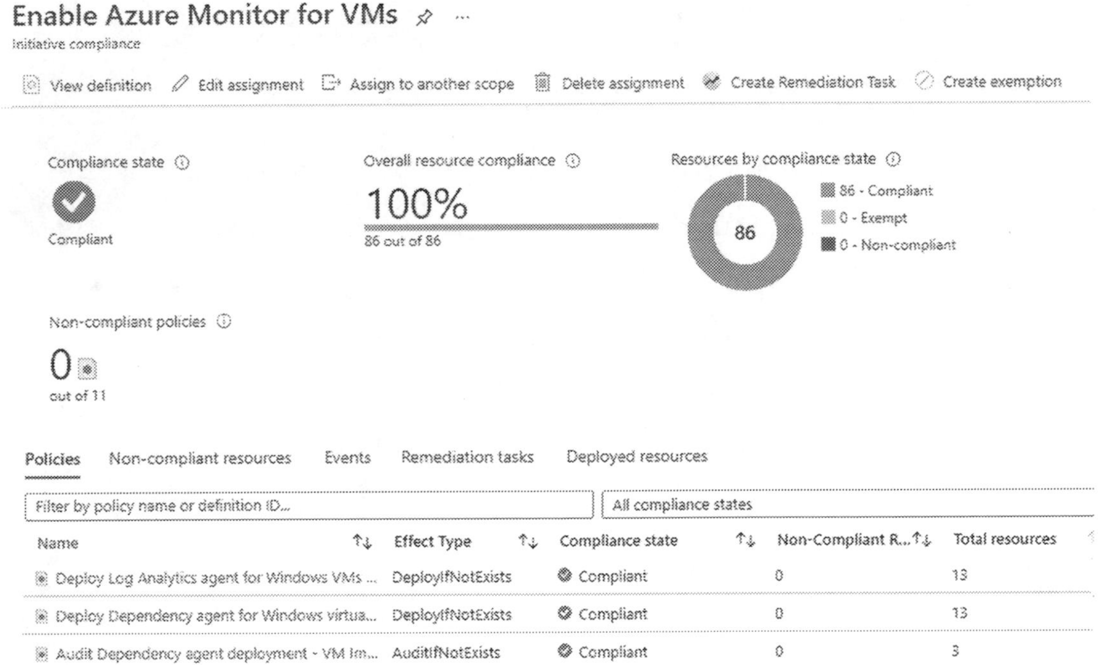

***Figure 6-4.** The Enable Azure Monitor for VMs policy initiative at 100% compliance in a resource group*

Azure Policy: Remediation Tasks

After assigning the **Enable Azure Monitor for VMs** initiative to the subscription or resource group, newly created resources (Azure VMs and Azure Arc servers) will be automatically remediated if non-compliant. For existing resources create **Remediation tasks** to push the necessary agents to their respective targets. Most servers will not have the Microsoft Management Agent (MMA) or the Dependency agent installed and configured for the target Log Analytics workspace. Indeed, Azure Policy is a two-step process for preexisting resources: Assign policy to identify noncompliant resources, and then launch remediation tasks to fix things.

Follow this protocol to deploy the solution with Azure Policy:

1. At Policy ➤ Compliance, select the **Enable Azure Monitor for VMs** initiative.
2. Click **Create Remediation task**.
3. For the Policy to remediate, select **Deploy Log Analytics agent for Windows VMs**.
4. Make sure the scope is correct (one computer, one resource group, or one subscription).
5. Check the Re-evaluate resource compliance before remediating.
6. Push **Remediate**.
7. Repeat from step 2 and select **Deploy Dependency agent for Windows virtual machines**.
8. Repeat steps 4, 5, and 6.
9. Repeat from step 2 again if appropriate for **Deploy Log Analytics agent for Linux VMs**, and then **Deploy Dependency agent for Linux virtual machines**.
10. After the first wave of remediation tasks, triage, and remedy failures, repeating remediation tasks as needed until all computers are in compliance. Create exceptions (covered next) as appropriate to boost the compliance percentage.

Unlisted Images

The default policies "fail-safe" to *noncompliant* when the precise source of the VMs OS disk is unknown to ARM. If some computers flag the audit policies for *VM Images (OS) unlisted*, it is necessary to clone the built-in initiative and create a custom initiative with custom policies for the Log Analytics Agent and Dependency agent policies. The custom policies will add your organization's custom *osDisk.creationOption* values so that the policy will accept and proceed to remediate.

For example, the following JSON code when spliced into the "policyRule": section of the will allow the use of attached and uploaded disk images:

```
{
  "allOf": [
    {
      "field": "Microsoft.Compute/virtualMachines/
      storageProfile.osDisk.createOption",
      "equals": "Attach"
    }
  ]
},
{
  "allOf": [
    {
      "field": "Microsoft.Compute/virtualMachines/
      storageProfile.osDisk.createOption",
      "equals": "FromImage"
    }
  ]
},
```

Multiple Management Groups

If MMA agent failure occurs during remediation tasks due to *multiple management groups*, you can install the VM Extension of the MMA manually using Azure PowerShell/Cloud Shell. The following example custom script adds the “"stopOnMultipleConnections" = $false” flag.

```
Connect-AzAccount

$PublicSettings = @{"workspaceId" = " fd75fd75-f70c-4fe5-bd39-afa5f70c
afa5";"stopOnMultipleConnections" = $false}
$ProtectedSettings =@{'workspaceKey' = 1234abcdxxxxxxxxxxxxxxxxxxxxxxx
xxxxxxxxxxxxxxxxxxxxxxxxxxxxxxxxxxxxxxxxxxxxxxx1234abcd=='}
```

```
Set-AzVMExtension -ResourceGroupName "MyResourceGroup" `
-VMName "MyAzureVM" `
-Publisher Microsoft.EnterpriseCloud.Monitoring `
-ExtensionType MicrosoftMonitoringAgent  `
-TypeHandlerVersion 1.0 `
-Settings $PublicSettings `
-ProtectedSettings $ProtectedSettings `
-Location "eastus2 `
-Name MicrosoftMonitoringAgent
```

For Azure Arc servers, if there is a large number of computers needing the modified VM Extension install policy, clone the built-in policy and create a custom initiative with custom policy for the Log Analytics Agent. Replace the built-in "resources" section of the policy with this code:

```
"resources": [
  {
    "name": "[concat(parameters('vmName'), '/', variables('
    vmExtensionName'))]",
    "type": "Microsoft.HybridCompute/machines/extensions",
    "location": "[parameters('location')]",
    "apiVersion": "2019-12-12",
    "properties": {
      "publisher": "[variables('vmExtensionPublisher')]",
      "type": "[variables('vmExtensionType')]",
      "settings": {
        "workspaceId": "[reference(parameters('logAnalytics'),
        '2015-03-20').customerId]",
        "stopOnMultipleConnections": "false"
      },
      "protectedSettings": {
        "workspaceKey": "[listKeys(parameters('logAnalytics'),
        '2015-03-20').primarySharedKey]"
      }
    }
  }
],
```

Azure Policy: Exemption

A policy may be assigned to a computer that will always report noncompliant but given the particulars should not decrement the noncompliant computer count when calculating overall policy compliance. In other words, a waiver of policy.

Follow this protocol to exempt a computer from an assigned Azure Policy:

1. At Policy ➤ Compliance, select the Enable Azure Monitor for VMs initiative.
2. Click **Non-compliant resources**.
3. Locate the computer to exempt and click the **Create Exemption** button.
4. Make sure the Exemption scope (one computer) is correct.
5. Select *Waiver* or *Mitigated* as appropriate.
6. Enter comments such as ticket number and click **Review + create** and then **Create**.

Azure Log Analytics

A single Log Analytics workspace is the focus of the solution. All monitoring artifacts point back to the designated workspace. A number of **Azure Log Analytics solutions** are installed in the workspace to contribute to the solution (Figure 6-5):

- ADAssessment
- ADReplication
- AgentHealthAssessment
- ChangeTracking (automatically installed by Azure Automation Change Tracking)
- DnsAnalytics
- LogicAppsManagement

- Security
- ServiceMap
- SQLVulnerabilityAssessment
- Updates (automatically installed by Azure Automation Updating Solution)
- VMInsights (automatically installed by linking the Log Analytics workspace with VM Insights)

The solutions that require manual installation are listed as follows. Follow these steps to add the solutions:

1. At Log Analytics workspace ➤ General ➤ Workspace summary, click the **Add** button.
2. At Marketplace, paste in the exact name of the solution in the search bar:
    a. Active Directory Health Check
    b. AD Replication Status
    c. Azure Log Analytics Agent Health
    d. DNS Analytics
    e. Logic Apps Management
    f. Security and Audit
    g. Service Map
    h. SQL Vulnerability Assessment
3. Locate the solution and click the Create button.
4. Select the Log Analytics Workspace and click Create again.

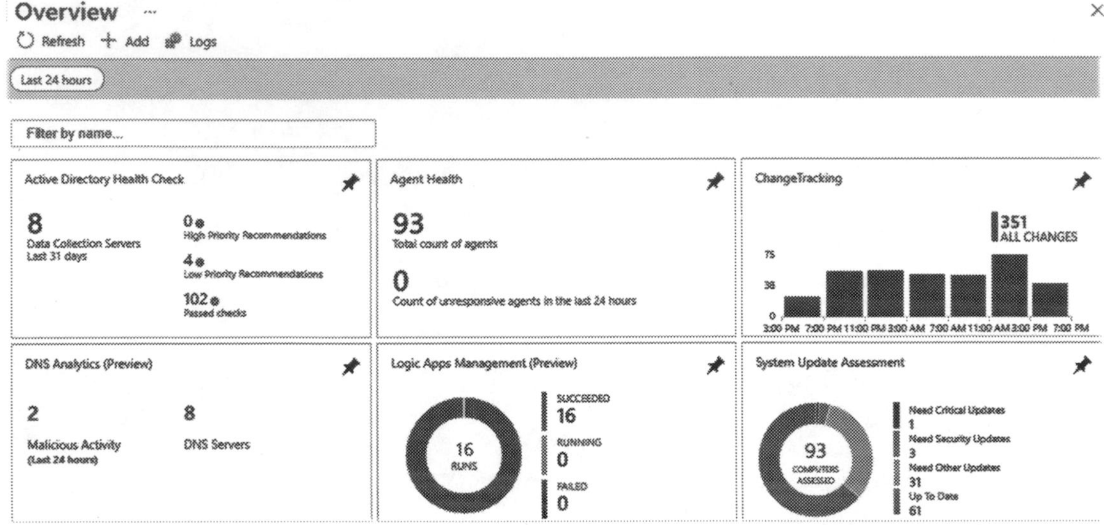

***Figure 6-5.** The Overview page of an Azure Log Analytics workspace with recommended solutions installed*

Log Analytics Workspace Additional Configuration

After installing the solutions in the Azure Log Analytics workspace, there are additional customizations to the Azure Log Analytics Agents configuration. For effective monitoring, it is necessary to collect the common event logs (System and Application) and selected additional disk and memory performance counters. Also, you will confirm the retention period for your workspace data.

Windows Event Logs

At Log Analytics workspace ➤ Settings ➤ Agent configuration ➤ Windows event logs, add the Application and System logs with all priority events (Figure 6-6).

Agents configuration ...

Windows event logs | Windows performance counters | Linux performance counters | Syslog | IIS Logs

Collect Windows event log data from standard logs, like System and Application, or add custom logs created by applications you need to monitor. Learn more

+ Add windows event log

Filter event logs

Log name	Error	Warning	Information	
Application	☑	☑	☑	🗑
System	☑	☑	☑	🗑

Figure 6-6. *Windows event logs to collect*

Windows Performance Counters

At Log Analytics workspace ➤ Settings ➤ Agent configuration ➤ Windows performance counters, add the settings as shown in Figure 6-7.

Windows event logs | Windows performance counters | Linux performance counters

Collect performance counters from Log Analytics agents at custom intervals to gain insight into the performance of hardware components, operating systems, and applications. Learn more
Click on the new counter name to edit it. ⓘ

+ Add performance counter

Filter performance counters

Performance counter name	Sample rate (seconds)	
LogicalDisk(*)\Avg. Disk sec/Transfer	60	🗑
LogicalDisk(*)\Current Disk Queue Length	60	🗑
Memory(*)\Pages/sec	60	🗑

Figure 6-7. *Collect these additional Windows performance counters*

Alternatively, the following Azure PowerShell example script (Add-PerfCounters.ps1) will create the Windows performance counters:

Add-PerfCounters.ps1

```
$ResourceGroup = "MyResourceGroup"
$WorkspaceName = "MyWorkspace"
New-AzOperationalInsightsWindowsPerformanceCounterDataSource
-ResourceGroupName $ResourceGroup -WorkspaceName $WorkspaceName -ObjectName
"LogicalDisk" -InstanceName "*" -CounterName "Avg. Disk sec/Transfer"
-IntervalSeconds 60 -Name "LogicalDisk(*)\Avg. Disk sec/Transfer"
New-AzOperationalInsightsWindowsPerformanceCounterDataSource
-ResourceGroupName $ResourceGroup -WorkspaceName $WorkspaceName -ObjectName
"LogicalDisk" -InstanceName "*" -CounterName "Current Disk Queue Length"
-IntervalSeconds 60 -Name "LogicalDisk(*)\Current Disk Queue Length"
New-AzOperationalInsightsWindowsPerformanceCounterDataSource
-ResourceGroupName $ResourceGroup -WorkspaceName $WorkspaceName -ObjectName
"Memory" -InstanceName "*" -CounterName "Pages/sec" -IntervalSeconds 60
-Name "Memory(*)\Pages/sec"
```

Data Retention

Confirm the retention period for Azure Log Analytics data matches your expectations. In the default offering, at no additional cost, logs are retained for 31 days. If you elect for longer retention, set that at Log Analytics workspace ➤ General ➤ Usage and estimated costs ➤ Data Retention. (Microsoft Sentinel includes free retention for 90 days.) Keeping data longer than the included/free retention periods will incur additional monthly Azure subscription billing.

Tip Here are *some rules of thumb* for estimating the additional cost of longer retention:

Azure Log Analytics:

50% additional per month to retain 1 year vs. 31 days. Example: $100 per month to retain 31 days, $150 per month to retain 1 year

Microsoft Sentinel:

20% additional cost per month to retain 1 year vs. 90 days. Example: $1000 per month to retain 90 days, $1200 per month to retain 1 year

---

The maximum retention for data in your Log Analytics workspace is 730 days (2 years). While your data remains in your workspace repository, it is subject to query and use in reporting like current data. If your data retention needs exceed 2 years, a supported solution is to enable **continuous data export** from Log Analytics to an Azure storage account or Azure event hub. For details on how this works, consult this URL:

`https://docs.microsoft.com/en-us/azure/azure-monitor/logs/logs-data-export`

Azure Automation

When an Azure Automation account is created, an "Azure Run as Account" is created as a service principal in Azure AD and granted the Contributor role to the subscription. Check the status of the Azure Run as Account at Automation Account ➤ Account Settings ➤ Run as accounts. The Service Principal should have *Contributor* role assigned at the Azure subscription.

As a one-time activity, link an Azure Automation account to the Azure Log Analytics workspace at Log Analytics workspace ➤ Related Resources ➤ Automation Account.

After linking an Azure Automation account to the Azure Log Analytics workspace, enable the **Update management** and **Inventory** solutions for *all available and future machines* as shown in Figure 6-8.

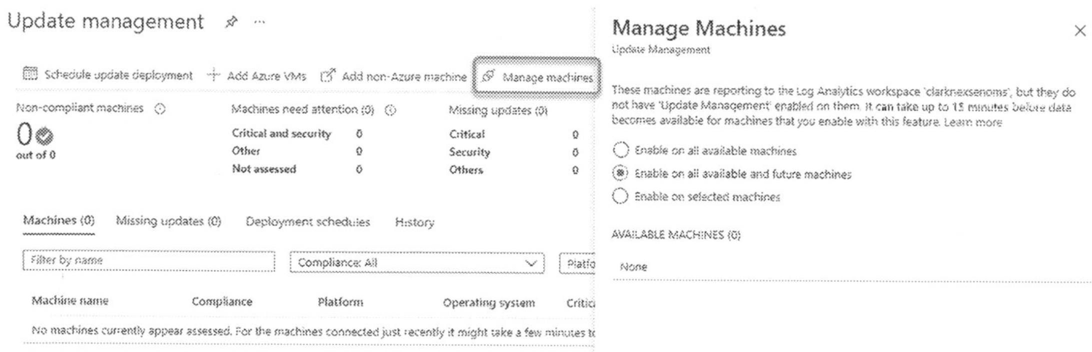

Figure 6-8. *Enable the Azure Automation Update management solution for all available and future machines*

When a computer enrolls in an Azure Automation solution, a system hybrid worker group is silently created for each machine. The system hybrid worker groups will have names like *MyComputer.mydomain.com_4fcd 9932-4206-4fcd-8842-4fcd 63874fcd*. This hybrid worker is authorized to run on the monitored computer in order to collect inventory, change and update data, and install updates if that option is turned on.

Azure Monitor

In this solution, two aspects of Azure Monitor are used for monitoring servers. These are the scheduled alert rules and Azure VM Guest health monitors. Together the rules and the monitors are the active sensors in the solution.

Azure Monitor Action Groups

Before importing a selection of scheduled alert rules, an Azure Monitor Action Group is created to receive the alerts and perform notification on them. When the alert rules are imported, the name of this action group is specified, so it must exist before importing the alert rules.

Action Group: Default-Alert-Action

The action group is created as follows:

1. Log Analytics workspace ➤ Monitoring ➤ Alerts ➤ Manage actions ➤ Add Action group.
2. For name, enter **Default-Alert-Action**.
3. For Short name, enter **DefAlertAct**.
4. Create a Notification action of type Email.
5. Add an email address of the notification endpoint.
6. Select Yes to Enable the common alert schema.
7. Click OK.
8. Click **Save Changes**.

Figure 6-9 is an extract from an Azure Monitor email alerting product; this is an example of a computer with loss of heartbeat.

FW: Fired:Sev2 Azure Monitor Alert Azure Monitor Heartbeat Failure on journey3 (microsoft.operationalinsights/workspaces)

Metric name	Heartbeat
Metric namespace	Microsoft.OperationalInsights/workspaces
Dimensions.Dimension name1	ResourceId
Dimensions.Dimension value1	/subscriptions/318b[illegible]46 6e/resourceGroups/rg-dev-eus/providers/Microsoft .OperationalInsights/workspaces/Journey3
Dimensions.Dimension name2	Computer
Dimensions.Dimension value2	Venus

Figure 6-9. *Subject and body extract from an email alert notification sent by Azure Monitor*

Action Group: VM Insights Health Alert

A second action group **VM Insights Health Alert** is created to launch a Logic App that postprocesses Azure VM Health monitor alerts. This group is created later in the solution deployment after the Logic App *Azure-Monitor-Guest-Health-Alerting* has been created. The action group has a single action: trigger the Logic App.

Azure Monitor Scheduled Alert Rules

Scheduled monitor alert rules run periodically (from every 5 minutes to once a day) and look back across log data for the presence of warning or critical alert indicators, or the absence of normal data indications. The solution includes 12 scheduled alert rules (Table 6-1). Figures 6-10 and 6-11 show the solution in action, displaying a day's worth of alert traffic in an active environment.

Table 6-1. *Azure Monitor Scheduled Alert Rules*

Name	Type/Freq	Condition
Azure Monitor Heartbeat Failure	Metric 5m @ 1m	Whenever the total heartbeat is less than or equal to 2 [in 5 minutes]
Logical Disk Current Queue Length is too High	Metric 15m @ 1m	Whenever the average average_current disk queue length is greater than 32
Logical Disk Transfer (reads and writes) Latency is too High	Metric 15m @ 1m	Whenever the average average_avg. disk sec/transfer is greater than 0.04
Memory Pages Per Second is too High	Metric 1h @ 5m	Whenever the average average_pages/sec is greater than 5000
(Core Windows Services Rollup) A service has stopped	Log 5m @ 5m	ConfigurationData | where SvcState == "Stopped" | where SvcName == "Browser" or SvcName == "DHCP" or SvcName =="DNSCache" or SvcName == "PlugPlay" or SvcName == "RpcSs" or SvcName == "lanmanserver" or SvcName == "LmHosts" or SvcName == "Eventlog" or SvcName == "MpsSvc" or SvcName == "WinRM" or SvcName == "Lanmanworkstation" | where SvcStartupType != "Disabled"
A previously running Windows service has stopped	Log 5m @ 5m	ConfigurationChange | where ConfigChangeType contains "WindowsServices" | where SvcStartupType contains "Auto" | where SvcState contains "Stopped" | where SvcPreviousState contains "Running" | where SvcName !in ("IaasVmProvider", "edgeupdate","RemoteRegistry","sppsvc", "TrustedInstaller","wuauserv")

(continued)

Table 6-1. (*continued*)

Name	Type/Freq	Condition
A Service has Entered into an Unpredictable State	Log 5m @ 5m	Event | where (EventLog == "System" and Source == "Service Control Manager") and (EventID == 7030 or EventID == 7037) | project Computer, TimeGenerated, AlertType_s = "A Service has Entered into an Unpredictable State", Severity = 4, SeverityName_s = "WARNING", AffectedCI_s = Computer, AlertTitle_s = strcat(Computer, ": A Service has Entered into an Unpredictable State"), AlertDetails_s = strcat("Event Description:\r\n", RenderedDescription)
Duplicate IP Address has been Detected	Log 5m @ 5m	Event | where (EventLog == "System" and Source == "Tcpip") and (EventID == 4198 or EventID == 4199) | project Computer, TimeGenerated, AlertType_s = "Duplicate IP Address has been Detected", Severity = 4, SeverityName_s = "WARNING", AffectedCI_s = Computer, AlertTitle_s = strcat(Computer, ": Duplicate IP Address has been Detected"), AlertDetails_s = strcat("Event Description:", RenderedDescription)
Malware threat detected on computer (Defender)	Log 10m @ 10m	ProtectionStatus | summarize ThreatStatusRank=max(ThreatStatusRank) by Computer, Time=bin(todatetime(DateCollected), 10m) | summarize(Time, ThreatStatusRank) = argmax(Time, ThreatStatusRank) by Computer | where ThreatStatusRank !in (150, 470) | project Computer, Rank = ThreatStatusRank

(*continued*)

Table 6-1. *(continued)*

Name	Type/Freq	Condition
NTFS - File System Corrupt	Log 30m @ 30m	Event | where EventLog == "System" and Source == "DISK" or Source == "Ntfs" and EventID == 55 | project Computer, TimeGenerated, AlertType_s = "NTFS - File System Corrupt", Severity = 4, SeverityName_s = "WARNING", AffectedCI_s = Computer, AlertTitle_s = strcat(Computer, ": NTFS - File System Corrupt"), AlertDetails_s = strcat("Event Description:", RenderedDescription)
One or more previously seen agents is unresponsive	Log 2h @ 2h	Heartbeat | summarize LastCall = max(TimeGenerated) by Computer | where LastCall < ago(24h)
Unexpected shutdown	Log 1d @ 1d	Event | where EventLog == "System" and EventID == 6008 | project Computer, TimeGenerated, AlertType_s = "Unexpected shutdown", Severity = 4, SeverityName_s = "WARNING", AffectedCI_s = strcat(Computer), AlertTitle_s = strcat(Computer, ": Unexpected Shutdown"), AlertDetails_s = strcat("Multiple shutdowns detected in the past 24 hours\r\nEventID: 6008\r\nEvent Description: ", RenderedDescription)

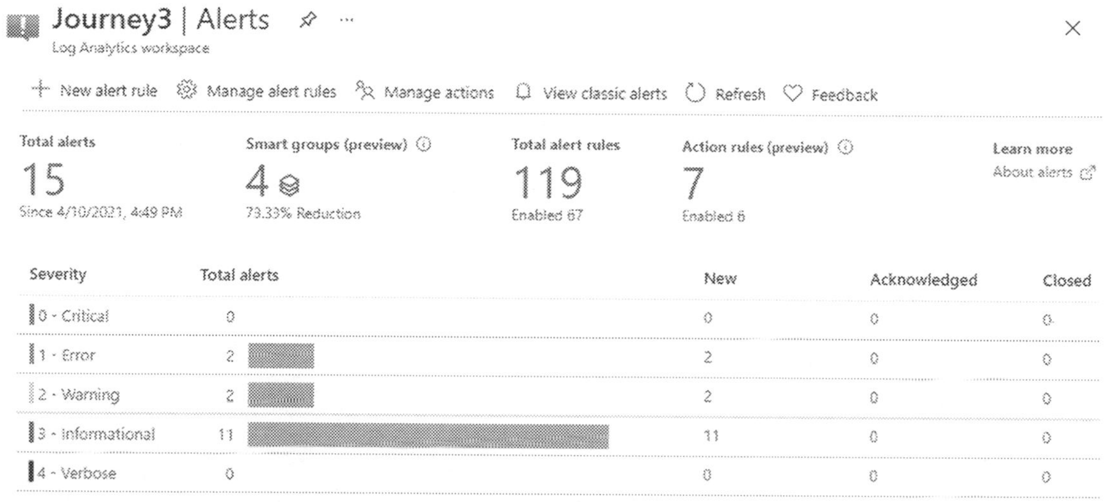

Figure 6-10. *Azure Monitor alerts console in the Azure portal*

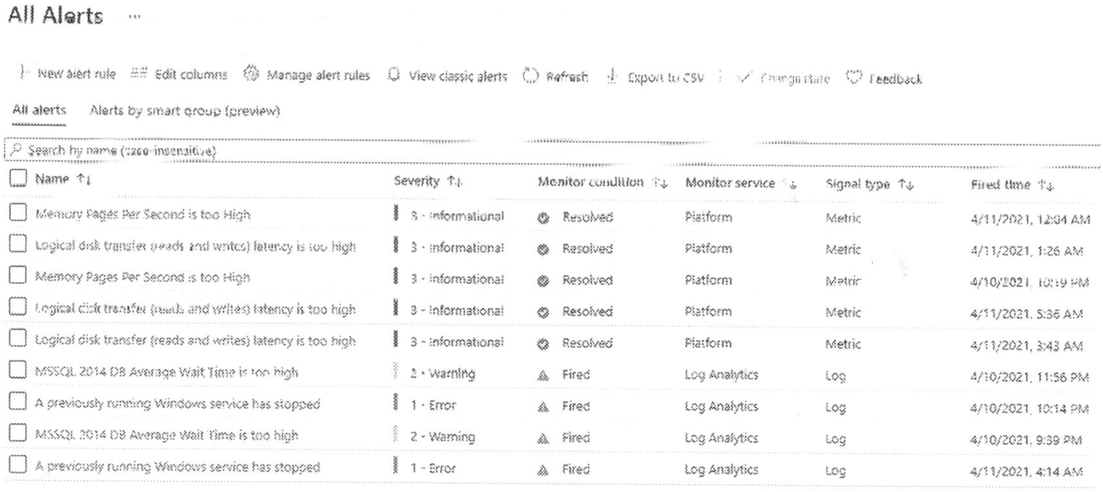

Figure 6-11. *All alerts list includes platform metric and Log Analytics log alerts*

Azure Monitor scheduled alert rules can be manually created as KQL queries using the information in Table 6-1 or imported into the Azure subscription using ARM templates. Find sample KQL queries to paste into scheduled alert rules you might create at this URL:

```
https://github.com/microsoft/AzureMonitorCommunity
```

Figure 6-12 shows the solution rules running in the Azure Log Analytics workspace after being imported.

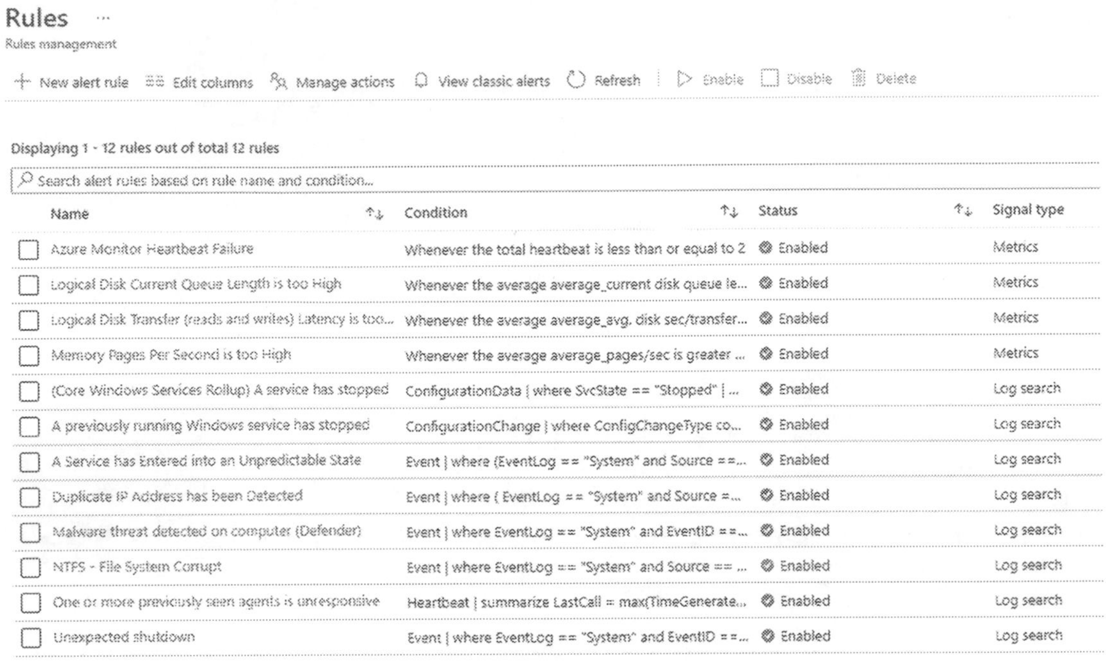

Rules ...
Rules management

+ New alert rule Edit columns Manage actions View classic alerts Refresh Enable Disable Delete

Displaying 1 - 12 rules out of total 12 rules

Search alert rules based on rule name and condition...

Name	Condition	Status	Signal type
Azure Monitor Heartbeat Failure	Whenever the total heartbeat is less than or equal to 2	Enabled	Metrics
Logical Disk Current Queue Length is too High	Whenever the average average_current disk queue le...	Enabled	Metrics
Logical Disk Transfer (reads and writes) Latency is too...	Whenever the average average_avg. disk sec/transfer...	Enabled	Metrics
Memory Pages Per Second is too High	Whenever the average average_pages/sec is greater ...	Enabled	Metrics
(Core Windows Services Rollup) A service has stopped	ConfigurationData | where SvcState == "Stopped" | ...	Enabled	Log search
A previously running Windows service has stopped	ConfigurationChange | where ConfigChangeType co...	Enabled	Log search
A Service has Entered into an Unpredictable State	Event | where (EventLog == "System" and Source ==...	Enabled	Log search
Duplicate IP Address has been Detected	Event | where (EventLog == "System" and Source =...	Enabled	Log search
Malware threat detected on computer (Defender)	Event | where EventLog == "System" and EventID ==...	Enabled	Log search
NTFS - File System Corrupt	Event | where EventLog == "System" and Source == ...	Enabled	Log search
One or more previously seen agents is unresponsive	Heartbeat | summarize LastCall = max(TimeGenerate...	Enabled	Log search
Unexpected shutdown	Event | where EventLog == "System" and EventID ==...	Enabled	Log search

Figure 6-12. *Azure Monitor scheduled alert rules performing monitoring in an environment*

Using ARM Templates for Rule Management

You might find it convenient to create a library of scheduled alert rules to import into Azure Log Analytics. Azure Monitor can be deployed and configured at scale using ARM templates. Each alert rule can be imported as an ARM template/parameter file pair. There are sample templates for different Azure Monitor features that can be modified for your particular requirements at this URL:

`https://docs.microsoft.com/en-us/azure/azure-monitor/resource-manager-samples`

Create a Library of Reusable Alert Rule Templates

The GitHub Management toolkit URL contains instructions to import dozens of common alert rule definitions, many of which are included in this Azure Monitoring solution. Follow the link to download the **Alert Toolkit for Legacy Log Alerts API** at this URL:

`https://github.com/microsoft/manageability-toolkits`

Consider this approach to developing your ARM template library:

1. Import all available rules from the manageability toolkit into Azure Log Analytics.
2. Disable the rules you don't need running for development.
3. Evaluate the rules you will use in production and export their contents to ARM templates.
4. Delete the rules imported into Azure Monitor by the manageability toolkit.
5. Reimport production rules using ARM templates for code-based management.
6. Use the ARM templates to deploy identical rule sets to other Azure Log Analytics workspaces, or use them as backup/documentation of your monitoring infrastructure.

Authoring Scheduled Alert Rule Templates

Log alert rules and metric alert rules have different structures. For a complete deployment of rules, you will need to prepare the following files:

1. Template files for log alerts
2. Template files for metric alerts
3. Template parameter file for log alerts
4. Template parameter file for metric alerts

There are detailed instructions and example templates at these URLs:

- Create a log alert with a Resource Manager template

  `https://docs.microsoft.com/en-us/azure/azure-monitor/alerts/alerts-log-create-templates`

- Create a metric alert with a Resource Manager template

  `https://docs.microsoft.com/en-us/azure/azure-monitor/alerts/alerts-metric-create-templates`

Tip Be sure to precreate the Azure Monitor Action Group that will perform default notification for alerts before importing rules via ARM template. (That's the *Default-Alert-Action* group covered in the Azure Monitor Action Group section of this chapter.) **How**: Specify the action group's resource group ID in the template parameter file to automatically enable your default notification channel when you import the alert rules. Your action group resource group ID will look something like this in the parameter file:

```
"actionGroupId": {
    "value": "/subscriptions/12341234-1234-1234-1234-
    123412341234/resourceGroups/RG-DEV-EUS/providers/
    microsoft.insights/actiongroups/Default-Alert-Action"
}
```

Deploying ARM Templates to Enable Monitoring

You can deploy your ARM templates (thus enabling monitoring) using any standard method for deploying Resource Manager templates. The following sections describe methods that use the Azure portal and Azure PowerShell to import standardized versions of scheduled log and metrics alert rules into Azure Log Analytics.

Import Rule Templates Using Azure Portal

1. Navigate to Home ➤ New ➤ Search the Marketplace.
2. Type "template" and from the drop-down list select **Template deployment (deploy using custom templates)**. Click **Create**.
3. At select a template, click **Build your own template in the editor**.
4. At *Edit template*, replace the entire contents of the code view with the template file contents and click **Save**.
5. Click Edit parameters; then at *Edit parameters*, replace the entire code section with the template parameter file contents and click **Save**.

6. At Custom deployment, select Resource group, click **Review + create**, and then click **Create**.

Import Rule Templates Using Azure PowerShell

Prepare input template and template parameter files for rules to be imported; then use the *New-AzResourceGroupDeployment* cmdlet to create the deployment. This example imports the log rule "Core service has stopped" from files "MonitorLogAlert-template-Core service has stopped.json" and "MonitorLogAlert-parameters.json":

```
New-AzResourceGroupDeployment -Name "LogAlertDeployment" -ResourceGroupName
MyResourceGroup -TemplateFile "MonitorLogAlert-template-Core service has
stopped.json" -TemplateParameterFile "MonitorLogAlert-parameters.json"
```

This example imports the metric rule "Azure Monitor heartbeat failure" from the files "MonitorLogAlert-template-Azure Monitor heartbeat failure-metric.json" and "MonitorMetricsAlert-parameters.json":

```
New-AzResourceGroupDeployment -Name "MetricAlertDeployment"
-ResourceGroupName MyResourceGroup -TemplateFile "MonitorLogAlert-template-
Azure Monitor heartbeat failure-metric.json" -TemplateParameterFile
"MonitorMetricsAlert-parameters.json"
```

Bundle all your deployments into one PowerShell script that runs New-AzResourceGroupDeployment once for each rule you are importing. Distribute the script along with the template and template parameter JSON files. Deploy the entire suite of alerting rules by executing the PowerShell .PS1 script.

Tip You can reuse the same parameter files for all rules deployed to the same environment. Prepare two template parameter files, one each in versions for log rules and for metric rules; then use those template files for all rule deployments. Example: to deploy 12 x rules that include both log and metric types, you will need to prepare 14 x files, two of which are template parameter files.

About Escaped Characters in ARM Template Files

When working with scheduled rule query ARM templates, pay attention to the need to "escape" the protected characters (", \, and /) with the backslash character (\) in the template file *description* and *query* fields. Table 6-2 lists the escaped character guidance you need to follow:

Table 6-2. *Escape Special Characters with a Backslash*

Special Character	Escaped Output
Quotation mark (")	\"
Backslash (\)	\\
Slash (/)	\/
New line	\n
Carriage return	\r

Here are before (un-escaped) and after (escaped) examples of ARM template *query* and *description* fields:

```
"query": "Event | where EventLevelName == "Error""
```

(escaping the "quotes" characters) becomes

```
"query": "Event | where EventLevelName == \"Error\""
```

```
"description": "Sample https://site.com link"
```

(escaping the "backslash" characters) becomes

```
"description": "Sample https:\/\/site.com link"
```

Azure Monitor Guest VM Health

In addition to the 12 Azure Monitor scheduled alert rules described so far in this chapter, a second and separate monitoring stack is deployed in the solution called **Guest VM Health**. This feature adds to the solution a hierarchical health monitor for CPU, memory, and logical disk space, with three alerting rules, one for each resource type, bringing to 15 the total number of alert-producing rules in the solution.

Guest VM Health monitors complement the scheduled metric and log alert rules for an efficient and effective core OS monitoring solution. Guest VM Health is a more flexible way of monitoring those performance metrics than using scheduled query metric alert rules.

The Guest VM Health feature works for Linux computers also, however only Ubuntu in the first release.

Tip If you have Azure Arc servers only, there is no need to install the Guest VM Health solution. However, if you are an all-Azure or a hybrid organization, you will deploy Guest VM Health in parallel to Azure Monitor scheduled alert rules. At the end of this section are listed Azure Monitor scheduled alert rules to deploy in lieu of Guest VM Health data collection rules.

Introducing the Azure Monitor Agent (AMA)

The Guest VM Health solution uses the new **Azure Management Agent** (AMA) rather than the classic MMA used by System Center Operations Manager (SCOM) and Azure Log Analytics. The AMA and the MMA can and do exist in parallel. In the solution, all agent components are installed using Azure VM Extensions by their respective machine agent. This technique leverages the built-in *Windows Azure Guest Agent* service to perform the software installations of the other agents on Azure VMs and the *Azure Connected Machine Agent* to perform the software installations of the other agents on Azure Arc servers.

Just as there are two software components to install inside a Windows VM for the classic Azure Log Analytics and VM Insights solution (the MMA and the Dependency agent), there are two different software components deployed inside a Windows VM when deploying the Guest VM Health solution:

1. The first is the Azure Monitoring Agent (AMA). The AMA runs as a Windows process separate from the MMA. The AMA (agent version 1.x) and the MMA (agent version 10.x) both send heartbeats to the same Log Analytics workspace.

2. The other is the Guest VM Health Agent. Deploying this agent combines the Azure VM Insights experience with the new Health monitor feature. This solution requires the AMA; it can't run on the MMA alone.

All four agents are installed in the solution by Azure VM Extensions, and all create Windows services. However, unlike the MMA and Dependency agent, which install as applications and appear in Control Panel ➤ Add/Remove Programs, the AMA and Guest Health Agent are installed by VM Extensions. Their presence is indicated by inspecting the list of installed Azure VM Extensions (Figure 6-13).

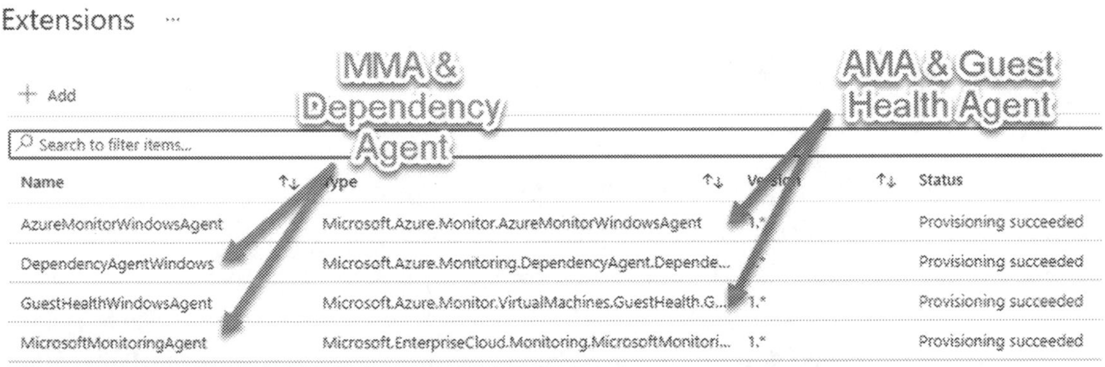

Extensions ...

MMA & Dependency Agent

AMA & Guest Health Agent

+ Add

Search to filter items...

Name	Type	Version	Status
AzureMonitorWindowsAgent	Microsoft.Azure.Monitor.AzureMonitorWindowsAgent	1.*	Provisioning succeeded
DependencyAgentWindows	Microsoft.Azure.Monitoring.DependencyAgent.Depende...	9.*	Provisioning succeeded
GuestHealthWindowsAgent	Microsoft.Azure.Monitor.VirtualMachines.GuestHealth.G...	1.*	Provisioning succeeded
MicrosoftMonitoringAgent	Microsoft.EnterpriseCloud.Monitoring.MicrosoftMonitori...	1.*	Provisioning succeeded

Figure 6-13. *Azure VM Extensions are the primary deployment tool for agents*

In the Windows file system for an Azure VM, the presence of the AMA and Guest Health Agent will be noted in the C:\WindowsAzure and C:\Packages\Plugins folders. Figures 6-14 and 6-15 show the Guest VM Health solution from the all-servers view and a detail view of one server experiencing a high CPU utilization Warning state.

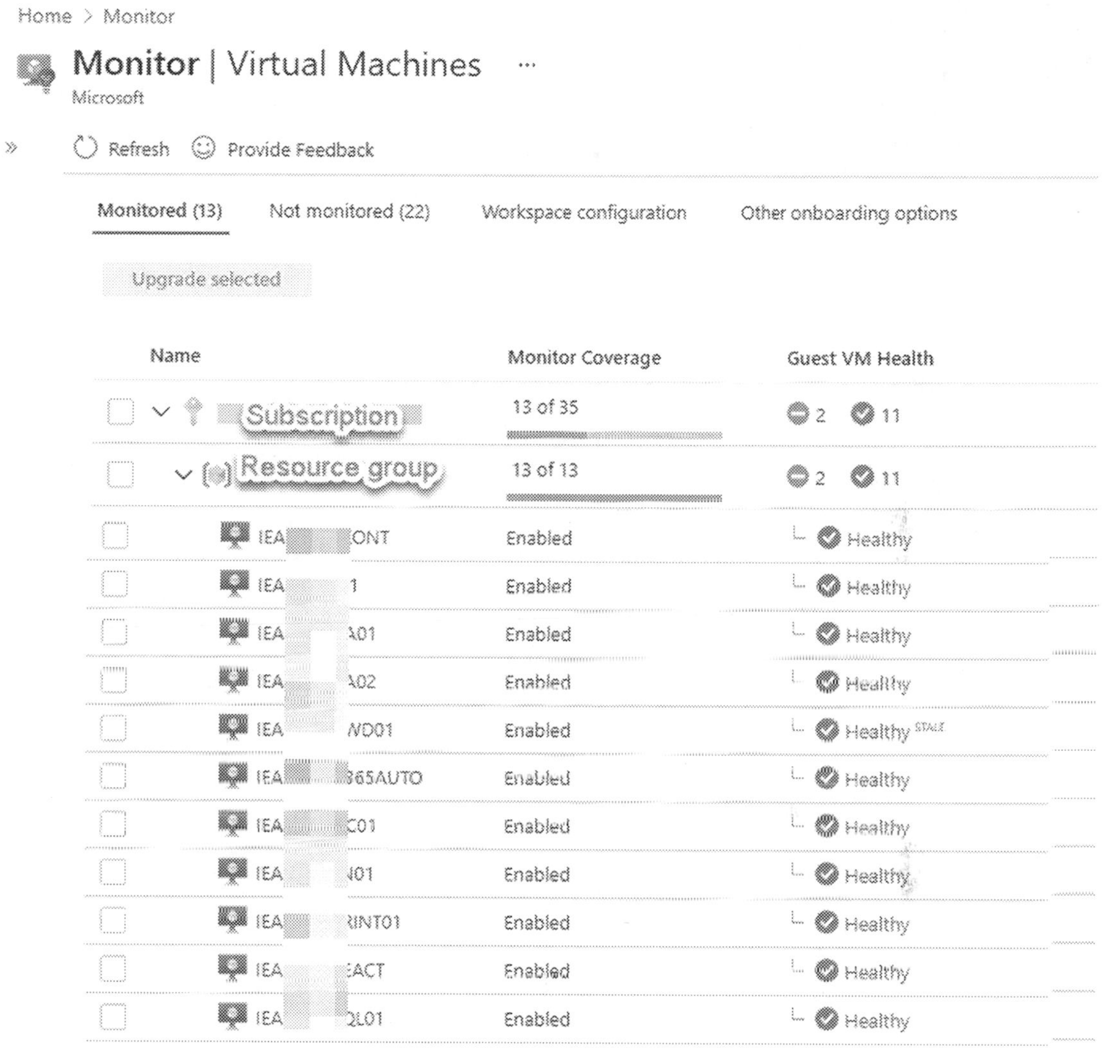

Home > Monitor

Monitor | Virtual Machines ...

Microsoft

Refresh Provide Feedback

Monitored (13) Not monitored (22) Workspace configuration Other onboarding options

Upgrade selected

Name	Monitor Coverage	Guest VM Health
Subscription	13 of 35	2 11
Resource group	13 of 13	2 11
IEA ONT	Enabled	Healthy
IEA 1	Enabled	Healthy
IEA A01	Enabled	Healthy
IEA A02	Enabled	Healthy
IEA VD01	Enabled	Healthy STALE
IEA 365AUTO	Enabled	Healthy
IEA C01	Enabled	Healthy
IEA I01	Enabled	Healthy
IEA RINT01	Enabled	Healthy
IEA EACT	Enabled	Healthy
IEA QL01	Enabled	Healthy

Figure 6-14. *Guest VM Health monitors running on all servers in a resource group*

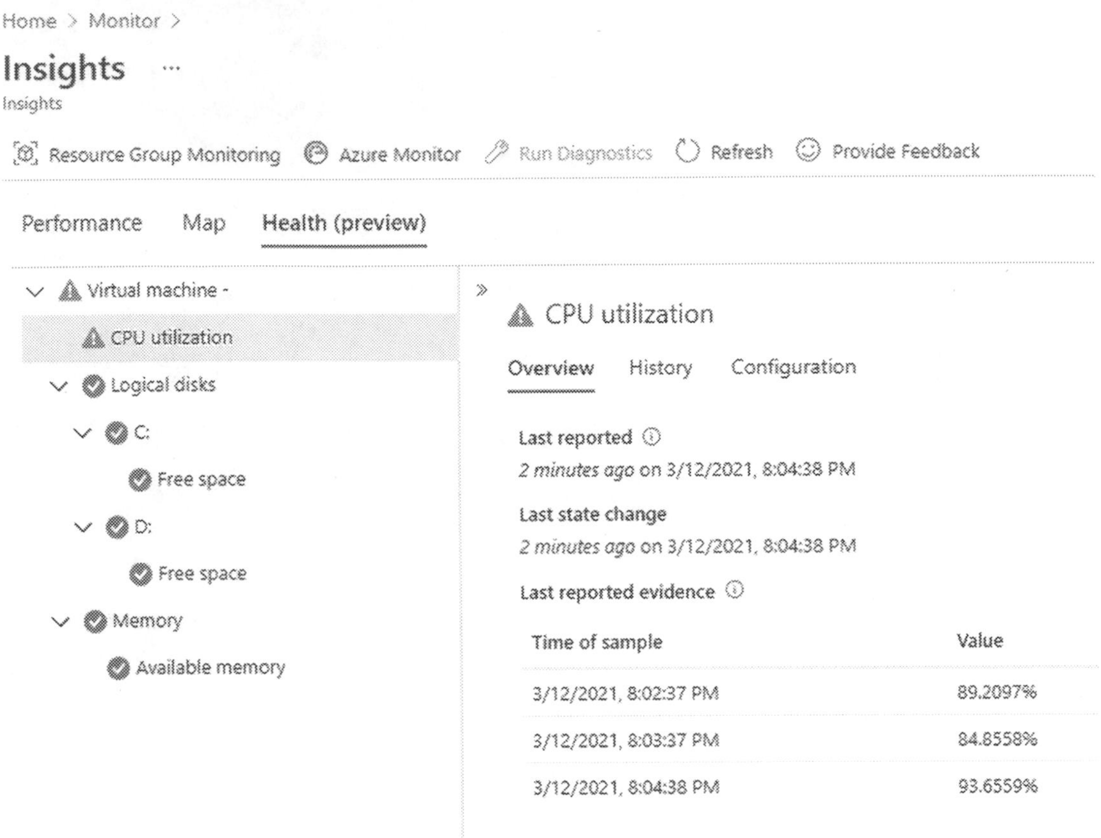

Figure 6-15. *Guest VM Health monitor with CPU utilization in a Warning state*

Azure Monitor Data Collection Rules

Guest VM Health monitors gather data on a computer using a combination of a Data Collection Rule (DCR) and a Data Collection Rule Association. DCR associations assign a DCR to one or more computers. A DCR defines what data is collected, and an association defines what computers are to use the DCR. Figure 6-16 demonstrates the Add data source step where you define what data to collect.

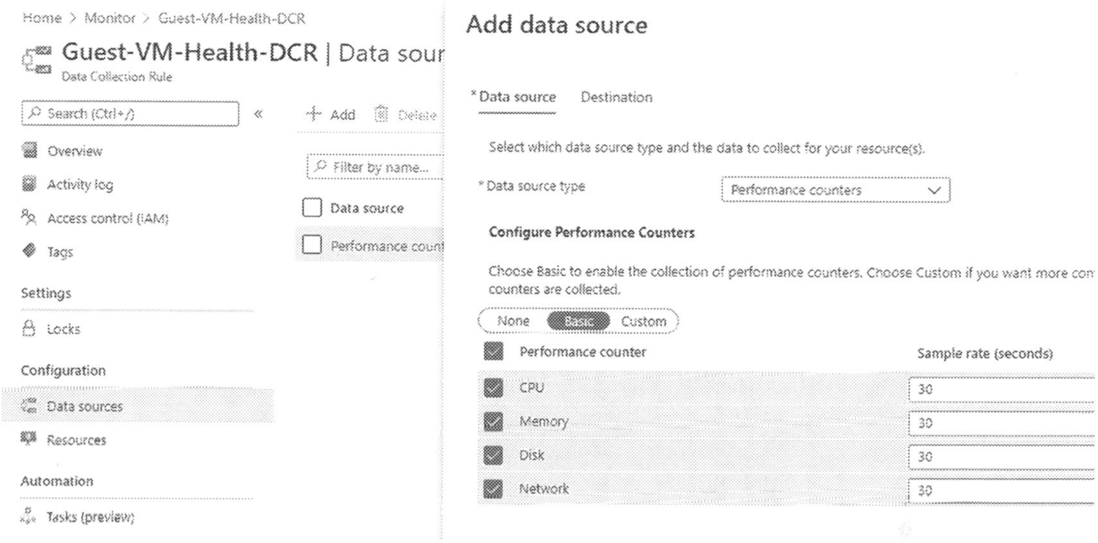

***Figure 6-16.** Add data source step when creating a custom Data Collection Rule*

If you enable Guest VM Insights on a computer using the Azure portal (at Home ➤ Monitor ➤ Insights ➤ Virtual Machines), a generic DCR is applied, which is the standard DCR with default settings. Default settings enable Critical alerts but not Warning alerts. To provide more proactive alerting, deploy a custom DCR that includes Warning thresholds as well as Critical thresholds for alerting purposes. To deploy a custom DCR, use the procedure "**Configure monitoring at scale in VM insights guest health using data collection rules**" at this URL:

`https://docs.microsoft.com/en-us/azure/azure-monitor/vm/vminsights-health-configure-dcr`

When creating a custom DCR, the recommended settings are listed in Table 6-3.

***Table 6-3.** Recommended VM Guest Health Performance Monitor Alerting Thresholds*

Monitor	Critical Threshold	Warning Threshold
CPU utilization	>90%	>80%
Logical disk free space	<5%	<10%
Memory	<100 MB	<200 MB

Scheduled Alert Rules for Azure Arc Servers (Until Guest VM Health Is Supported)

Since the VM Guest Health solution does not support Azure Arc servers, to provide equivalent monitoring to non-Azure servers, it is necessary to augment the scheduled alert rules previously detailed in Table 6-1. Table 6-4 defines three additional rules that replace the monitoring provided by the Guest VM Health solution that is not available for Azure Arc servers.

Table 6-4. *Additional Scheduled Alert Rules for Azure Arc Servers*

Alert Name	Monitor Configuration and Threshold	Performance Counters to Collect
Alert - High CPU Usage	AveCpu >85% at 30-minute intervals over a 4-hour period	Process(*)\% Processor Time Sample rate: 60 seconds
Low Disk Space Windows - Critical	Min % Free Space <10% in last 30 minutes, drives C:, E:, F:, and G:.	LogicalDisk(*)\% Free Space Sample rate: 300 seconds
Alert - Low Memory	minAvailableMB <1024 MB at 30-minute intervals over a 4-hour period	Memory(*)\Available Mbytes Sample rate: 1800 seconds

To deploy these additional rules

1. Extract the rule query definitions from the GitHub manageability toolkit as described earlier in the "Using ARM Templates for Rule Management" section of this chapter.
2. Add the listed performance counters to the Log Analytics agents configuration as seen previously in Figure 6-7.
3. To avoid dual monitoring and alerting from computers that are enrolled in Azure VM Guest Health, limit the scope of the additional rules to only Azure Arc servers. As a workaround,

add a line to the KQL of the alert rule that excludes computers with name patterns indicating they are Azure VMs; for example, `"| where Computer notcontains "AZ""` would not alert on computers with the letters "AZ" in their names.

4. Modify the thresholds as appropriate for your environment and deploy the additional rules for production monitoring of computers that cannot participate in the Azure VM Guest Health solution.

Azure Monitor Data Collection Rule Associations

DCR Associations link a computer to the collection ruleset. Associated computers show up in the Data Collection Rule ➤ Configuration ➤ Resources panel as seen in Figure 6-17.

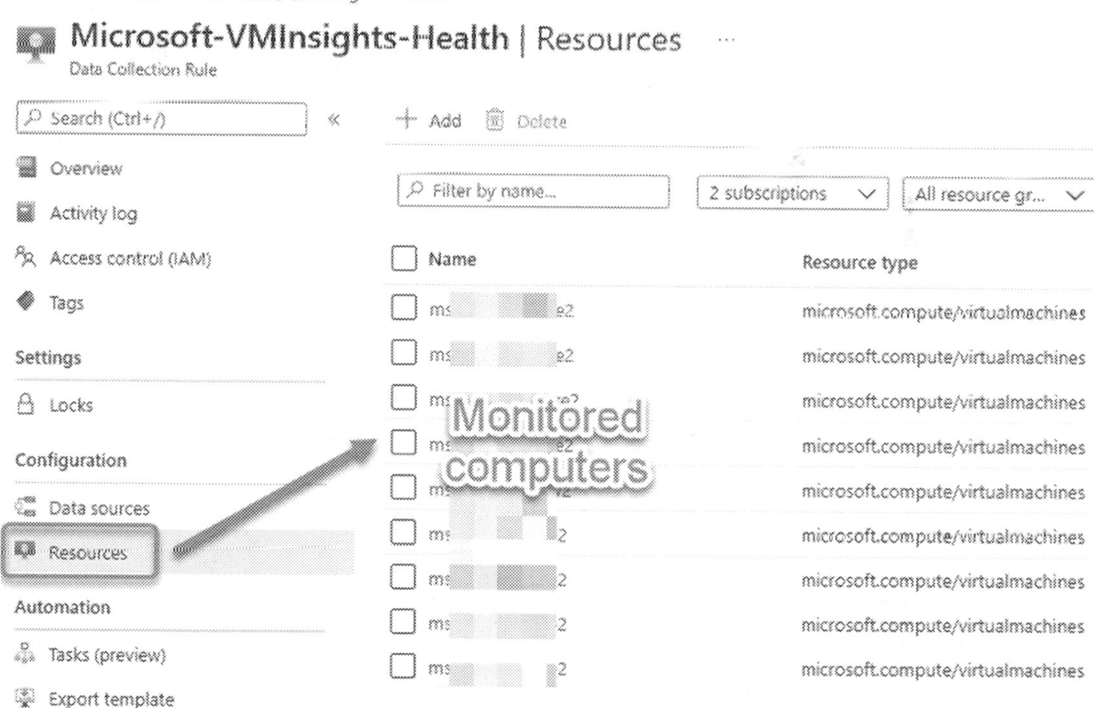

__Figure 6-17.__ List of computers (resources) associated to this DCR. All these servers will share the same VM Guest Health settings

Azure Monitor Action Rules

Accessed at Monitor ➤ Alerts ➤ Manage actions ➤ Action rules, these are rules that are created for suppressing notifications from alerts and for enabling alerting actions at scale. In the Azure Monitor solution, action rules are used in both modes.

Create Action Rule for Action Group

There is one action rule created, **Notify administrators when alert fires**, to catch state changes in Azure Guest VM Health monitors. Follow these steps to create the "action group" action rule:

1. Navigate to Log Analytics ➤ Alerts ➤ Manage actions ➤ Action rules and click **New action rule**.
2. Scope: Select the subscription.
3. Filter:
    a. Monitor condition Equals *Fired*
    b. Monitor service Equals *VM Insights-Health*
4. Define on this scope: Action group.
5. Action group: VM Insights Health Alert.
6. Name: Notify administrators when alert fires.
7. Click Save.

Azure Monitor Action Rule (Suppression): Overrides

This is an important part of the Azure Monitor solution; it is how "overrides" are introduced to reduce false positives and thus reduce alert fatigue. Accessed at Monitor ➤ Alerts ➤ Manage actions ➤ Action rules, these are specific override rules that are created for suppressing notifications from alerts. Overrides are simple to create and human readable from the Azure portal.

Figure 6-18 illustrates three overrides for performance monitors during daily backup windows, as well as the "Notify administrators when alert fires" action rule created in the previous step.

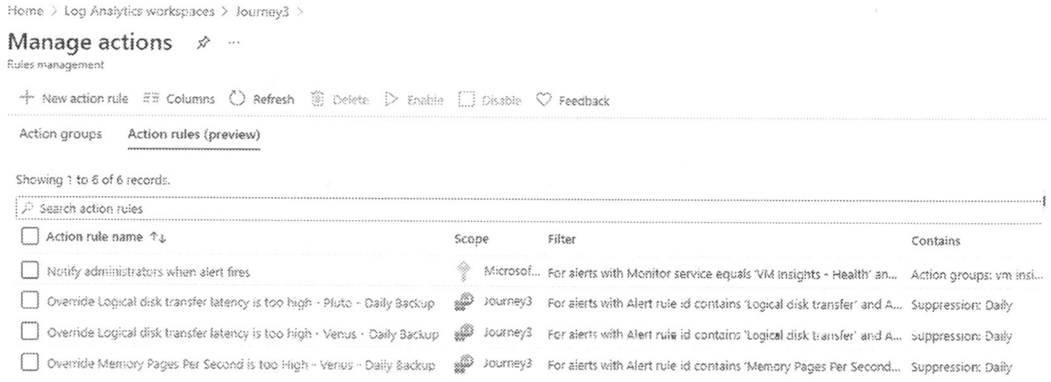

Figure 6-18. *Server-specific, rule-specific overrides deployed as Action rules*

Create Action Rule for Suppression

Follow these steps to create an action rule for suppression:

1. Navigate to Log Analytics workspace ➤ Alerts ➤ Manage actions ➤ Action rules and click **New action rule**.

2. Scope is the Log Analytics workspace.

3. Notice the *Rules matching to this scope* will show a number, such as 123 Alert rules.

4. Click on the Filter **Add** button (Figure 6-19).

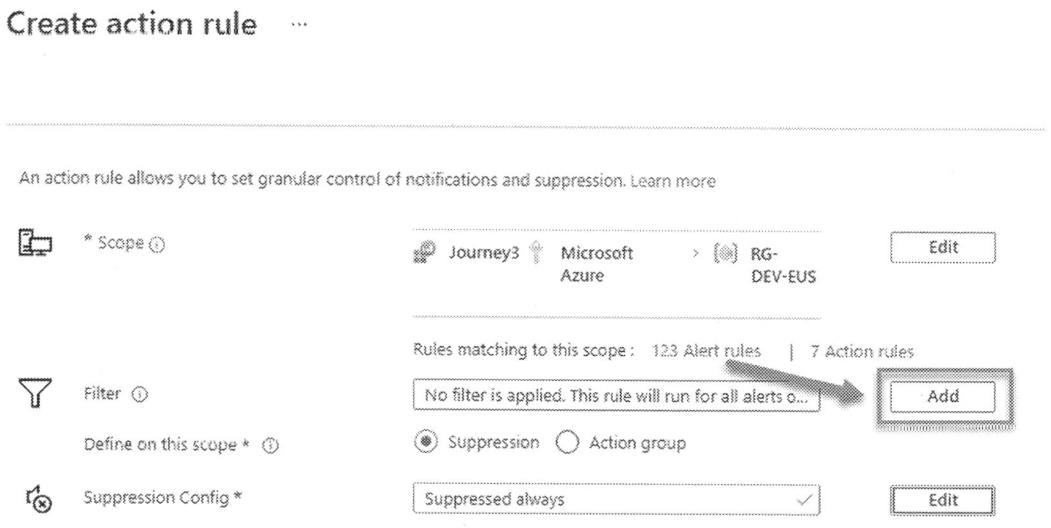

Figure 6-19. *Selecting the rule that is the target of the override*

5. At **Add Filters**, add this information (Figure 6-20):

   a. Alert Rule Id contains the name of the alert to override (the name must exist the list of Alert rules).

   b. Alert Context (payload) contains the computer name for the override.

   c. Give the Action rule the name "Override <name of override> - <computer name> - <reason>".

   d. Save the action rule in the resource group of the Log Analytics workspace and click **Create**.

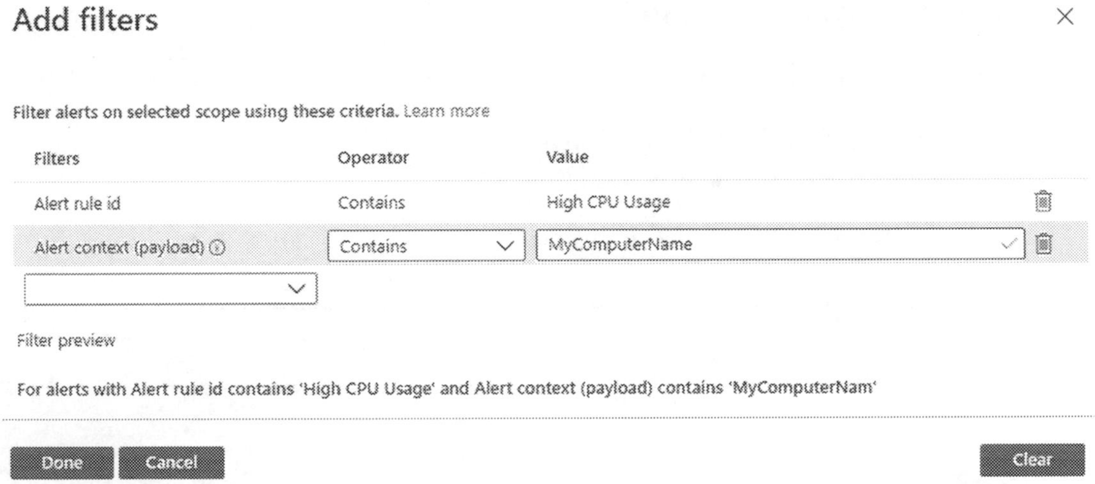

Figure 6-20. *Creating an override with the alert rule name and server name to suppress alerting*

Azure Logic Apps

An Azure Logic app is a cloud microservice that can be used to schedule, automate, and orchestrate tasks, business process, and workflows. Along with Azure Automation and Azure Functions, Azure Logic Apps are a primary tool in the Azure Monitoring solution. Notably, Azure Logic Apps are the only inline automated response option for Microsoft Sentinel incidents and alerts.

A logic app deployed in this solution is **Azure-Monitor-Guest-Health-Alerting** (Figure 6-21). This logic app extracts actionable data from Azure VM Guest Health alerts and makes the results easily readable by humans. The logic app postprocesses the output of the alert action rule.

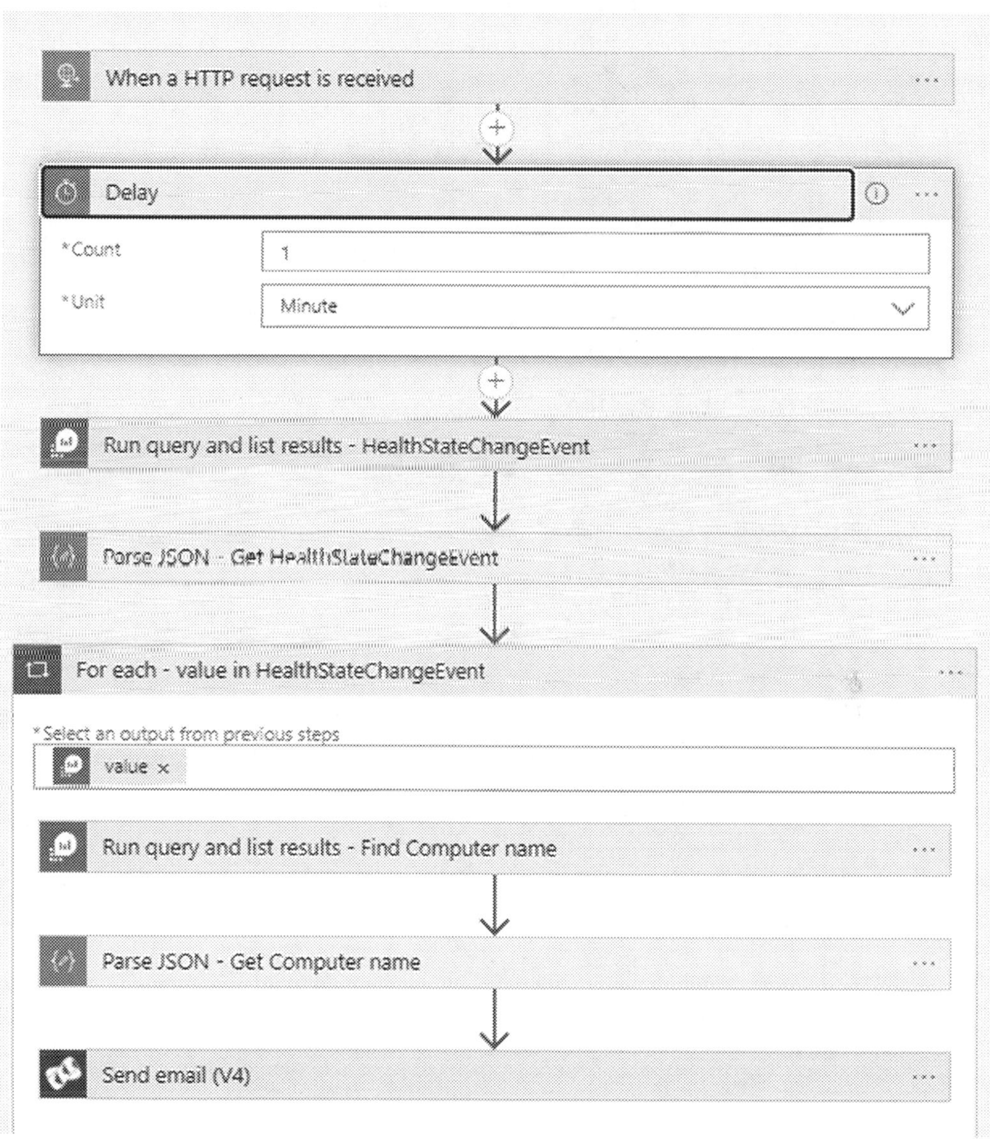

Figure 6-21. *Azure Logic App: Azure-Monitor-Guest-Health-Alerting formats the alert and emails it*

Author Logic App

The logic app is specified as the *Azure Monitor Action Rule* to run when an Azure VM Guest Health alert fires. The logic app is composed of these steps:

1. When a new alert arrives, delay 1 minute for the alert to appear in the Azure Log Analytics database.

2. Run an Azure Log Analytics query to see what VM Guest Health state change events fired in the previous 5 minutes.

```
HealthStateChangeEvent

| where ( MonitorName contains "logical-disks" and MonitorType
contains "free-space" ) or ( MonitorName contains "memory" and
MonitorType contains "available" ) or ( MonitorName contains "cpu" and
MonitorType contains "utilization" )
| where CurrentMonitorState == "critical" or CurrentMonitorState
== "warning"
| where EvaluationTimestamp > ago(5m)
```

3. Parse the JSON out of the query response for the *Azure resource* reporting the alert.

```
@{body('Run_query_and_list_results_-_HealthStateChangeEvent_')}
```

4. Run another Azure Log Analytics query to see what the *Name* of the Azure resource is (the Computer name).

```
Heartbeat
| where ResourceId contains "@{items('For_each_-_value_in_
HealthStateChangeEvent')?['_ResourceId']}"
| distinct Computer
```

5. Parse the JSON out of the query response for the computer name.

```
@{body('Run_query_and_list_results_-_Find_Computer_name')}
```

6. Send email notification (Figure 6-22) with the name of the server, the last three values of the performance counter, and the threshold value that was exceeded.

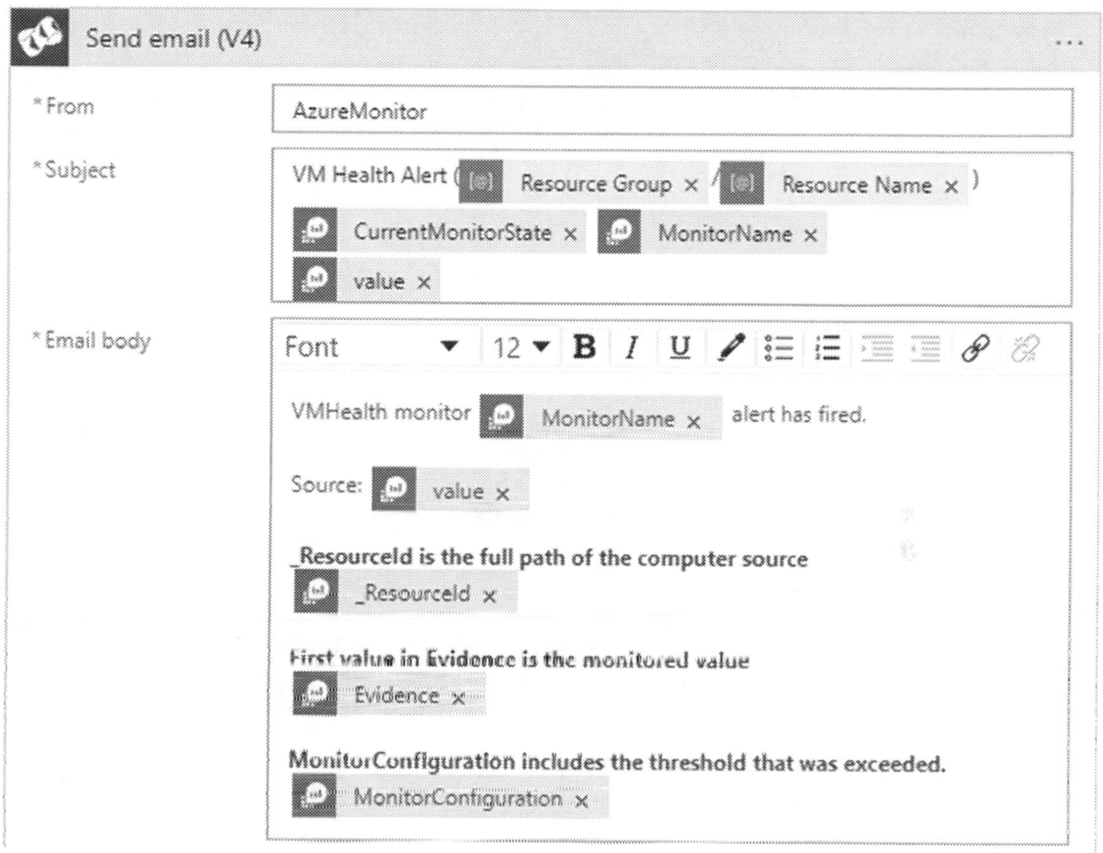

***Figure 6-22.** The Send email step at the end of the logic app*

Guest VM Health Alerting: End to End

The *Azure Monitor Acton Rule* **Notify administrators when alert fires**—which runs when a VM Guest Health monitor has a Warning or Critical state change—calls the *Azure Monitor Action Group* **VM Insights Health Alert**,which launches the *Logic App* **Azure-Monitor-Guest-Health-Alerting** that performs notification. Figure 6-23 shows what the final email notification product looks like. In production, your solution might perform notification to an ITSM product using an API connection rather than email.

From: AzureMonitor
Sent: Saturday, March 13, 2021 2:05 PM

Subject: VM Health Alert (Microsoft Azure/RG-DEV-EUS) warning memory|available [{"Computer":"obelia"}]

VMHealth monitor **memory|available** alert has fired.

Source: **[{"Computer":"OBELIA}]**

_ResourceId is the full path of the computer source
/subscriptions/12341234-1234-1234-1234-123412341234/resourcegroups/RG-DEV-EUS/providers/microsoft.compute/virtualmachines/obelia

First value in Evidence is the monitored value
{"samples":[{"value":176.969,"timestamp":"2021-03-13T20:01:10.7690000Z"},{"value":189.953,"timestamp":"2021-03-13T20:02:10.7730000Z"},{"value":195.574,"timestamp":"2021-03-13T20:03:10.7750000Z"}],"reason":{"code":2200,"message":"Collected samples met warning condition for this monitor."}}

MonitorConfiguration includes the threshold that was exceeded.
{"defaultVersion":"free-mem.1","overrides":[{"source":{"ruleResourceId":"/subscriptions/12341234-1234-1234-1234-123412341234//resourceGroups/RG-DEV-EUS/providers/Microsoft.Insights/dataCollectionRules/Microsoft-VMInsights-Health","version":"2021-03-13T04:18:17.3450000Z"},"values":{"monitorConfiguration":{"warningCondition":{"isEnabled":true,"operator":"<","threshold":200}},"alertConfiguration":{"isEnabled":true}}}]}

Figure 6-23. *Alert notification from Azure Logic App*

Azure Workbooks

As a finishing touch to solution deployment, a selection of Azure Monitor workbooks is deployed, configured, and saved into the subscription. Workbooks are deployed centrally to the Log Analytics workspace, not to the generic Azure Monitor or other scoped console. See a sample workbook in Figure 6-24 (*CPU Heatmap*).

***Figure 6-24.** Azure Monitor workbook: CPU Heatmap features "honeycomb" visualization*

There are eight recommended workbooks to install (Figure 6-25):

1. Virtual Machine Performance
2. VM Updates Summary
3. Server Availability
4. VM Security and Audit
5. CPU Heatmap
6. VM Connection Records

7. VM Network Dependencies
8. VM Network Failed Connections

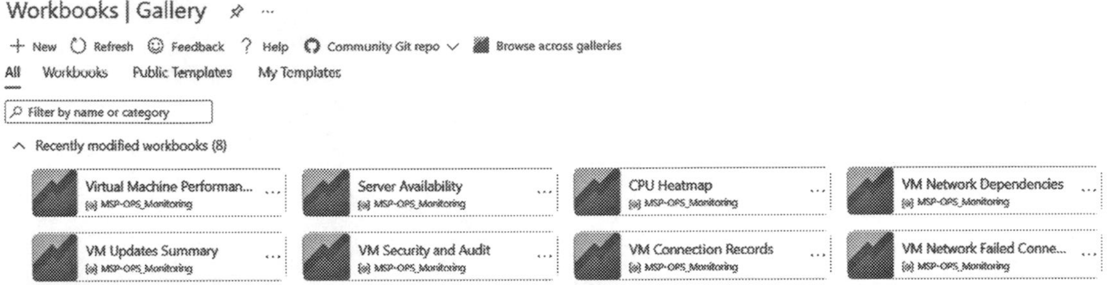

Figure 6-25. *Workbooks to install into the Log Analytics workspace*

Download the workbooks from this URL:

`https://github.com/microsoft/Application-Insights-Workbooks/tree/master/Workbooks/Virtual%20Machines`

Workbooks are installed from Log Analytics workspace ➤ General ➤ Workbooks ➤ New ➤ Edit ➤ Code view. Paste the entire contents of a Workbook template into the code editor and click **Save**. Click **Done Editing** and then **Save** again. Give a workbook the same *name* as its workbook *title* and save to the Azure subscription as a *shared workbook*.

Summary

It is possible to achieve cost-effective, reliable, and effective monitoring of server core OS functions using the native tools and services in Azure. This chapter covered the following actions that together create the Azure Monitoring solution.

1. Define core monitoring requirements for servers.
2. Connect Azure Arc servers to Azure Log Analytics using Azure Policy.
3. Configure Azure Log Analytics workspace for monitoring.
4. Engage and leverage Azure Automation for server OS updating.

5. Deploy relevant and actionable alerting using Azure Monitor.
    a. Create Action group to perform alert notification.
    b. Deploy Scheduled alert rules.
    c. Configure Guest VM Health solution.
6. Create Azure Monitor Action Group Action rule to alert on VM Insights Health Alert state changes.
7. Create Azure Monitor Suppression Action rules to override specific rules on specific servers.
8. Author an Azure Logic app for postprocessing of raw alerts to render more readable alert notifications.
9. Import Azure Workbooks to showcase server monitoring data.

The next chapter, "Regulatory and Security Compliance for Azure Arc Servers," extends the Azure Monitoring solution to include Microsoft Sentinel, Microsoft Defender for Cloud, and Azure Arc SQL Server integrations.

CHAPTER 7

Regulatory and Security Compliance for Azure Arc Servers

In the previous chapter, "Hybrid Server Monitoring Solution," you built out your Azure-based server management capability. You can now perform economical and efficient server infrastructure monitoring of Azure VMs and Azure Arc servers using Azure Monitor. A parallel and significant opportunity to leverage your Azure management investment exists: to achieve compliance with regulatory and security frameworks. The Azure Arc and Microsoft monitoring agents and Azure Policy operations covered in detail in this book are also foundational to adopting best practice Microsoft enterprise security solutions.

In this chapter, we will showcase how the Azure Arc agent communicates with Microsoft Defender for Cloud to deliver solid and substantial security coverage to include integrated vulnerability scanning. Then you will learn how Microsoft Sentinel installs as a solution within Azure Log Analytics to create the best modern Security Incident and Event Management (SIEM) for the hybrid estate.

We'll finish the chapter with a look at the security aspects of Azure Arc SQL Server. You will gain an appreciation for how Azure Arc server and Azure Arc SQL Server fit into the larger Microsoft Azure Arc road map for unified management of hybrid resources that even includes Azure Stack HCI (hyperconverged infrastructure)

Microsoft Defender for Cloud for Azure Arc Servers

Microsoft packages and delivers its recommended best practice and comprehensive enterprise security solutions using an Azure portal feature: *Microsoft Defender for Cloud.*

S. Buchanan and J. Joyner, *Azure Arc-Enabled Kubernetes and Servers*,
https://doi.org/10.1007/978-1-4842-7768-3_7

- In the Azure Arc scenario, *Microsoft Defender for Cloud* is where workload protection for servers is enabled.
- In this chapter, we will focus on the *Regulatory compliance* and *Microsoft Defender for Cloud for servers* components of Microsoft Defender for Cloud.

Microsoft Defender for Cloud

Microsoft Defender for Cloud is a unified infrastructure security management system that provides advanced threat protection across hybrid workloads in the cloud–whether they're in Azure or not–as well as on premises. Microsoft Defender for Cloud is a top-level console in the Azure portal as seen in Figure 7-1.

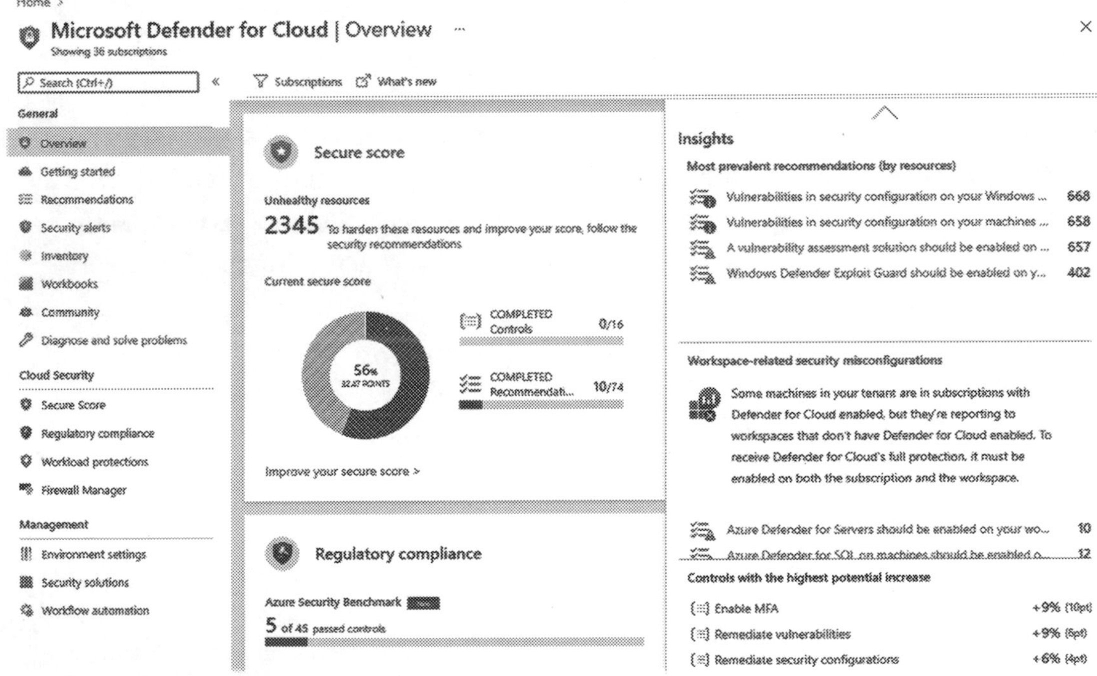

Figure 7-1. *Microsoft Defender for Cloud manages workload protection on Azure Arc servers*

In understanding the role of Microsoft Defender for Cloud, alternative and competing products similar to Microsoft Defender for Cloud include Qualys Cloud Platform, AlienVault USM, Tripwire Enterprise, Nessus, and Tenable.io. These platforms manage, orchestrate, and report on enterprise security posture. These products include or support *cloud workload protection platforms* (CWPPs) used to secure server workloads in public cloud infrastructure. Well-known CWPPs include Microsoft Defender for Cloud, Trend Micro Deep Security and Cloud One, VMware Carbon Black, Sophos Central, and Palo Alto Networks Prisma Cloud.

In practice, Microsoft Defender for Cloud is your tool and your friend. Use it and depend on it to guide, focus, and understand security issues across all platforms in all locations. If you want to exercise due diligence in your security responsibilities, you can't invest too much in the resources available from Microsoft Defender for Cloud.

Microsoft Defender for Cloud will interact with Azure Arc servers using Azure Policy. The policies applied will correspond with the controls appropriate for the regulatory framework(s) the enterprise needs to be compliant with. This is known as *coverage* or *protection*. Microsoft Defender for Cloud coverage is applied to Azure subscriptions, and then Microsoft Defender for Cloud plans can be enabled for "protectable" resource types found in the covered subscription(s).

Microsoft Defender for Cloud workload protections

Microsoft Defender for Cloud's integrated cloud workload protection platform (CWPP), **Microsoft Defender for Cloud**, delivers advanced, intelligent, protection of Azure and hybrid resources and workloads. Notice controls for Microsoft Defender for Cloud surface in the lower portion of the portal in Figure 7-1.

Microsoft Defender for Cloud provides security alerts and advanced threat protection for specific Azure resource types, and hybrid computers are an included resource type. Azure Arc servers are first-class citizens (alongside Azure VMs) when it comes to available ARM-based security protections from Microsoft Defender for Cloud. Consider that you are extending to your own on-premises servers the same security umbrella Microsoft has proven to be secure and effective for its hyperscale cloud.

Figure 7-2 is the Microsoft Defender for Cloud overview page and makes clear how a wide variety of security-sensitive resources (top third) are managed together to produce a consolidated collection of cross-platform security alerts (middle third). The lower third surfaces controls for the *Advanced protection* additional features bundled with Microsoft Defender for Cloud.

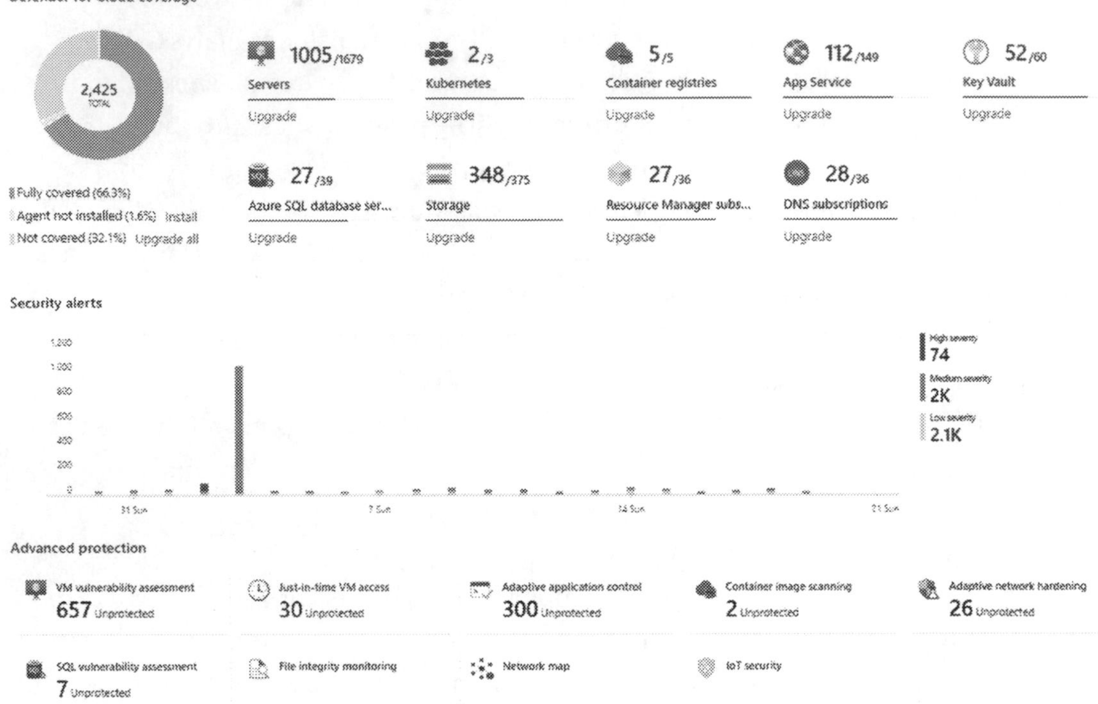

***Figure 7-2.** Microsoft Defender for Cloud is the delivery system for security policy and enforcement to servers, apps, and services everywhere*

Microsoft Defender for Cloud abstracts compute, data, and service layers in your environment so that discreet *Microsoft Defender for Cloud*nical goals (compliance policies) can be applied across these heterogenous resource types:

- Microsoft Defender for Cloud workload protection for servers
- Microsoft Defender for Cloud workload protection for App Service
- Microsoft Defender for Cloud workload protection for Storage
- Microsoft Defender for Cloud workload protection for SQL
- Microsoft Defender for Cloud workload protection for Kubernetes
- Microsoft Defender for Cloud workload protection for container registries
- Microsoft Defender for Cloud workload protection for Key Vault

- Microsoft Defender for Cloud workload protection for Resource Manager
- Microsoft Defender for Cloud workload protection for DNS

Microsoft Defender for Cloud for Servers

Microsoft Defender for Cloud for servers adds threat detection and advanced defenses for Windows and Linux computers. Microsoft Defender for Cloud workload protection for servers as a product was formerly known as Azure Security Center (ASC) Standard, and you can use the terms *Azure Defender for Servers* and *ASC Standard* interchangeably with Microsoft Defender for Cloud workload protection for servers.

There is a granular cost to use Microsoft Defender for Cloud, the principal one being $15 per month per server. This is the cost of the Microsoft cloud workload protection platform, and it is a tremendous value in today's cybersecurity market. It's the same cost for in-Azure servers and Azure Arc servers. Microsoft Defender for Cloud integrates these Azure services to monitor and protect Azure Arc servers:

- Integrated license for **Microsoft Defender for Endpoint** (Windows only): Microsoft Defender for Cloud for servers includes Microsoft Defender for Endpoint. Together, they provide comprehensive endpoint detection and response (EDR) capabilities.
- **Vulnerability assessment scanning for VMs**: The vulnerability scanner included with Microsoft Defender for Cloud is powered by Qualys. (We cover this in detail in the next section of this chapter, "Microsoft Defender for Cloud's integrated vulnerability assessment solution.")
- **Just-in-time (JIT) virtual machine (VM) access**: When you enable Microsoft Defender for Cloud for servers, you can use just-in-time VM access to lock down the inbound traffic to your VMs, reducing exposure to attacks while providing easy access to connect to VMs when needed.
- **File integrity monitoring (FIM)**: When you enable Microsoft Defender for Cloud for servers, you can use FIM to validate the integrity of Windows files, your Windows registries, and Linux files.

- For Linux, Microsoft Defender for Cloud collects audit records from **Linux machines** by using *auditd*, a common Linux auditing framework. Microsoft Defender for Cloud integrates functionalities from the auditd package within the Log Analytics agent. Microsoft Defender for Cloud also performs **Docker host hardening** by identifying unmanaged containers hosted on IaaS Linux VMs, or other Linux machines running Docker containers.
- **Adaptive application controls (AAC) and adaptive network hardening (ANH)**: AAC are an intelligent and automated solution for defining "allow lists" of known-safe applications for your machines. ANH further improves the security posture by hardening NSG rules based on the actual traffic patterns.

Onboarding Microsoft Defender for Cloud workload protection for servers

To enable Microsoft Defender for Cloud on your Azure subscription:

1. From Microsoft Defender for Cloud's sidebar, select **Getting started** (see Figure 7-3).
2. The *Upgrade* tab lists subscriptions eligible for onboarding.
3. From the *Select subscriptions to enable Microsoft Defender for Cloud on* list, select the subscriptions to upgrade and click the **Upgrade** button to enable Microsoft Defender for Cloud.

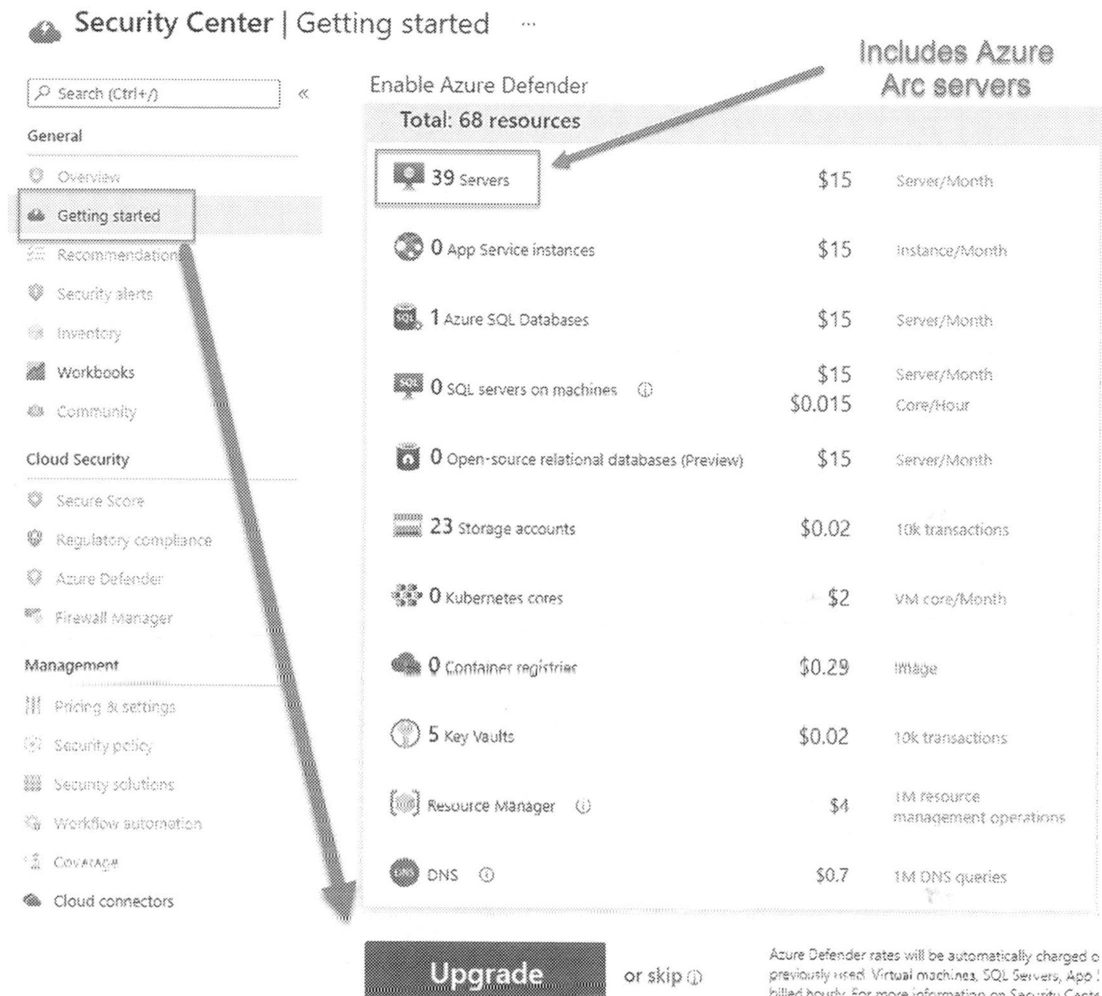

***Figure 7-3.** Turning Microsoft Defender for Cloud on to enable server workload protection on an Azure subscription*

Roles and Permissions

Prepare your internal teams organizationally to begin using Microsoft Defender for Cloud, and Azure Policy features. To use Microsoft Defender for Cloud in production, you need to name a team that is responsible for monitoring and governing Azure and non-Azure environments from a security perspective.

- Assign team members Security Admin, Contributor, or Reader roles as appropriate for their jobs.

- Conduct key stakeholder and operator training on accessing and using the solution. Cover using the Azure portal, ARM templates, Azure PowerShell, Azure CLI (command-line interface), and/or REST API as appropriate for how your organization will operate Microsoft Defender for Cloud.

Tip There are only two Azure RBAC security roles that have the authority to enable Microsoft Defender for Cloud on a subscription: *Owner* and *Security Admin*. Additionally, *Owner* is the only role that can add and assign regulatory compliance standards.

Assign and Customize the Microsoft Defender for Cloud Default Policy

Activating Microsoft Defender for Cloud registers a subscription to the Microsoft Defender for Cloud Resource Provider *Microsoft.Security*. This action also triggers the assignment of the Azure Security Benchmark policy initiative on the subscription, if the Azure Security Benchmark policy initiative has not already been assigned neither to the subscription itself nor to a management group higher up in the hierarchy.

Azure Security Benchmark

This default policy will have a name like *"ASC Default (subscription: 2cb51234-d53f-48f3 -1234-2cfd189e1234)."* Microsoft recommends that you review each of the security recommendations in this default initiative to determine whether they are appropriate for the various subscriptions and resource groups in your organization. The policy will assign the *Azure Security Benchmark* initiative.

The Azure Security Benchmark initiative represents the policies and controls implementing security recommendations defined in Azure Security Benchmark v2; see `https://aka.ms/azsecbm`. It is the Microsoft Defender for Cloud default policy initiative. There are about 200 or more policies in the initiative, including policies that detect Azure Arc computers without the Log Analytics agent installed (Figure 7-4).

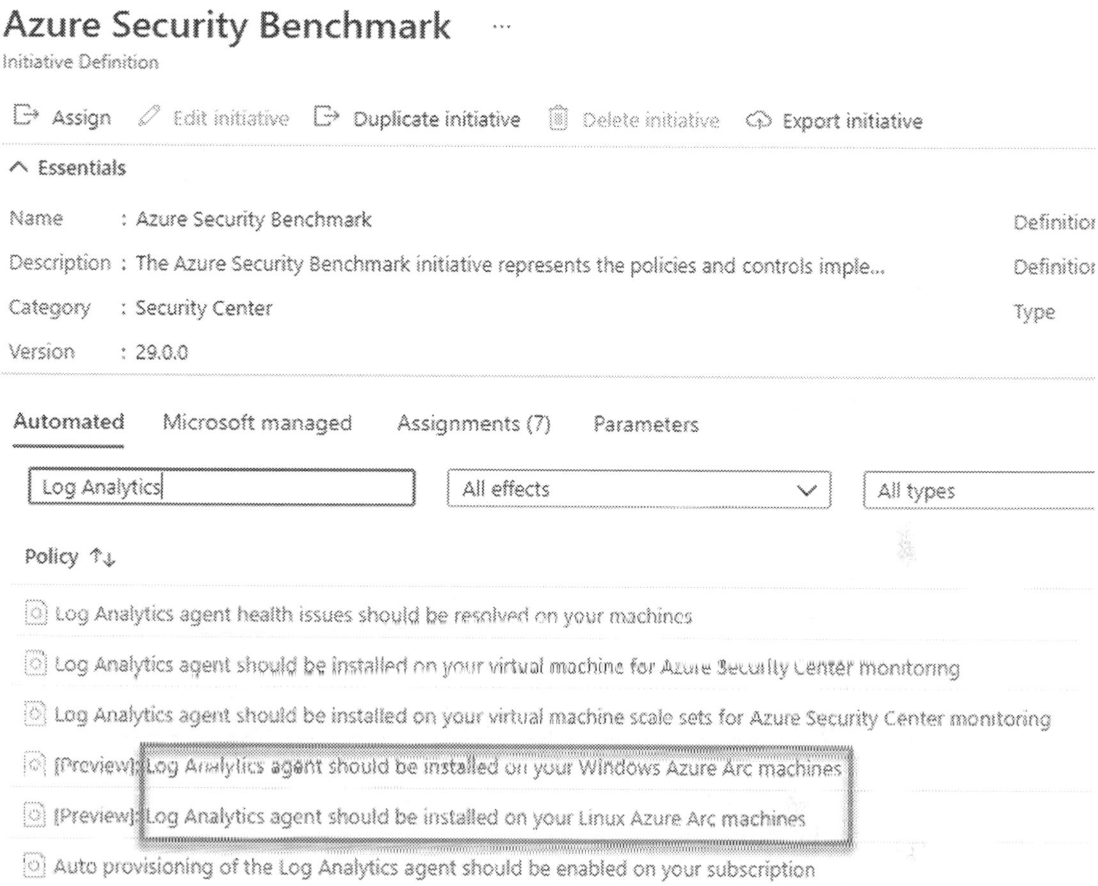

Azure Security Benchmark ...
Initiative Definition

Assign | Edit initiative | Duplicate initiative | Delete initiative | Export initiative

Essentials

Name : Azure Security Benchmark
Description : The Azure Security Benchmark initiative represents the policies and controls imple...
Category : Security Center
Version : 29.0.0

Definitior
Definitior
Type

Automated | Microsoft managed | Assignments (7) | Parameters

Log Analytics | All effects | All types

Policy

Log Analytics agent health issues should be resolved on your machines
Log Analytics agent should be installed on your virtual machine for Azure Security Center monitoring
Log Analytics agent should be installed on your virtual machine scale sets for Azure Security Center monitoring
[Preview]: Log Analytics agent should be installed on your Windows Azure Arc machines
[Preview]: Log Analytics agent should be installed on your Linux Azure Arc machines
Auto provisioning of the Log Analytics agent should be enabled on your subscription

Figure 7-4. *Policies in the Azure Security Benchmark include Azure Arc servers*

Upon assigning the Azure Security Benchmark to the subscription or resource group containing your Azure Arc servers, each Azure Arc server will begin to report its compliance state. Both overall compliance with the initiative and individual compliance on each specific policy in the initiative are displayed at the Azure Portal ➤ Azure Arc server ➤ Operations ➤ Policies blade.

Assess Policy Compliance

If you have followed the procedures in this book, your Azure Arc servers are already covered by the *Enable Azure Monitor for VMs* policy initiative (see the "Azure Policy" section of Chapter 6, "Hybrid Server Monitoring Solution"). In that case, an Azure Arc server policy blade might look like Figure 7-5.

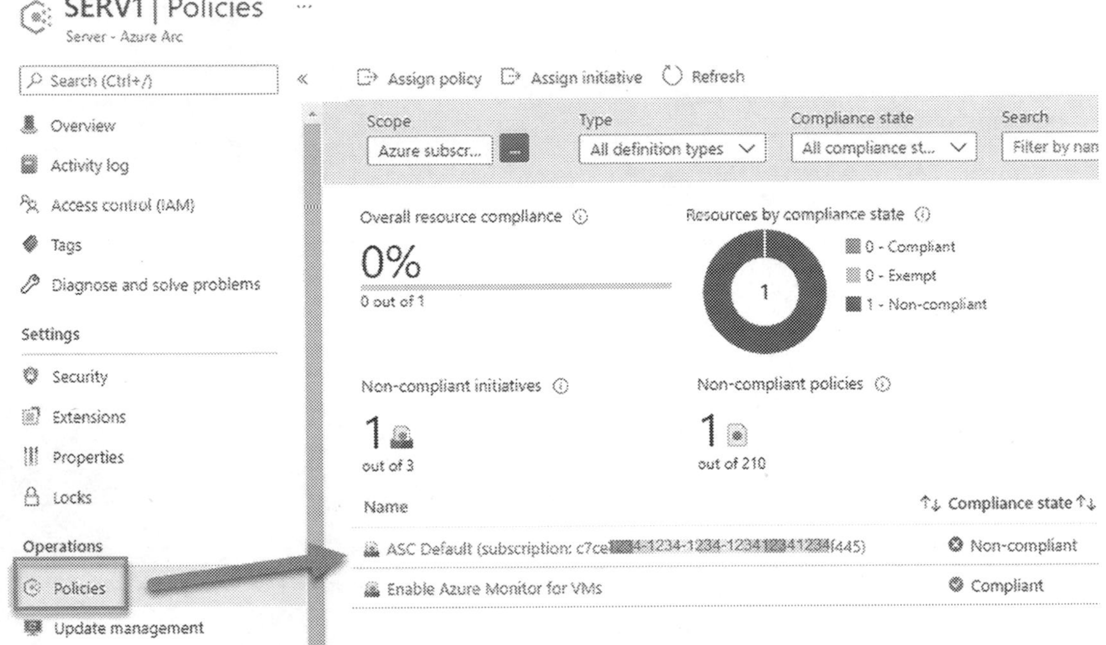

Figure 7-5. The Azure Security Benchmark assigned to an Azure Arc server

The Azure Arc server in Figure 7-5 is compliant with the *Enable Azure Monitor for VMs* policy but not fully compliant with the *ASC Default subscription* policy. Clicking through on the *ASC Default subscription* initiative proceeds to a list of all the policies in the initiative. Policies that the server is not in compliance with are sorted at the top (Figure 7-6).

Non-compliant policies

1

out of 199

Groups Policies Non-compliant resources Events

Filter by group name... Subgroup : **All subgroups** Compliance state : **7 selected**

Name	Compliance	Subgroup	Non-compliant poli...	Total policies
Perform software vulnerability assessments	Non-compliant	Posture and Vulnerability ...	1	1
Implement security for internal traffic	Compliant	Network Security	0	0

Figure 7-6. The Azure Security Benchmark assigned to an Azure Arc server

Notice at the top of Figure 7-6 that the server is only out of compliance with one policy out of 199 policies in the initiative. At the top of the list is the one noncompliant policy: *Perform software vulnerability assessments*. The Azure Arc server is already in compliance with the Log Analytics Agent policy we saw in Figure 7-4 because the Enable Azure Monitor for VMs initiative contains the same individual policy! The only additional thing you need to do is deploy a vulnerability assessment, and we will cover how to do that in this chapter, coming up in the "Integrated Vulnerability Assessment" section.

Tip There are parameters that need to be verified or set when using compliance standards, including even the *ASC Default*. For example, CMMC requires you to declare what accounts should be in the local admin group; then it audits to ensure that only those accounts are in the local admin group.

Choose Industry Standards and Enable Compliance

Azure has the industry's broadest and deepest compliance portfolio. Azure compliance offerings are global, with over 60 offerings specific to over 20 regions and countries. Azure is also built for the specific needs of key industries and complies with over 50 compliance offerings specific to the health, government, finance, education, manufacturing, and media industries. The complete list of over 100 Azure compliance offerings can be found at this URL:

```
https://docs.microsoft.com/en-us/azure/compliance/
```

A subset of those compliance offerings is either included by default in Microsoft Defender for Cloud or can be easily imported to the regulatory compliance dashboard and then assigned to a subscription. Using the regulatory compliance dashboard in Microsoft Defender for Cloud, you can compare the configuration of your resources with the requirements of industry standards, regulations, and benchmarks.

The ability to translate specific industry and regional requirements into actionable and auditable security controls is a strategic value-add for the Microsoft Defender for Cloud platform. Table 7-1 lists the offerings in each category.

Table 7-1. *Regulatory Frameworks That Can Appear on the Microsoft Defender for Cloud Compliance Dashboard*

Out-of-the-box offerings	Prebuilt offerings can be added
Azure Security Benchmark	NIST SP 800-53 R4 & 171 R2
PCI DSS 3.2.1	CMMC Level 3
ISO 27001	UKO and UK NHS
SOC TSP (SOC 2 Type 2)	Azure CIS 1.1.0 & 1.3.0
	Canada Federal PBMM
	HIPAA HITRUST
Custom offerings	SWIFT CSP CSCF v2020
Any custom initiative as an offering	ISO 27001:2013
	New Zealand ISM Restricted

To add one of the prebuilt offerings, disable one of the out-of-the-box offerings, or add a custom initiative, navigate to Microsoft Defender for Cloud ➤ Cloud Security ➤ Regulatory compliance, and click the **Manage compliance policies** button as seen in Figure 7-7.

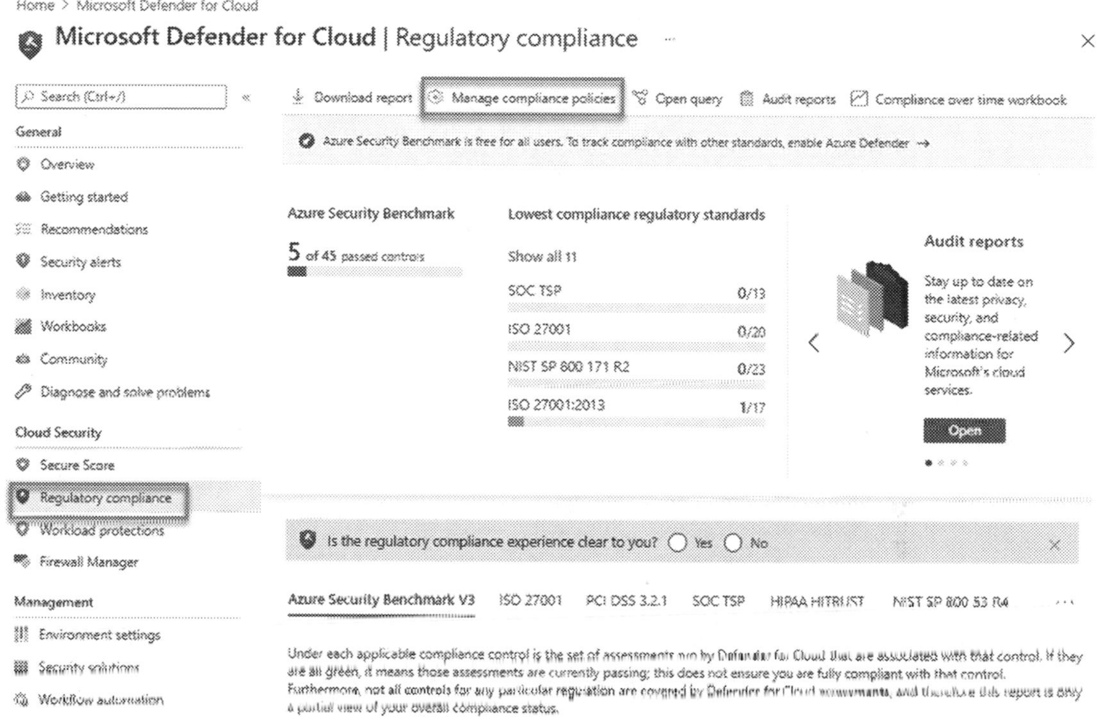

Figure 7-7. *Accessing the Manage compliance policies functions*

You can build your own custom offering using the prebuilt offerings as guides. A custom offering is a custom policy initiative that contains all the individual policies that constitute that compliance standard. Your custom offering might include many of the prebuilt individual policies as well as some additional custom policies you might add, to create a custom mix of policies, some built-in and some custom.

Tip Out of scope for this book but of interest to cybersecurity professionals is another major Microsoft security solution: **Microsoft Compliance Manager**, an end-to-end compliance management solution inside the Microsoft 365 compliance center. Learn more at this URL:

`https://docs.microsoft.com/en-us/microsoft-365/compliance/compliance-manager`

Assess Regulatory Compliance

If you want to consult your organizational compliance with one of the "out-of-the-box" standards, or after you have added a prebuilt or custom standard, navigate to Microsoft Defender for Cloud ➤ Regulatory compliance and click the tab that corresponds to the offering you want to review. Figure 7-8 shows that after assigning the HIPAA HITRUST standard, 11 of 27 VMs and Azure Arc servers are missing change tickets demonstrating patch testing and validation prior to production deployment.

Azure Security Benchmark
ISO 27001
PCI DSS 3.2.1
SOC TSP
HIPAA HITRUST
Under each applicable compliance control is the set of assessments run by Security Center that are associated with that control. If they are all green, it means those assessments are currently passing; this does not ensure you are fully compliant with that control. Furthermore, not all controls for any particular regulation are covered by Security Center assessments, and therefore this report is only a partial view of your overall compliance status.
10. Control of Operational Software
10.m. Control of Technical Vulnerabilities
0713.10m2Organizational.5. Patches are tested and evaluated before they are installed.
Control details
Customer responsibility
Resource type
Failed resources
Resource complianc...
Vulnerabilities in security coı
VMs & servers
11 of 27

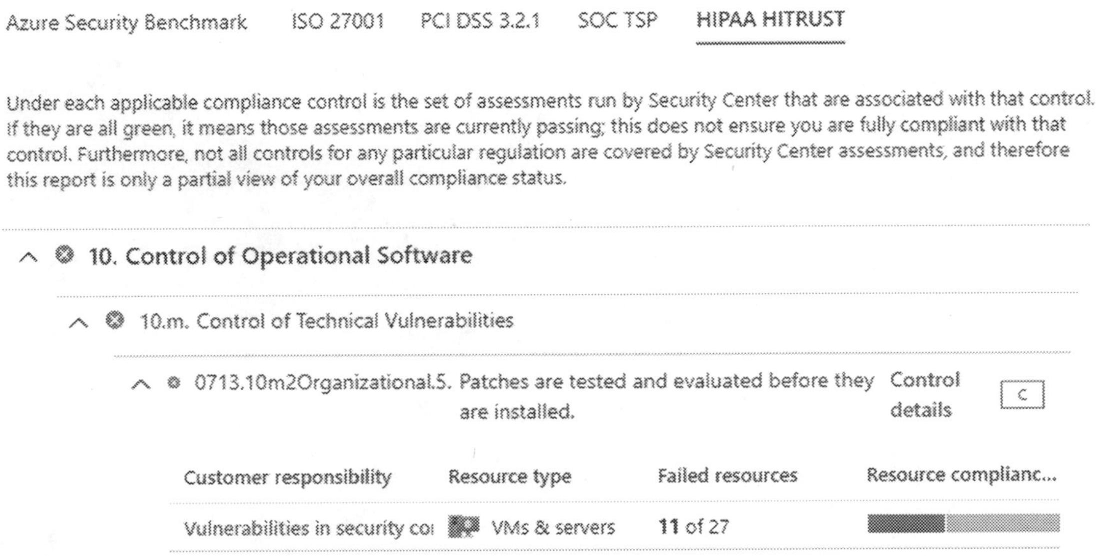

Figure 7-8. Assessing organizational compliance with specific regulatory standard controls

An individual Azure Arc server will surface Microsoft Defender for Cloud integration at the Azure Arc server ➤ Settings ➤ Security blade as seen in Figure 7-9. Recommendations based on policies applied from the enabled regulatory standard(s) are listed. If this server has been involved with any security incident or alert in the previous 21 days, that will be reflected on this page.

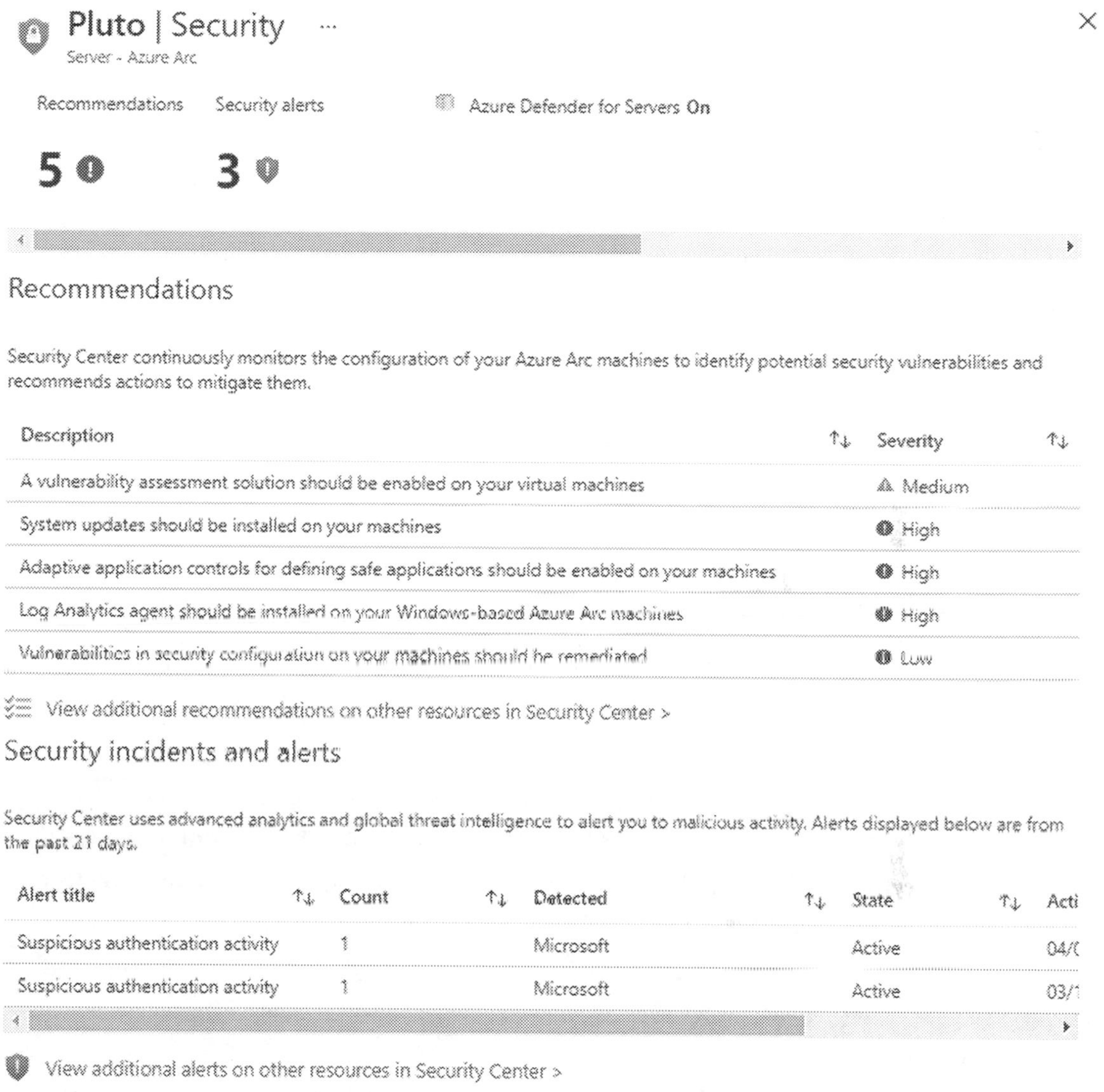

Pluto | Security ...

Server - Azure Arc

Recommendations Security alerts Azure Defender for Servers **On**

5 **3**

Recommendations

Security Center continuously monitors the configuration of your Azure Arc machines to identify potential security vulnerabilities and recommends actions to mitigate them.

Description	Severity
A vulnerability assessment solution should be enabled on your virtual machines	Medium
System updates should be installed on your machines	High
Adaptive application controls for defining safe applications should be enabled on your machines	High
Log Analytics agent should be installed on your Windows-based Azure Arc machines	High
Vulnerabilities in security configuration on your machines should be remediated	Low

View additional recommendations on other resources in Security Center >

Security incidents and alerts

Security Center uses advanced analytics and global threat intelligence to alert you to malicious activity. Alerts displayed below are from the past 21 days.

Alert title	Count	Detected	State	Acti
Suspicious authentication activity	1	Microsoft	Active	04/(
Suspicious authentication activity	1	Microsoft	Active	03/1

View additional alerts on other resources in Security Center >

***Figure 7-9.** Microsoft Defender for Cloud for servers, active on an Azure Arc server*

The deceptively simple interface of Microsoft Defender for Cloud hides some amazingly powerful security tools. Clicking on the *View additional recommendations on other resources in Security Center* link under the recommendations section opens a new window with an interactive view of all the policies you are not in compliance with (Figure 7-10).

Recommendations ...

Download CSV report Guides & Feedback

Each security control below represents a security risk you should mitigate.
Address the recommendations in each control, focusing on the controls worth the most points.
To get the max score, fix all recommendations for all resources in a control. Learn more >

Controls	Max score	Current Score	Potential score incre...	Unhealthy resources	Resource health
Enable MFA	10	10	+ 0% (0 points)	None	
Secure management ports	8	8	+ 0% (0 points)	None	
Remediate vulnerabilities	6	0	+ 11% (6 points)	17 of 19 resources	
Apply system updates	6	2.82	+ 6% (3.18 points)	9 of 17 resources	
Enable encryption at rest	4	0	+ 7% (4 points)	5 of 5 resources	
Manage access and permissions	4	0	+ 7% (4 points)	1 of 1 resources	
Remediate security configurations	4	0.67	+ 6% (3.33 points)	15 of 25 resources	
Encrypt data in transit	4	2.67	+ 2% (1.33 points)	4 of 12 resources	
Restrict unauthorized network access	4	3.2	+ 1% (0.8 points)	1 of 5 resources	

***Figure 7-10.** Microsoft Defender for Cloud for servers active on an Azure Arc server*

What's so powerful about this view is that the potential increase–that the contribution to security each specific recommendation would achieve–is scored. The more serious the impact, multiplied by the number of instances needing remediation, yields a numeric value that helps you prioritize your security work. In this manner, the otherwise gigantic task of enforcing enterprise security in a distributed and hybrid environment is made more achievable. Focus at each opportunity on remediating the next most impacting unmitigated security risk(s) until none remain.

Create Compliance Exceptions

When you remediate a security risk by performing the recommended action, you are rewarded with seeing the result in the compliance dashboard report–because your compliance score improves (assessments run approximately every 12 hours). But some policies simply don't apply to your environment or, after due diligence, are accepted as known risks. In these cases, you can create exceptions to specific policies.

- For policies that are built into Microsoft Defender for Cloud and included in the secure score, you can create exemptions for one or more resources directly in the portal as follows:

1. Open the recommendations details page for the specific recommendation, such as "Log Analytics agent should be installed on your Windows-based Azure Arc machines."

2. From the toolbar at the top of the page, select **Exempt** (Figure 7-11).

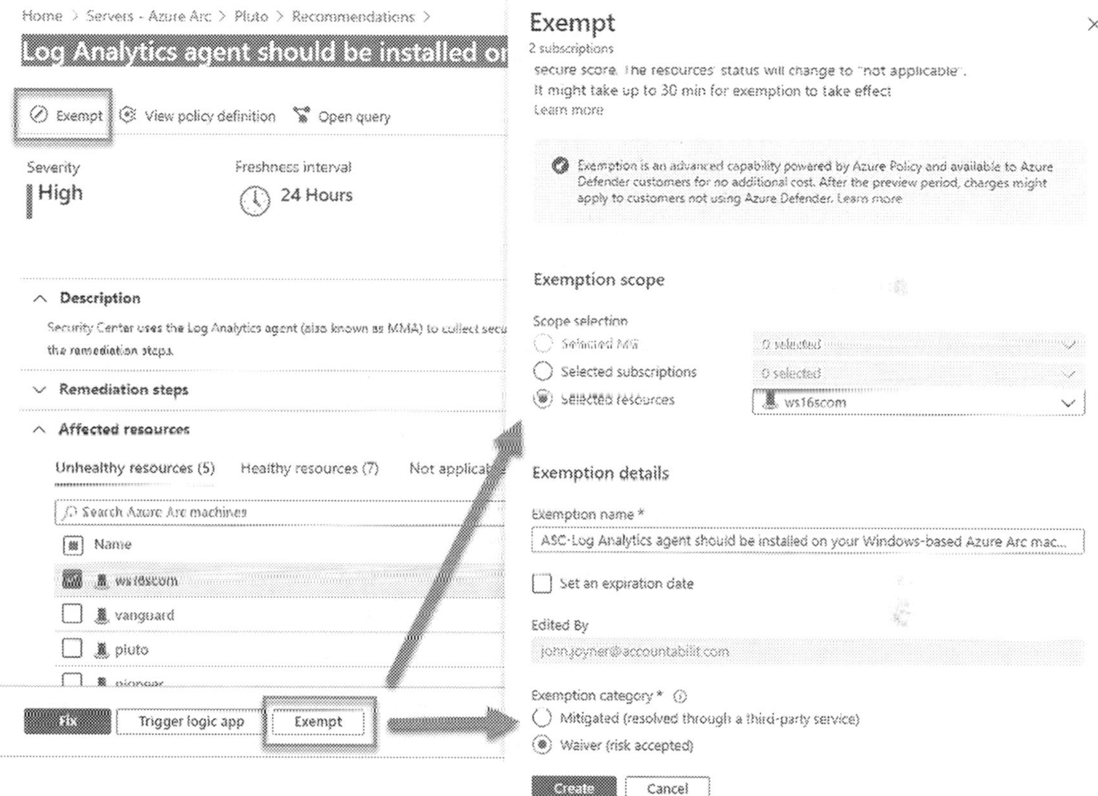

Figure 7-11. *Exempting an Azure Arc server from a specific recommendation*

3. Click the Exempt button at the bottom of the blade; then select the resource(s) to exempt.

4. Select either *Mitigated or Waiver* and click the **Create** button.

For other policies, you can create an exemption directly in the policy itself by following the instructions for Azure Policy exemption. We covered this procedure in the "Azure Policy: Exemption" section of Chapter 6, "Hybrid Server Monitoring Solution."

Tip There's no clear way to review existing exemptions from Microsoft Defender for Cloud. In order to review exemptions you have created, consult Policy ➤ Authoring ➤ Exemptions. Note than an exemption is created for each applicable compliance standard for the resource and policy.

Integrated Vulnerability Assessment

Overview

The integrated vulnerability scanner in Microsoft Defender for Cloud is a tremendous value and should be included in your organization's cyberdefense plan. Generically, a vulnerability scanner is a piece of software that discovers weaknesses in other entities, like networks and computers. In common practice, they are used in the identification and detection of vulnerabilities arising from misconfiguration or flawed programming within a network-based asset such as a firewall, web server, or application server.

Internal and External Vulnerability Scans

Think of failing to apply a security patch or make system modifications without properly updating related security. These rare but predictable situations create vectors for exploitation. Many hostile compromise and ransomware events could have been avoided if more organizations tested their environments using vulnerability scanners. For this reason, PCI DSS 11.2, among other regulatory compliance frameworks, requires organizations that store, process, and/or transmit cardholder data electronically to run internal and external vulnerability scans.

PCI DSS requires two independent methods of vulnerability scanning: internal and external. An external vulnerability scan is performed outside of your network (e.g., at your network perimeter), and it identifies known weaknesses in network structures. An internal vulnerability scan is performed within your network, and it looks at other hosts on the same network to identify internal vulnerabilities.

Microsoft Defender for Cloud and Internal Scanning

Deploying and using the integrated vulnerability scanner that is bundled with *Microsoft Defender for Cloud for servers* can help your organization achieve the internal scanning goal on Windows and Linux servers. This is accomplished by offloading the vulnerability scanning to the Qualys cloud service as illustrated in Figure 7-12.

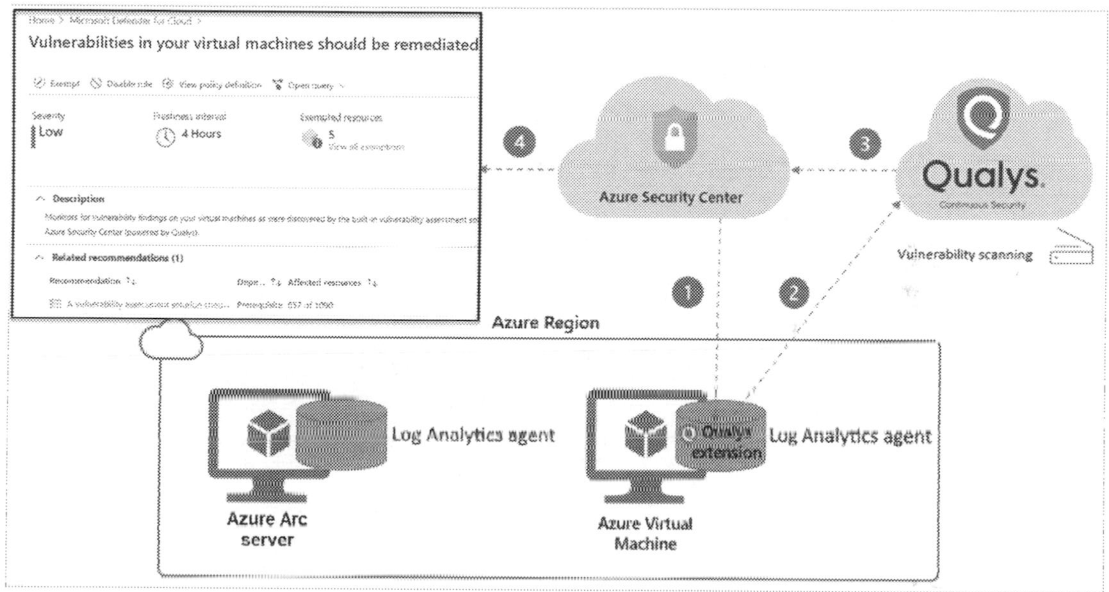

Figure 7-12. *How the integrated vulnerability scanner works. (Source: Microsoft)*

The vulnerability scanner included with ASC is powered by third-party service provider **Qualys**. Qualys' scanner is an industry-leading tool for real-time identification of vulnerabilities. It's only available with Microsoft Defender for Cloud workload protection for servers. You don't need a Qualys license or even a Qualys account–everything's handled seamlessly inside Microsoft Defender for Cloud. Note that scanning is only for devices running the agent and that there are no "device discovery" or "agentless scanning" components.

The vulnerability scanner extension workflow is as follows (steps numbered in Figure 7-12):

1. Deploy Azure Policy from Microsoft Defender for Cloud to perform vulnerability assessments.

2. Azure VMs and Azure Arc servers forward telemetry for analysis to the Qualys cloud service in the defined region.

3. Qualys' cloud service conducts the vulnerability assessment and sends its findings to Microsoft Defender for Cloud.

4. Findings are reported in Microsoft Defender for Cloud and will guide your remediation priorities and actions.

Deploy the Integrated Scanner to Your Azure Arc Servers

Follow these steps to start using the Qualys vulnerability scanner with your servers protected by Microsoft Defender for Cloud:

1. Navigate in your Azure Portal to Home ➤ Microsoft Defender for Cloud.

2. From the Microsoft Defender for Cloud menu, open the **Recommendations** page.

3. Type "vulnerability" in the Search recommendations box as shown in Figure 7-13. Locate and click on the recommendation "**A vulnerability assessment solution should be enabled on your virtual machines**."

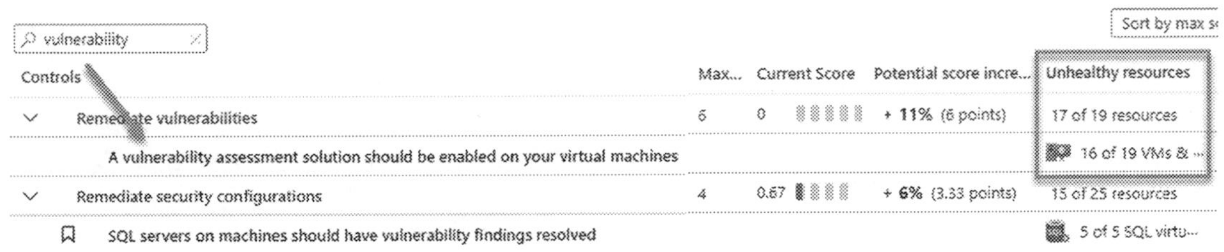

Figure 7-13. *Locate the control that will enable the vulnerability scans*

- Notice that some or all of your computers will be classified as *Unhealthy resources* for the recommendation. Unhealthy in this list means a vulnerability scanner <u>can</u> be deployed to the machine.

- You might see some computers classified as *Not applicable resources*. Machines listed here can't have a vulnerability scanner extension deployed. Reasons could be it's an image in an AKS cluster, it's part of a virtual machine scale set (VMSS), or it's not running one of the supported operating systems for the integrated vulnerability scanner.

4. A blade will open listing the Unhealthy resources as seen in Figure 7-14. Notice all the computers from your hybrid estate will be listed uniformly—Windows and Linux, in-Azure and Azure Arc. From the list of unhealthy machines, select the ones to receive a vulnerability assessment solution and click the **Fix** button.

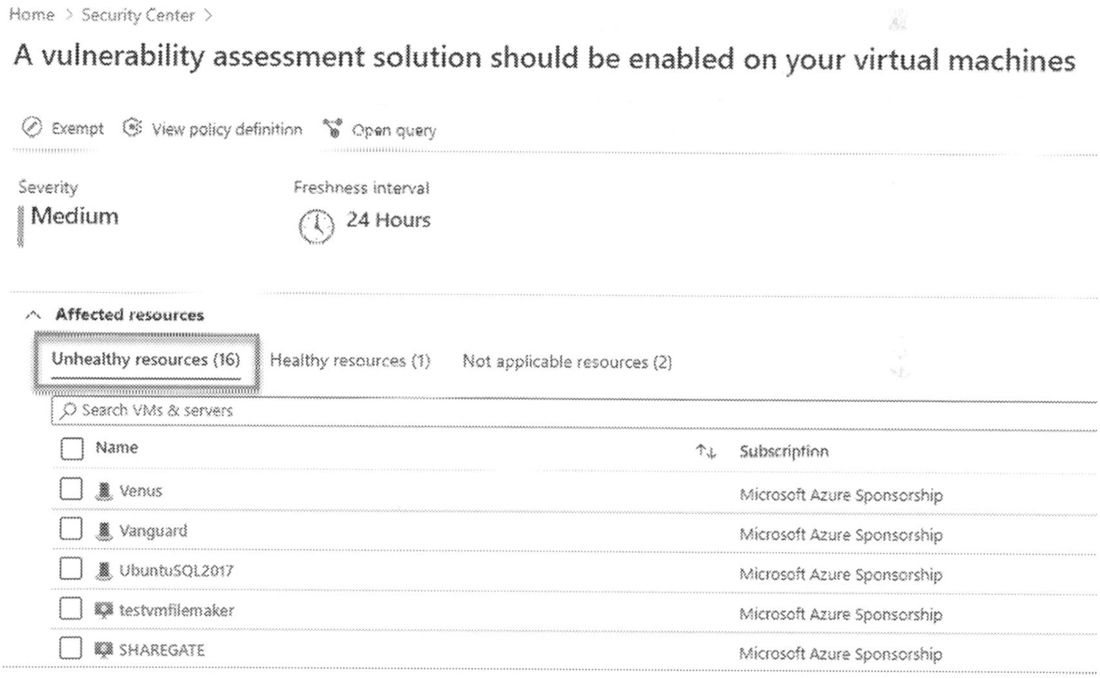

Home > Security Center >

A vulnerability assessment solution should be enabled on your virtual machines

Exempt View policy definition Open query

Severity
Medium

Freshness interval
24 Hours

Affected resources

Unhealthy resources (16) Healthy resources (1) Not applicable resources (2)

Search VMs & servers

Name	Subscription
Venus	Microsoft Azure Sponsorship
Vanguard	Microsoft Azure Sponsorship
UbuntuSQL2017	Microsoft Azure Sponsorship
testvmfilemaker	Microsoft Azure Sponsorship
SHAREGATE	Microsoft Azure Sponsorship

Figure 7-14. *Select the machines to receive a vulnerability assessment solution*

5. Confirm the quantity of resources being remediated and that you are deploying the Microsoft Defender for Cloud integrated vulnerability scanner powered by Qualys (included with Microsoft Defender for Cloud workload protection for servers) as seen in Figure 7-15 and click **Proceed**.

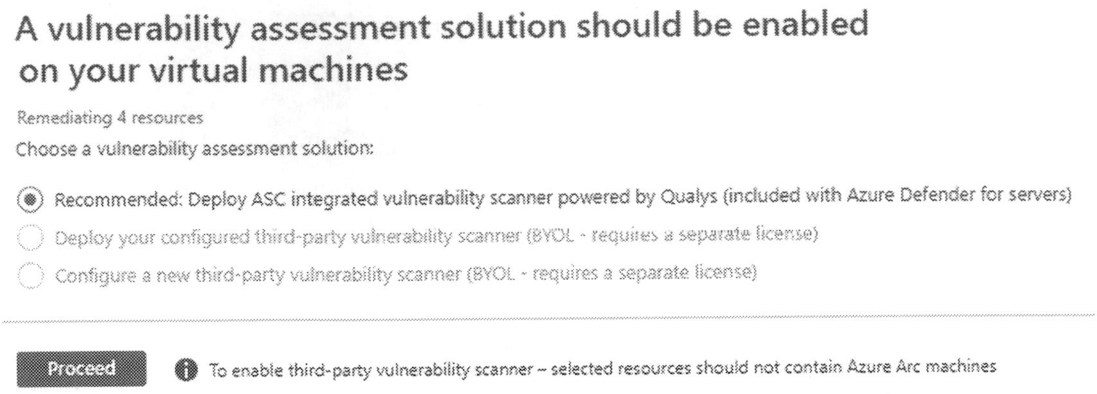

A vulnerability assessment solution should be enabled on your virtual machines

Remediating 4 resources

Choose a vulnerability assessment solution:

(•) Recommended: Deploy ASC integrated vulnerability scanner powered by Qualys (included with Azure Defender for servers)

( ) Deploy your configured third-party vulnerability scanner (BYOL - requires a separate license)

( ) Configure a new third-party vulnerability scanner (BYOL - requires a separate license)

Proceed | To enable third-party vulnerability scanner – selected resources should not contain Azure Arc machines

Figure 7-15. *Deploy the integrated vulnerability scanner powered by Qualys*

6. At the Fixing Resources page, confirm the selected resources are the servers you want to onboard to the solution and click the ***Fix resources*** button as shown in Figure 7-16.

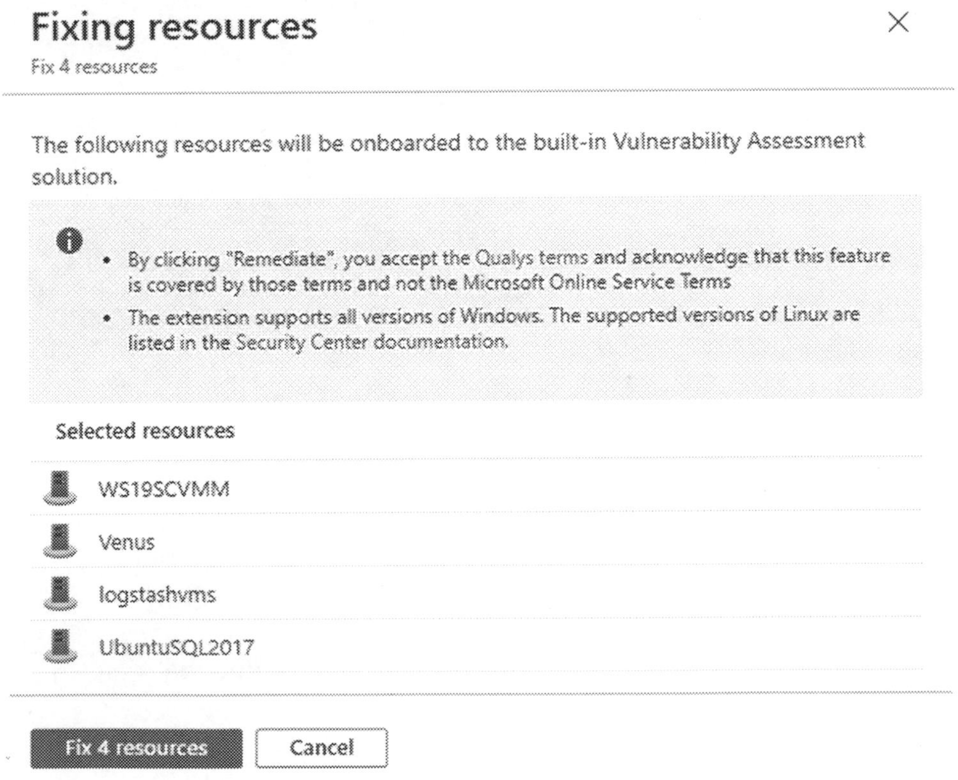

Fixing resources

Fix 4 resources

The following resources will be onboarded to the built-in Vulnerability Assessment solution.

- By clicking "Remediate", you accept the Qualys terms and acknowledge that this feature is covered by those terms and not the Microsoft Online Service Terms
- The extension supports all versions of Windows. The supported versions of Linux are listed in the Security Center documentation.

Selected resources

WS19SCVMM

Venus

logstashvms

UbuntuSQL2017

Fix 4 resources | Cancel

Figure 7-16. *Onboarding Windows and Linux Azure Arc servers to the built-in Vulnerability Assessment solution*

7. The *fix resources* command launches an Azure Resource Manager (ARM) deployment of the provider type *Write ServerVulnerabilityAssessment* for each machine.

   - Windows machines will have the *WindowsAgent.AzureSecurityCenter* extension installed by the ARM deployment. For Linux machines, the extension is named *LinuxAgent.AzureSecurityCenter*.
   - You'll see the extensions being created on the Settings ➤ Extensions page of the Azure Arc server. You can also follow the progress of the ARM deployment in the Azure subscription's activity log (Home ➤ Activity log).
   - Windows computers will show the application **Qualys Cloud Security Agent**, published by Qualys, Inc., in Control Panel ➤ Programs and Features. Linux computers will list **qualys-cloud-agent** when you run the *apt list--installed* command.

8. Scanning begins automatically as soon as the extension is successfully deployed. Scans will then run at 4-hour intervals. This interval isn't configurable.

Tip Target machines must be able to communicate with Qualys' cloud service. If you control Internet access from servers to be scanned, add the following IPs to allow lists (protocol HTTPS, TCP port 443):

64.39.104.113—Qualys' US data center

154.59.121.74—Qualys' European data center

If the machine is in a European Azure region, its artifacts will be processed in Qualys' European data center. Artifacts for machines located elsewhere are sent to the US data center.

Automate At-Scale Deployments

The steps in the preceding section, "Deploy the Integrated Scanner to Your Azure Arc Servers," can be repeated manually as often as needed to keep all production servers enrolled in the solution. For larger environments, there are a variety of at-scale automation tools available to deploy the solution.

Azure Resource Manager (ARM)

This method is available from the Microsoft Defender for Cloud *Recommendations* blade. Return to the view seen in Figure 7-14, and just above the *Affected resources* section of the page, in the *Remediation steps* section, click the **View remediation logic** button. The *Automatic remediation script content* will be displayed. The content is the ARM template to deploy the solution; copy the content out and save as a text file with the ".JSON" extension. Use the JSON-formatted template for whatever automation solution your organization prefers.

Azure Policy

Import the custom policy **Deploy Qualys vulnerability assessment solution on virtual machines** at this GitHub URL into your Azure subscription:

```
https://github.com/Azure/Azure-Security-Center/tree/master/Remediation%20
scripts/Enable%20the%20built-in%20vulnerability%20assessment%20solution%20
on%20virtual%20machines%20(powered%20by%20Qualys)/Azure%20Policy
```

You can assign this policy (seen in Figure 7-17) at the level of Azure subscription, resource groups, or management groups.

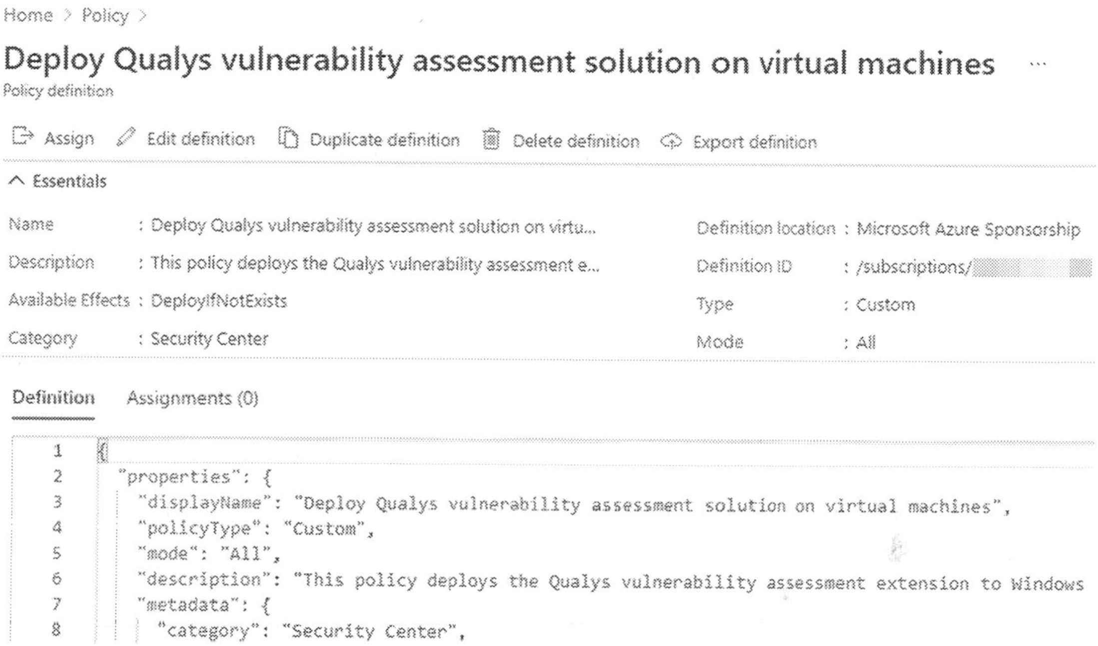

Figure 7-17. *Assign this custom DeployIfNotExists policy to enable a remediation task that deploys the solution to machines*

Azure PowerShell

Use the **qualys-remediate-unhealthy-vms.ps1** script to deploy the extension for all unhealthy virtual machines. To install on new resources, consider automating the script with Azure Automation. The script finds all unhealthy machines discovered by the ASC recommendation and executes an ARM call to deploy the solution. Download the script from this GitHub URL:

```
https://github.com/Azure/Azure-Security-Center/tree/main/Remediation%20
scripts/Enable%20the%20built-in%20vulnerability%20assessment%20solution%20
on%20virtual%20machines%20(powered%20by%20Qualys)/PowerShell
```

Azure Logic App

Use Microsoft Defender for Cloud's workflow automation tools to trigger a logic app like that seen in Figure 7-18 to deploy the scanner whenever the *A vulnerability assessment solution should be enabled on your virtual machines* recommendation is generated for a resource.

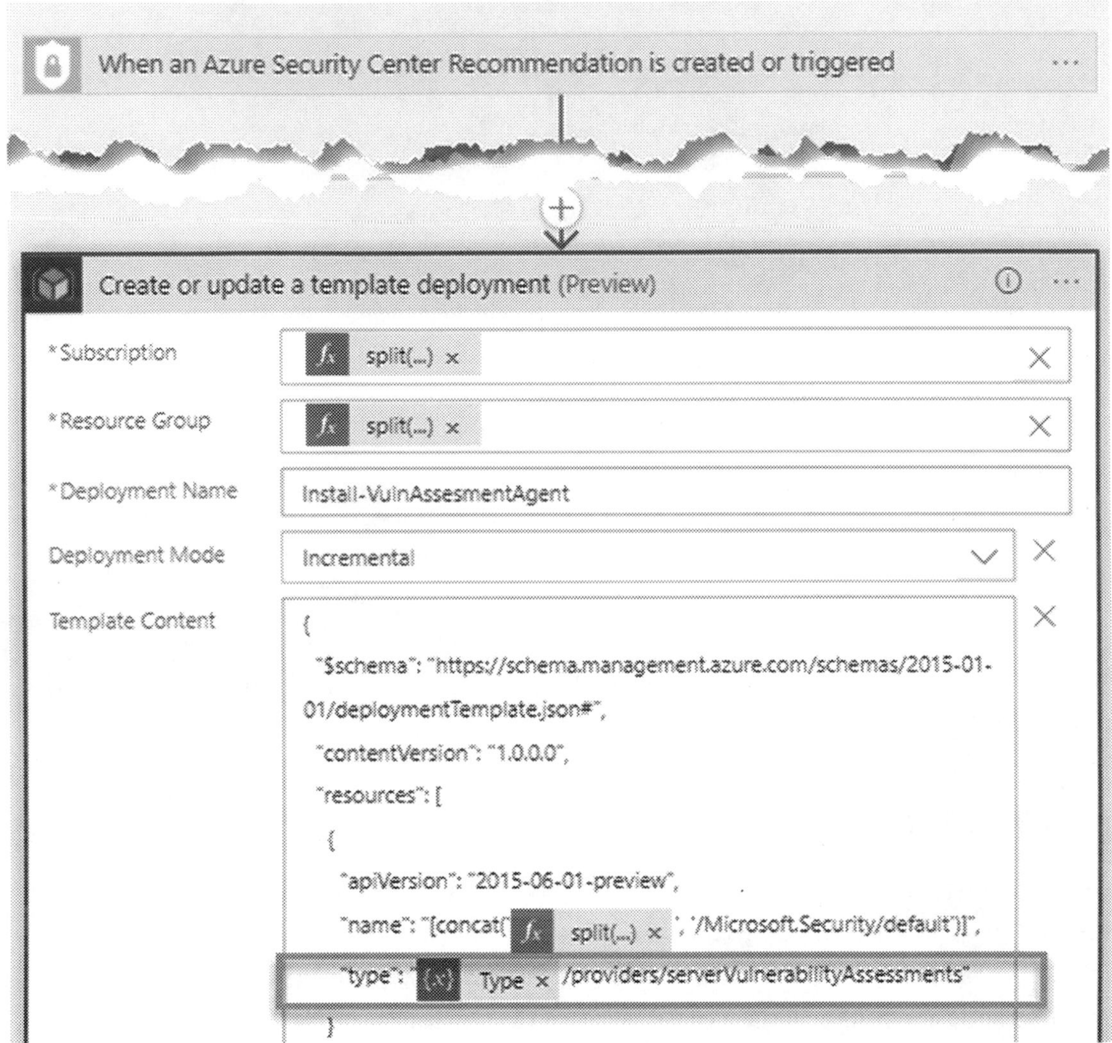

Figure 7-18. *Azure Logic App triggered by a Microsoft Defender for Cloud recommendation*

Build a logic app based on the **Install-VulnAssesmentAgent** sample app you can deploy from this GitHub location:

`https://github.com/Azure/Azure-Security-Center/tree/main/Workflow%20automation/Install-VulnAssesmentAgent`

After you import the logic app, you do need to edit the logic app and customize the *Create or update a template deployment* step with an API connection credential that has permission to write to your Azure VM or Azure Arc server resources. Following that customization, anywhere in the Microsoft Defender for Cloud console where a recommendation is presented, you can click the **Trigger** button to deploy the solution as shown in Figure 7-19.

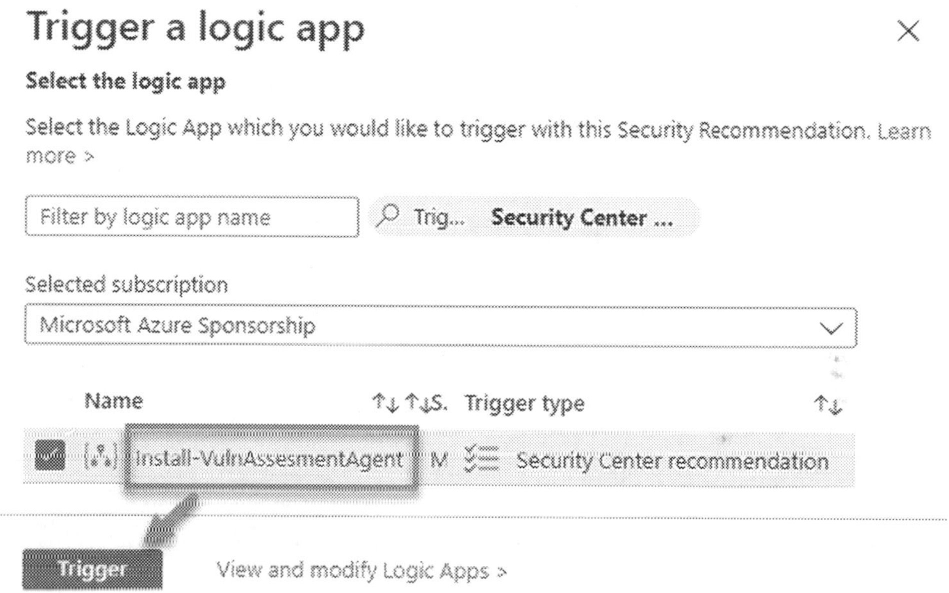

***Figure 7-19.** Manually triggering the logic app to install the extension on a machine*

Azure REST API

To deploy the integrated vulnerability assessment solution using REST API, make a PUT request for the following URL and add the relevant resource ID:

```
https://management.azure.com/<resourceId>/providers/Microsoft.Security/
serverVulnerabilityAssessments/default?api-Version=2015-06-01-preview
```

Trigger an On-Demand Scan

You can trigger an on-demand scan from the machine itself using local or remote scripts or Group Policy Object (GPO). Alternatively, you can integrate an on-demand scan into your software distribution tools at the end of a patch deployment job. The following commands trigger an on-demand scan:

Windows

```
REG ADD HKLM\SOFTWARE\Qualys\QualysAgent\ScanOnDemand\Vulnerability /v
"ScanOnDemand" /t REG_DWORD /d "1" /f
```

Linux

```
sudo /usr/local/qualys/cloud-agent/bin/cloudagentctl.sh
action=demand type=vm
```

View and Remediate Findings

When the vulnerability assessment tool reports vulnerabilities, Microsoft Defender for Cloud presents the findings and related information as *recommendations*. In addition, the findings include related information such as remediation steps, relevant CVEs, CVSS scores, and more. Follow these steps to view and remediate findings from vulnerability assessment scans on your machines:

1. Navigate in your Azure Portal to Home ➤ Microsoft Defender for Cloud.
2. From the Security Center menu, open the **Recommendations** page.
3. Type "vulnerabilities" in the Search recommendations box. Locate and click on the recommendation "**Vulnerabilities in your virtual machines should be remediated**."
4. Expand *Security Checks* and see your vulnerabilities listed in the *Findings* tab as seen in Figure 7-20.

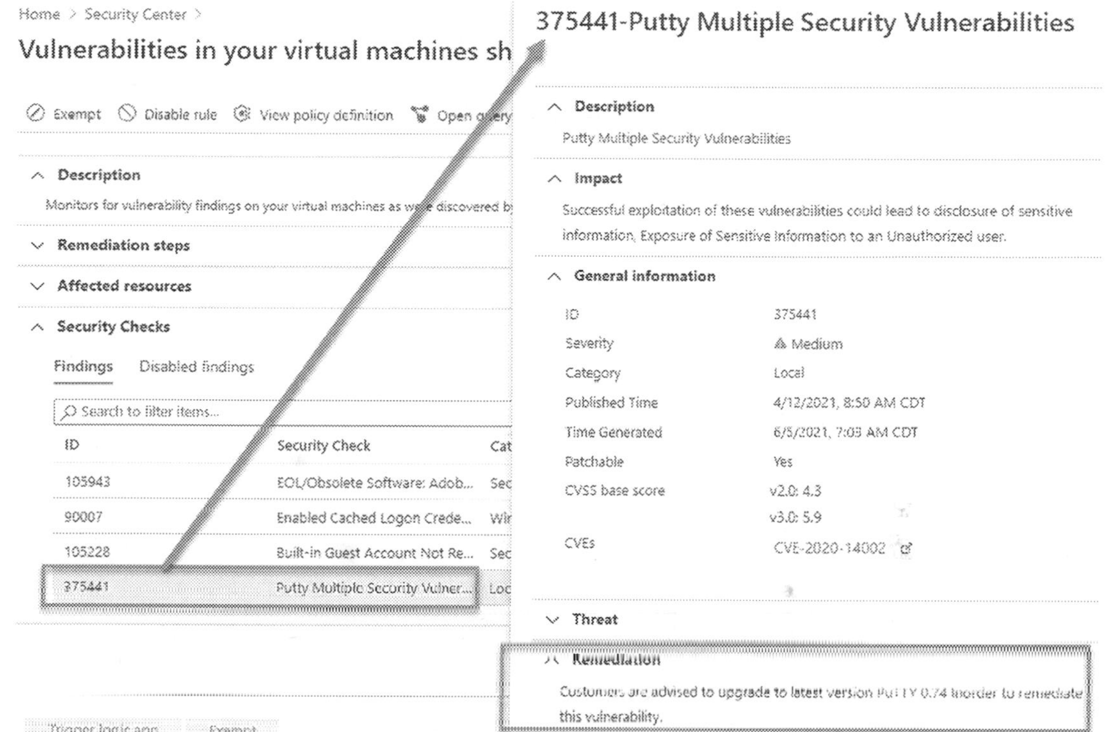

Figure 7-20. *Microsoft Defender for Cloud will provide remediation instructions for discovered vulnerabilities*

Figure 7-20 also illustrates how Microsoft Defender for Cloud materially helps you achieve compliance more rapidly. In this example, the Qualys scanner has identified a vulnerable version of the popular SSH tool **PuTTY**. Expanding *Remediation* specifically lists what safe version of PuTTY to upgrade to and even has a hyperlink to the download site.

Disable Specific Findings

If you have an organizational need to ignore a finding, rather than remediate it, you can optionally disable it. Disabled findings don't impact your secure score or generate unwanted noise.

An example scenario might be an organization that needs to keep using *Adobe Flash Player* because a critical line-of-business application still uses it. After performing due diligence to accept the risk and possibly implementing other mitigations or protections, proceed to disable the finding:

1. From the recommendations detail page for *Vulnerabilities in your virtual machines should be remediated,* select **Disable rule**.

2. Select the relevant scope, such as your subscription.

3. Define your criteria. You can use any of the following criteria:

    - Finding ID
    - Category
    - Security check
    - CVSS scores (v2, v3)
    - Severity
    - Patchable status

    For this example, we use "105943" *Finding ID* that corresponds to this PuTTY vulnerability.

4. Optionally enter a Justification in the provided area and click the **Apply rule** button. New disable rules applied to a subscription might take up to 30 minutes to take effect. After the disable rule takes effect, the item will drop from the list of findings.

5. A list of all *Disabled findings* is available as seen in Figure 7-21. Notice your justification comments are preserved in the *Reason* column.

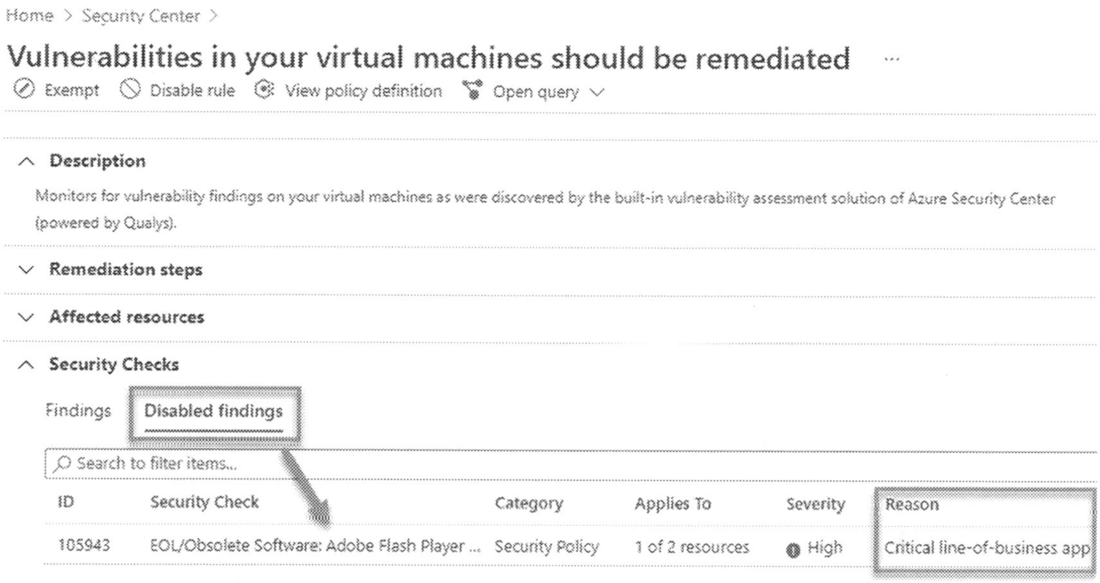

Figure 7-21. *Disabled findings are a way to track what recommendations you have elected to ignore*

Microsoft Sentinel and Azure Arc Server

Every organization with two or more sources of security data needs a SIEM (Security Information and Event Management) tool, which means every organization. The SIEM is where dissimilar but security-sensitive platforms send their real-time security data to, for purposes of central collection and analysis. If you don't have an actual SIEM solution, your ITSM ticketing system or your email inbox might be standing in as your SIEM. At some point, all organizations mature to the point where they can and must deploy a dedicated security tool to perform security event and incident correlation and investigation.

Microsoft Sentinel is a cloud-based SIEM and the only native cloud SIEM. Competing cloud SIEMs include Splunk Security Cloud, AT&T AlienVault USM Anywhere, and IBM QRadar on Cloud. If your organization *has not* invested in one of these or similar SIEMs and you *have* deployed the solutions described in this book such as Azure Arc, Azure Monitor, Azure Log Analytics, and Microsoft Defender for Cloud, then the decision to add Microsoft Sentinel to your security stack should be an easy one. You will gain perhaps the best SIEM available in the world today at a fraction of the cost of adding a third-party enterprise SIEM.

If you have servers outside Azure, a primary reason for adopting Azure Arc might be to deploy Microsoft Sentinel as your enterprise SIEM. If you are performing a best-practice Microsoft Sentinel deployment–and your IT assets include on-prem servers, private cloud and hosted servers, or servers in AWS and/or Google cloud—you should begin your Microsoft Sentinel deployment with an Azure Arc deployment. The high-level steps to roll out Microsoft Sentinel as your SIEM are the following:

1. Install **Azure Arc** agents on non-Azure servers to give them the same out-of-band control using VM Extensions that Azure VMs have.

2. Assign **Azure Policy** to all servers in all clouds that connect them to a specific Azure Log Analytics workspace using VM Extensions.

3. In your Azure subscription, install a **Microsoft Sentinel** instance in the Log Analytics workspace all your servers are connected to.

It's really that simple: Microsoft Sentinel is a superset of Azure Monitor and Azure Log Analytics that both (1) correlates security data from servers with security data from other platforms such as firewalls and cloud service logins like Office 365 and (2) processes the server security data itself for anomalies and threat indicators.

Adding Microsoft Sentinel to a Log Analytics instance will about double the cost of Azure monthly services for a given group of servers. Microsoft Sentinel is an additive cost on top of what your servers might already be consuming in log volume. Table 7-2 gives you an idea; at higher utilization (>50 GB/month), precommitment tiers provide volume discounts. (You get the 100-GB price break starting at 50 GB of utilization.)

Table 7-2. *Comparison of Azure Monitor to Microsoft Sentinel Ingestion Costs*

(East US, 90-day retention)	Azure Monitor	Azure Sentinel
50 GB/month	$3,438.50	$3,000.00 (+87% additional)
100 GB/month	$5,880.00	$3,000.00 (+51% additional)
200 GB/month	$11,040.00	$5,400.00 (+48% additional)

Export Microsoft Defender for Cloud Data to Microsoft Sentinel

Microsoft Defender for Cloud is connected to Microsoft Sentinel very easily. There is a fully functional no-cost connection mode and an optional mode that does incur microcharges for log ingestion.

Complementary Microsoft Defender for Cloud Integration

In the Microsoft Sentinel console, navigate to Configuration ➤ Data connectors. Locate Microsoft Defender for Cloud and click the **Open connector page** button. In the Subscription list, move the slider to the Connected position as shown in Figure 7-22.

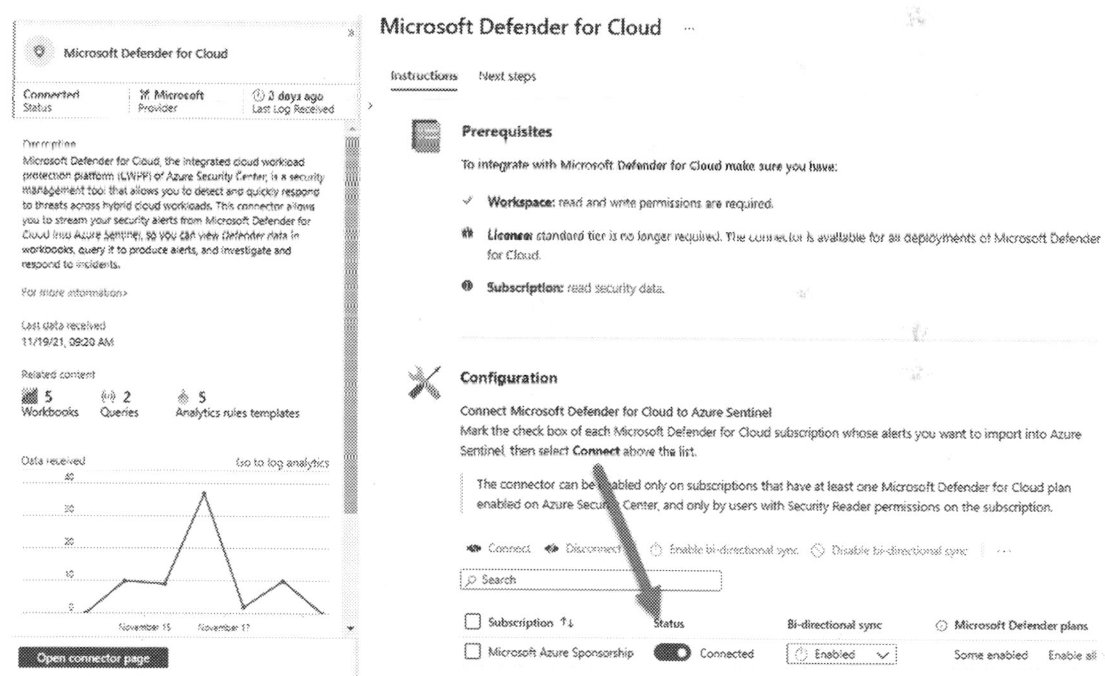

Figure 7-22. *Connect Microsoft Defender for Cloud to Microsoft Sentinel in one click*

The integration shown in Figure 7-22 will cause Security Alerts from Microsoft Defender for Cloud to surface in the Azure Log Analytics instance where Microsoft Sentinel is installed. A Microsoft Sentinel analytics rule (*Create incidents based on Azure Security Center alerts*), when enabled per best practice, will create a Microsoft Sentinel incident when a Microsoft Defender for Cloud alert fires.

There is no cost to enable this integration; that is, there is no Microsoft Sentinel data ingestion charge. This mode is sufficient for many environments, and Microsoft Sentinel incidents will be created in real time when Microsoft Defender for Cloud fires an alert.

Figure 7-23 is a Microsoft Defender for Cloud-sourced Microsoft Sentinel incident from an Azure Arc server. The *Suspicious authentication activity* incident, when investigated, was found to be from an Exchange server, and in the IIS logs, there was a dictionary attack attempting SMTP authentication in order to relay spam.

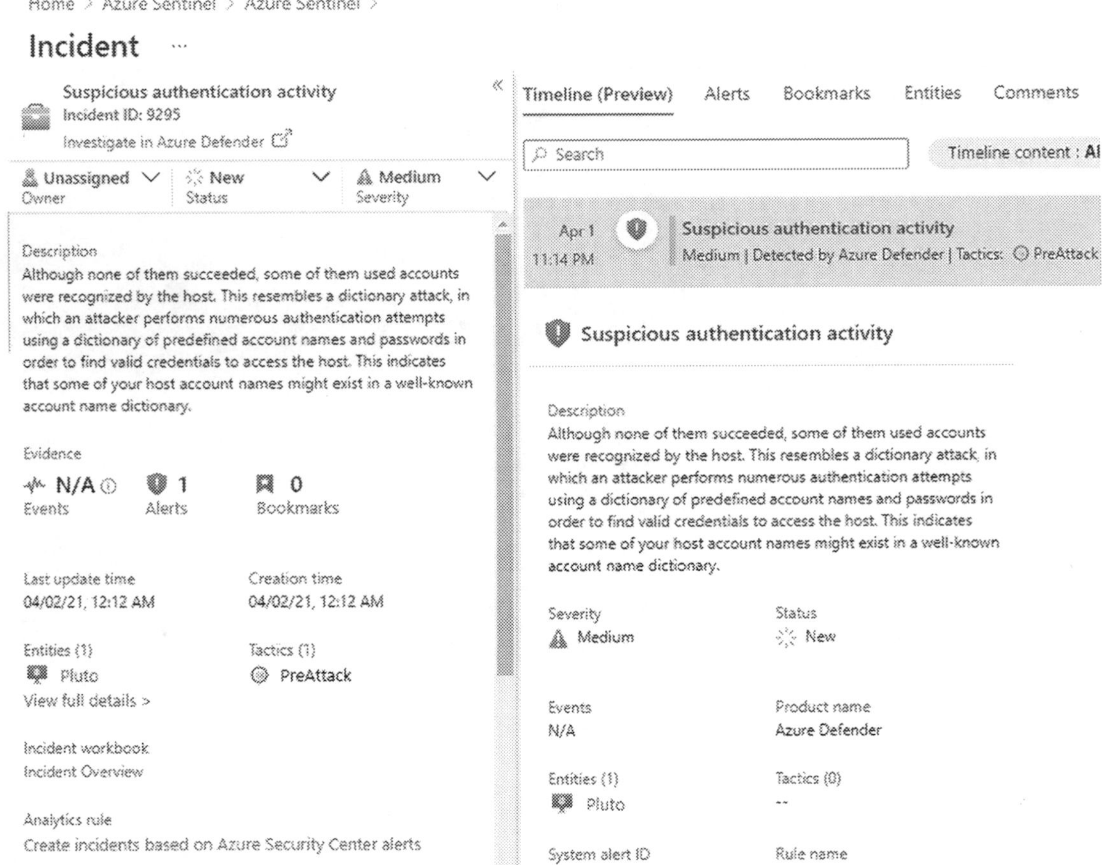

Figure 7-23. *Security incident discovered by Azure Defender on an Azure Arc server*

Tip Using Microsoft Sentinel to receive and manage incidents arising from Microsoft security services incurs no data processing cost. Even if your organization is not going to use Microsoft Sentinel for other purposes, connecting these services will provide a single pane of glass for these ten heterogenous data sources essentially for free:

Azure Activity Logs

Office 365 Audit Logs (SharePoint and Exchange activity)

Microsoft 365 Defender

Microsoft Defender for Office 365

Microsoft Defender for Identity

Microsoft Defender for Endpoint

Microsoft Defender for Cloud

Microsoft Defender for Cloud Apps

Azure Information Protection (AIP)

Additional Microsoft Defender for Cloud Data Export

In addition to the Microsoft Sentinel integration with Microsoft Defender for Cloud alerts, you can optionally export other Microsoft Defender for Cloud products like vulnerability assessment findings, secure score, and regulatory compliance messages to Azure Log Analytics. If you have Microsoft Sentinel installed in the same workspace, Microsoft Sentinel will also ingest the additional data, but there is no automatic support for incident creation like there is for Microsoft Defender for Cloud alerts.

Enabling this mode of logging does incur Azure Log Analytics and possibly Microsoft Sentinel per-GB volume-based processing charges. While very modest microcharges are incurred for the expected volume of these types of messages, for most environments, the cost is trivial (but nonzero).

To enable additional data export from Microsoft Defender for Cloud to Azure Log Analytics:

1. Navigate to Home ➤ Microsoft Defender for Cloud ➤ Management ➤ Environment Settings ➤ <Subscription name> ➤ Continuous export.
2. Select the Log Analytics workspace tab and turn *Export enabled* **On**.
3. Select *Exported data types* as desired; an example is seen in Figure 7-24. Avoid exporting the *Security alerts* type if you have enabled the default Microsoft Sentinel integration to avoid double-alerting on those incidents.
4. Select the resource group and target workspace and click the **Save** button.

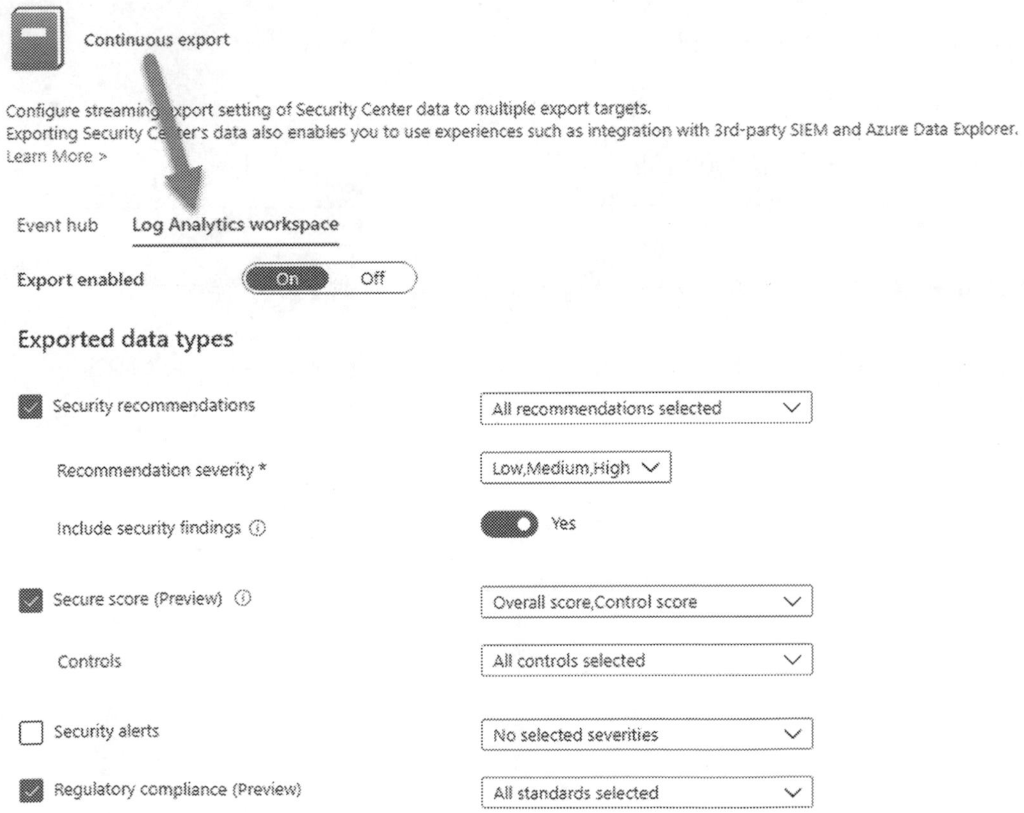

Figure 7-24. *Enabling export of additional Microsoft Defender for Cloud data to an Azure Log Analytics workspace*

Optionally create Azure Monitor Log Alerts based on Log Analytics queries to view exported types in Azure Monitor and trigger alert rules, such as when a vulnerability assessment contains a high-priority finding.

Get a head start creating Azure Monitor alert rules using the built-in wizard:

1. After you enable continuous export, scroll all the way to the bottom of the *Continuous export* setup page and click the link **Continue integration with Azure Monitor**.

2. Select the Log alert *Create alert rules for exported recommendations* and click the **Create** button.

3. Navigate to Home ➤ Log Analytics workspace ➤ Alert rules and locate the rule *[Azure Security Center] New Security Recommendation*. Click to edit the rule.

4. In the Condition section, click the connection name *Whenever the average custom log search is greater than 0*.

5. In the *Evaluated based on* section, change both the period and frequency from 5 minutes to 60 minutes. (This will reduce the cost of the monitor rule itself from $1.50 per month to under $0.15 per month.)

6. In the Actions section, click **Add action groups**, and then select and add your preferred notification action group. You can create an action group if you don't have one yet–there is a *Create action group* control at the top of the page.

7. Click the **Save** button.

Microsoft Defender for Cloud vulnerability scans log data of the *SecurityRecommendation* type when reporting scan results. When future data of the SecurityRecomendation type is found in the Log Analytics database during the hourly checks, you will receive a notification.

Tip If you only want to receive alerts when there is a *high* severity finding, edit the query in the alert rule as follows:

```
SecurityRecommendation
| where RecommendationSeverity contains "High"
```

Microsoft Sentinel Analytics Rules for Azure Arc Servers

Microsoft Sentinel has built-in connectors for over 120 services and cloud applications. The selection of which connectors to enable is based on the sources of security data in your organization. Microsoft Sentinel *Data connectors* that are particularly relevant for Azure Arc servers are

- Microsoft Defender for Cloud
- DNS
- Security Events
- Windows Firewall

These are the same connectors that apply to Azure VMs running Windows and Linux and performing IaaS roles. Enabling these connectors is recommended when you have either or both Azure VMs and Azure Arc servers being monitored.

Tip When enabling the *Security Events* data connector, a recommendation is to start with the *Common* events setting. The *All Events* setting can be quite expensive, and the *Minimal* setting doesn't provide a full audit trail.

Each data connector presents a list of *Relevant analytic templates* on its Open connector page ➤ Next steps tab. The following are the Analytics Active rules that are recommended to enable, assembled from the relevant connectors' template lists.

Analytics Active Rules

These Microsoft Sentinel Analytics alert rules are especially relevant for Azure Arc servers:

- All GALLIUM, IRIDIUM, ZINC, PHOSPHORUS, THALLIUM, CERIUM, STRONTIUM, BARIUM, and NOBELIUM rules
- Create incidents based on Azure Defender alerts
- Potential DGA detected
- Rare client observed with high reverse DNS lookup count
- Solorigate Network Beacon

- TI map Email entity to SecurityAlert
- TI map URL entity to SecurityAlert data
- TI map Domain entity to SecurityAlert

Anomaly Rules

Anomaly rules must be activated before they will generate anomalies. Once the anomaly rule is activated, detected anomalies will be stored in the *Anomalies* table in the *Logs* section of your Microsoft Sentinel workspace.

- Each anomaly rule has a training period, and anomalies will not appear in the table until after that training period. You can find the training period in the description of each anomaly rule (usually 7 or 14 days).
- Once the anomaly rules start producing anomaly detections, like that shown in Figure 7-25, you can optionally create alerting rules that are tailored to your environment.

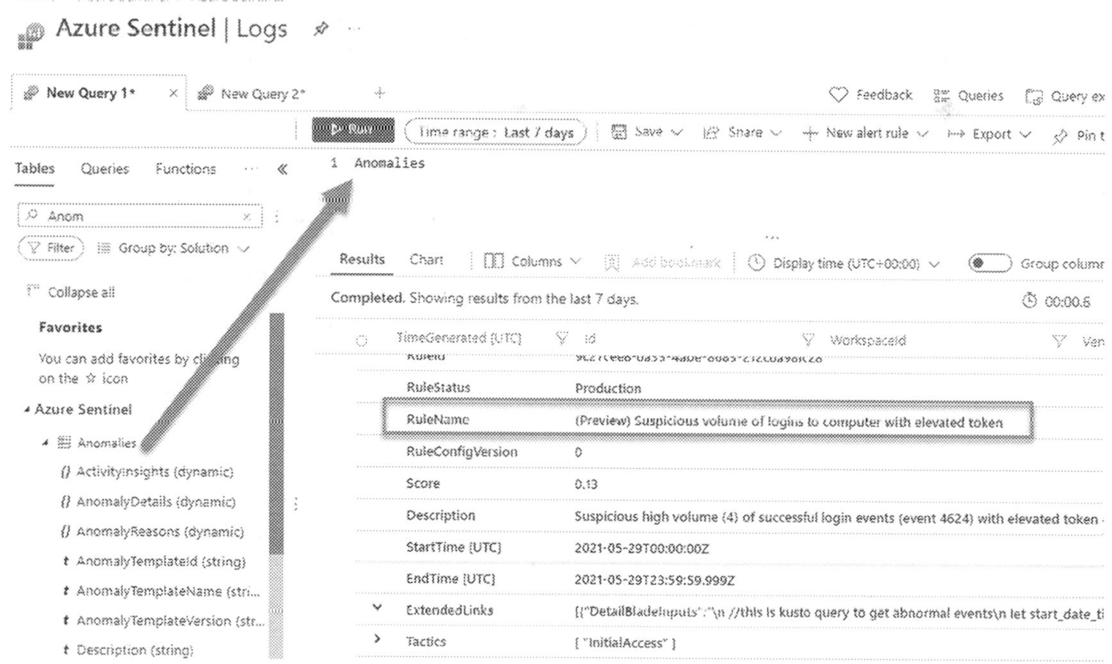

Figure 7-25. *An entry in the Anomalies table about an Azure Arc server*

For more information about using Anomaly rules, consult this reference URL:

`https://docs.microsoft.com/en-us/azure/sentinel/work-with-anomaly-rules`

These Microsoft Sentinel Anomaly rules are especially relevant for Azure Arc servers:

- Attempted user account and computer brute force
- Suspicious volume of logins to user account and computer
- Suspicious volume of logins to user account with elevated token
- Suspicious volume of logins to user account by logon type
- Attempted user account brute force per logon type
- Suspicious volume of logins to computer with elevated token
- Detect machine generated network beaconing behavior
- Unusual network volume anomaly
- Excessive data transfer anomaly
- Anomalous web request activity
- Attempted user account brute force per failure reason

Prepare and Deploy Logic Apps

As a user of Microsoft Sentinel, you are going to need to deploy one or more *Playbooks* that are Azure *Logic Apps* to interact with Microsoft Sentinel incidents. Azure Logic Apps are the only mechanism available for advanced notification, automation, and incident workflow in Microsoft Sentinel.

Locating and Deploying Playbooks

Every production Microsoft Sentinel environment over time will collect and adopt playbooks to increase security team efficiency and effectiveness. Most start with a single playbook that performs a basic notification action. As incident processing needs and automation opportunities emerge, additional and more complex playbooks are introduced.

Fortunately, there is a wealth of community resources to draw from in creating your custom collection of logic apps. There are hundreds of playbooks ready to import at this GitHub URL:

`https://github.com/Azure/Azure-Sentinel/tree/master/Playbooks`

Example Playbook Employment

As an example of how an Azure Arc server reporting into Microsoft Sentinel can gain value from a playbook, consider the **Get-GeoFromIpAndTagIncident** playbook at the preceding URL. This playbook will take the IP address entities from the incident and query a Geo-IP API to geo-locate the IP address. It will write the City and Country to a tag on the Incident. This playbook will save you the time of performing a geographic lookup on the source IP of a possible threat when investigating an incident.

Once you import the playbook to your Microsoft Sentinel instance, you need to edit the playbook and provide necessary security credentials to playbook tasks so the playbook has rights to add tags to Microsoft Sentinel incidents. Additionally, edit the settings of the *For each* task (the lowest task) as follows:

1. Right-click the ellipse "..." control and click **Settings**.
2. Set the *Concurrency Control* to **On** and the *Degree of Parallelism* to **1**.
3. Click **Done**.

Then **save** the playbook, and it's ready to be run against existing incidents.

Using Get-GeoFromIpAndTagIncident

- To tag existing incidents containing IP addresses with the city and county code the addresses correspond to:
    1. Select the incident and click the **View full details** button.
    2. Click the Alerts tab and scroll all the way to the left to expose the **View playbooks** link; then click on the link.
    3. Locate the *Get-GeoFromIpAndTagIncident* playbook and click the **Run** button.

Using Get-GeoFromIpAndTagIncident-Auto

- To automatically tag future incidents containing IP addresses:

    1. At Microsoft Sentinel ➤ Configuration ➤ Automation ➤ Playbooks, locate the *Get-GeoFromIpAndTagIncident* playbook and click it to open the logic app.
    2. Click the **Clone** button and name the clone *Get-GeoFromIpAndTagIncident-Auto*. Click **Create**.
    3. Now open the cloned playbook *GeoFromIpAndTagIncident-Auto* and click the **Edit** button.
    4. Delete the top-level task, *When a response to an Azure Sentinel alert is triggered*. (Right-click the ellipse "..." control and select **Delete**.)
    5. Add the trigger *When Azure Sentinel incident creation rule was triggered* in its place as the top-level task.
    6. Replace the second-level task with new task *Get incident* and use Incident ARM ID: *Incident ARM ID*.
    7. Replace the third-level task with new task *Entities - Get IPs* and use Entities list: *Entities*.
    8. Replace the lowest-level task (For each) with a new *For each 2*.
        - Select the output from previous steps: `@body('Entities_-_Get_IPs')?['IPs']`
        - Copy the HTTP GET to an HTTP2 GET step using the URI `http://ip-api.com/json/@{items('For_each_2')?['Address']}`
        - Copy the Parse JSON to a Parse JSON 2 step using Content: `@{body('HTTP_2')}`. Also copy and paste the Schema from Parse JSON to Parse JSON 2.
        - Create a new lowest-order step *Update incident*.
            - Incident ARM id: *Incident ARM ID*

- Tags to add tag – 1: `@body('Parse_JSON_2')?['city']`
- Tags to add tag – 2: `@body('Parse_JSON_2')?['country']`

9. Delete from the logic app canvas any steps remaining from the original logic app and click ***Save***. Figure 7-26 shows on the left the original logic app and on the right the edited clone.

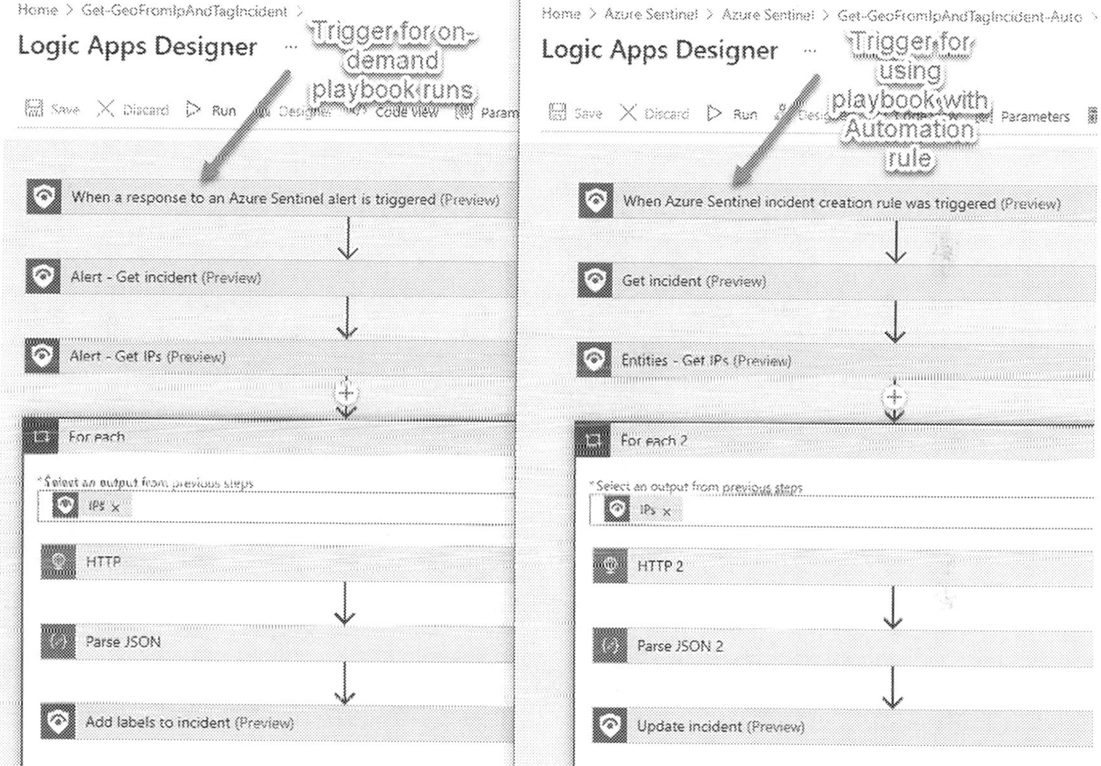

Figure 7-26. *Two versions of the logic app, one for manual runs and one for automatic employment*

10. At Microsoft Sentinel ➤ Configuration ➤ Automation, select *Create* ➤ **Add new rule.**
11. Name the automation rule *Geo-tag all incidents with IP addresses.*
12. At Actions, select Run playbook. Select the playbook *Get-GeoFromIpAndTagIncident-Auto*. (Only playbooks with the *When Azure Sentinel incident creation rule was triggered* trigger are available to be selected.)

13. Type an *Order* number that is not the highest numbered order (this should not be the last automation rule to run) and click the **Apply** button.

Now when you either run the playbook *Get-GeoFromIpAndTagIncident* manually or cause the automation rule *Geo-tag all incidents with IP addresses* to run the playbook *Get-GeoFromIpAndTagIncident-Auto* programmatically, incidents will be tagged with the city and country as seen in Figure 7-27.

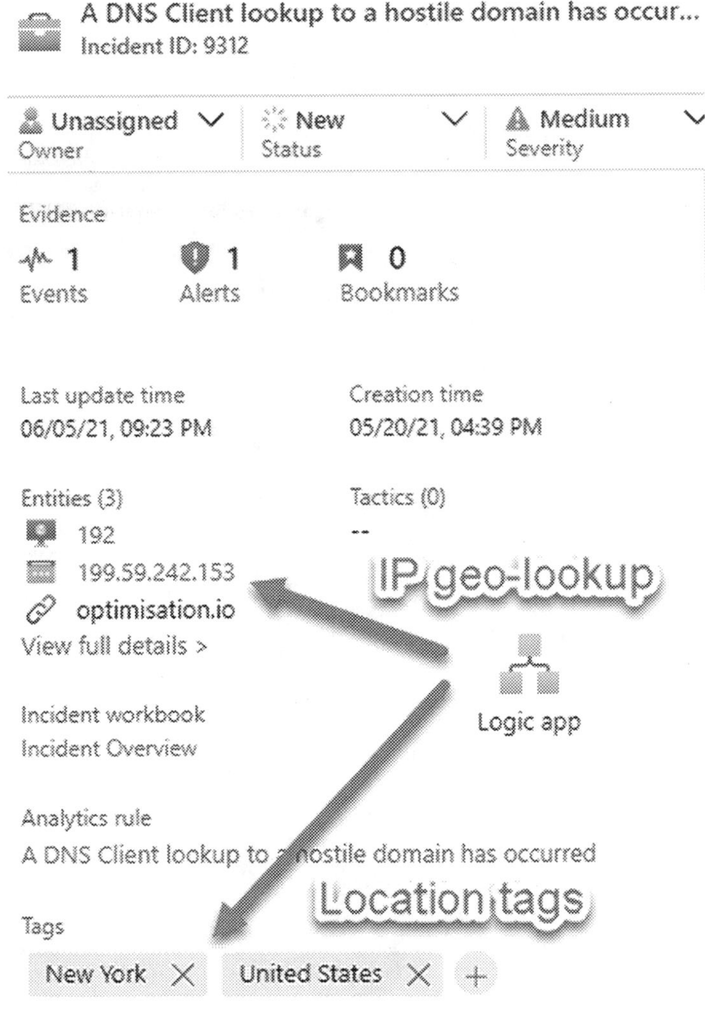

Figure 7-27. *City and country tags added to the incident by the playbook*

Tip The Get-GeoFromIpAndTagIncident playbooks will work as configured but will throw an error when one or more of the IPs are in the private IP ranges, like 10.x or 192.168.x. To avoid the error message, add a new *Condition* step after *Parse JSON* (or *Parse JSON 2*). The Condition step is the following: And `@body('Parse_JSON')?['status']` or `@body('Parse_JSON_2')?['status']` does not contain **fail**. Move the lowest task (*Add labels to incident* or *Update incident)* into the *True* outcome task and leave the *False* outcome task empty.

Workbooks and Dashboards

Microsoft Sentinel, like Azure Monitor, leverages Azure Workbooks for interactive visualization. Especially for Azure Arc servers, there are some specific workbook templates you should consider saving to your subscription and using in your routine security management duties.

1. Find the workbook templates in the Microsoft Sentinel console at Threat management ➤ Workbooks ➤ Templates.
2. Select each workbook you want to start using and click the **Save** button.
3. Saved workbooks are found at Threat management ➤ Workbooks ➤ My workbooks.
4. Use your saved workbooks by clicking on the **View saved workbook** button.

Table 7-3 lists the recommended workbooks associated with each of the best practice data connectors for Azure Arc servers.

***Table 7-3.** Microsoft Sentinel Workbooks Especially Useful for Azure Arc Servers*

Data Connector	Recommended Workbooks
Microsoft Defender for Cloud	• Cybersecurity Maturity Model Certification (CMMC) • Zero Trust (TIC 3.0)
DNS	• DNS • SolarWinds Post Compromise Hunting
Security Events	• Identity & Access • Insecure Protocols
Windows Firewall	• Windows Firewall (shown in Figure 7-28)

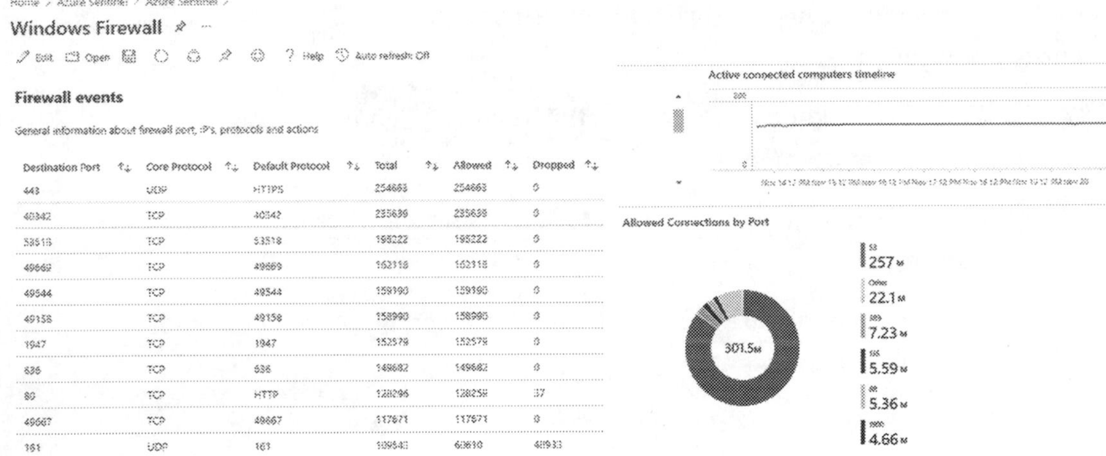

***Figure 7-28.** The Windows Firewall workbook combines Azure VM and Azure Arc server firewall logs*

Tip Even if your organization does not use the Windows Firewall component on your Windows servers, you can leverage the collection of firewall logs for high value security indications. Figure 7-29 shows a suggested Group Policy Object (GPO) that will enable firewall logging when you enable the Windows Firewall data connector in Microsoft Sentinel. The key settings are:

- Size limit (KB): 1,024
- Log dropped and successful connections: Yes

It's important that the size limit is small (1 KB) since the logs are only uploaded to Microsoft Sentinel when they reach the selected size. Smaller logs sizes result in more rapid ingestion to Microsoft Sentinel.

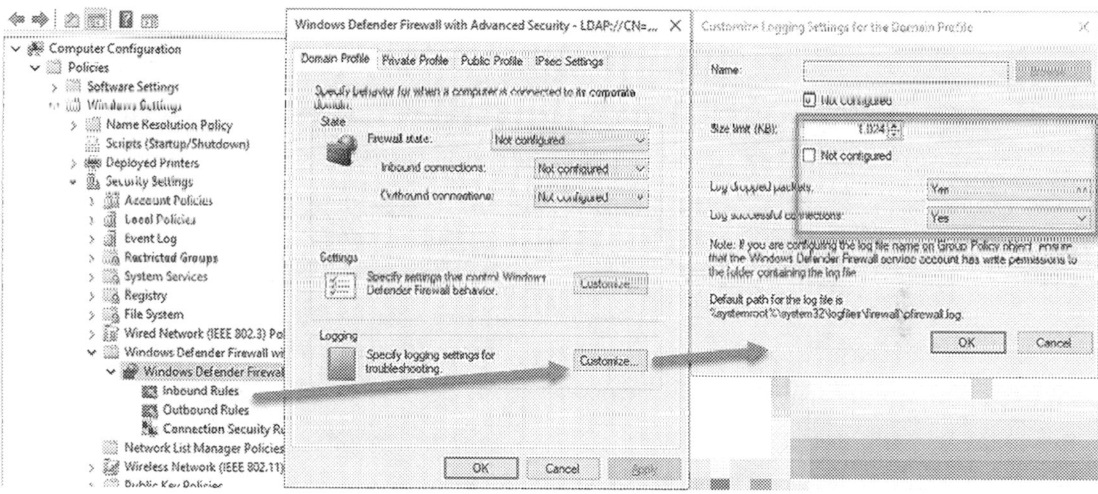

Figure 7-29. Configure Windows Firewall logging using a GPO

Azure Arc SQL Server

Recall that the top-level Azure portal page for Azure Arc (Figure 7-30) includes menu items for Servers and Kubernetes clusters, and these two Azure Arc features are the focus of this book. We will round out the chapter with a close look at another member of the Azure Arc family: Azure Arc SQL Server.

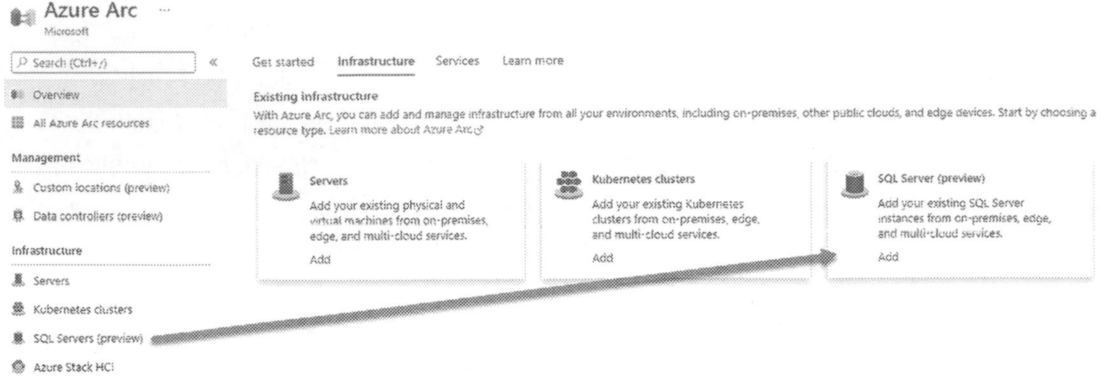

Figure 7-30. *Adding an Azure Arc SQL Server to your Azure subscription*

Overview

Microsoft's vision for Azure Arc can be appreciated once you start adding multiple Azure Arc resource types to your Azure subscription(s). Just as an *Azure Arc server* is functionally equivalent to an *Azure VM*, an on-prem SQL Server is just like an in-Azure IaaS VM running SQL Server. **Azure Arc SQL Server** is a step toward achieving parity of management between in-*Azure SQL virtual machines* and on-prem *SQL Servers*.

Azure SQL Virtual Machines

The comparison with Azure Arc server refers specifically to the Azure offering "Azure SQL virtual machine." This is a premium Microsoft Azure service offering on top of Windows Server and SQL Server IaaS provisioning. The primary characteristic of this offering is an Azure resource type:

```
Microsoft.SqlVirtualMachine/sqlVirtualMachines
```

That resource type permits management of the SQL Server application from the Azure portal or other supported Azure management tools like PowerShell and REST API. Advanced SQL features like *Always On* for high availability and utility functions like backups and patching are managed from the Azure control plane, not the server OS. Azure communicates with the SQL application using the VM extension `Microsoft.SqlServer.Management.SqlIaaSAgent` installed by the *Windows Azure Guest Agent*, which runs on all Azure VMs.

Azure Arc SQL Servers

Azure Arc-enabled SQL Server allows you to manage your global inventory of SQL servers, protect SQL Server instances with Microsoft Defender for Cloud workload protection for servers, and periodically assess and tune the health of your SQL Server configurations. The Azure Arc SQL Server solution is based on this Azure resource type:

```
Microsoft.AzureArcData/sqlServerInstances
```

Just like the in-Azure original, this resource type permits management of the SQL Server application from the Azure portal or other supported Azure management tool—even with the IaaS VM or physical SQL Server running in your on-prem data center! This first version of Azure Arc SQL Server uses the `CustomScriptExtension` VM extension to run scripts in the OS of the SQL Server. Recall that running on every Azure Arc server is the *Guest Configuration Extension service,* which performs the identical function as the Windows Azure Guest Agent when it comes to installing, modifying, and removing VM extensions.

Focus on SQL Server Assessment

Just as both Azure VMs and Azure Arc servers share the same need for uniform OS management and security, both in-Azure and non-Azure SQL Servers require identical application and database configuration assessment. Microsoft has selected the On-Demand Assessment aspect of SQL Server management to lead off their Azure Arc SQL Server initiative. If you have followed this book's recommendations and deployed Microsoft Defender for Cloud workload protection for servers, adding workload protection for Azure Arc SQL Server to your security plan is a natural evolution.

Throughout this book, we have shown how parity in management features for non-Azure Windows and Linux servers and Kubernetes clusters adds security and increases efficiency. Now consider that directing uniform assessment coverage to SQL resources–of all types in all locations—will achieve a substantial increase in your organization's database readiness and security.

Azure Arc SQL Server: A Superset of Azure Arc Server

Figure 7-31 shows Windows and Linux Azure Arc servers–and Windows and Linux Azure Arc SQL Server resources–all in one view.

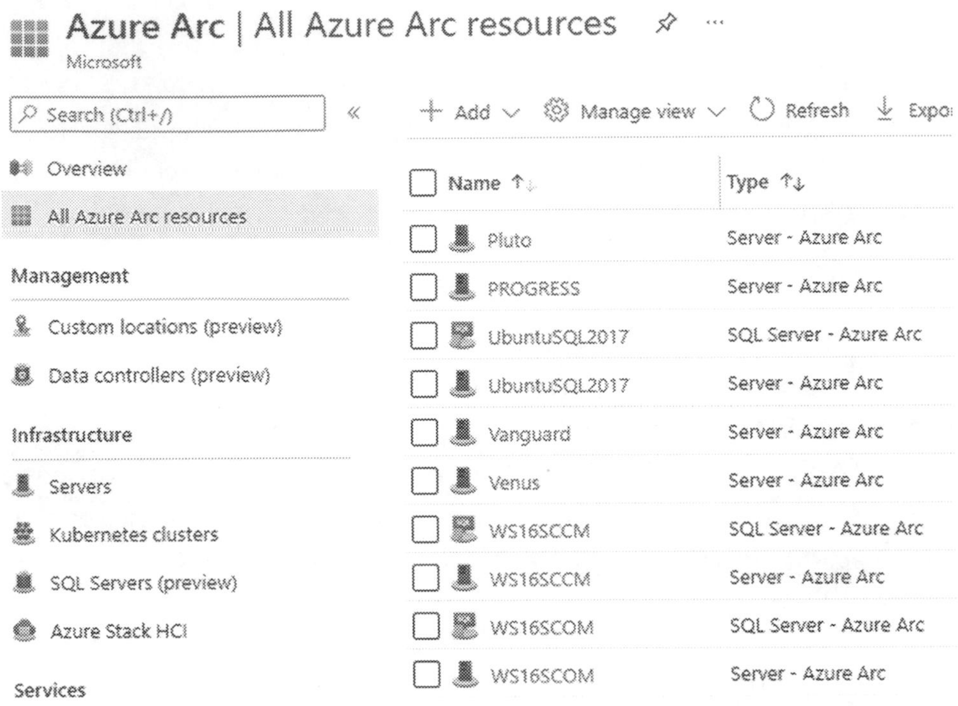

Azure Arc | All Azure Arc resources
Microsoft

Name	Type
Pluto	Server - Azure Arc
PROGRESS	Server - Azure Arc
UbuntuSQL2017	SQL Server - Azure Arc
UbuntuSQL2017	Server - Azure Arc
Vanguard	Server - Azure Arc
Venus	Server - Azure Arc
WS16SCCM	SQL Server - Azure Arc
WS16SCCM	Server - Azure Arc
WS16SCOM	SQL Server - Azure Arc
WS16SCOM	Server - Azure Arc

Figure 7-31. *Azure Arc server and Azure Arc SQL Server resources*

Non-Azure servers enrolled in Azure Arc server, which are also running SQL Server, can optionally be enrolled as well in Azure Arc SQL Server. This creates two Azure Arc resources: One represents the server itself, and the other represents the SQL Server application. Again, this is exactly how Microsoft does it with in-Azure SQL VMs. Figure 7-32 was produced by Microsoft to explain how Azure Arc SQL Server works.

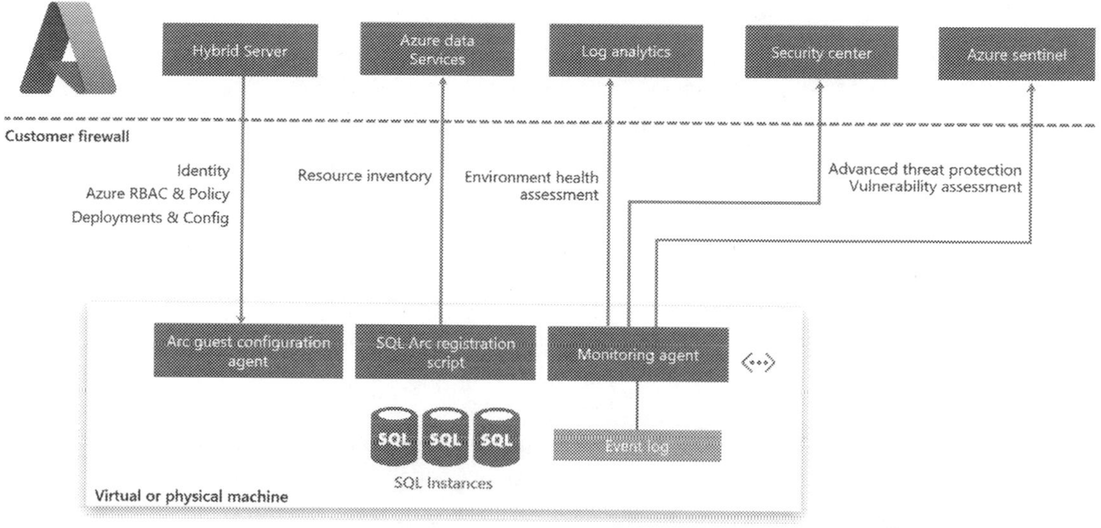

Figure 7-32. *How the SQL Arc extension works. (Source: Microsoft)*

The left portion of Figure 7-32 (Hybrid Server) should be familiar as the Azure Arc server component, described in Chapter 4 of this book, "Azure Arc Servers: Getting Started." The right portion (Log Analytics, Security Center, Microsoft Sentinel) was covered in Chapter 6, "Hybrid Server Monitoring Solution," and previous sections of this chapter, *Regulatory and Security Compliance for Azure Arc Servers*. What's specific to Azure Arc SQL Server is the *Azure Data Services* piece in the middle.

Connect Your SQL Server to Azure Arc

Follow these steps to get started with Azure Arc SQL Server:

1. Prepare your Azure subscription by registering the Microsoft. AzureArcData resource provider using one of these methods:

    - Azure Portal

        i. Navigate in the Azure portal to Home ➤ Subscription ➤ Settings ➤ Resource providers.

        ii. Search for `Microsoft.AzureArcData` and select **Register.**

- Azure PowerShell

```
Login-AzAccount
Set-AzContext -SubscriptionId <SubscriptionId>
Register-AzResourceProvider -ProviderNamespace
Microsoft.AzureArcData
```

- Azure CLI

```
az account set --subscription "{Your Subscription Name}"
az provider register --namespace Microsoft.AzureArcData
```

2. Navigate in your Azure portal to Home ➤ Azure Arc ➤ SQL Servers and click **Create**.

Tip The first time you create the onboarding script for Azure Arc SQL Server, there is a confirmation prompt at the very top of the fourth page where you generate the script to "activate" Azure Arc SQL Server. You hit accept on that and never have to think about it again. It is easily missed.

---

3. Select the resource group, region, and OS of the Azure Arc SQL Server(s) to onboard and click **Next** and **Run script**.
4. Copy the script to your clipboard and save the contents as *OnboardAzureArcSqlServerScript.ps1* on the SQL Server to be onboarded.
5. Prepare the SQL Server as follows:
   - SQL Server requires .NET Framework 4.7.2 or later to run Az PowerShell cmdlets.
     i. Download .NET Framework 4.8 at this link: `https://go.microsoft.com/fwlink/?linkid=2088631`
     ii. System restart is required.

- Run these PowerShell commands in an elevated session and restart your PowerShell session afterward:

  ```
  Install-PackageProvider -Name NuGet -MinimumVersion
  2.8.5.201 -Force

  Install-Module -Name Az -AllowClobber -Force

  Import-Module -Name Az.Accounts
  ```

6. Run the OnboardAzureArcSqlServerScript.ps1 script in an elevated PowerShell session.
   - The script will install and configure files and at a certain point will prompt you to enter a URL in a browser and enter a code.
   - When prompted, log into Azure using a credential that has permissions in your Azure subscription to create Azure Arc and Azure Arc SQL Server resources in the Azure resource group you selected when creating the script.
   - You do not have to use a browser on the computer where the script is running; any browser with Internet connectivity is fine.
7. The script performs these actions:
   - Checks connectivity from your environment to Azure and specified machine using PowerShell
   - Onboards the host machine as an Azure Arc server by deploying the Azure Connected Machine agent if not already onboarded
   - Initiates SQL Server instance discovery
   - Adds SQL Server instances on your target machine to Azure

When the script completes successfully, you will see this message:

```
SQL Server - Azure Arc resource: <servername> created
```

After you register SQL Server instances with Azure Arc-enabled SQL Server (preview), go to the Azure portal and view the newly created Azure Arc resources. You will see a new Machine (Azure Arc for each connected machine) and a new SQL Server (Azure Arc resource for each registered SQL Server instance).

Figure 7-33 shows what you can expect to see on the overview page of an Azure Arc SQL Server resource. The arrows point to the two locations where you will find inventory information about your SQL server.

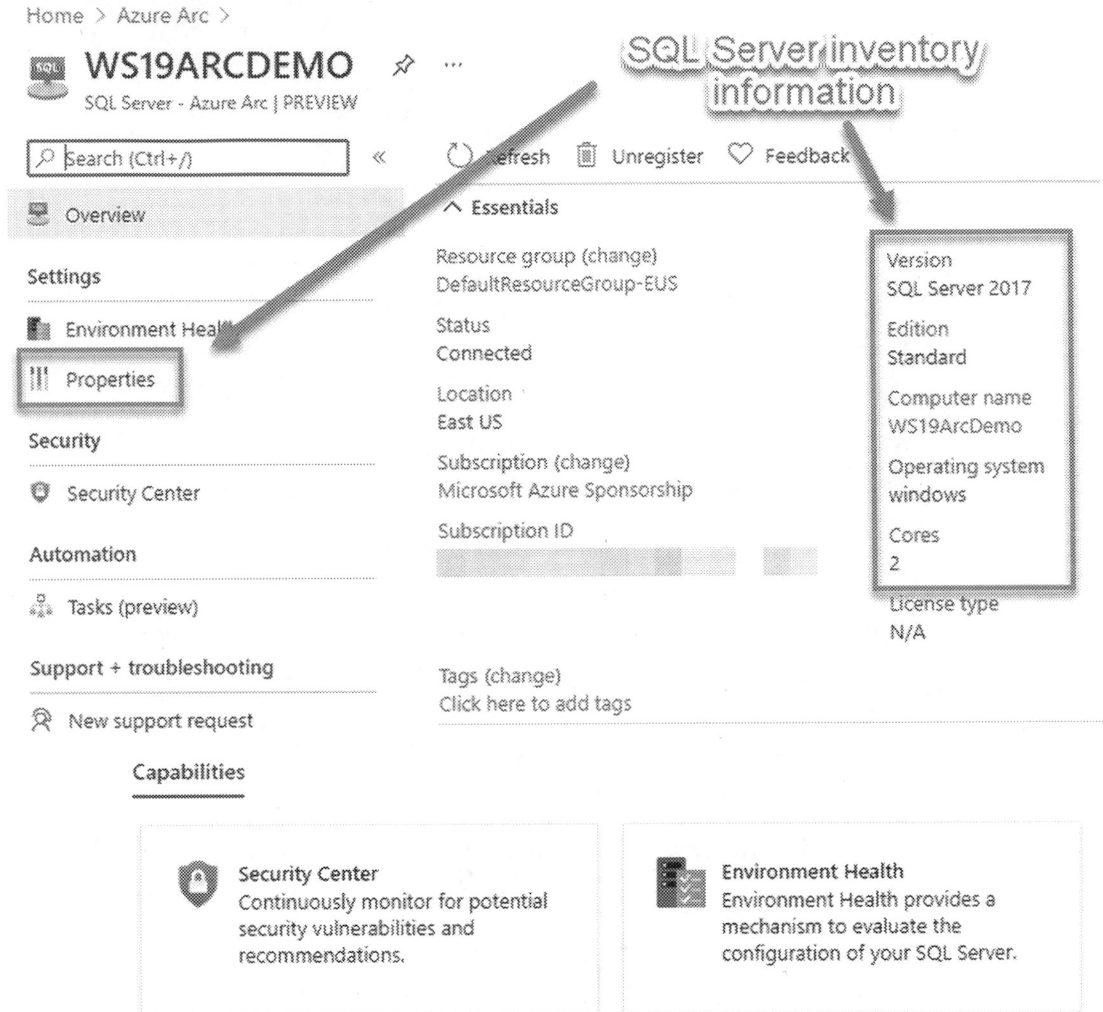

Figure 7-33. *Azure Arc SQL Server helps you track SQL inventory across clouds*

At this point, modify the tags on the Azure Arc server and/or Azure Arc SQL Server object(s) to fit in with any existing tag management schemes in your organization.

Connect Azure Arc SQL Server for Linux

The RegisterSqlServerArc script connects the Linux computer to both Azure Arc server and Azure Arc SQL server.

1. Copy RegisterSqlServer.Arc.sh to the Linux server and make the file executable:

   ```
   chmod 700 RegisterSqlServerArc.sh
   ```

2. Run the script:

   ```
   sudo ./RegisterSqlServerArc.sh
   ```

3. When prompted, select Y to install the Azure CLI.

Tip Azure Arc SQL Server support for Linux versions of SQL Server is minimal in the current preview release. The *Environment Health* and *Security Center* features of Azure Arc SQL Server are grayed out for Linux. The value-add for Linux SQL Servers is limited to inventory and tagging features.

SQL Server Inventory in Azure Resource Graph

One of the compelling features of Azure Arc is the projection of your hybrid assets' configuration into Azure Resource Manager (ARM). That means you can use all the management tools in Azure as you see fit to get your work done. **Azure Resource Graph Explorer** in the Azure portal lets you browse your Azure resources and optionally export data for use in other record and reporting systems.

To view your Azure Arc SQL Server inventory data using Azure Resource Graph Explorer, navigate to this page: `https://portal.azure.com/#blade/HubsExtension/ArgQueryBlade`

In the search box, filter on resource type *Microsoft.azurearcdata/sqlserverinstances (SQL Server - Azure Arc)*, click on the resource type to populate the *Query* window, and click **Run query**. The result as seen in Figure 7-34 includes information about SQL server edition, version, instance name, TCP port, and collation type.

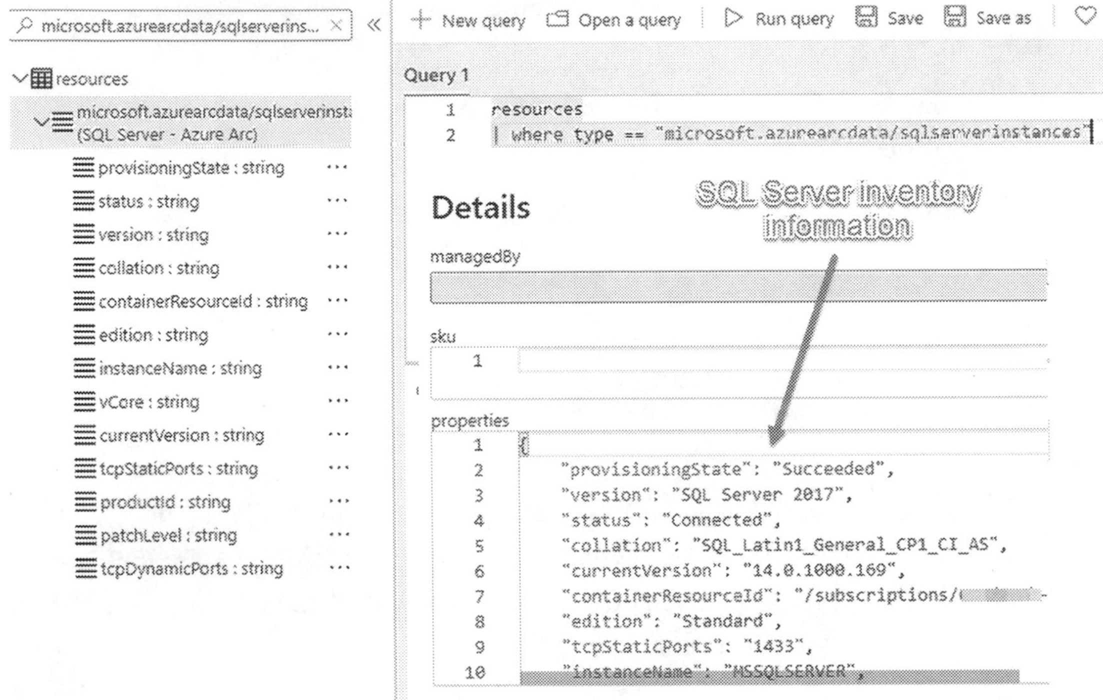

Figure 7-34. *Azure Arc SQL Server properties in Azure Resource Graph Explorer*

Click **Download as CSV** in the *Results* area to get an offline record copy of your SQL inventory like that seen in Figure 7-35.

NAME	PROPERTIES
UbuntuSQL2017	{"provisioningState":"Succeeded","version":"Microsoft SQL Server 2019","status":"Connected","containerResourceId":"UbuntuSQL2017","currentVersion":"15.0.4102.2","tcpStaticPorts":"1433","edition":"Standard","vCore":"2"}
WS16SCCM	{"provisioningState":"Succeeded","version":"SQL Server 2017","status":"Connected","collation":"SQL_Latin1_General_CP1_CI_AS","containerResourceId":"/subscriptions/00000000-0000-0000-0000-000000000000/resourceGroups/RG-DEV-EUS/providers/Microsoft.HybridCompute/machines/WS16SCCM","currentVersion":"14.0.1000.169","tcpStaticPorts":"1433","instanceName":"MSSQLSERVER","edition":"Standard","patchLevel":"14.0.2037.2","productId":"00394-30000-00000-AB479","vCore":"2"}
WS16SCOM	{"provisioningState":"Succeeded","version":"SQL Server 2014","status":"Connected","collation":"SQL_Latin1_General_CP1_CI_AS","containerResourceId":"/subscriptions/00000000-0000-0000-0000-000000000000/resourceGroups/RG-DEV-EUS/providers/Microsoft.HybridCompute/machines/WS16SCOM","currentVersion":"12.0.6024.0","tcpStaticPorts":"1433","instanceName":"MSSQLSERVER","edition":"Standard","patchLevel":"12.3.6433.1","productId":"Mpcld-004-0590034-02847"}
WS19SCVMM	{"provisioningState":"Succeeded","version":"SQL Server 2017","status":"Connected","collation":"SQL_Latin1_General_CP1_CI_AS","containerResourceId":"/subscriptions/00000000-0000-0000-0000-000000000000/resourceGroups/RG-DEV-EUS/providers/Microsoft.HybridCompute/machines/WS19SCVMM","currentVersion":"14.0.1000.169","tcpStaticPorts":"1433","instanceName":"MSSQLSERVER","edition":"Standard","patchLevel":"14.0.2037.2","productId":"00394-30000-00000-AB070","vCore":"2"}

Figure 7-35. *Azure Arc SQL Server inventory dumped from Azure Resource Graph*

Connect SQL Server Instances to Azure Arc at Scale

You can adapt the Azure Arc SQL Server installation script to register SQL Server instances on multiple machines. See the details of the at-scale registration method at this URL:

```
https://docs.microsoft.com/en-us/sql/sql-server/azure-arc/connect-at-
scale?WT.mc_id=Portal-Microsoft_Azure_HybridData_Platform&view=sql-
server-ver15
```

The process is identical to that described in Chapter 5 of this book, "Azure Arc Servers: Using at Scale," in that you will create a service principal in Azure AD, grant permissions to the service principal, and modify the at-scale installation script to use the credential of the service principal.

Run On-Demand SQL Assessment

The centerpiece of Azure Arc SQL Server is its integration with the SQL Server Assessment. Azure Arc SQL Server provides a mechanism to deploy the SQL Server assessment solution at scale. There are two ways to deploy the SQL Server Assessment to your Azure Arc SQL Servers: automatically using Azure VM extensions or by running a script on each SQL Server. The Environment Health page of the Azure Arc SQL Server seen in Figure 7-36 is where you start to use either method.

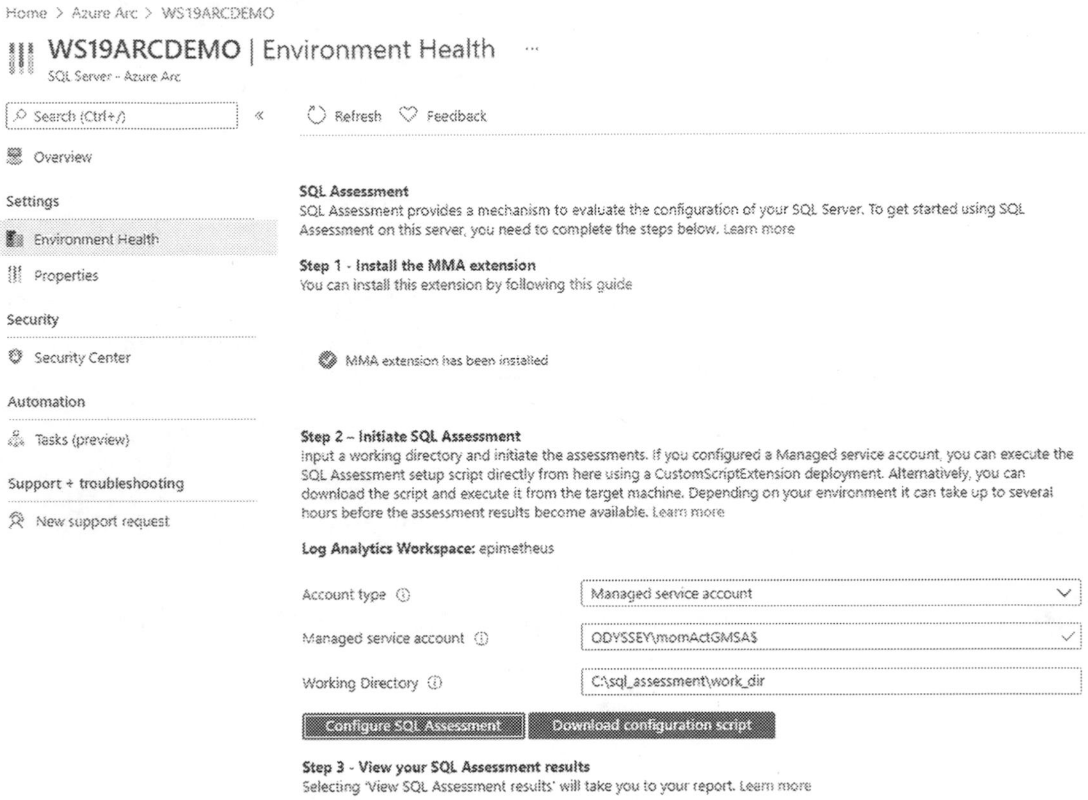

***Figure 7-36.** Configure SQL Assessment from the Azure Arc SQL Server Environment Health page*

Whichever method you use, automatic or manual, the solution creates a Scheduled Task that runs the SQL Server Assessment once per week and uploads the report data to an Azure Log Analytics workspace.

Services Hub Connection

Consult the *Prerequisites* section at this URL before attempting to run a SQL Server Assessment:

`https://docs.microsoft.com/en-us/sql/sql-server/azure-arc/assess`

In particular, you must make sure that you have linked your Azure subscription to **Microsoft Services Hub** and added the SQL Server Assessment. You must be registered on services hub and have Owner or Contributor rights on an Azure subscription registered through the same email-enabled account.

Automatic Deployment Using Managed Service Account

Follow these steps to produce and view an assessment on an Azure Arc SQL Server when you can use the managed service account (MSA) method:

1. Specify a managed service account to activate the Configure SQL Assessment button.
    - This will initiate the assessment from the Portal by deploying a CustomScriptExtension. Because only one CustomScriptExtension can be deployed at a time, the script extension for SQL Assessment will be automatically removed after execution.
    - If you already have another CustomScriptExtension deployed to the hosting machine, the Configure SQL Assessment button will not be activated.
2. Enter the managed service account in the format DOMAIN\MSAname$ and confirm the working directory, which, by default, is C:\sql_assessment\work_dir.
3. Click the **Configure SQL Assessment** button.
4. A VM extension named CustomScriptExtension is then installed in the Azure Arc server. The CustomScriptExtension runs the PowerShell onboarding script on the Azure Arc SQL Server.
5. In about 1 to 2 hours, the **View SQL Assessment** result button will become un-grayed. Clicking on the button will open the assessment results in a new blade as seen in Figure 7-37.

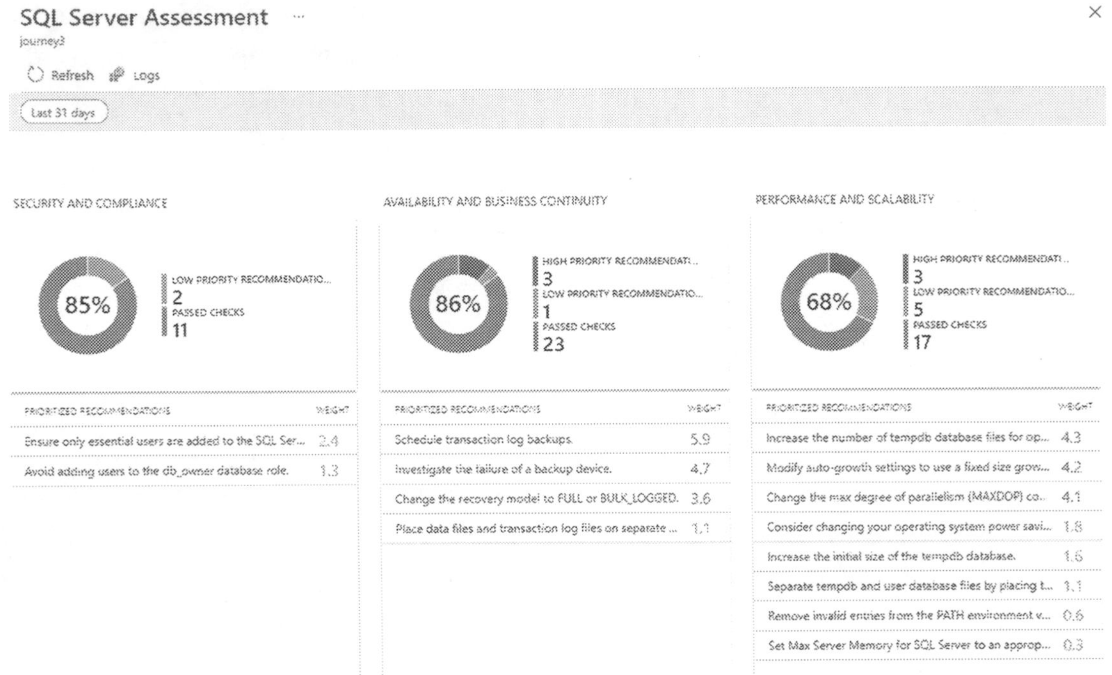

Figure 7-37. *Reviewing SQL Server Assessment results in the Azure portal*

Manual Deployment Using a Configuration Script

Follow these steps to produce and view an assessment on an Azure Arc SQL Server when you are using the *download configuration script* method:

1. Click the **Download configuration script** button from the Azure Arc Server Environment Health page.

2. Save the **AddSqlAssessment.ps1** file and copy it to the Azure Arc SQL Server. The script will look something like this:

```
Add-SQLAssessmentTask -SQLServerName "WS19ArcDemo.odyssey.
com" -WorkingDirectory "C:\sql_assessment\work_dir"
-RunWithManagedServiceAccount $True -ScheduledTaskUsername
"ODYSSEY\momActGMSA$" -ScheduledTaskPassword (new-object System.
Security.SecureString)
```

3. Observe a scheduled task like that shown in Figure 7-38 is created on the server in the path Task Scheduler ➤ Task Scheduler Library ➤ Microsoft ➤ Operations Management Suite ➤ AOI-<GUID> ➤ Assessments ➤ SQL Assessment.

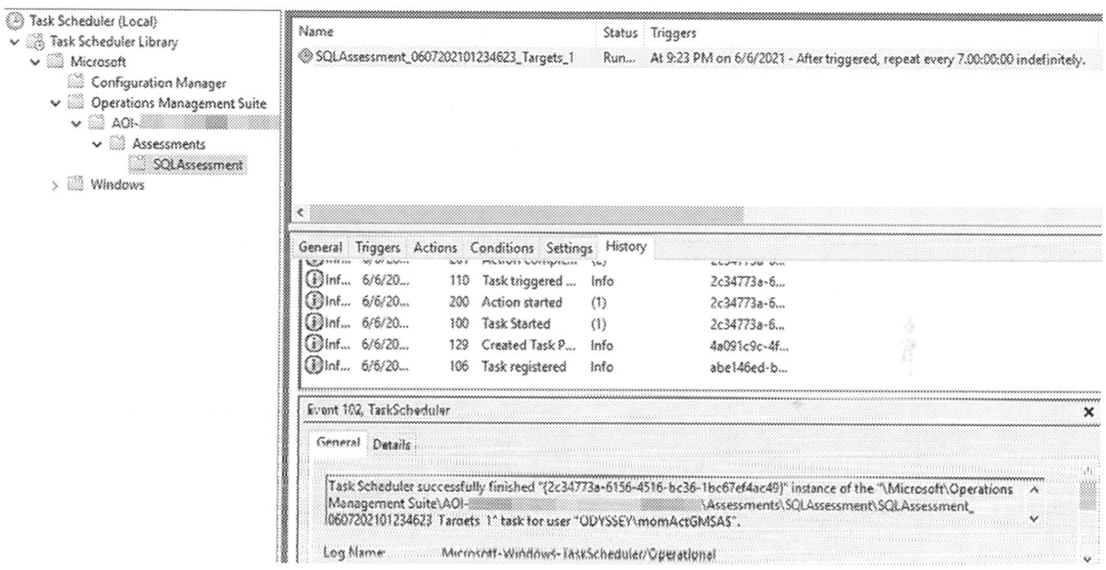

Figure 7-38. Confirming a successful weekly run of the SQL Assessment scheduled task

4. Soon after the scheduled task completes on the Azure Arc SQL Server, if you return to the Azure Arc SQL Server's Azure portal page and click on the *Environment Health* menu item again, you will see the same report view shown in Figure 7-37.

Enable Microsoft Defender for Cloud for SQL Server

In addition to inventory, tagging, and SQL Assessment benefits of Azure Arc SQL Server, there is an additional high-value feature in the solution. This is the surfacing of Microsoft Defender for Cloud workload protection for SQL Server recommendations and security alerts from Microsoft Defender for Cloud on Azure Arc SQL Server blades in the Azure portal.

As seen in Figure 7-39, Azure Arc SQL Server will confirm that Microsoft Defender for Cloud for SQL is **On** and any recommendations or alerts from Microsoft Defender for Cloud are easy to find and act on.

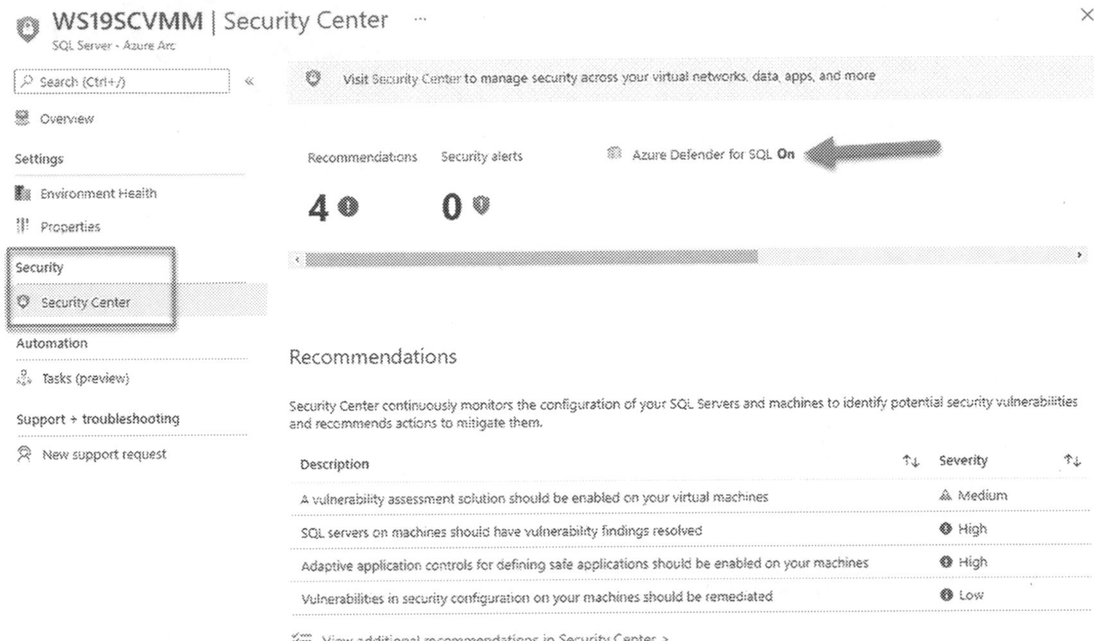

***Figure 7-39.** Microsoft Defender for Cloud workload protection for SQL Server adds valuable content to Azure Arc SQL Server*

As recommended earlier in the “Microsoft Defender for Cloud” section of this chapter, as a best practice, you will enable Microsoft Defender for Cloud protection for all covered resource types, including Azure Defender for SQL Server.

- Microsoft Defender for Cloud workload protection for SQL Server detects anomalous activities indicating unusual and potentially harmful attempts to access or exploit databases.
- Security alerts fire when there are suspicious database activities, potential vulnerabilities, or SQL injection attacks, and anomalous database access and query patterns.

Summary

This chapter focused on how Azure Arc can be a key provider of security services for your organization. We started by explaining how Azure Arc extends to your non-Azure servers all the security benefits of Microsoft Defender for Cloud workload protection for servers.

Then we detailed how to use the integrated vulnerability assessment from Qualys to provide internal scanning coverage, view scan results, and remediate findings.

Next, we covered how to optimally configure Microsoft Sentinel for protection of Azure Arc servers. Best practice methods for selecting analytic and anomaly rules were explained, and we made a deep dive into customizing Azure Logic Apps as Microsoft Sentinel playbooks. Finally, we took a look at another member of the Azure Arc family, Azure Arc SQL Server, and gained an appreciation for how Microsoft is delivering new management experiences in the hybrid space.

The next chapter, "GitOps Insights," is all about *infrastructure as code*. You will be introduced to the GitHub platform and the concept of GitOps. You will learn how to deploy a CI/CD solution using GitOps to create a configuration on an Azure Arc-enabled Kubernetes cluster using a Git repository.

CHAPTER 8

GitOps Insights

Deploying and managing Kubernetes clusters is only a part of the life cycle of running Kubernetes clusters even when spread across multiple clouds. You also will need to deploy and run your applications on Kubernetes. This is a critical aspect of a Kubernetes life cycle, and this is because the real value Kubernetes brings to the business is through the applications running on it.

In order to understand how a team can deploy and run an application on Kubernetes, it is important to understand some of the DevOps tooling that is out there. Understanding this tooling will help you understand GitOps.

In this chapter, we are going to dive into three topics including Git, GitHub, and finally GitOps. We are going to explore these topics and tools in greater detail, tying this all back together to gain an understanding of GitOps.

Git Overview

If you are reading this book, chances are you are not a developer. You are probably a cloud engineer or a DevOps type. Git may or may not be something new to you. If it is not new for you, then this section will be a good review on the topic of Git. If this is new to you, take some time and dig into the topic of Git as it is at the core of the world of tech these days from developing software, to infrastructure as code (IaC), and now GitOps. Git is a core skill to have and will serve you well along your cloud journey.

Git is an open source version control system. It was created in 2005. It is the most popular version control system used today. It is a distributed version control system, meaning a developer has a local snapshot of the code in a full-fledged repository. The developer can work on code locally and then sync with the repository on a server. Git tools are supported and run on pretty much every major operating system (OS) out there. The overall goals of Git are the following:

S. Buchanan and J. Joyner, *Azure Arc-Enabled Kubernetes and Servers*,
https://doi.org/10.1007/978-1-4842-7768-3_8

Speed

Git should help teams have faster releases of the software they develop. This allows companies to push out software to their customers faster and innovate quicker, giving them a competitive edge in their marketplace.

Distributed

Git should be distributed in nature vs. the centralized version control systems of the past. This makes it easier to have remote and distributed teams consisting of multiple developers working in parallel, allowing developers to continue to work even when mobile such as flying on an airplane realizing the ultimate level of flexibility when developing software.

Integrity

Git should maintain data integrity in its repositories. Git checksums all data before it is stored and referred to using that checksum, making it impossible to modify a file or directory without Git knowing about the changes.

There are various ways to use Git such as a graphical user interface, add-ons into other tools such as Microsoft VS Code as well as other developer tools, and the Git command line, the most common. The Git command line is the most robust containing all of the Git commands. So it is recommended to become familiar with the Git commands as you dive deeper into learning Git. Five key Git commands you will use the most are the following:

```
git clone
```

This command will create a local copy of a repository from a remote repository.

```
git add
```

This command will perform a stage of changes that have been made as the first part of the change tracking process. These staged changes will become a part of the next commit and a part of the repository's history.

```
git commit
```

This command creates the snapshot of changes, a.k.a. the commit to the repository completing the change tracking process.

```
git push
```

This command will update a remote repository with commits that have been made locally to a branch.

```
git pull
```

This command will update the local commit line of a branch with updates from its remote repository counterpart.

An always up-to-date full reference list of Git commands can be found here: `https://git-scm.com/docs/git#_git_commands`.

Two key features of Git are Branches and Commits. A Branch is a pointer to the lasted commit in a main branch. Here is a visual of what this looks like (Figure 8-1).

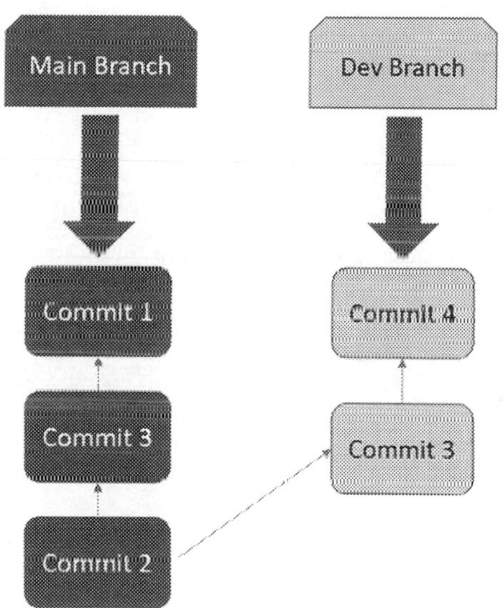

Figure 8-1. *Visual representation of Git Branches*

Here is a breakdown of the Branching image. At the start, the developer made commit 1 as well as commit 2 in the main branch. A new branch named dev was created after commit 2 from the main branch. Commit 3 and commit 4 were then made in the Dev branch. Notice our Dev branch is now ahead of the Main branch. In order to bring the code from the Dev branch back into the Main branch, we need to perform a merge.

A merge is when Git combines multiple sequences of commits from two branches into one unified history typically in a main branch. Merging takes independent development paths from separate branches and puts them into a single branch.

So for our example using the git command line, we would run the following to merge Dev into the Main branch:

```
git checkout main
```

then run

```
git merge test
```

That is a very basic example of how branches and merge work in Git. Now let's learn what a commit is. There are different types of merges that are outside of the scope of this book.

A commit is how you record changes to a repository. It is the record of what changes a developer has made since the last time a commit was made. In Git, as a developer modifies code, Git will see the changes; these changes will be ready to be staged, which is controlled by the developer, and, once staged, then committed to a repository using the `git commit` command.

That wraps up the overview of Git. There is a lot more to Git and working with Git. This section is designed to give you a starter overview of Git to pique your interest and give you enough foundational knowledge for a better understanding of GitOps. For full end-to-end breakdown of Git, refer to this documentation on the official Git site: `https://git-scm.com/book/en/v2`.

GitHub Overview

You just learned what Git is and at a high level how it works. Git is a version control system consisting of tools and commands that can only take software development/ DevOps/cloud teams so far by itself. The next step in the journey of using Git is to have a platform to host your code. Some platforms that use Git are Azure DevOps, Bitbucket, AWS CodeCommit, GitLab, and many more. In this chapter, we are going to cover GitHub specially.

GitHub is a platform for hosting Git repositories online powered by Git. GitHub was created in 2007, and Microsoft acquired GitHub in October of 2018. GitHub hosts the remote repository and comes with additional features that teams use to collaborate on projects. GitHub as the remote repository becomes the unified source of truth for teams. GitHub is widely used with a base of 40 million+ users and 190 million+ repositories. GitHub has free accounts commonly used for open source projects or paid accounts for organizations to use for projects. The core of GitHub is GitHub.com. There is a GitHub Enterprise that functions like GitHub.com but is self-hosted so that an organization can run it internally on its own hardware. GitHub is more commonly used over GitHub Enterprise. Figure 8-2 shows what a Git repository looks like on GitHub.com.

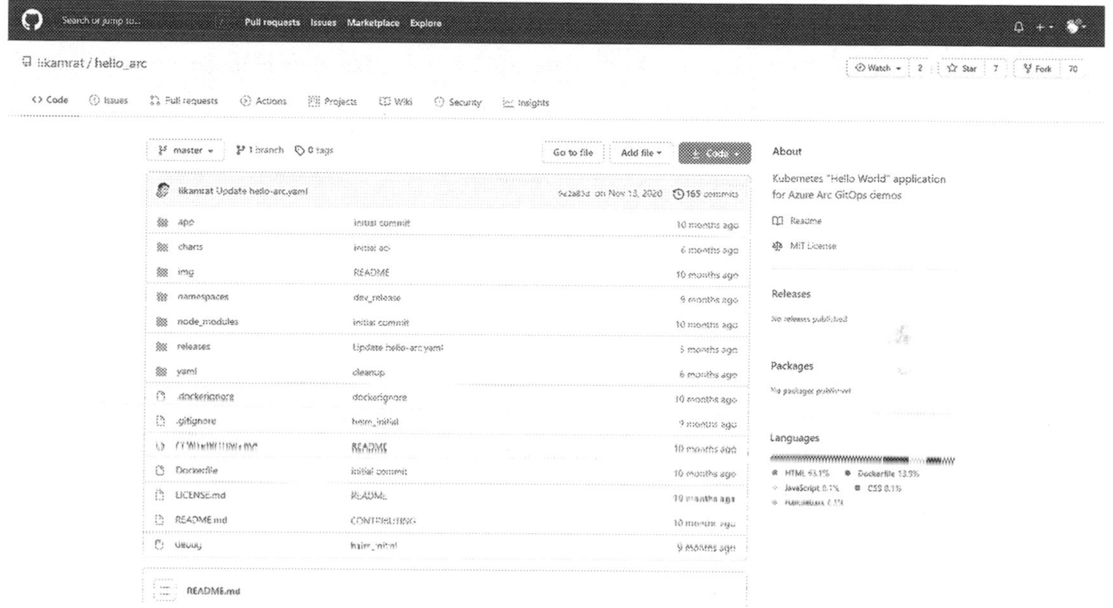

Figure 8-2. *GitHub.com website*

With GitHub.com, there is core functionality such as access control, bug tracking, feature requests, task management, continuous integration, and more. GitHub.com repositories can be accessed using Git command line. There are also many desktop clients, developer tools such as VS Code, and Git plug-ins that can be used with GitHub.com. So overall many teams use GitHub to host their code in Git repositories and collaborate on projects. Since Microsoft has acquired GitHub, they have worked to expand the functionality of GitHub and added more features and products. Here is a breakdown of additional GitHub features and products:

GitHub Pages
A service to host static web pages.

GitHub Actions
A service that automates and executes development workflows in repositories hosted on GitHub.

GitHub Discussions

A project community communication forum for the around an open source project.

GitHub Packages

A public or private software package hosting and management service.

GitHub Insights

A service for metrics and analytical reports of software delivery processes on GitHub Enterprise.

GitHub Desktop

A desktop application used to interact with GitHub, utilizing a GUI instead of the Git command line or through a web browser.

GitHub CLI

A command-line interface used to interact with GitHub.

Also, GitHub has a GitHub Marketplace with free and for-purchase apps to extend the functionality of GitHub.

That wraps up the overview of GitHub. There is definitely more to learn about GitHub. The best way to learn both Git and GitHub is to jump in and start working with it. Teams that utilize GitOps will often use GitHub to host their code in Git, so it is important to have a solid understanding of Git and GitHub before you look at adopting GitOps.

GitOps Overview

In this section, we will get to the core of this chapter covering GitOps! Before we actually dive into GitOps, let's explore a couple of problems that GitOps solves, helping understand the need for GitOps.

Problem: In this DevOps cloud-native era, the lines between ops and devs are blurring, resulting in ops-related activities shifting to devs. Devs need to be convinced, enabled, and trained on how to perform ops-related activities. This does not always go well as it can be an uphill task to get devs to using ops tools, understanding ops practices, and taking on these activities.

Solution: GitOps serves as an abstraction of the ops tooling, automates the ops practices, and makes it easier for devs to take on the ops activities via the layer of abstraction and making Git the source of truth and keeping it as the core tool.

Problem: When it comes to deployments to Kubernetes, dev teams will build an application, package it, and then hand it to an ops team for deployment. An ops team will then update their IaC config scripts and use them to deploy the application to the Kubernetes cluster. This method results in the code in the Git repository being disconnected from the live environment. For example, when an update to the application or environment configuration is needed, the ops team will make updates to the IaC configuration scripts and apply them manually to the live environment. This is a risk because changes may not always be properly tracked and configuration drift can occur.

Solution: Application and configuration deployments are performed via GitOps, making Git the source of truth, ensuring the application and environment configuration in the live environment matches the desired state specified in the code within the Git repository.

Those are just two examples of problems that GitOps solves. GitOps has many additional benefits and use cases. Some more use cases for GitOps are

- Service Rollouts
- Infrastructure management, that is, K8s clusters, fleets, and microservices
- Cloud Native App Management, that is, "CD" in CI/CD

Now let's jump into what GitOps is. GitOps was created by a company named Weaveworks. Weaveworks had been using the GitOps operating model pattern in their Kubernetes environments for a while before they blogged about it publicly in 2017. GitOps can be described as follows:

> *GitOps is an operating model pattern for cloud native applications & Kubernetes storing application & declarative infrastructure code in Git as the source of truth used for automated continuous delivery.*

GitOps is a logical extension of DevOps taking the best practices from DevOps such as version control, collaboration, and continuous deployment, applying these to environment automation including application deployment, configuration, and infrastructure. GitOps makes Git the source of truth where you describe the desired state of your entire system. The GitOps Principles and Practices are not new, but the name and some of the tools are. For example, a GitOps principle is for the desired state of your environment to be described declarativity in code. This is not new as we have been using this and applying it to our environments with tools such as Chef and Puppet. The main difference is that GitOps treats Git as the source of truth while the other tools did not. Here are the GitOps Principles and Practices:

GitOps Principles:

- **Declarative configuration**
    - System state described declaratively
- **Version controlled, immutable storage**
    - Git as the source of truth.
    - Desired system state is versioned in git.
- **Automated delivery**
    - Git as the single place for operations (create, change, delete) performed by autonomous agents
- **Software agents**
    - Software known as operators enforce desired state and alert on drift.
- **Closed loop**
    - Automated delivery of approved system state changes

GitOps Practices:

- Pull over Push.
- 2 Repos per App. One for App Source Code and one for Config (manifests).
- Have a plan for secrets management regardless if this will be in Kubernetes secrets or another secrets management solution.
- Ensure testing is included in your GitOps process.

The way GitOps works is that within Git, there is code that describes the state of your system like the applications and configurations. In the context of Kubernetes, the code in the Git repository would be Kubernetes manifest files in YAML format for the application pods and for any other configurations in the Kubernetes cluster like secrets, configmaps, deployments, services, ingress, etc.

From there, a software agent known as a GitOps operator would watch the Git repository for any changes, performs a pull, and will apply the changes to the Kubernetes cluster through Kubectl or Helm. This ensures the state of live environment matches the desired state that is described in Git. Let's take a look at the visual representation of a GitOps workflow (Figure 8-3).

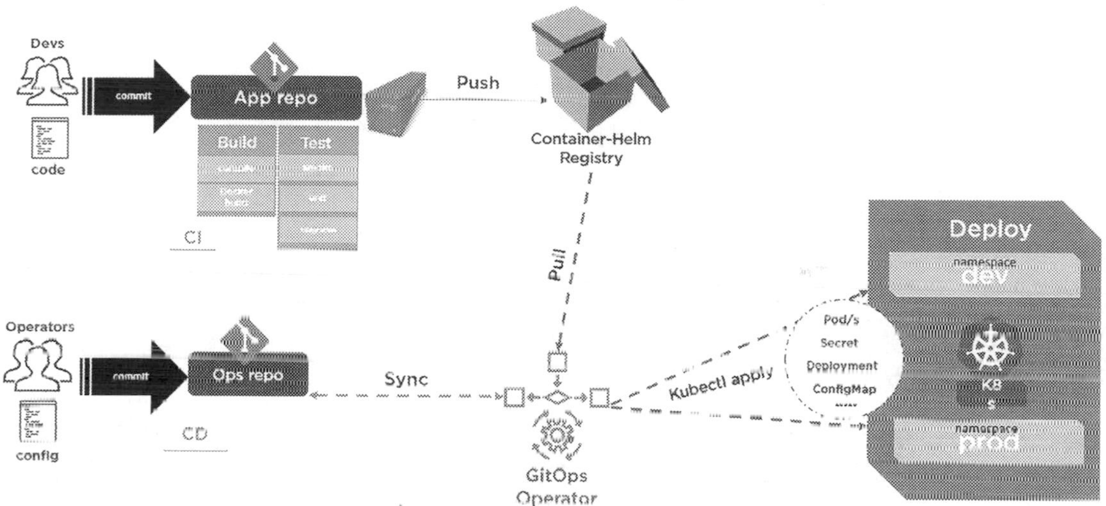

***Figure 8-3.** Example GitOps workflow*

There are many GitOps operators out there, but the two main ones are Flux and Argo CD. The Flux and Argo CD GitOps operators are designed to work with Kubernetes

A question that comes frequently is, "My organization is not using Kubernetes. Does GitOps still apply to us?" Yes, GitOps does apply to you. The GitOps operating model is not limited to just Kubernetes. You can actually use GitOps with any system that can be observed and described declaratively.

Currently, the majority of GitOps operators have been built for Kubernetes, but there are some operators out there for Terraform for example. Two GitOps operators that work directly with Terraform are Kubestack and Atlantis. Kubestack is a Terraform GitOps Framework for building Kubernetes on any platform. Atlantis is a GitOps operator for cloud via Terraform Pull Request Automation.

Now let's take a look at the key benefits of GitOps as this is important to understand how GitOps will benefit your team and organization. The key benefits of GitOps are the following:

- **Git as the source of truth** gives an enhanced Developer Experience and easy adoption.
- **Continuous sync** results in more reliability for your environment.
- **Everything tracked in Git** results in a full audit trail, meeting compliance, and better stability.
- **Continuous security** shifting access to the GitOps operator; security becomes code; credential and state segregation become reality.
- **Everything as a code** results in easier rollback, more consistency, & standardization.

Let's now explore GitOps and Azure Arc-enabled Kubernetes. Azure Arc-enabled Kubernetes (Arc K8s) does utilize GitOps. Arc K8s uses GitOps in two ways: the first way is for configuration of Kubernetes, and the second way is for the deployment of applications to a Kubernetes cluster. Arc K8s uses Flux. Flux is an open source GitOps operator. Weaveworks built Flux and open sourced it. Flux is a part of a Cloud Native Computing sandbox project.

The Flux operator runs on a Kubernetes cluster as a pod. The Flux operator takes a pull-based approach to syncing the Git repository with a Kubernetes cluster. The Flux operator can perform create, change, and delete operations on the Kubernetes cluster you give it permission to. The Flux operator can also continuously poll a container registry or Helm repository for additions or changes needed in a Kubernetes cluster.

This Flux operator is used to sync Kubernetes cluster configuration and configuration with the desired state in the Git repository with the goal to match the two through create, change, and delete operations.

The connection for the Arc K8s cluster and Git repository is housed in Azure Resource Manager. This connection is an extension resource named *Microsoft.KubernetesConfiguration/sourceControlConfigurations*. This connection resource is stored in an Azure Cosmos DB database. This connection is encrypted at rest. The connection can be set up using the Azure portal or through Azure Command Line Interface (CLI). The *sourceControlConfiguration* has the following properties:

- Configuration name

- Operator Instance name
- Operator namespace
- Repository URL
- Operator scope (Namespace/Cluster)
- Operator type
- Operator params
- Helm (Enabled/Disabled)

You can have multiple *sourceControlConfigurations in* each Arc K8s cluster. These configurations can be scoped to namespaces or at the cluster level. This is useful when an organization has multienvironment or multitenancy needs.

Summary

This brings us to a close of this chapter. In this chapter, we took a journey into the world of Git, exploring what it is and how it works. We then moved into an overview of GitHub, its history, how it works, and it various features and products.

We then rounded out this chapter, taking a turn into GitOps, breaking down why it's needed, what it is, its benefits, principles, and practices, as well as how it comes into play with Azure Arc. The goal of this chapter was to give you the needed background into Git and GitHub, bringing it full circle with GitOps, so you will be ready as you explore Azure Arc-enabled Kubernetes and learn how it leverages GitOps.

CHAPTER 9

Azure Arc-Enabled Kubernetes: Getting Started

Welcome to the "Azure Arc-Enabled Kubernetes: Getting Started" chapter. Azure Arc-enabled Kubernetes is a newer service in Azure that is gaining a tremendous amount of traction. In this chapter, we are going to take a deep dive into the work of using Azure Arc with Kubernetes clusters.

In this chapter, we are going to start with an overview of what Azure Arc-enabled Kubernetes is and its use cases, and we will explore its architecture. We will then move on to how you can set up Azure Arc-enabled Kubernetes as well as connect it to external Kubernetes clusters. You will also gain knowledge on how to utilize Azure Arc to manage your external Kubernetes clusters across on-premises or multiclouds. We will unpack how to extend monitoring, security scanning/protection, Azure Active Directory RBAC controls, and policy for compliance of Kubernetes clusters.

We will wrap up this chapter on a journey into utilizing GitOps and Azure Arc-enabled Kubernetes to deploy configurations and applications to external Kubernetes clusters.

Let's get going as we have a chapter packed full of important information on Azure Arc-enabled Kubernetes.

S. Buchanan and J. Joyner, *Azure Arc-Enabled Kubernetes and Servers*,
https://doi.org/10.1007/978-1-4842-7768-3_9

What Is Azure Arc-Enabled Kubernetes

Azure Arc is a cloud solution that responds to the on-premises and multicloud management needs of organizations. Azure Arc extends Azure capabilities to environments outside of Azure. Azure Arc enables you to create and manage resources as well as workloads on the following:

- On-premises
- Non-Azure clouds (i.e., GCP, AWS, Alibaba, etc.)
- Microsoft Hybrid (Azure Stack Hub, Azure Stack HCI, Azure Stack Edge)

Azure Arc-enabled Kubernetes (Arc K8s) allows you to connect Kubernetes clusters to Azure that are running on either on-premises or non-Azure clouds. Arc K8s brings a unified Azure management experience to workloads running anywhere.

Azure Arc has several offerings with some being in a GA state, while some are in private preview, and some are in public preview. Azure Arc-enabled Kubernetes has moved to GA. The pricing for Azure Arc-enabled Kubernetes offering is unique in that it is currently offered at no additional cost when managing Azure Arc-enabled servers and Azure Arc-enabled Kubernetes clusters. Azure Arc control plane functionality for servers and Kubernetes is offered for free. The services that are considered as a part of the Azure Arc Control plane include

- Attaching servers and Kubernetes clusters to Azure
- Resource organization through Azure management groups and Tagging
- Searching and indexing through Resource Graph
- Access and security through Azure RBAC and Azure subscriptions
- Environments and automation through ARM templates and Azure extensions

As of right now, Azure Arc-enabled Kubernetes is available in the following specific regions:

- East US
- West Europe

- West Central US
- South Central US
- Southeast Asia
- UK South
- West US 2
- Australia East
- East US 2
- North Europe
- Central US
- US Gov Virginia
- France Central
- Korea Central
- Japan East
- East Asia

Microsoft will add more and more supported regions for Azure Arc-enabled Kubernetes over time. It is recommended to check the official Microsoft documentation here: `https://docs.microsoft.com/en-us/azure/azure-arc/kubernetes/overview#supported-regions` for the most up-to-date information on the list of supported regions for Azure Arc-enabled Kubernetes.

Azure Arc-enabled Kubernetes supports any Kubernetes distributions that are Cloud Native Computing Foundation (CNCF)-certified Kubernetes. Here is a sample list of on-premises and cloud-based Kubernetes that are supported by Azure Arc-enabled Kubernetes:

- Kind
- MicroK8s
- Rancher K3s
- AKS (Azure Kubernetes Service)
- AKS on Azure Stack HCI
- EKS (Amazon Elastic Kubernetes Service)

- GKE (Google Kubernetes Engine)
- ACK (Alibaba Cloud Container Service for Kubernetes)
- Azure Red Hat OpenShift

Azure Arc-enabled Kubernetes brings many of Azure's native capabilities to projected Kubernetes clusters via extensions and GitOps. These include

- Utilizing Azure Monitor and Microsoft Defender for Cloud with Arc to monitor and protect projected Kubernetes clusters
- Administering projected Kubernetes clusters using Azure Arc and Azure Policy
- Utilizing Azure Active Directory RBAC for authorization and access to projected Kubernetes clusters
- Integration with GitOps (Flux GitOps operator) and projected Kubernetes clusters
- Deploying applications and configurations to projected Kubernetes clusters via GitOps
- Deploying Helm charts to projected Kubernetes clusters via GitOps
- Deploying IoT workloads to the edge
- Run Azure App Service, Functions, Event Grid, Azure API Management, and Logic Apps on any Arc-enabled Kubernetes cluster
- Service Mesh on projected Kubernetes clusters with mTLS security, fine-grained access control, traffic shifting, tracing with Jaeger functionality via Microsoft Open Service Mesh

---

Note Microsoft continues to add more functionality and capabilities to Azure Arc all the time, so the preceding list will grow over time as the life cycle of Azure Arc-enabled Kubernetes continues to mature.

The last topic we want to discuss about Azure Arc-enabled Kubernetes is a comparison of Azure Arc-enabled Kubernetes and other products. These come up as questions all the time when discussing Azure Arc-enabled Kubernetes.

Azure Arc K8s vs. Rancher

Azure Arc-enabled Kubernetes centralizes management of Kubernetes clusters on on-premises or public clouds including Azure, GCP, AWS, edge, IoT, and Hybrid (Azure Stack) and extends Azure native tooling and GitOps to external Kubernetes clusters.

Rancher centralizes management and provisioning of Kubernetes clusters on-premises or public clouds including Azure, GCP, and AWS. Extends Rancher interface, application catalog, GitOps, and open source tooling to external Kubernetes clusters.

Azure Arc K8s vs. Azure Stack Hub/AWS Outposts

Azure Arc extends Azure capabilities to environments outside of Azure such as your data center and other clouds like AWS and GCP.

Both Azure Stack Hub/AWS Outposts and Azure Arc enable hybrid cloud scenarios. Azure Stack is a hybrid cloud platform that lets you run Azure in your own data center. AWS Outposts makes the same claim for running AWS out of your data center.

Azure Arc K8s vs. Anthos

Google offers Anthos as a managed application platform extending GCP container services to any environment. The GCP approach is to move workloads to containers running on GKE.

In contrast with Anthos, Azure Arc allows customers to run virtual machines or containers. Arc extends the Azure control plane to both and serves as the overarching management layer for resources. The Azure Arc approach provides flexibility, allowing you to run resources on-premises or run them on other clouds.

Azure Arc-Enabled Kubernetes Use Cases

According to the "The State of the Kubernetes Ecosystem 2nd edition" report by The New Stack, 61% of Kubernetes users at organizations with 5,000 or more employees have more than five clusters, and the percentage of Kubernetes users with more than five clusters rose from 34% in 2017 to 39% in 2019.

This is important information in regard to Azure Arc-enabled Kubernetes as many organizations today are choosing to adopt a multicloud strategy including running Kubernetes across multiple clouds. Managing Kubernetes clusters across on-premises and multiple clouds can be disjointed and overly complicated. Azure Arc-enabled Kubernetes sets out to solve this and reduce the headache that comes with managing multiple Kubernetes clusters across on-premises and multiple clouds.

Several use cases that Azure Arc-enabled Kubernetes helps with are the following:

- App consistency across Azure, Google Cloud Platform, and Amazon Web Services clouds
- Centralized management of IoT app for managing equipment across many edge locations for mining company
- Bringing Azure PaaS services on-premises to meet additional compliance

Note that is not an exhaustive list of the use cases that Azure Arc-enabled Kubernetes helps with.

Azure Arc-Enabled Kubernetes Architecture

Azure Arc-enabled Kubernetes is a PaaS service running in Azure that is used to manage multiple Kubernetes clusters regardless of where they are. Azure Arc-enabled Kubernetes architecture consists of Azure services, resources, tools, agents, and a number of deployments and pods running on a projected Kubernetes cluster. Let's take a look now into the Azure Arc-enabled Kubernetes architecture and agent.

In Azure, the following Resource Providers are needed in the Azure subscription that you are running Azure Arc-enabled Kubernetes in to support Azure Arc-enabled Kubernetes:

- `Microsoft.Kubernetes`
- `Microsoft.KubernetesConfiguration`
- `Microsoft.ExtendedLocation`

A projected Kubernetes cluster will have an Azure Arc-enabled Kubernetes agent running on it. In order for the Agent to work, the following Network ports and protocols/Endpoint outbound URLs need to be allowed on the projected Kubernetes cluster network:

Ports:

- TCP on port 443 and TCP on port 9418

Endpoint (DNS) allowed outbound from projected Kubernetes cluster:

- `https://management.azure.com`

- `https://eastus.dp.kubernetesconfiguration.azure.com`
  `https://westeurope.dp.kubernetesconfiguration.azure.com`
- `https://login.microsoftonline.com`
- `https://mcr.microsoft.com`
- `https://eus.his.arc.azure.com`
- `https://weu.his.arc.azure.com`

There will be a namespace running on the projected Kubernetes cluster named "azure-arc" after the projected Kubernetes cluster is onboarded.

Also, there will be operators running on the projected Kubernetes cluster in the azure-arc namespace as deployments:

- **config-agent**

It monitors the project Kubernetes cluster to update the compliance state when sourceControlConfiguration resources are applied on the projected cluster.

- **controller-manager**

It orchestrates interactions between Azure Arc components. An operator used to operate other operators.

- **metrics-agent**

It gathers metrics from other Arc agents to measure performance and ensure it is optimal.

- **cluster-metadata-operator**

It collects versions of clusters and Azure Arc agents, cluster metadata, and node count.

- **resource-sync-agent**

It syncs the metadata collected by the cluster-metadata-operator with Azure Arc.

- **clusteridentityoperator**

This operator holds a Managed Service Identity (MSI) certificate that is used by the other operators to communicate with Azure.

- **flux-logs-agent**

As a part of the sourceControlConfiguration, Flux operators are deployed to the projected Kubernetes cluster(s), and this agent collects the logs from them.

There will be some pods running on the projected Kubernetes cluster in the azure-arc namespace including

- **cluster-metadata-operator**-b88f6695d-rf998
- **clusteridentityoperator**-6459fd778c-4wx66
- **config-agent**-6cc967f5-kd8b8
- **controller-manager**-557d758b9f-f69vw
- **flux-logs-agent**-5db8bff9d4-gktl4
- **metrics-agent**-997cf95d5-h96gd
- **resource-sync-agent**-587b999567-4kz64

That concludes the components that make up Azure Arc-enabled Kubernetes. The architecture includes Azure services, resources, tools, agents, and a number of deployments and pods.

Connecting Kubernetes Clusters to Azure Arc

Before you can start utilizing Azure Arc-enabled Kubernetes with your external Kubernetes cluster(s), you need to first connect it to Azure Arc. The process for connecting external Kubernetes clusters to Azure Arc is fairly straightforward. Before you connect it, you do need to have some prerequisites in place. The prerequisites for Connecting K8s to Azure Arc are the following:

- Create an Azure Service Principal (SP).
- Azure Arc-enabled Kubernetes resource providers enabled.
- Need the kubectl (Kubernetes command-line) tool installed.
- kubeconfig file (kubectl context) configured to connect with your K8s cluster.
- Install/update Helm 3 or above.
- Install/update Azure CLI to version 2.15.0 or above.
- Azure CLI extension connectedk8s and k8s-configuration installed.

Let's take a journey on how to get the prerequisites installed and set up before you can connect Arc to Kubernetes:

First off, you will need to create a Service Principal (SP) in your Azure subscription. This SP will need read and write permissions on the `Microsoft.Kubernetes/connectedClusters` resource type in the subscription.

You are also going to use this SP with the az login and az connectedk8s connect. You can create this SP with one line of syntax by running it in Azure Cloud Shell. When you create the SP, you will need to copy the output somewhere safe as you will need to use this later on. You can use the following syntax to create the SP with a name and assign it to a specific subscription:

```
az ad sp create-for-rbac --name <SPNNAME> --role contributor --scope
/subscriptions/<SUBSCRIPTIONID>
```

Example of output:

```
{
  "appId": "138r8633-v9g3-4f90-80d9-hg7924c823f9",
  "displayName": " SPNNAME ",
  "name": "http:// SPNNAME",
  "password": "5g2c85va-43ds-31f0-o6c6-rbg2c5av472g",
  "tenant": "9uh4qq35-q432-4j2v-h20r-6o24b11p53TW"
}
```

Again, be sure to copy the output so that you have it ready when needed.

Next up, you need to register some resource providers for Azure Arc-enabled Kubernetes in our Azure subscription.

```
az provider register --namespace Microsoft.Kubernetes
az provider register --namespace Microsoft.KubernetesConfiguration
az provider register --namespace Microsoft.ExtendedLocation
```

You then need to install Helm. There are multiple ways to install Helm depending on the platform that you are installing it on. Because the install will differ based on your platform, it is best to refer to the Helm install link for the latest updates on this process. This is the official link for the Helm install: `https://helm.sh/docs/intro/install`.

Next, install/update Azure CLI to version 2.15.0 or above. You can install in Azure CLI in Windows, macOS, and Linux environments, or you can run it as a Docker container. It is also preinstalled in Azure Cloud Shell:

```
https://docs.microsoft.com/en-us/cli/azure/install-azure-cli
```

Install the Azure Arc K8s CLI extensions to manage the external Kubernetes clusters.

```
az extension add --name connectedk8s
az extension add --name k8s-configuration
```

That sums up what we need to do in regard to the Azure Arc-enabled Kubernetes prerequisites.

Connect Azure Arc to Azure Kubernetes Service Clusters

Now let's go ahead and connect the Kubernetes cluster to Azure Arc. Use the SP to log into your Azure subscription. Run this from a shell where your external Kubernetes cluster is, that is, GCP cloudshell.

```
az login --service-principal --username SPID --password SPPWD --tenant
SPTENANTID
```

Create a resource group for the projected Kubernetes cluster.

```
az group create -location LOCATIONHERE --name RGNAME --subscription
SUBSCRIPTIONID
```

We now can connect the external Kubernetes cluster to Azure Arc K8s.

```
az connectedk8s connect --name ARCK8SCLUSTERNAME --resource-group RGNAME
--location LOCATIONHERE --tags 'Environment=dev-arc-cluster1'
```

After it is connected, it becomes a projected K8s cluster showing in the Azure portal.

The projected Kubernetes cluster(s) will show in the Azure portal in the following ways:

- It appears as a resource in the Azure portal.
- It has tags like other Azure resources.

- It shows in your Azure subscription and resource group.
- In the portal, it has an Azure Resource Manager ID and a Managed Identity.

Monitoring Kubernetes Clusters with Azure Arc and Azure Monitor

Monitoring your projected Kubernetes clusters and the containers running on them is critical in ensuring your environments are healthy. Azure Monitor Container Insights is able to provide monitoring of projected Kubernetes clusters that are connected to Azure Arc-enabled Kubernetes.

Azure Monitor for Containers gives you performance visibility and will collect memory and CPU utilization metrics from your projected Kubernetes nodes and containers. At the time of this writing, Azure Monitor for Containers does not support Live Data.

Azure Monitor Container Insights can

- Monitor performance of Kubernetes clusters and their nodes.
- Identify containers that are running on nodes and their average processor and memory utilization.
- Identify where the container resides in a controller or a pod.
- Understand the behavior of the cluster under average and heaviest loads.
- Integrate with Prometheus to view application and workload metrics it collects from nodes and Kubernetes using queries.

Before onboarding projected Kubernetes cluster(s) into Azure Monitor Container Insights.

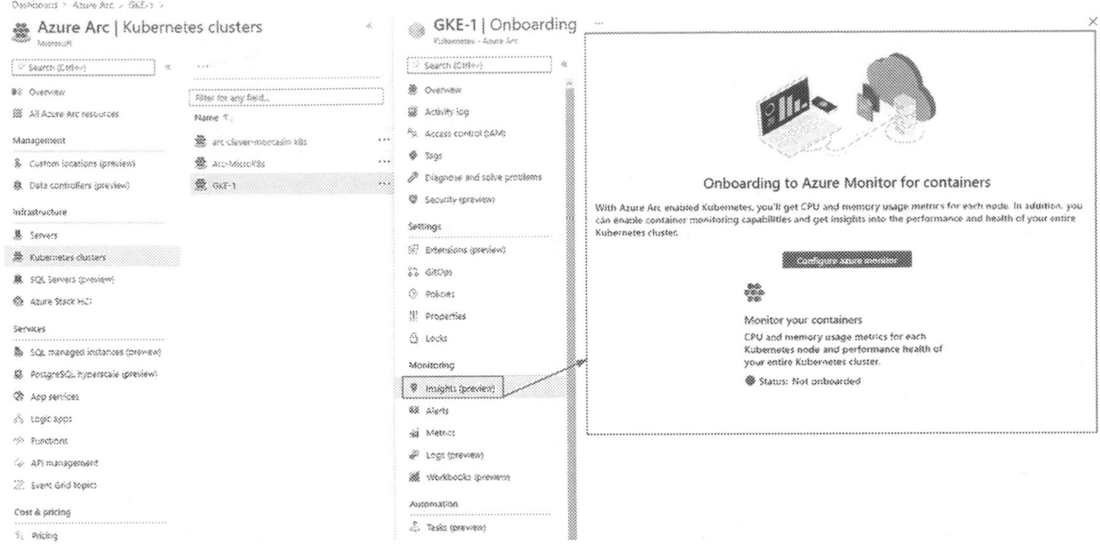

Figure 9-1. *Azure Monitor Container Insights before onboarding*

Before you are able to enable Azure Monitor Container Insights monitoring, you will need to have some prerequisites in place:

- A Log Analytics workspace configured with Azure Monitor for containers.
- At a minimum, you need to be a member of the Azure Contributor role in the Azure subscription.
- A member of the Log Analytics Contributor role of the Log Analytics workspace configured with Azure Monitor for containers.
- A member of the Contributor role on the Azure Arc cluster resource.
- A member of the Log Analytics reader role permission.
- HELM client to onboard the Azure Monitor for containers chart for the specified Kubernetes cluster.
- The following Microsoft Monitoring Endpoints need to be allowed through any firewalls:

  ```
  *.ods.opinsights.azure.com
  *.oms.opinsights.azure.com
  dc.services.visualstudio.com
  ```

```
*.monitoring.azure.com
login.microsoftonline.com
port 443 for all of them
```

Let's walk through the three ways to onboard a projected Kubernetes cluster for Azure Monitor Container Insights:

#1 From Azure Monitor blade

- In the Azure portal, navigate to the "Monitor" blade, and select the "Containers" option under the "Insights" menu.
- Select the "Unmonitored clusters" tab to view the Azure Arc-enabled Kubernetes clusters that you can enable monitoring for.
- Click on the "Enable" link next to the cluster that you want to enable monitoring for.
- Choose the Log Analytics workspace and select the "Configure" button to continue.

#2 From Projected K8s cluster resource blade

- In the Azure portal, select the projected Kubernetes cluster that you want to monitor.
- Select the "Insights (preview)" item under the "Monitoring" section of the resource blade.
- On the onboarding page, select the "Configure Azure Monitor" button.
- You can now choose the Log Analytics workspace to send your metrics and logs data to.
- Select the "Configure" button to deploy the Azure Monitor Container Insights cluster extension.

#3 From Projected K8s cluster resource

Go ahead and download the "enable monitoring AKA OMS" script named enable-monitoring.sh using the following syntax:

```
curl -o enable-monitoring.sh -L https://aka.ms/enable-monitoring-bash-
script
```

Next, retrieve the Azure Arc Connected Cluster Azure Resource ID using the following syntax:

```
export azureArcClusterResourceId=$(az resource show --resource-group
PROJECTEDK8SRESOURCEGROUP --name PROJECTEDK8SCLUSTERNAME --resource-
type "Microsoft.Kubernetes/connectedClusters" --query id -o tsv)
```

Retrieve the projected Kubernetes cluster credentials from the current KubeContext using the following syntax:

```
export kubeContext="$(kubectl config current-context)"
```

Run the enable-monitoring.sh script with the following syntax:

```
bash enable-monitoring.sh --resource-id $azureArcClusterResourceId
--client-id SPNID --client-secret SPNPASSWORD --tenant-id TENANTID
--kube-context $kubeContext
```

After onboarding projected Kubernetes cluster(s) into Azure Monitor Container Insights.

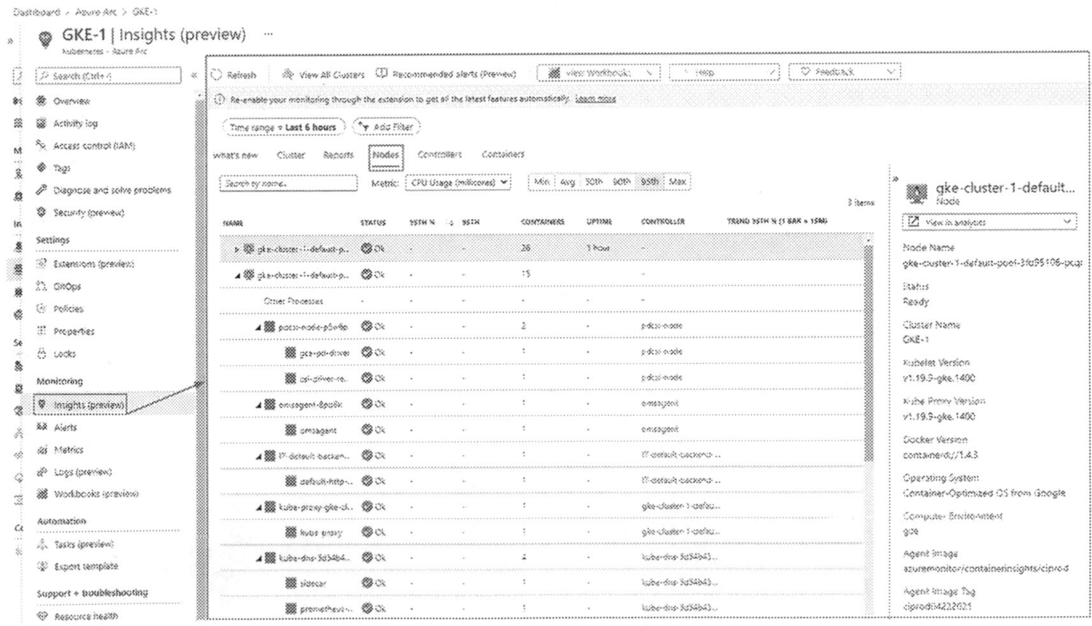

Figure 9-2. Azure Monitor Container Insights after onboarding

Configure RBAC on Kubernetes Clusters with Azure Arc and Azure AD RBAC

One of the many benefits of Azure Arc-enabled Kubernetes is the ability to utilize Azure Active Directory (AAD) for the identity provider for authorization and access to your projected Kubernetes clusters. With the RBAC and Azure Arc-enabled Kubernetes, you can use Azure AD and role assignments to control who can read, write, and delete Kubernetes objects like deployments, pods, and services. You can use AAD RBAC and role assignments to define and control authorization to your projected Kubernetes clusters vs. the built-in RoleBinding and ClusterRoleBinding that come with Kubernetes. Natively, in Kubernetes, RoleBinding and ClusterRoleBinding are typically used to define and control authorization.

Note The Azure AD RBAC integration with Kubernetes does not work with non-Azure managed Kubernetes services such as AKE and GKE. This is because with services such as GKE and AKE, you don't have access to the Kubernetes cluster API server.

Prerequisites to Azure AD and Azure Arc Projected K8s Integration:

- Azure CLI installed.
- Connectedk8s extension installed.
- Connect to your existing Azure Arc projected Kubernetes cluster.

There are two steps to setting up Azure AD and Azure Arc Projected K8s Integration

#1 Set up Azure AD applications

- Create a server application.
- Create a client application.
- Create a role assignment for the server application.

#2 Enable Azure AD RBAC on the K8s cluster

Run the following command on your projected K8s cluster to enable the Azure AD RBAC feature: az connectedk8s enable-features -n ARCK8sNAME -g RGNAME --features azure-rbac --app-id SPAPPID --app-secret SPPWD

Azure AD RBAC integration has role assignments that can be assigned to the projected Kubernetes cluster and can be done using the Access Control (IAM) blade of the projected cluster resource on the Azure Portal>Azure Arc. The role assignments are the following:

- **Azure Arc Kubernetes Viewer**
  - Allows read-only access to see most objects in a namespace. This role doesn't allow viewing secrets.
- **Azure Arc Kubernetes Writer**
  - Allows read/write access to most objects in a namespace. This role doesn't allow viewing or modifying roles or role bindings.
- **Azure Arc Kubernetes Admin**
  - Allows admin access. It's intended to be granted within a namespace through RoleBinding.
- **Azure Arc Kubernetes Cluster Admin**
  - Allows superuser access to execute any action on any resource.

You can create a custom role definition to use in Azure AD role assignments. It is a three-step process:

Step #1 is to create a **customrole.json** file with the following syntax:

```
{
    "Name": "Arc Deployment Viewer",
    "Description": "Lets you view all deployments in cluster/namespace.",
    "Actions": [],
    "NotActions": [],
    "DataActions": [
        "Microsoft.Kubernetes/connectedClusters/apps/deployments/read"
    ],
    "NotDataActions": [],
    "assignableScopes": [
        "/subscriptions/<subscription-id>"
    ]
}
```

Step #2 is to create the **role definition** from the customrole.json file using the following command:

az role definition create --role-definition mycustomrole.json

Step #3 is to create the **role assignment** using the custom role definition you created in step #1. You will use the following command to create the role assignment:

```
az role assignment create --role "Arc Deployment Viewer" --assignee
<AZURE-AD-ENTITY-ID> --scope $ARM_ID/namespaces/<namespace-name>
```

There are two ways to connect to the projected K8s cluster:

#1: The Cluster Connect feature (az connectedk8s proxy)

```
az connectedk8s proxy -n ARCK8sNAME -g RGNAME
```

Can run kubectl commands after the preceding command is run.

#2: Use the kubeconfig file

Set the credentials for the user:

```
kubectl config set-credentials user@domain.com \
--auth-provider=azure \
--auth-provider-arg=environment=AzurePublicCloud \
--auth-provider-arg=client-id=SPCLIENTID \
--auth-provider-arg=tenant-id=TENANTID \
--auth-provider-arg=apiserver-id=SPAPPID
#2 Add the config-mode setting under user > config -
name: user@domain.com
user:
    auth-provider:
    config:
        apiserver-id: $SERVER_APP_ID
        client-id: $CLIENT_APP_ID
        environment: AzurePublicCloud
        tenant-id: $TENANT_ID
        config-mode: "1"
    name: azure
```

Can run kubectl commands now.

Protect Kubernetes Clusters with the Microsoft Defender for Cloud and Azure Arc

The Microsoft Defender for Cloud for Kubernetes clusters extension is able to protect your projected Kubernetes clusters running on-premises or even in other clouds. Defender offers the same threat detection and capabilities that are available for Azure Kubernetes Service (AKS) clusters.

Items received and analyzed by Security Center include

- Audit logs from the API server
- Raw security events from the Log Analytics agent
- Cluster configuration information from the projected Kubernetes cluster
- Workload configuration from Azure Policy (via the Azure Policy add-on for Azure Arc projected Kubernetes)

Let's take a look at the prerequisites for Microsoft Defender for Cloud for Azure Arc-enabled Kubernetes:

- Microsoft Defender for Cloud for Kubernetes is enabled on your subscription.
- Your external Kubernetes cluster is connected to Azure Arc.
- Meet the prerequisites already for the generic cluster extensions (Azure CLI, connectedk8s and k8s-extension extensions, projected K8s cluster connected to Arc).

Deploy Microsoft Defender for Cloud extension for Arc K8s.

We need to run the following code on the Azure Arc projected Kubernetes cluster to enable it for Defender.

Note You should run "az login" and "az account set" before running this code.

```
az k8s-extension create --name microsoft.azuredefender.kubernetes
--cluster-type connectedClusters --cluster-name ARCK8sCLUSTERNAME
--resource-group RGNAME --extension-type microsoft.azuredefender.kubernetes
```

Enforce Compliance of Kubernetes Clusters Using Azure Policy, Azure Arc, and GitOps

Azure Policy can be utilized to enforce compliance on Kubernetes clusters. It was originally utilized for Azure Kubernetes Service clusters. With the introduction of Azure Arc-enabled Kubernetes, Azure Policy for Kubernetes was extended to external Kubernetes clusters. Azure Policy can also be used with GitOps. This is done by utilizing a GitOps Azure Policy definition that will set GitOps configurations on your projected Kubernetes clusters.

Azure Policy for projected Kubernetes clusters can do two things:

1. Apply policies to enforce and safeguard your projected Kubernetes clusters in a centralized, consistent manner.

2. Apply GitOps configurations at scale on Azure Arc projected Kubernetes clusters.

Currently, Azure Policy for Kubernetes only supports Linux node pools and built in policy definitions.

Example Azure Policies for Kubernetes:

- Kubernetes cluster containers should only use allowed images.
- Azure Kubernetes Service Private Clusters should be enabled.
- Kubernetes clusters should not use the default namespace.
- Authorized IP ranges should be defined on Kubernetes Services.

There are prerequisites for Azure Policy for Kubernetes that need to be met before it can be deployed and used. These prerequisites are the following:

- Azure CLI version 2.12.0 or later installed.
- Azure Policy provider registered in your subscription:
    - az provider register --namespace 'Microsoft.PolicyInsights'
- Kubernetes cluster version 1.14 or higher.
- Helm 3 or higher.
- Your external Kubernetes cluster is connected to Azure Arc.

- The Azure Resource ID of the Azure Arc-enabled Kubernetes cluster is needed.
- Assign "Policy Insights Data Writer (Preview)" role assignment to the Azure Arc-enabled Kubernetes cluster.

Let's explore how Azure Policy for projected Kubernetes works. Azure Policy for K8s is based on the Open Policy Agent implementation called Gatekeeper. Azure Policy for K8s is made up of two components:

- Gatekeeper component
- Azure-policy component

When the Azure Policy extension for Kubernetes is added, a namespace called gatekeeper-system is created with two pods deployed into it:

1. gatekeeper-audit pods
2. gatekeeper-controller pods

Gatekeeper components are installed in the gatekeeper-system namespace, while the azure-policy components are installed in the kube-system namespace.

Azure Policy for Kubernetes has two types of effect(s): audit and deny. These break down as such:

1. By default, the gatekeeper-audit pod will check the cluster for violations.
2. The gatekeeper-controller pods perform enforcement when the action is set to deny.

When a deployment fulfills all Azure Policy for Kubernetes policy conditions, it is allowed to be deployed. When a deployment does not fulfill all policy conditions, it denies the deployment. In order to install the Azure Policy add-on for Arc Projected Kubernetes clusters, you will need to add the Azure Policy add-on repo to Helm and then install the Azure Policy add-on Helm chart. You should run the code for adding the add-on to the Helm repo and installing the helm chart from your Azure Arc projected Kubernetes cluster. Run the following syntax to Azure Policy add-on repo to Helm:

```
helm repo add azure-policy https://raw.githubusercontent.com/Azure/azure-policy/master/extensions/policy-addon-kubernetes/helm-charts
```

In order to install the Azure Policy add-on Helm chart, run the following syntax:

```
helm install azure-policy-addon azure-policy/azure-policy-addon-arc-clusters \
    --set azurepolicy.env.resourceid=<AzureArcClusterResourceId> \
    --set azurepolicy.env.clientid=<ServicePrincipalAppId> \
    --set azurepolicy.env.clientsecret=<ServicePrincipalPassword> \
    --set azurepolicy.env.tenantid=<ServicePrincipalTenantId>
```

After installing the Azure Policy for Kubernetes add-on, the next step is to assign an Azure Policy to a projected Kubernetes cluster. You can do this using the following steps:

- In the Azure portal, click All services in the left pane and then search for Policy.
- In the left pane under Authoring, click on Definitions.
- In the Category drop-down list box, click Select all to clear the filter and then type Kubernetes in the filter box to scope to Kubernetes. Click on Kubernetes.
- Select the policy definition; then select the Assign button.
- Scope to where the Kubernetes is (i.e., management group, subscription, resource group) to apply policy assignment.
- Give your policy assignment a Name and Description.
- Set the Policy enforcement to either "Enabled" or "Disabled" and click next.

Note If the enforcement mode is set to disabled, then the policy effect isn't enforced (i.e., deny policy won't deny resources). However, compliance assessment results will still be available.

- Set your parameters (if needed).
    - By default, the kube-system, gatekeeper-system, and azure-arc namespaces are set to be excluded. This will exclude these namespaces from policy evaluation. It is recommended to keep this in place.
- Click on Review + create.

The other use for the Azure Policy for Kubernetes add-on is to use Azure Policy for Kubernetes to Apply GitOps. With Azure Policy for Kubernetes, you can assign a GitOps configuration to your projected Kubernetes cluster(s). You can also use Azure Policy to apply GitOps configurations (`Microsoft.KubernetesConfiguration/sourceControlConfigurations` resource type) at scale on Azure Arc projected K8s clusters (`Microsoft.Kubernetes/connectedclusters`).

To use GitOps with Azure Policy for Kubernetes, you would use the built-in GitOps policy definition and create a policy assignment on your Kubernetes cluster. You would need to set the needed parameters such as

```
Operator instance name
Operator namespace
Operator scope
Operator type
Operator parameters
Repository URL
...
```

Understanding GitOps and Azure Arc-Enabled Kubernetes Architecture and Workflow

It is important to restate what GitOps is. “GitOps is an operating model pattern for cloud native applications and Kubernetes storing application and declarative infrastructure code in Git as the source of truth used for automated continuous delivery.” Azure Arc-enabled Kubernetes utilizes Flux, an open source GitOps operator built by Weaveworks. GitOps in Azure Arc-enabled Kubernetes is a connection between a projected Kubernetes cluster and a Git repository through a Flux operator running on the Kubernetes cluster as a pod. This Flux operator is used to sync Kubernetes cluster configuration and configuration with the desired state in the Git repository with the goal to match the two through create, change, and delete operations.

This sync is accomplished with the Flux operator via a pull-based approach where Flux will continuously poll the Git repository for anything new or changes and will enact any creation or updates to the Kubernetes cluster. Azure Arc-enabled Kubernetes utilizes GitOps to cover two things:

#1 For the configuration of Kubernetes

- Configuration can include objects such as namespaces, configmaps, secrets, ingress controllers, ingress, and more.

#2 For the deployment of applications to Kubernetes

- An application can be things such as deployments, pods, services, Helm charts, and more.

The Azure Arc-enabled Kubernetes cluster and Git repository connection lives in ARM as an extension resource named `Microsoft.KubernetesConfiguration/sourceControlConfigurations`. This is stored in an Azure Cosmos DB database encrypted at rest. For each Azure Arc-enabled Kubernetes cluster, you can have multiple `sourceControlConfigurations`. These can be scoped to namespaces. This helps in multienvironment and multitenancy scenarios.

The **sourceControlConfiguration properties** consist of

- Configuration name
- Operator Instance name
- Operator namespace
- Repository URL
- Operator scope (Namespace/Cluster)
- Operator type
- Operator params
- Helm (Enabled/Disabled)

GitOps can also be used with Azure Arc-enabled Kubernetes to manage configuration of large amounts of Kubernetes clusters at scale. This is accomplished by using Azure Policy to apply required sourceControlConfigurations on projected Kubernetes clusters as soon as they are onboarded into Azure Arc. One may use this if you want to apply the same configurations across multiple Kubernetes clusters such as monitoring agents, ingress controllers, service mesh, and more. We can either set up this configuration via the Azure portal or through Azure CLI. The following image is a GitOps workflow/architecture with Azure Arc-enabled Kubernetes.

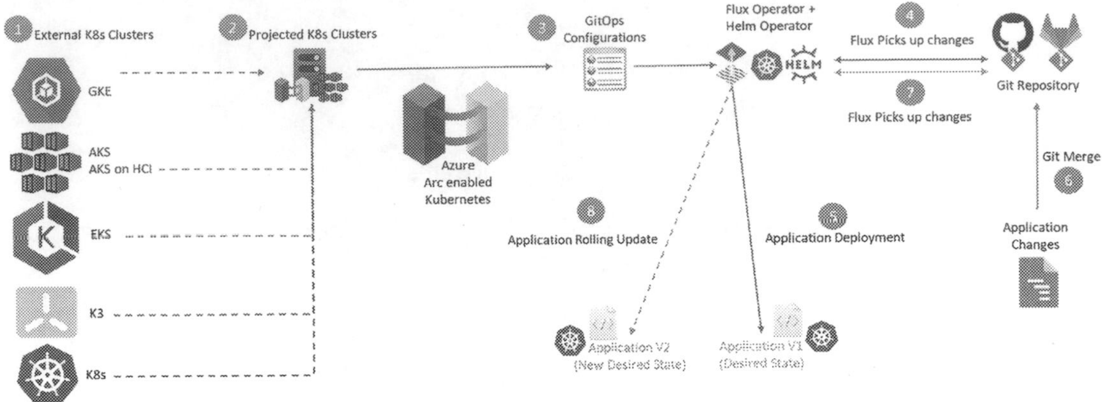

Figure 9-3. *Azure Arc-enabled Kubernetes GitOps workflow*

Setting Up a GitOps Configuration in Azure Arc

The GitOps setup in Azure Arc-enabled Kubernetes is straightforward. It simply needs some core information about your configuration such as the URL for your GIT repository, the login info if it is private, scoping to a namespace or at the cluster level, and more. You have two options to set it up. You can either set it up via a GUI or through command line. The setup works using the following options:

Option #1 is to run code on the projected Kubernetes cluster. For example, if you are running GKE, you could save the following code to a file named "az_k8sconfig_gke.sh" and run it via Google Cloud Shell:

```
az k8s-configuration create \
--name hello-arc \
--cluster-name $arcClusterName --resource-group $resourceGroup \
--operator-instance-name hello-arc --operator-namespace prod \
--enable-helm-operator \
--helm-operator-params='--set helm.versions=v3' \
--repository-url $appClonedRepo \
--scope namespace --cluster-type connectedClusters \
--operator-params="--git-poll-interval 3s --git-readonly --git-
path=releases/prod"
```

Option #2 is to enable the GitOps configuration via the Azure portal. Go to Azure Arc ➤ Kubernetes clusters ➤ GitOps.

Click on Add Configurations and complete the required properties and optional properties (if needed):

- Configuration name
- Operator Instance name
- Operator namespace
- Repository URL
- Operator scope (Namespace/Cluster)
- Operator type
- Operator params
- Helm (Enabled/Disabled)

Click Add.

Note The GitOps configuration state will show as pending and can take up to 10 minutes to change to Installed status.

Using GitOps and Azure Arc to Deploy an Application to a Projected Kubernetes Cluster

You can utilize GitOps with Azure Arc-enabled Kubernetes to deploy an application to your projected Kubernetes cluster(s). The process is straightforward once you have GitOps set up with Azure Arc-enabled Kubernetes on your projected Kubernetes cluster. The following steps break down the steps taken to deploy an app on your projected Kubernetes cluster:

- The developer writes application or the DevOps engineer writes code for configuration of Kubernetes cluster.
- The developer pushes the code to a remote branch on the application repository and opens a pull request for review.
- There is a review of the pull request to approve or deny the merge.

- Changes are validated as needed.
- The lead or team signs off on the pull request, and the change is merged into the main Git repository.
- In a short time (interval set by you), Flux will notice a new change in the Git repository that is connected to the Flux GitOps operator.
- The Flux GitOps operator will pull the changes and apply them to the projected Kubernetes cluster, resulting in a deployment of the application and configuration.

Understanding How Azure Arc and GitOps Work with Helm

The deployment of a Helm-based application to a projected Kubernetes cluster via GitOps and Azure Arc-enabled Kubernetes is similar to deploying an application using a Kubernetes manifest file. There are some differences starting with what Helm is. Let's look at some key points to understanding Helm charts and Azure Arc-enabled Kubernetes:

- Helm is a package manager for Kubernetes.
- Helm is used to manage the life cycle of applications on Kubernetes.
- The Helm operator in Azure Arc-enabled Kubernetes provides an extension to Flux that automates Helm chart releases.
- Helm is set to either disabled or enabled in Arc K8s GitOps configuration.
- The operator utilizes the "HelmRelease" Custom Resource Definition (CRD).
- HelmRelease can input specific values to a helm chart, making it easy to values for different environments like dev, stage, prod, etc.

Understanding How Azure Arc and GitOps Work with IoT Edge Workloads

Azure has an offering that moved cloud analytics and custom business logic to devices. This offering is known as Azure IoT Edge. IoT Edge packages services in containers running on the edge devices. These containers can run Azure services, third-party services, or your own custom code. IoT Edge works with IoT Hub and other services in Azure. IoT edge runs Kubernetes as an operating environment that IoT Edge applications can run on. Azure Arc-enabled Kubernetes can manage the Kubernetes clusters on IoT Edge. GitOps can be utilized to deploy IoT Edge Workloads to IoT Edge via Azure Arc-enabled Kubernetes. The key points of Azure Arc-enabled Kubernetes and IoT Edge include the following:

- With IoT Edge, you bring your own K8s cluster and register the IoT Edge Custom Resource Definition (CRD) controller in it.
- Arc K8s can be used to operate the K8s cluster running IoT Edge including remotely deploy/manage workloads at scale via GitOps and perform bidirectional ingest to and from cloud services, that is, IoT Hub.
- All IoT Edge components are scoped to a specific Kubernetes namespace, allowing you to use a single cluster for multiple edge devices.

Summary

This brings us to a close of the last chapter of this book. This book has been a journey into the world of Azure Arc and two of its key offerings: servers and Kubernetes. In this chapter, we started with an understanding of Azure Arc-enabled Kubernetes and various use cases for it and explored Azure Arc-enabled Kubernetes architecture, connecting Arc to Kubernetes clusters, monitoring them, securing them, and enforcing compliance on projected Kubernetes clusters. We also jumped into GitOps and Azure Arc-enabled Kubernetes including what GitOps is, how it works with Azure Arc-enabled Kubernetes, and how to use GitOps to deploy configurations and applications to projected Kubernetes clusters. Thank you for taking this journey through Azure Arc throughout this book.

Index

A

S. Buchanan and J. Joyner, *Azure Arc-Enabled Kubernetes and Servers*,
https://doi.org/10.1007/978-1-4842-7768-3

B

C

J

K

L

M, N, O

P, Q

R

S

T, U

V

W, X, Y, Z

Printed in the United States
by Baker & Taylor Publisher Services